# Ius Comparatum – Global Studies in Comparative Law

Volume 41

As globalization proceeds, the significance of the comparative approach in legal scholarship increases. The IACL / AIDC with almost 800 members is the major universal organization promoting comparative research in law and organizing congresses with hundreds of participants in all parts of the world. The results of those congresses should be disseminated and be available for legal scholars in a single book series which would make both the Academy and its contribution to comparative law more visible. The series aims to publish the scholarship emerging from the congresses of IACL / AIDC, including: 1. of the General Congresses of Comparative Law, which take place every 4 years (Brisbane 2002; Utrecht 2006, Washington 2010, Vienna 2014, Fukuoka 2018 etc.) and which generate (a) one volume of General Reports edited by the local organizers of the Congress; (b) up to 30 volumes of selected thematic reports dealing with the topics of the single sections of the congress and containing the General Report as well as the National Reports of that section; these volumes would be edited by the General Reporters of the respective sections; 2. the volumes containing selected contributions to the smaller (2-3 days) thematic congresses which take place between the International Congresses (Mexico 2008; Taipei 2012; Montevideo 2016 etc.); these congresses have a general theme such as "Codification" or "The Enforcement of Law" and will be edited by the local organizers of the respective Congress. All publications may contain contributions in English and French, the official languages of the Academy.

More information about this series at http://www.springer.com/series/11943

Académie Internationale de Droit Comparé
International Academy of Comparative Law

Guillaume Tusseau
Editor

# Debating Legal Pluralism and Constitutionalism

## New Trajectories for Legal Theory in the Global Age

Springer

*Editor*
Guillaume Tusseau
Sciences Po Law School
Paris, France

ISSN 2214-6881 ISSN 2214-689X (electronic)
Ius Comparatum – Global Studies in Comparative Law
ISBN 978-3-030-34431-3 ISBN 978-3-030-34432-0 (eBook)
https://doi.org/10.1007/978-3-030-34432-0



This Springer imprint is published by the registered company Springer Nature Switzerland AG.
The registered company address is: Gewerbestrasse 11, 6330 Cham, Switzerland

# Contents

# Debating Legal Pluralism and Constitutionalism: New Trajectories for Legal Theory in the Global Age

**Guillaume Tusseau**

**Abstract** Globalisation has disrupted most of the intellectual and practical tools jurists had devised. Yesterday's "high definition" law has given way to a new "low definition" law. The main features of the latter have debased such paradigmatic concepts as the authority of the State legislator, the dichotomy between internal and external legal norms, the distinction between public and private sources of law, the image of the Kelsenian pyramid of norms, and the centrality of legal obligation. Legal pluralism and constitutionalism have frequently been presented as the two main competing orientations to meet the challenges of the global age. Whereas the former insists on diversity, the latter insists on common values. The legal, empirical, and doctrinal information gleaned from nine national reporters about the respective situations of Argentina, Botswana, Brazil, Cyprus, Germany, Greece, Singapore, the Solomon Islands, and the United Kingdom tend to prove that no clear-cut distinction between pluralism and constitutionalism is evident. Nor are the strategies these two perspectives embody totally successful to meet the demands of the day. Section 2 of this general report sets the stage for the study of legal interactions in the global age. It sheds light on the degree of pluralism each of the studied legal systems admits, both in its relations with other legal systems that reach beyond the States, and in its relations with more or less autonomous inner forms of legal normativity. Section 3 tackles the forms of interactions that take place among legal actors in the context of an increasingly plural landscape, and how they contribute to changing legal mentalities. By focusing respectively on legal actors' reasoning and on legal scholarship, understood as the interacting members of a unified epistemic community, Sects. 4 and 5 contribute to highlighting what "thinking like a lawyer" means today. Finally, Sect. 6 identifies how little neutral, and how value-laden, the current discussion about pluralism and constitutionalism is. The very concepts that are currently used to confront today's major legal changes testify to the ideological dimension of legal analysis.

G. Tusseau (✉)
Sciences Po Law School, Paris, France
e-mail: guillaume.tusseau@sciencespo.fr

 
G. Tusseau (ed.), *Debating Legal Pluralism and Constitutionalism*, Ius Comparatum – Global Studies in Comparative Law 41, https://doi.org/10.1007/978-3-030-34432-0_1

> Non è forse giunto il momento di liberarsi del decrepito schema della gerarchia delle fonti oggi che l'assetto delle fonti smentisce, nel fervore dell'esperienza, quello schema e ne vive un altro?[1]

# 1 Introduction: General Perspective

Western legal culture faces many challenges. Yesterday's "high definition" law has given way to a globalised "low definition" law.[2] The imagination of the first,[3] at least in the continental tradition, was centered on some essential pillars:

(a) an authority – the figure of the State legislator –,
(b) a source of law – the national legislation –,
(c) a robust legal dogmatics made of concepts, clear reasoning and dichotomies (internal v. external, public v. private, etc.),
(d) a legal architecture of which the Kelsenian pyramid offered the paradigmatic image, and
(e) a modality of normativity based on coercion and obligation.

On the contrary,

> the scenario of global law involves different dynamics and different types of legal rationalities, as well as more numerous and more diverse subjects than those that characterized the modern legal scenario. The multiplicity of forms that the global law can take, the multiplication of the sources that produce it, and the subjects that populate it tend to give the impression of a crowded environment, in which the distinctive features fade away or are not very formalized, and are subject to frequent changes and high levels of precariousness.[4]

Thus the new paradigm of global law appears as a law of absence:

(a) absence of legislation expressing the will of politically identified authors and development of multiple sources of law, both public (legislative, judicial, etc.) and private (companies, NGOs, activists, etc.), national, supranational, international, and transnational, and even "unofficial";
(b) absence of mandatory, general and abstract substantive standards and development of a soft, essentially procedural, law, based on the negotiated respect of agreed standards;
(c) absence of clear static and dynamic hierarchies and perfectly stable and defined modes of connection between these normativities;
(d) absence of a geographic space of reference and decline in the territorial dimension of legal intercourse;
(e) absence of a unitary society and appearance of various subjectivities and multiculturalism, sources of multiple and mobile allegiances.[5]

---

[1]Grossi (2007), p. 8.

[2]On this image, see Ferrarese (2012), p. 32. For a general presentation, see also Domingo (2008), Walker (2015), Frydman (2012, 2014) and Cotterrell (2006).

[3]On the complexity and polycentricity of the common law, see esp. Samuel (2003, 2013).

[4]Ferrarese (2012), pp. 52–53.

[5]See also Yeh and Chang (2008), pp. 104–108.

Up to now, legal theory has not met these significant challenges successfully. Most of what is at stake, both empirically and epistemologically, remains adrift in a cloudy space. Drawing data from the national reports, this general report takes a step in this direction.

Contemporary constitutionalism can summarily[6] be characterised by the apparition of a normative standpoint.[7] The constitution is understood as a type of law that prescribes what agents ought to do. Like any other norm, a constitution cannot be automatically efficient. Only a system of implementation can guarantee compliance with its prescriptions. In *Marbury v. Madison*,[8] John Marshall established the necessity for a jurisdictional guarantee of constitutions in order for constitutional norms to really impose themselves as "the supreme law of the land".[9]

From a formal point of view, the constitution closes the legal system. It defines the characteristics that all the other elements of the system must exhibit to belong to it. Moreover, it presents itself as a superior norm because of both its active capacity to repeal other norms and its passive capacity to resist being repealed by other norms.[10] From a substantive point of view, the constitution is considered to be a document in which the most important values, the main commitments and the most fundamental principles that society wants to protect are established and guaranteed. It is indeed in that respect that human rights protection is provided for in it. Louis Henkin offers the following picture of the key elements of the paradigm that has conquered the world:

> In general, modern prescriptive constitutions reflect and give effect to 'constitutionalism' and 'the rule of law.' Constitutionalism is nowhere authoritatively defined, but, as commonly used, a constitution designed to reflect constitutionalism will have common elements, with variations. It declares the sovereignty of the people and derives its authority from the will of the people. It prescribes a blueprint for representative government responsible and accountable to the people through universal suffrage at periodic elections. Governmental authority is to be exercised only in accordance with law established pursuant to constitutional processes and consistent with constitutional prescriptions and limitations. Government is for the people, but is limited by a bill of individual rights. Many constitutional systems fractionate governmental authority by some separation of powers or other checks and balances. (Some systems divide authority 'vertically' by forms of federalism.) Increasingly, constitutions provide for constitutional review by a court or other independent institutions with authority to monitor compliance with constitutional prescriptions and to provide remedies against their violation. Constitutionalism implies also that the constitution cannot be suspended, circumvented or disregarded by political organs of government, and

---

[6]Introducing further important conceptual discussions, see Kombos, Legal Pluralism and Constitutionalism in the Cypriot Example.

[7]On the major trends in constitutionalism, see McIlwain (1940), Wormuth (1949), Fioravanti (1999, 2009), Grimm (1991, 2016), Mohnhaupt and Grimm (2002) and Bastid (1985).

[8]5 US 137 (1803).

[9]Article VI of the US Constitution. On constitutional supremacy, see esp. Del Rosario-Rodríguez (2011).

[10]See e.g. Kelsen (1962) and Merkl (1962).

> that it can be amended only by procedures appropriate to change of constitutional character and that give effect to the will of the people acting in a constitutional mode.[11]

Today however, the link that used to connect all those concepts has become more tenuous. This phenomenon goes far beyond the "weakening of the State" or the "crisis of sovereignty" before other economic, supranational or subnational powers. It is not exceptional nor illegitimate anymore for authors, NGOs, institutions, firms, practitioners, or activists to think of a multiplicity of non State-related contexts through the ideas of constitution, constitutionalisation, or constitutional law. Associated with each other by a family resemblance,[12] those ideas form a conceptual nebula the fields of application of which seem to be multiplying and to result in an inescapable situation of plurality. What follows is an attempt at charting these "atypical legal constructs".[13]

At the international or supranational level, a supra-national sort of constitutionalism[14] is emerging. Increasingly numerous international norms relate to human rights, which gives them a constitutional dimension. They overlap in many respects with the *jus cogens*[15] norms which, being at the apex of the pyramid of international norms, confer upon the international legal system the formal structure of a constitutional system. Treaties that do not belong to the strict framework of inter-State reciprocity and favour forms of majority decision-making are multiplying.[16] Several authors do not hesitate to consider that the United Nations Charter is a world constitution[17] and the World Trade Organisation Agreement the economic constitution of the world,[18] while the European Court of Human Rights and the European Court of Justice present themselves as agents of a form of constitutionalism. For example, the ECtHR presented the European "Convention as a constitutional instrument of European public order,"[19] whereas according to the ECJ, "the European Economic Community is a community based on the rule of law, inasmuch as neither its member States nor its institutions can avoid a review of the question whether the measures adopted by them are in conformity with the basic constitutional charter, the Treaty."[20] More recently, the ECJ considered that "The EU has a new kind of legal order, the nature of which is peculiar to the EU, its own constitutional framework

---

[11]Henkin (1998), pp. 11–12.

[12]See e.g. Wittgenstein (2010), p. 57; Wittgenstein (2014), pp. 64–65.

[13]Kombos, Legal Pluralism and Constitutionalism in the Cypriot Example.

[14]Helfer (2003), Kadelbach and Kleinlein (2006), St. John Macdonald and Johnston (2005), Frishman and Muller (2010), Schwöbel (2011) and Queiroz (2011).

[15]Art. 53 of the Vienna Convention on the Law of Treaties of 1969. See e.g. Orakhelashvili (2010).

[16]Tomuschat (1993) and Simma (1994).

[17]Fassbender (2009), Dupuy (1997), Doyle (2009) and Chemain and Pellet (2006).

[18]Schneiderman (2008), Cass (2005), Petersmann (2000, 2011), McGinnis and Movsesian (2000) and Trachtman (2006).

[19]ECHR, 23 March 1995, Loizidou v. Turkey (Preliminary objections), (Application no. 15318/89), § 75. See e.g. Walter (1999), Alkema (2000) and Stone Sweet (2009).

[20]ECJ, 23 April 1986, Parti écologiste "Les Verts" v. European Parliament, Case 294/83, § 23.

and founding principles, a particularly sophisticated institutional structure and a full set of legal rules to ensure its operation."[21] The European communities and the European Union offer paradigmatic examples of international organisations that have progressively evolved from intergovernmentality to constitutionalism.[22]

What is most remarkable is the emergence of what some authors analyse as spontaneous forms of constitutionalisation and constitutionalism which are appearing independently of States. Private law and private actors find themselves involved in the protection of fundamental rights.[23] Under what is called "corporate social responsibility" or "corporate citizenship", many norms which belong to soft law thus aim to make sure that economic agents protect human rights.[24] Regarding these institutions, Gunther Teubner has identified several forms of autonomous constitutionalisation in different sectors (economy, health, tourism, sports, culture, new technologies, etc.). He accounts for them in the idea of "societal constitutionalism".[25] As he remarks, "Here we are, [...] faced with a curious phenomenon – Stateless self-constitutionalisation." Sectors of the global society are progressively developing their own constitutional norms. Urgent social problems which appear within autonomous global systems engender social conflicts which lead to legal norms being conferred constitutional features. Over time, those norms are then brought together under the form of "sectorial constitutions of the global society."[26] Those spheres become *de facto* relevant from the perspective of global governance.[27] They have stable relationships the one with the other, agree on behavioural standards and conflict settlement, for themselves and in relation to third parties, develop a set of fundamental principles that all their other decisions must comply with, and settle their conflicts in a way that is close, in diverse degrees, to that of a jurisdictional process.[28] As Horatia Muir Watt puts it, "In redistributing regulatory power, globalisation disrupts the neat ordering of normative space: groups with diverse economic or ideological interests bypass State courts to claim protection in the international arena; private international arbitration has succeeded in creating a parallel system of justice which is gaining ground in many fields where State interests where thought to be paramount; transnational agreements between public

---

[21]ECJ, 18 December 2014, Opinion 2/13.

[22]Weiler (1999), Weiler and Wind (2003), Schütze (2012), Rosas and Armati (2012), Von Bogdandy and Bast (2010) and Bailleux (2014).

[23]Alston (2005), Clapham (2006), Gatto (2011) and Palombella (2012).

[24]Nolan (2009). See also the Norms on the Responsibilities of Transnational Corporations and Other Business Enterprises with regard to Human Rights of 2003, https://digitallibrary.un.org/record/501576, and the United Nations Global Compact, https://www.unglobalcompact.org/. See e.g. Rasche (2010).

[25]Teubner (2004, 2012, 2016).

[26]Teubner (2010, 2013). On sectorial constitutionalisation, see also Tuori (2015), pp. 125–318.

[27]See e.g. Zumbansen (2010, 2011), Hall and Biersteker (2011), Cutler (2003), Tuori (2013) and Maduro et al. (2014).

[28]Scott et al. (2011), Schepel (2004, 2005) and Peters et al. (2009).

authorities fall either side of the public/private divide."[29] Important parts of the *lex digitalis*, of the *lex constructionis*, etc. thus turn out to be real "transnational corporate constitutions".[30]

Lastly, at the infra-national level, the dynamics of the "new constitutionalism",[31] as it is emerging in Latin America, leads to the identification of new forms of acknowledgement of the constitutional autonomy of the first nations. It goes beyond the forms of normative autonomies that have hitherto been granted to entities such as churches, native communities or professional organisations when they collectively decide on labour conditions.[32] These claim to allow for a more sincere and inclusive taking into account of the specific cultures of the people who have until then been more or less violently colonised and whose ways of life and *Weltanschauungen* have been ignored, silenced, excluded, despised, or even fought against. Based on tolerance and multiculturalism, this sort of infra-national constitutionalism allows for new forms of interaction between State law and the normative practices of indigenous communities.[33] As well as the constitution of Ecuador,[34] the Bolivian "plurinacional" constitutionalism offers a telling example of this ambition, which results in various devices of vertical and horizontal separation of powers, and more crucially in the constant affirmation of a strong commitment to a specifically inclusive ideology, especially intending to benefit from the traditional knowledge and philosophy, in particular regarding its conception of harmony among human beings, animals and their environment (*Pacha Mama*), in order to revive the general political culture.[35]

Today, the very grammar of constitutionalism is quite clearly being redirected towards other legal, political and social "spheres," "sites of authority" or "sites of normativity"[36] which introduce multiplied forms of legal pluralism in opposition to the traditionally bilateral relation that used to exist between the State and the constitution. Animated by a double function of distributing and limiting normative powers, on the one hand, and preserving fundamental rights, on the other hand, international, supranational or transnational constitutions meet the definition of Article 16 of the Declaration of the Rights of Man and the Citizen, according to which "Any society in which no provision is made for guaranteeing rights or for the separation of powers, has no Constitution." From this brief outline,[37] two major characteristics of the different constitutional spheres can be identified. Those norms first claim formal and substantive (axiological or value-based) primacy in their own

[29]Muir Watt (2004), p. 274.

[30]Teubner (2011). See also Robé (2012, 2013).

[31]See e.g. Storini and Alenza García (2012) and Corrêa Souza de Oliveira and Luiz Streck (2014).

[32]See esp. De Sousa Santos (2002).

[33]See e.g. Neves (2009), pp. 216–229.

[34]See e.g. Andrade et al. (2009), Ávila Santamaría et al. (2008) and López Freire et al. (2009).

[35]See e.g. Acosta (2013), Pigrau Solé (2013) and Bagni (2013).

[36]See also Yeh and Chang (2008).

[37]See also Klabbers et al. (2009).

legal sphere. Then the constitutional systems assert their independence and autonomy towards other legal spheres. That is why they do not have hierarchical relations the one with the other—on the contrary, their relations are "heterarchical". In other terms, a situation of pluralism emerges.

The fact that legal spaces that were unused up to now are adopting similar self-descriptions indeed implies the implementation of specific links among them. Thus the simple plurality of constitutional and constitutionalised spheres, which is quite static, also quite naturally includes a more dynamic dimension of pluralism.[38] Only a polycentric model can account for this situation, while insisting, from a dynamic viewpoint, on ideas such as cooperation, networks, mobility, etc. They are revealed in the way the actors try to comprehend one another when, quite unavoidably, they have to regulate, each from its own point of view, a same set of facts or, in Robert M. Cover's words, when situations of "jurisdictional redundancy"[39] arise.

The pluralism of constitutional norms, which has become quite apparent, calls for an *aggiornamento* of legal practices and legal reasoning. Potentially important conflicts result from it. It is not difficult to imagine a situation in which, regarding a professional sportsperson, the constitutional law of a State (e.g. the principles of tax collection or the workers' fundamental rights), sports constitutional law (e.g. the principles of repressive measures against doping or measures for equality among clubs) and European constitutional law (e.g. the principle of free movement of workers) are in conflict. The absence of a hierarchy among the different systems does not make it *a priori* possible to foresee any obvious solution. The situation becomes even more complicated and tensions stronger when some of the multiple constitutional spheres are able to assert what Pedro Cruz Villalón presents as forms of "meta constitutionality".[40] That word refers to the capacity for a constitutional system to assert something about another and require that it comply with its demands (such as primacy and direct effect in EU law), while, very often, the targeted system is also able to make meta constitutional claims towards the other. In such a situation, the constitutional intertwining and the tensions that result from them distort in quite a serious way the analysis grids that are associated to the classic constitutional paradigm. The reflection that has developed about "global constitutionalism,"[41] "constitutionalism in the global realm,"[42] "constitutional pluralism,"[43] "transnational constitutionalism,"[44] "multi-level constitutionalism,"[45]

[38]On pluralism, see among others, MacCormick (1995, 1999), Walker (2002, 2016), Teubner (1997) and Berman (2009).

[39]Cover (1981).

[40]Cruz Villalón (2004), p. 73.

[41]Fischer-Lescano (2005), Schwöbel (2011), Lang and Wiener (2017) and Belov (2018).

[42]Kjaer (2014).

[43]Avbelj and Komárek (2008, 2012) and Millet (2018).

[44]Stein (1981), Tsagourias (2007), Zumbansen (2012a, b), Goderis and Versteeg (2013) and Yeh and Chang (2008).

[45]Pernice (1999, 2002), Freixes et al. (2012), Piattoni (2010), Walker (2012a), Cerri and Donnarumma (2014) and Navas Castillo and Florentina Navas Castillo (2016).

"transconstitutionalism,"[46] "post-national constitutionalism,"[47] "societal constitutionalism,"[48] "composite constitutionalism[49]", "network constitutionalism,"[50] "interordinal constitutionalism,"[51] "multi-vocal constitutionalism,"[52] "harmonic law,"[53] etc., precisely aims to face that issue.

Manuel Atienza for example underlines to what extent "constitutionalism" and "globalisation" are both phenomena and ways of conceptualising those phenomena.[54] That double dimension is at the core of this report's topic. The objective of this work on "Debating legal pluralism and constitutionalism: new trajectories for legal theory in the age of globalisation" is to measure to what extent the mutations of legal systems today are upsetting the operation of positive law. At a deeper level, it aims at understanding how the intellectual or cultural backgrounds, which are at the basis of the perception of those mutations, are affected. Its objective is to determine and understand how legal phenomena, when tackled through "constitutionalism", "pluralism", "constitutional pluralism", etc., presuppose, trigger, accompany, impose or hinder the development of renewed ways not only of finding practical solutions to cases, both within a legislative and litigation framework, but, at a deeper level, of questioning the theories, concepts, categories, methods, intellectual tools, reasoning, and arguments which have been called upon to conceive, analyse, understand and describe them. Its goal is to allow the presentation of the new reasoning and elements of legal theory that have been implemented, invented from the beginning or rediscovered in the light of the history of legal practices and jurisprudence—in other words, to try and comprehend whether there is any emergence of a new legal rationality (e.g. the idea of *jus commune*, of *comitas gentium*, the theories of legal pluralism, etc.).

In front of globalisation, legal theory has undergone—or should have undergone—a radical paradigm shift.[55] In a somewhat oversimplified presentation, two main orientations are commonly identified in the literature: constitutionalism and pluralism. Whereas constitutionalism is mostly based on the foregoing considerations, it tends to unify the legal landscape by organising it from the formal viewpoint and imposing on it a specific substantive *telos*. From a genealogical perspective, it inevitably derives from the pattern of the State. Constitutionalism

---

[46]Neves (2009, 2015).

[47]Shaw (2011), Krisch (2011) and Walker (2012b).

[48]Teubner (2003).

[49]Besselink (2006, 2007); Pernice and Mayer (2000); Claes and De Visser (2012), p. 144.

[50]Bustos Gisbert (2005).

[51]Gordillo Pérez (2014).

[52]Jackson (2010), p. 91.

[53]Letsas (2012).

[54]Atienza (2013), pp. 31–60. See similarly Zumbansen (2012a, b).

[55]De Julios-Campuzano (2009). For an overview of the current theoretical efforts, see Kombos, Legal Pluralism and Constitutionalism in the Cypriot Example, § 2.

can thus be presented as a factor of order, which tends to offer a vernacular that is apt to remedy global fragmentation. Indeed,

> Trying to outline the results of the studies on fragmentation, one could say that the pluralist theorists consider fragmentation essentially from two different points of view. On the one hand, fragmentation can be understood as a multi-layered fragmentation, along a vertical axis composed by the States, the supranational or regional bodies, and the international organizations. It is a fragmentation across different levels of governance, from global, through international, supranational, and finally domestic spheres. On the other hand, fragmentation can be intended as a segmentation in a wide range of single regulatory regimes, placed side by side or overlapping on a horizontal plane in the global sphere, each exercising recognizably public governance functions.[56]

Constitutionalism is classically said to belittle the significance of autonomy. As Lucrezia Palandri notices, global constitutionalism "does not reflect, least of all respect, the pluralistic nature of reality, rather tends to neutralize and negate it, driven by the ambition of a utopian reduction to unity, claiming to re-impose order and re-establish hierarchy."[57] On the contrary, pluralism tends to be presented as rejecting any dimension of hierarchy or even of order, and as admitting disorder, and even welcoming it as evidence of social vitality and equal consideration for varying forms of institutionalisation of social spaces. Whereas constitutionalism tends to impose a single narrative that results from the national States' historical experience alone, pluralism seems to be more welcoming, more tolerant, and more open-minded regarding the contemporary blurring of traditional intellectual and practical patterns. It is committed to a common and reciprocal recognition of the other party, whatever its own specificities. As a consequence, pluralism is not satisfied with merely admitting, from a somehow static viewpoint, that a plurality of sites of authority exists. It also embraces a more dynamic description and insists on the fruitfulness of the interactions among them.

In a seminal article, John Griffiths has defined pluralism as

> a concomitant of social pluralism: the legal organization of society is congruent with its social organization. 'Legal pluralism' refers to the normative heterogeneity attendant upon the fact that social action always takes place in a context of multiple, overlapping 'semi-autonomous social fields', which, it may be added, is in practice a dynamic condition.
>
> A situation of legal pluralism – the omnipresent, normal situation in human society – is one in which law and legal institutions are not all subsumable within one 'system' but have their sources in the self-regulatory activities of all the multifarious social fields present, activities which may support, complement, ignore or frustrate one another, so that the 'law' which is actually effective on the 'ground floor' of society is the result of enormously complex and usually in practice unpredictable patterns of competition, interaction, negotiation, isolationism, and the like.[58]

In the context of the debate regarding legal globalisation, Kaarlo Tuori has distinguished three types of pluralism. The "pluralism of legal sources" implies the

---

[56]Palandri (2013), pp. 61–62.

[57]Palandri (2013), p. 67.

[58]Griffiths (1986), pp. 38–39.

multiplication of sources of law, the appearance of new legal actors and the polycentric[59] creation of the law. The "pluralism of legal orders" addresses the situation where several legal orders claim authority on a given social space. The "pluralism of legal systems" calls into question the exclusivity and primacy of State law.[60] When compared with constitutionalism, which is adamant that the protection of fundamental values calls for the establishment of a supreme norm and, consequently, of a hierarchy of organs with a supreme one at its apex, the lexicon of pluralism is based on multiplicity, fragmentation, idiosyncrasies, interdependence, and autonomy. It seems to be less reluctant to draw inspiration from the current legal phenomena in order to reform theoretical and practical mindsets, to give up previous lenses and concepts (such as that of sovereignty, the explicative and normative value of which seems to be decreasing). Even tentatively, pluralism promotes new ones that will need to readapt as things change and call for new imaginative efforts. As a consequence, constitutionalism and pluralism seem to offer competing viewpoints or strategies to address the challenges of the global age.[61]

Some authors have tried to offer a sort of middle-ground between these two conflicting poles.[62] For example Palandri has put forward the following proposal:

> This theory aims at the reconciliation of plurality in constitutionally meaning terms. To this end, it goes through various stages. Firstly, constitutional pluralist scholars realize the pluralistic essence of the contemporary legal world, making use of the outcomes of the legal pluralism studies as a starting point. Secondly, they recognize to each non-State legal order its own independent constitutional claims, and respect every distinct constitutional site – national, supranational, international –. Thirdly, they provide a normative sense to the global space, recognizing not only single constitutional identities but also the proper constitutional quality of their mutual relationships. The cooperative dimension between constitutional units cannot be represented anymore either by the old Westphalian order of fully sovereign States, or by an equally fully sovereign global State with a global constitution that absorbs and replaces the existing different sites of authority, repositioning the one-dimensional sovereign order. Constitutional pluralism provides an alternative interpretation of these connections, playing a crucial role in fostering the conditions under which these connections may occur, and thus progressively stabilizing them.[63]

Neil Walker, one of the leading proponents of new theories to address legal globalisation, has offered the following presentation:

> Briefly stated, [Constitutional Pluralism] in its original European context maintains the following:
>
> 1. The overall complex of law pertaining to the EU embraces multiple sites (i.e. the supranational site of the EU and the national sites of each of its 28 member States), each with its own claim to constitutional authority;

[59]See esp. Petersen and Zahle (1995).

[60]Tuori (2013). See also Tuori and Sankari (2010).

[61]Kennedy (2008).

[62]See e.g. Walker (2002, 2016); Cohen (2012), esp. pp. 21–79.

[63]Palandri (2013), p. 68.

2. There is, in fact, no dominant understanding of this complex that holds across these multiple sites, according to which the claims to constitutional authority associated with each site would be ordered within a hierarchy or otherwise reconciled and resolved by reference to a single meta-authoritative standard; rather, each site is associated with a plausible claim to ultimate constitutional authority that stands independently of the other claims
3. In order to sustain the overall complex in a constitutionally optimal fashion, each site ought to acknowledge and somehow accommodate the claims of the others as independent sites of constitutional authority—thereby ensuring the continuing absence of a single dominant authoritative framework.[64]

However, according to a logic of "bipolar errors" identified by Gaston Bachelard,[65] each of the two alternatives leads to a stalemate, which the other alternative cannot remedy without falling into an abyss of difficulties which are themselves solvable only by means of the antagonistic strategy, itself doomed to failure. Whichever approach is chosen, there is an antinomy the structure of which is comparable to those that Alf Ross has highlighted in *Towards a Realistic Jurisprudence*.[66] In an article summing up in French the perspective of this work, he writes:

> On this fundamental dualism of the notion of source of law it is possible to develop a whole series of antinomies. [...]
>
> *First antinomy*
>
> Thesis: The propositions of the doctrine of the sources of law do not themselves belong to positive law, but are valid independently of a given positive system of law.
>
> Antithesis: The propositions of the doctrine of the sources of law vary from one legal system to another, and must therefore be parts of these.
>
> The proof of the thesis is easy, because if the propositions of the doctrine of the sources of law belong themselves to positive law, they must then be recognized by the very sources of law, which leads obviously to a vicious circle, that is, to an infinite regression. It follows that the question What is a source of law? can only be resolved on the basis of the notion of law itself.
>
> But the antithesis seems to be as obvious, because experience undoubtedly teaches us that the sources of law vary according to the systems and can develop in different ways; it does not seem that there is a single historical phenomenon that could be said, in a general way, to be a source of law and should be. Legislation itself, whatever the vagueness of that term, does not constitute a necessary and absolute form of the law. [...] The origin of this antinomy can be stated most succinctly in the following way: the propositions of the doctrine of the sources of law are, in their content, conditioned by positive law but at the same time in their form (as the basis of knowledge for any positive rule), they are independent from them.[67]

In the present case, one could attempt to formulate the antinomy in the following way:

---

[64] Walker (2016), pp. 333–334.

[65] Bachelard (1967), p. 20. See Ost and Van de Kerchove (1988); Ponthoreau (2010), pp. 203–206.

[66] Ross (1946).

[67] Ross (2004), pp. 29–30.

> *Thesis*: Pluralism implies respect for the autonomy of self-emerging legal spheres and excludes the external superimposition of hierarchical authority in the name of paramount substantive fundamental values.
>
> *Antithesis*: Constitutionalism allows legal spheres to organise their own autonomy through internal supremacy and external equality, depending on their values, in order to interact with other legal entities.

According to the thesis, pluralism implies autonomy and excludes constitutionalism, whereas according to the antithesis, constitutionalism is one of the ways to express autonomy. As Lorenzo Zucca puts it, "The irony of global constitutional law is that it inevitably defines itself as tolerant and pluralist."[68] More puzzlingly, Hans Kelsen has even suggested that the pluralist standpoint is somehow self-defeating. Pluralism implies that several distinct legal systems enjoy separate scopes of application. But as Christoph Kletzer recently put it with a Kelsenian touch, "the fact that a norm does not apply somewhere is not a brute fact but a legal fact. Thus, there has to be an even higher norm that stipulates that the seemingly highest norm applying to the one legal system does not apply to the other legal system. This higher norm, by definition, applies to both legal systems and establishes legal monism. So, as soon as we think we have established pluralism (our highest norm does not apply there), what we have actually established is monism (there is a higher norm applying to both systems)."[69]

From a descriptive viewpoint, one that is not committed to the more or less explicit normative standpoints that respectively lie beneath those conceptions, this antinomy allows to surmise a relatively deflationist approach. Both perspectives are entwined with one another. As Mireille Delmas-Marty explained, the global age is the age for multiple practices that are "ordering pluralism".[70] Pluralism implies overlap, conflict, frictions, responsiveness, which are regulated by norms that are materially constitutional. The patterns of interconnection that ensue are justified by substantive values that are constitutional. Even the most cherished values of pluralism, such as autonomy and self-sufficiency, can be regarded as fundamental constitutional requisites. The very independence which legal spheres enjoy in a pluralist landscape needs to be constructed and legitimised. Independence is frequently conquered through a discourse that tends to bestow constitutional properties on the social sphere in question. That is why, according to François-Xavier Millet,

> it is remarkable that the doctrines of constitutional pluralism – and, more broadly, all pluralist theories that do not belong to radical pluralism – tend to take into account systematic considerations and institutional (rather than textual) constraints, thus allowing the judge, who is the central character in these theories imbued with realism, to resolve disputes. Courts are therefore called on to reconstruct substantive hierarchy, which, far from being fixed, will necessarily fluctuate according to the circumstances.[71]

[68]Zucca (2018), p. 5.

[69]Kletzer (2018), p. 96.

[70]Delmas-Marty (2006).

[71]Millet (2018), p. 128.

Conversely, the intellectual and practical tools of legal pluralism are necessary to acknowledge the coexistence of the constitutional spheres that tend to proliferate and manage their interactions.

Consequently, the distinction between constitutionalism and pluralism should not be regarded as a clear-cut opposition, but would be more fruitfully looked at from a scalar perspective. Current legal practice may illustrate *hic et nunc* one more than the other, but each necessarily seems to imply the other, and *vice versa*.

With this general background in mind, the following general report tries and offers a picture of the current tensions and accommodations between constitutionalism and pluralism. It has greatly benefited from the information and analysis gleaned from nine national reporters about the respective situations, difficulties, achievements, standpoints, perspectives, etc., of Argentina, Botswana, Brazil, Cyprus, Germany, Greece, Singapore, the Solomon Islands, and the United Kingdom.

Although they frequently follow, or draw, from one another, the report successively addresses five major groups of topics. Section 2 sets the stage for the study of legal interactions in the global age. It sheds light on the degree of pluralism each of the studied legal systems admits, both in its relations with other legal systems that reach beyond the States, and in its relations with inner more or less autonomous forms of legal normativity. Section 3 tackles the forms of interactions that take place among legal actors in the context of an increasingly plural landscape, and how they contribute to changing legal mentalities. Sections 4 and 5 do not follow a clear-cut distinction. Section 4 focuses on legal actors' legal reasoning, whereas Sect. 5 addresses legal scholarship. It is obvious however that legal doctrines and legal thought evolve thanks to (or because of) the simultaneous and joined efforts of legal actors and legal scholars, understood as members of a more or less unified epistemic community. In several countries, it is not exceptional for law professors to become judges or conversely, nor is it exceptional for legal actors, especially judges, to quote legal scholars.[72] At a deeper level, a sort of interactive and cyclical process appears according to which (a) legal actors make a decision that somehow changes previous modes of reasoning, (b) legal scholars comment on this decision and help explain its presuppositions and implications, so that (c) new decisions by legal actors refine their reasoning, which (d) calls for new comments by legal scholars, etc. The conceptual framework that is in force in a given society thus results from both sources. That is why even though they may seem to draw too sharp a distinction between legal actors and legal scholars, both parts contribute to highlighting what "thinking like a lawyer"[73] means today. Finally, Sect. 6 identifies how little neutral, and how value-laden, the current discussion about pluralism and constitutionalism as it appears in the legal systems under review is. The very concepts that are currently used to confront today's major legal changes testify to the ideological dimension of legal analysis. But as the final part of the document proves by using comparative

[72]See e.g. Pegoraro and Figueroa Mejía (2017).

[73]Schauer (2009).

methodology, making that clear does not necessarily allow one to avoid ideology. At best, it helps to be minimally aware of its possible impact on legal discourses.

## 2 The Statics of the Relations Among Legal Spheres in Positive Law: Multifaceted Pluralism

This part of the report intends to tackle the following issues. What is the position of national law regarding international and transnational law? Is it open or closed (e.g. monistic or dualist), and to what extent, to their interference in terms of regulation of behaviours? Is its attitude uniform or does is vary depending on the types of international norms (e.g. customary law, principles of international law, international treaties, EU law, international human rights law, etc.)? What type of hierarchy of norms (e.g. place of international and supranational law regarding the constitution or the law) or norm combination (e.g. degree of contractual freedom in the choice of applicable law and litigation resolution, autonomy granted to professionals in collective bargaining, admission of normativities from traditional cultures, native communities or churches, etc.) is established? Are relations among norms mainly founded on the idea of a binding force of the norms of other legal spheres or rather on the idea of a weaker "persuasive"[74] force? Are specific appeals organised at the internal level in order to give external norms prevailing force (e.g. distinction and combination of conventionality review and judicial review; preliminary rulings; consequences of the concept of public order on contractual freedom, etc.)? Have those aspects of the relations among legal norms evolved over the past few years?

With respect to these questions, one might suspect that in spite of the very respectable tradition of legal thought it is related to,[75] "pluralism" is at best a vague catchword—or at least an "elusive ism"[76]—to address many different phenomena whenever some sort of *dis*order appears in what sets out to be an order, and especially some disagreement or conflict among various norms.[77] William Twining for example notices: "it is important to distinguish between (a) 'State legal pluralism' (recognition within a State legal system of different bodies of law, such as religious or customary law, applying to members of particular groups for given purposes); (b) 'legal polycentricity' (the eclectic use of sources in different sectors of a State

[74]Glenn (1987) and Flanders (2009). On the distinction between "must-", "should-", and "may-" sources of law, see also Peczenik (2009).

[75]See esp. Ehrlich (1913) and Romano (2002).

[76]Twining (2009).

[77]For critical efforts at conceptual clarification, see for example Griffiths (1986), Merry (1988), Petersen and Zahle (1995), Tamanaha (1993, 2008), Teubner (1992, 1997) and Berman (2009).

legal system); and (c) legal pluralism as the co-existence of discrete or semi-autonomous legal orders in the same time-space context."[78]

Considering the national reports, and with a view to exposing the gathered data without silencing the various perspectives they express, two main interpretations of "pluralism" seem appropriate. Both start from what remains—even though its relevance is sometimes called into question—the major reference point for legal thought, i.e. the State. The first ideal-type can be called "outward pluralism". It is related to the interconnections between the State, understood as the dominant, classical or prototypical legal system, and other normative orders that reach beyond the State, i.e. classically international, supranational, and transnational legal orders (Sect. 2.1). The second ideal-type can be called "inward pluralism". It is related to the ways States make room for diverse forms of autonomy that allow taking norms which are not immediately those of the State into account in domestic law (Sect. 2.2).

## 2.1 *Outward Pluralism: Perspectives on the Relationship Between Domestic and International, Supranational, and Transnational Legal Orders*

Over the past few years, one has witnessed a general internationalisation of legal systems due to the increasing impact of international law.[79] One of the important teachings of the national reports is related to the very little value of the fundamental divide between "monist" and "dualist" States, no matter their definition.[80] As a matter of example, Millet proposes the following definition:

> Dualism refers to separate, autonomous legal orders that are self-contained and theoretically perfect. This doctrine presupposes that the only addressees of international law are the States, and that the international and domestic legal orders do not overlap but, at best, operate side by side. It implies that an external law norm cannot be applied until it has been transformed into an instrument of domestic law, in accordance with the procedures that the latter has laid down for that purpose.
>
> Under the monist doctrine, the suggestion is that there is only a single legal order, which is made up of 'suborders', also sometimes called 'partial' legal orders. Although this approach does not offer any conclusive elucidation as to which legal order enjoys primacy, it indicates that international law is supposed to be, as such, directly applied in the domestic legal order without having to be formally implemented by the State organs through legislative or administrative measures.

In several respects, most of the examples prove how weak this dichotomy is from descriptive and explicative viewpoints. What is interesting moreover is that when

---

[78] Twining (2009), p. 28. See also Twining (2000), pp. 82–88, 224–233.

[79] See e.g. Fombad (2012) and Killander (2017).

[80] See generally Shelton (2011). See also Killander and Adjolohoun (2010) and Ramadi Dinokopila (2017).

one focuses on the specificities presented by the national reports, the validity of this dichotomy is called into question from various angles and in various ways.

At the most monist end of the spectrum, Cyprus offers an almost unique example of constitutional deference to supranational law. Whereas the constitution is classically presented as the supreme law of the land,

> following the 2006 fifth amendment of the Constitution,[81] the acquis communautaire acquired precedence over the Constitution. More specifically, the fifth amendment inserted a new provision, namely Article 1A which envisages that '[n]o provision of the Constitution shall be deemed to annul laws enacted, acts done or measures taken by the Republic which become necessary by reason of its obligations as a member State of the European Union, nor does it prevent Regulations, Directives or other acts or binding measures of a legislative character, adopted by the European Union or the European Communities or by their institutions or competent bodies thereof on the basis of the Treaties establishing the European Communities or the Treaty of the European Union, from having legal effect in the Republic'.[82]

This amendment was meant to curb a ruling by the Supreme Court that had overruled a lower court judgement. This judgement had made national measures that implemented EU legislation an extension of EU law, and had allowed them to benefit from the latter's primacy.[83] Pursuant to Article 169 of the Constitution, the remainder of international law only enjoys primacy regarding ordinary statutes, but not the Constitution itself. This distinction has led some authors to debate the monist or dualist perspective of Cyprus' legal system. But Constantinos Kombos downplays the intrinsic importance of this divide.[84] An appropriate example is offered by the constitutional human rights provisions. The ECHR was a source of inspiration when they were drafted, so that their domestic interpretation heavily relies on an attitude of openness towards the ECtHR's rulings.[85] More generally, there is evidence of an important internal perception of the need to change domestic law, including constitutional law, when the evolution of "contemporary aspirations, interests and desires,"[86] as they may be expressed at the global level, call for it.

After offering a picture of the complex Greek path and current situation, Ioannis A. Tassoupoulos accurately remarks, regarding the monist/dualist divide, that: "The transition from a monist view of supremacy of domestic law over international law, to the dualist position of two independent legal orders, which do not interpenetrate, to the monist view of preponderance of international law, or to non-hierarchical 'interacting systems,' marks the interplay between the *constitutionalization of international law* or the *internationalization of constitutional law,* more prominent in the tensions between universalization of human rights, democracy, and market

[81] Law relating to the Fifth Amendment of the Constitution, (Law No. 127(I)/2006).

[82] Kombos, Legal Pluralism and Constitutionalism in the Cypriot Example, § 3.2.1.

[83] Attorney General v. Costas Constantinou (2005) LCR 1356, quoted by Kombos, Legal Pluralism and Constitutionalism in the Cypriot Example, § 3.3.2.3.

[84] Kombos, Legal Pluralism and Constitutionalism in the Cypriot Example, § 3.2.2.

[85] Kombos, Legal Pluralism and Constitutionalism in the Cypriot Example, § 3.2.2.

[86] Kombos, Legal Pluralism and Constitutionalism in the Cypriot Example, § 3.3.2.3.

globalization."[87] He thus insists on the very fluidity of the matter. Greece for its part has adopted what can be characterised as a monist position. Pursuant to Article 28 of the Constitution,

1. The generally recognised rules of international law, as well as international conventions as of the time they are sanctioned by statute and become operative according to their respective conditions, shall be an integral part of domestic Greek law and shall prevail over any contrary provision of the law. The rules of international law and of international conventions shall be applicable to aliens only under the condition of reciprocity.
2. Authorities provided by the Constitution may by treaty or agreement be vested in agencies of international organizations, when this serves an important national interest and promotes cooperation with other States. A majority of three-fifths of the total number of Members of Parliament shall be necessary to vote the law sanctioning the treaty or agreement.
3. Greece shall freely proceed by law passed by an absolute majority of the total number of Members of Parliament to limit the exercise of national sovereignty, insofar as this is dictated by an important national interest, does not infringe upon the rights of man and the foundations of democratic government and is effected on the basis of the principles of equality and under the condition of reciprocity.

Brazil also seems to clearly endorse a position of strict constitutional primacy.[88] Nevertheless, among the States covered in this report, it is one of the clearest examples of a monist approach to the relationship among legal systems. Pursuant to Article 49 of the Constitution and constitutional custom, the Congress needs to approve any international treaty or agreement and the President needs to endorse it. Once these steps have been followed, the international norm is integrated into the domestic legal system without any need for a further incorporation through a dedicated legislation. The ensuing hierarchy of norms is not uniform but threefold. Since 2004, treaties which specifically deal with human rights and which are approved following the same procedure as constitutional amendments have been granted a constitutional value. Human rights conventions and treaties approved before that date have an infraconstitutional but supralegislative status. Other international norms merely have a legislative status, and can generally be derogated pursuant to the *lex posterior* maxim.[89]

Argentina offers an original case. Following a constitutional amendment in 1994, which had been foreshadowed by the case-law of the Supreme Court, a monist position was clearly adopted.[90] Pursuant to Article 75 of the Constitution, the general rule is that treaties prevail over domestic acts. Moreover, regarding specific human rights conventions and declarations, the Constitution even states that these have the same value as the constitution itself.[91] Among these norms one can find

[87]Tassopoulos, Between Constitutionalism and Legal Pluralism: Perspectives from Greece, § 1.

[88]See also infra, § 3.

[89]STF, RE 349.703; STF, RE 466.343. See De Barcelos, Brazil and Its Many Realities. Courts and State-Centrism; Administrative Agencies and International Cooperation, § 2.

[90]Ucín, A Particular Dialogue Between Systems. The Argentinian Case.

[91]Ucín, A Particular Dialogue Between Systems. The Argentinian Case, § 1.ii.

some of the international norms and documents that have also deserved specific attention in other countries covered in this report. Article 75, 22 of the Constitution remarkably provides that:

> The American Declaration of the Rights and Duties of Man; the Universal Declaration of Human Rights; the American Convention on Human Rights; the International Pact on Economic, Social and Cultural Rights; the International Pact on Civil and Political Rights and its empowering Protocol; the Convention on the Prevention and Punishment of Genocide; the International Convention on the Elimination of all Forms of Racial Discrimination; the Convention on the Elimination of all Forms of Discrimination against Woman; the Convention against Torture and other Cruel, Inhuman or Degrading Treatments or Punishments; the Convention on the Rights of the Child; in the full force of their provisions, they have constitutional hierarchy, do no repeal any section of the First Part of this Constitution and are to be understood as complementing the rights and guarantees recognized herein.

This means that they are also above other international instruments that only enjoy an ordinary legislative value. This testifies to Argentina's evident openness to international and supranational spheres. That is why it "is integrated into other supranational organizations. It is part of the MERCOSUR (*Mercado Común del Sur*) since 1991, the UNASUR (*Unión de Naciones Sudamericanas*), the CELAC (*Comunidad de Estados Latinoamericanos y Caribeños*) and the OEA (*Organización de Estados Americanos*)."[92]

At the other end of the spectrum, the United Kingdom is frequently presented as the *locus classicus* of dualism. As Athanasios Psygkas makes clear, however, things are more complex depending on which source of international law is concerned. This position clearly corresponds to the relationships between international treaties and domestic law, because of the need for a national parliamentary act of incorporation. But insofar as domestic courts accept it, custom is automatically incorporated into English law unless it conflicts with an Act of Parliament.[93] In the famous *Miller* case, the UK Supreme Court made clear that, except in the case of peace treaties and, according to some judges, human rights treaties, "The first [proposition] is that treaties between sovereign States have effect in international law and are not governed by the domestic law of any State. [...] The second proposition is that, although they are binding on the United Kingdom in international law, treaties are not part of UK law and give rise to no legal rights or obligations in domestic law."[94] The major exception to this pattern, which adds to the complexity of the picture, is European Union law. Because of the special nature of this supranational legal

[92]Ucín, A Particular Dialogue Between Systems. The Argentinian Case, § 1.

[93]Psygkas, Accommodating Legal Pluralism and 'Pluralizing' the Constitution: The Example of the United Kingdom, § 2.1.

[94]R (Miller) v Secretary of State for Exiting the European Union [2017] UKSC 5 [55], quoted by Psygkas, Accommodating Legal Pluralism and 'Pluralizing' the Constitution: The Example of the United Kingdom, § 2.1.

order,[95] the foundation of which is the European Communities Act 1972 in the United Kingdom, EU norms enjoy primacy over domestic norms. Nevertheless, the Judiciary is adamant that this primacy results from the express consent of the British Parliament, so that the fundamental constitutional "rule of recognition" of the system remains unaltered.[96] Once completed, Brexit is expected to put an end to the existing interaction.

In the same vein, Botswana illustrates the traditional English common law approach to the relationships between legal systems. As Charles M. Fombad emphasises, "Botswana is a dualist country. Treaties and other international instruments signed and ratified by Botswana only take effect at the domestic level after they have been incorporated into national law by an Act of Parliament."[97] But this does not prevent some more informal or softer ways for international norms from having an influence on the domestic legal system. As Fombad continues, the interpretation of obscure statutes is frequently made on an "international law"-friendly basis, an interpretation of a domestic norm that is consistent with international law being preferred to another one.[98] A form of presumption according to which the Parliament cannot be presupposed to have wanted to violate international law thus ensures a minimal harmony between the two. Moreover, a monist approach is adopted as to customary international law. As is traditional in English law, customary norms are automatically incorporated into domestic law, provided they do not conflict with Acts of Parliament.

Singapore has also adopted a dualist perspective regarding the incorporation of international law. It cannot be automatic, but needs the passing of specific implementing acts.[99] Such a position was clearly affirmed by the High Court in *Public Prosecutor v Tan Cheng Yew*.[100] Nevertheless, as Jaclyn L. Neo, drawing from earlier writings of hers, makes clear, this general dualist attitude is not in itself uniform. It can encompass a complex gradation of legal consequences regarding the hierarchy of norms:

> First, a dualist State may completely view international law as being entirely irrelevant to domestic law, a position that I have called '*absolute non-relevance*'. Secondly, a dualist State may see international law as relevant but as not hierarchically superior, and thus would

[95]See ECJ, 5 February 1963, Van Gend & Loos (26/62); ECJ, 15 July 1964, Flaminio Costa v ENEL (6/64); ECJ, 17 December 1970, Internationale Handelsgesellschaft (11/70); ECJ, 9 March 1978, Simmenthal (106/77).

[96]Psygkas, Accommodating Legal Pluralism and 'Pluralizing' the Constitution: The Example of the United Kingdom, § 2.3, alluding to Hart (2012).

[97]Fombad, Reconciling Legal Pluralism and Constitutionalism: New Trajectories for Legal Theory in the Age of Globalisation in Botswana, § 2. See also Tshosa (2007).

[98]Attorney-General v. Dow [1992] BLR 119, 154, quoted by Fombad, Reconciling Legal Pluralism and Constitutionalism: New Trajectories for Legal Theory in the Age of Globalisation in Botswana, § 2. See also Ramadi Dinokopila (2017), pp. 239–240.

[99]Neo, Legal Pluralism in Centralist Singapore, § 2.

[100]Public Prosecutor v Tan Cheng Yew [2013] 1 SLR 1095 at [56], quoted by Neo, Legal Pluralism in Centralist Singapore, § 2.

> not override or supersede national statutes and the common law. In other words, '*domestic law prevails*'. Thirdly, a dualist State may see international law as relevant, but that it could not override or supersede the supreme constitution of the State. This means that the '*constitution prevails*' at all times, although international law may supersede national statutes or the common law.[101]

In view of this taxonomy, it appears that Singapore courts have decided to make domestic law prevail. That is why even if domestic law should be, as far as possible, interpreted consistently with international norms, this operation has inherent limits. Even *jus cogens* cannot prevail over a domestic statute.[102] Generally, thus, "Singapore courts have declined to apply interpretive incorporation,"[103] i.e. to allow international law to "slip into" the legal system more or less informally.

Nothing specific is said about the relationship between domestic and international law in the Constitution of Solomon Islands. However, due to the British heritage, a dualist model, according to which international law needs to be incorporated into domestic legislation, seems to be natural.[104] A lack of political will, stemming perhaps from a defensive attitude to its newfound sovereignty, coupled with a lack of resources, explain why Solomon Islands has not ratified many human rights treaties since its independence, and why most of the international conventions adopted by Solomon Islands have not been implemented through domestic legislation.[105] According to *K v. Regina*, the Constitution prevails over international law.[106] On a case-by-case basis, the implementing legislation may establish a system to solve conflicts and ensure, like the legislation related to the Regional Assistance Mission to Solomon Islands, that domestic legislation yields to the norms of the international law being implemented.[107]

Germany offers another example of the need to go beyond the monist/dualist divide. It is presented as adopting a "moderate dualist position".[108] Pursuant to Article 25 of the Basic Law, the general rules of international law, which include customary law and the general principles of law, prevail over domestic statutes. Treaties become part of the domestic system as soon as they have been approved by the government and ratified by the parliament. But they rank as ordinary statutes, so that the relationships between them and statutes are governed by the *lex posterior* principle. Nevertheless, more recently, the Federal Constitutional Court considered that even posterior statutes should be interpreted in conformity with international

---

[101]Neo, Legal Pluralism in Centralist Singapore, § 2. See also Neo (2012).

[102]Yong Vui Kong v Public Prosecutor [2015] 2 SLR 1129, quoted by Neo, Legal Pluralism in Centralist Singapore, § 2.

[103]Neo, Legal Pluralism in Centralist Singapore, § 2.

[104]Corrin, Constitutionalism and Customary Law in Solomon Island, § 3.1.

[105]Corrin, Constitutionalism and Customary Law in Solomon Island, § 4.1.

[106]Quoted by Corrin, Constitutionalism and Customary Law in Solomon Island, § 4.3.

[107]Corrin, Constitutionalism and Customary Law in Solomon Island, § 4.3.

[108]Viellechner, 'Friendliness' Towards Others: How the German Constitution Deals with Legal Pluralism, § 2.2.1.

obligations.[109] In particular, international human rights treaties should offer an "interpretive aid".[110] In the *Görgülü* case, the authorities had to take into account international treaties and their interpretation by supranational courts.[111] According to Lars Viellechner, this amounted to a constitutional entrenchment of international treaties.[112] But the recent case-law of the Federal Constitutional Court seems to parallel the British insistence on parliamentary sovereignty by implying that democracy requires that the parliament be able to override international norms.[113] As in the UK, EU norms enjoy a specific and "privileged" status. Their authority is based on Article 23 of the Basic Law, which also sets limits to European integration by requiring that the supranational legal order conform to "democratic, social and federal principles, to the rule of law, and to the principle of subsidiarity." Article 79.3 of the Basic Law imposes a limit on constitutional amendment as well as on European integration.[114] German authorities, and especially the parliament, "must retain competences of sufficient weight in both extent and substance so as to keep the scope of democratic action meaningful."[115] In Germany, transnational law is recognised and respected.[116]

Whatever the prevalent conception of the relationship between domestic and international orders, it appears that all the States covered in this report start from the same basic assumption: even though some examples testify to varying degrees of openness to international norms, this very position results from what has been decided in the States' constitutions. This principle of constitutional supremacy is clear for example in Botswana[117] and Brazil.[118] Similarly, even though the British constitutional scene can be presented as an "awesome mess",[119] the principle of parliamentary sovereignty remains the arch-principle ordering the whole system. As

[109]BVerfGE 58, 1, 34 (1981); BVerfGE 64, 1, 20 (1983), quoted by Viellechner, 'Friendliness' Towards Others: How the German Constitution Deals with Legal Pluralism, § 3.1.3.

[110]BVerfGE 74, 358, 370 (1987); BVerfGE 128, 282, 306 (2011), quoted by Viellechner, 'Friendliness' Towards Others: How the German Constitution Deals with Legal Pluralism, § 3.1.3.

[111]BVerfGE 111, 307, 315 (2004), quoted by Viellechner, 'Friendliness' Towards Others: How the German Constitution Deals with Legal Pluralism, § 3.1.3.

[112]Viellechner, 'Friendliness' Towards Others: How the German Constitution Deals with Legal Pluralism, § 3.1.3.

[113]See Cossalter and Klement (2016) and Cossalter et al. (2017).

[114]Viellechner, 'Friendliness' Towards Others: How the German Constitution Deals with Legal Pluralism, § 2.2.2.

[115]Viellechner, 'Friendliness' Towards Others: How the German Constitution Deals with Legal Pluralism, § 3.1.4.

[116]Viellechner, 'Friendliness' Towards Others: How the German Constitution Deals with Legal Pluralism, §§ 3.1.6 and 3.2.3.

[117]Fombad, Reconciling Legal Pluralism and Constitutionalism: New Trajectories for Legal Theory in the Age of Globalisation in Botswana, § 2.

[118]De Barcelos, Brazil and Its Many Realities. Courts and State-Centrism; Administrative Agencies and International Cooperation, § 2.

[119]Wright, quoted by Psygkas, Accommodating Legal Pluralism and 'Pluralizing' the Constitution: The Example of the United Kingdom, § 1.

Athanasios Psygkas expresses it: “Even as the UK legal order ceded ground to external normative sources as a matter of practical outcomes, the key national constitutional actors self-consciously justified this move, as a matter of formal constitutional principle, by express reference to domestic constitutional principles and sources. Briefly put, the simplified version of the argument was that it is ‘*our* Parliament and *our* courts’ making the conscious decision to establish links between these normative spheres which, in turn, may result in national law being set aside.”[120] This is a crude way of expressing it, but one cannot but consider that domestic constitutional sovereignty appears as the necessary building block providing its legal basis to the development of supranational sources. The British case thus allows to make this logical necessity explicit.

## 2.2 *Inward Pluralism: Perspectives on the Internal Consistency of Domestic Legal Systems*

Inward legal pluralism involves several legal, historical and social issues. It deals for example with the openness and receptiveness of the States’ legal systems vis-à-vis indigenous, local, and spontaneous normative orderings. Following Kelsen, these can be expressed by the dimensions of centralisation and decentralisation of the legal system. Dynamic centralisation and decentralisation depend on the number of authorities which are empowered to produce legal norms. The more they are, the more decentralised the system is. Static centralisation and decentralisation depend on the scope of validity of the legal norms. The wider their personal, territorial or material scope of application, the more centralised the system is. In the study of concrete examples, both dimensions need to be associated and combined. For example, as a Federal State, Germany implies from its very inception the admission of a degree of pluralism. On the dynamic axis, it can be seen in the existence of several layers of government: the *Bund* and the *Länder*. On the static axis, each of these authorities is given specific normative powers regarding specific subject matters. Such is also the case in Brazil and in Argentina. Regarding the States covered by this report, two major forms of inward pluralism can be identified.

Due to the circumstances of the historical formation of the State, and especially to former colonisation, it is by no means exceptional for a given legal system to have been submitted to various cross-influences. Such is the case of Botswana, which “received two entirely different and potentially conflicting legal traditions, the English common law and the Roman-Dutch law.”[121] This State consequently

[120]Psygkas, Accommodating Legal Pluralism and ‘Pluralizing’ the Constitution: The Example of the United Kingdom, § 1.

[121]Fombad, Reconciling Legal Pluralism and Constitutionalism: New Trajectories for Legal Theory in the Age of Globalisation in Botswana, § 1.

qualifies as a "mixed jurisdiction" or a "mixed legal system".[122] That has resulted in the judiciary being more trained either in one or the other law. The domestic legal system thus expresses an inbuilt pluralism, as it is a compound not only of various substantive norms, coming from various social perspectives, but also a compound of various sources of law, legal methodologies and ways of conceiving the legal regulation of behaviour.

In the UK, the former mother country, the multi-layered character of constitutional and legal sources does not seem to be a major novelty.[123] Indeed, that kingdom is made up of several nations which have enjoyed an increased legal empowerment thanks to the devolution process.

Also a former part of the British Empire, Solomon Islands offers another type of inward pluralism. As was frequent when the British Empire was dissolved, a written constitution was drafted by Order in Council in 1978.[124] This State consists of 26 main islands and about 900 smaller ones, and its population is about 550,000 persons speaking about 80 vernacular languages. Solomon Islands inherited English law including UK legislation, the common law and equity. It is also the host of several customary communities whose normative autonomy gives a specific appearance to the whole legal system: "Solomon Islands has a plural legal system wherein State laws co-exist with customary laws."[125] That is why inward pluralism is a more acute issue than outward pluralism. As Jennifer Corrin remarks: "rather than being challenged by limits imposed at an international or supranational level, governmental power is being challenged by local initiatives designed to promote the authority of traditional leaders and the customary laws which they promulgate."[126] The colonial administration allowed these customs to develop and be enforced by "native" (now "local") courts. According to the Constitution, which is the supreme law of the land pursuant to Article 1, these customary laws are to be preferred to common law in case of incompatibility. This is linked to the global philosophy that is expressed by the Preamble to the Constitution. In this text, the people of Solomon Islands claims to be "proud of the wisdom and the worthy customs of our ancestors, mindful of our common and diverse heritage and conscious of our common destiny" and to "cherish and promote the different cultural traditions within Solomon Islands." According to the High Court, customary norms and Acts of the UK Parliament rank equally in the hierarchy of norms, so that which one prevails is determined on a case-by-case basis.[127] In practice nevertheless, things seem not to be so clear, as common law is

---

[122]See for example Tetley (2000), Reid (2003), Du Plessis (2006), Palmer and Mattar (2015) and Palmer (2012).

[123]Psygkas, Accommodating Legal Pluralism and 'Pluralizing' the Constitution: The Example of the United Kingdom, § 1.

[124]Corrin, Constitutionalism and Customary Law in Solomon Island, § 1.

[125]Corrin, Constitutionalism and Customary Law in Solomon Island, § 1.

[126]Corrin, Constitutionalism and Customary Law in Solomon Island, § 1. See also ibid., § 7.

[127]K v T [1985–1986] SILR 49, quoted by Corrin, Constitutionalism and Customary Law in Solomon Island, § 3.4.

routinely enforced, while the government at the same time is reluctant to enforce legislation when it conflicts with customary norms.[128]

The Constitution of Cyprus is reminiscent of the previous examples, as this country also gained its independence from the British Empire in 1960 and still uses common law and equity, provided it is compatible with the Constitution. It is also an original mixed legal system, as it embodies a specific type of inward pluralism, resulting from the coexistence of the two Greek and Turkish communities. As Kombos puts it, "the assumed absolute mistrust between the two communities (Greek and Turkish) [...] resulted in a lengthy, detailed, rigid and permanent Constitution that has at its epicentre two principles: protected bi-communalism and a system of multiple checks and balances to ensure that the status quo remains intact and that minority rule is safeguarded."[129] On a daily basis, ordinary politics is afflicted with tensions and disagreements, so that coexistence does not seem to result in any form of legal hybridation. Freedom of contract is a constitutional right, as well as the right to collective bargaining. Two communal chambers, one Greek and one Turkish, were provided for in the Constitution in order to ensure the self-government of the respective communities regarding topics such as education, culture, religion, etc., but the Turkish community decided to withdraw from all State organs in 1964. Five religions enjoy constitutional status: the Orthodox Christian religion, the Islamic religion, the Maronites, the Roman Catholics, and the Armenians, the two main religious groups being granted special autonomy. Religious pluralism is thus secured, and other religions or rites enjoy religious freedom.[130]

In Greece, the Muslim minority in Thrace enjoys an increased autonomy. The validity of its customary law and sharia law is accepted, which has an important impact on personal law. As Ioannis A. Tassopoulos comments, this is the only European example where sharia law is valid.[131]

Although Brazil is a federal State like Germany, pluralism there does not seem to be a heated issue regarding the relationship between the domestic and international orders, nor regarding native communities. Nevertheless, according to Ana Paula de Barcellos there is room for a pluralism of a sort in slums, where the "lack of State's authority leaves room to other kinds of norms, organized by the community itself and frequently defined and imposed by criminal groups."[132] More originally, the concept of pluralism seems to be adequate when addressing the autonomy of public administrations, and especially of powerful administrative agencies. The latter have developed a sort of administrative diplomacy by joining cooperative international agencies, such as the International Coalition of Medicines Regulatory Agencies, the International Cooperation on Cosmetics Regulation, or the Financial Action Task

[128]Corrin, Constitutionalism and Customary Law in Solomon Island, § 3.4.

[129]Kombos, Legal Pluralism and Constitutionalism in the Cypriot Example, § 3.1.

[130]Kombos, Legal Pluralism and Constitutionalism in the Cypriot Example, § 3.2.4.

[131]Tassopoulos, Between Constitutionalism and Legal Pluralism: Perspectives from Greece, § 5.

[132]De Barcelos, Brazil and Its Many Realities. Courts and State-Centrism; Administrative Agencies and International Cooperation, § 1.

Force. The regulations which are drafted by the Brazilian agencies are "framed through international cooperation in the administrative level without much control or even participation from Congress."[133] Councils for professional supervision in various sectors also enact regulatory norms which tend to exceed the legislative power, and are sometimes considered void by Courts precisely for that reason. Private forms of autonomy can also be exercised pursuant to the constitutional recognition of professional collective bargaining, the autonomy of sports controlling entities and associations. Some attention to traditional communities is given by the Constitution, which tends to recognise and protect their social organisations, customs, languages, creeds, and traditions.[134] Although not provided for in the Constitution, some judicial recognition of their own normative orders seems to be implicit in court decisions where charges against members of indigenous people were dismissed because they had already been punished within their own communities.[135] In Argentina as well, the discussion regarding the compatibility between Aborigines' institutions and cosmovision and domestic law is important.[136]

Singapore offers an example that combines the two previous situations of colonial heritage on the one hand, and of taking account of social diversity on the other hand. This State is also a former British colony and supports the inheritance of English law. Nevertheless, as Neo makes clear, "first, English statute passed after the Second Charter [of Justice of 1826] was not to become part of Singapore law; and secondly, the reception of English law was subject to suitability to local circumstances and could be modified where its application would cause injustice or oppression."[137] Singapore also borrowed from other commonwealth jurisdictions, such as India and Australia. More fundamentally, this had important consequences on the general attitude of Singapore legal authorities towards accommodating local customary law and religious practices. From the institutional perspective, Islam is specifically taken into account because of the establishment of Shariah courts, which are under the supervision of the Ministry of Social and Family Development rather than constitute the Judiciary as such, and the existence of an Islamic Religious Council and the Registry of Muslim Marriages. Pursuant to the Administration of Muslim Law Act 1966, Shariah courts have jurisdiction over marriage, divorce, family, and inheritance questions, where all parties are Muslims or were married under Islamic law.[138] A strong form of pluralism seems to be guaranteed, as pursuant to the Supreme Court of Judicature Act 1969, "the High Court shall have no jurisdiction

---

[133]De Barcelos, Brazil and Its Many Realities. Courts and State-Centrism; Administrative Agencies and International Cooperation, § 2.

[134]De Barcelos, Brazil and Its Many Realities. Courts and State-Centrism; Administrative Agencies and International Cooperation, § 2.

[135]De Barcelos, Brazil and Its Many Realities. Courts and State-Centrism; Administrative Agencies and International Cooperation, § 2.

[136]Ucín, A Particular Dialogue Between Systems. The Argentinian Case, § 1.iii.

[137]Neo, Legal Pluralism in Centralist Singapore, § 1.

[138]Neo, Legal Pluralism in Centralist Singapore, § 3.

to hear and try any civil proceeding which comes within the jurisdiction of the Sariah Court." The case-law shows some contradictions and uncertainties regarding the exact boundaries of the respective jurisdictions. Amendments to the Supreme Court of Judicature Act and the Administration of Muslim Law Act led to increase the scope of concurrent jurisdiction between Shariah courts and civil courts. This did not really clarify or stabilise the relationships between the two types of institutions. As Neo documents, "Despite these legislative changes, jurisdictional and normative conflicts between these two legal systems continue to arise."[139] Civil courts are reluctant to admit that religious norms prevail over secular statutes. According to the Court of Appeals, "legislation and the common law prevail over personal laws."[140] Specific legal provisions also address the situations of the Catholic Church and Sikh and Hindu properties, which is evidence of a form of in-built institutional and substantive pluralism within the domestic legal system.

## 3 The Dynamics of the Relations Among Legal Spheres in Positive Law

This part of the report intends to tackle the following issues. Has the reorganisation of the interactions among norms imposed by globalisation happened in a natural, consensual way and "softly" or "smoothly", or in a more difficult, chaotic, or even conflict-ridden way? Have all the legal actors (constitutional courts, ordinary courts, legislative bodies, administrations, local authorities, etc.) adopted a homogenous attitude in that respect? Is there any consistency between the hierarchy of norms and models of interaction, articulation and collision of norms that have thus been set up and those established, suggested or imposed by the other legal spheres, or is each sphere trying to impose its own supremacy or way of understanding the combination of legal systems upon the other? How are conflicts solved? Is there any idea of transconstitutional "dialogues"? Are they vertical types of dialogues (e.g. between a national and a supranational court) or horizontal ones (e.g. between two national or two supranational courts)? Is it possible to perceive substantial influences, that is, ways for different actors to draw inspiration from one another? Are those types of interaction explicit and openly claimed or are they rather implicit, or even hidden? Has the case-law or the (constitutional or infraconstitutional) legislation gone through a spasmodic evolution? Has this evolution been marked by important decisions, or even by the existence of periods of time or phases that were characterised by different attitudes?

Whatever its exact shape, pluralism necessarily leads to a dynamic form of interaction among legal systems that claim to enjoy some form of autonomy

[139]Neo, Legal Pluralism in Centralist Singapore, § 3.

[140]Shafeeg bin Salim Talib and another v Fatimah bte Abud bin Talib and others [2010] 2 SLR 1123, quoted by Neo, Legal Pluralism in Centralist Singapore, § 3.

vis-à-vis one another. This is connected to the issue of the "*relational aspect* of the constitutional debate" identified by Kombos.[141] The major conceptual tool that has been developed to address that issue is that of "dialogue".[142] It tries and accommodates the more or less conflicting perspectives according to which each legal sphere endeavours to preserve its independence, while it simultaneously needs to take into account the others, which are understood to be partners as well as competitors. Traditionally, two forms of dialogues are identified. Dialogue can take a horizontal form, i.e. between authorities of the same type or co-equal authorities, for example between national constitutional judges or between international judges. In a context that presupposes some sort of integration and, possibly, some claim of hierarchisation, it can also take a vertical form, i.e. between authorities intervening on a separate territorial or legal level, for example between national judges and international or supranational judges.[143]

Horizontal dialogues frequently take the form of cross-quotation between legal actors. Three aspects of this practice need to be distinguished.

First, it is essential in certain cases that domestic judges pay attention to extrasystemic sources, especially international law or foreign law. Here, it seems to be necessary for them to apply or examine foreign sources. Municipal judges may have to deal with cases endowed with a transnational legal dimension, for example when they have to deal with private international law or conflict of laws. In these cases, which are increasingly numerous because of the increasing circulation of persons, national judges are compelled to use and confront materials coming from several legal orders. National judges also have to look at foreign law in the context of extradition procedures. That is not really new, nor can it be regarded as a significant aspect of transconstitutionalism and translegalism. Here resorting to foreign sources is mandatory under national sources, and seems to be intrinsic to this type of litigation.

Secondly, it is frequently natural for domestic actors to resort to foreign sources in the contexts where they have to enforce an international norm, such as a human rights treaty (ECHR, EU treaties, Inter-American Convention on Human Rights, etc.). Paying attention to what other parties to the treaty do, and especially to how they interpret and implement it locally is not really mandatory, but it seems quite rational if the aim of an international treaty is to foster uniform or at least convergent practices. This seems internal to the practice of having international relations. Such is for example Justice Scalia's opinion, in spite of all the prejudices he had against legal cosmopolitanism: "I will use it [foreign] law in the interpretation of a treaty."[144]

[141]Kombos, Legal Pluralism and Constitutionalism in the Cypriot Example, § 2.1.

[142]See infra, §§ 4 and 5.

[143]For illustrations, see e.g. Burgorgue-Larsen (2009); Ayala Corao (2012), pp. 128–129.

[144]Scalia-Breyer Debate on Constitutional relevance of foreign court decisions, available at http://www.freerepublic.com/focus/news/1352357/posts.

Thirdly, what is more significant of emerging transnational legal phenomena is the following, which may be called "incidental" involvement with extrasystemic sources. More and more often, it appears that judges will make their decisions, even in a strictly national context for national judges or in a strictly international context for international judges, with reference to foreign, international, supranational, transnational, comparative, etc., legal materials which they are not obliged to use. It is entirely contingent on the actors' *choice*. Essential and natural involvements with foreign law do not immediately result in an increase in incidental cross quotation. It needs to be interpreted as an important move in legal reasoning. For example, in *Calvin's Case*, Edward Coke reported the following: "Also in their arguments of this cause concerning an alien, they told no strange histories, cited no foreign laws, produced no alien precedents, and that for two causes; the one, for that the laws of England are so copious in this point, as, God willing, by the report of this case shall appear; the other, lest their arguments concerning an alien born should become foreign, strange, and an alien to the state of the question, which being quæstio juris concerning freehold and inheritance in England, is only to be decided by the laws of this realm."[145] There, Coke praised the judges for dealing with the condition of the children born in Scotland after James VI of Scotland had acceded to the English throne under the name of James I, i.e. with the concept of a stranger, without resorting to foreign considerations. Coke's *dictum* here represents the anti-global perspective. On the contrary, today, one precisely needs to concentrate on the legal actor that looks at a local matter through extra-local eyes. The voluntarily outward-looking reasoning can be regarded as a significant dimension of the emergence of new global legal characters.[146]

Most of the time, the tendency to take into account extra-systemic sources has led to what is regarded as progressive jurisprudence in terms of human rights protection.[147] That explains why, for example, it is only after South Africa adopted a democratic constitution in 1996 that judges in Botswana appeared to adopt a more cooperative attitude than before. It led them to rely on South African precedents, and to establish a "cross-judicial dialogue". This practice is known to have been quite important and quite natural among the Commonwealth countries, because for most of them, the supreme court sat at London. That is why the UK seems to have widely benefited from the case-law of other common law jurisdictions such as Australia, the

[145]7 Coke Report 1a, 77 ER 377 (1608).

[146]These remarks follow from a project developped with Horatia Muir Watt and Mikhaïl Xifaras, about "Emerging Global Legal Characters: Arbitrators, Judges and Transnational Legal Analysis", presented at the Institute for Global Law and Public Policy Workshop of 2011.

[147]See for example Supreme Court of the United States, Lawrence v. Texas 539 U.S. 558 (2003); Roper v. Simmons 543 U.S. 551 (2005); Constitutional Court of South Africa, State v T Makwanyane and M Mchunu, Case No. CCT/3/94; Supreme Court of Canada, R. v. Morgentaler, [1988] 1 S.C.R. 30. For a more critical account, see also infra, § 6.

United States, Canada, and New Zealand,[148] as much as, generally speaking, the former colonies benefited from the former metropole's law.

But the States under review in this report seem not to have embraced this practice without restrictions. In Brazil, although it is more evident in the case of lower judges than in that of superior judges, the judicial dynamics seems to favour domestic norms over international or supranational ones. It is clear for example in some cases of obvious disregard for rulings of the Inter-American Court of Human Rights by the Brazilian Supreme Court.[149] Similarly, State law is generally preferred to native community law, except in the States where native communities live, as States are more sensitive to the latter's perspectives. Judicial quotation of foreign precedents is irregular and depends on the inclinations of the individual judge.[150] The German Federal Constitutional Court also happens to quote from other courts that belong most of the time to the Western liberal tradition.[151] Nevertheless, it has led to the identification of a fifth method of constitutional interpretation, in addition to those classically mentioned by Savigny.[152] According to Viellechner, "Frequently, the [comparative] approach appears random and arbitrary. [...] In a more sympathetic appraisal, [commentators] detect mere decoration of a result already found."[153] Cyprus is presented as particularly open to external influence. Domestic courts have not hesitated, especially when human rights were concerned, to pay attention to foreign law and to engage in important dialogues with the ECtHR.[154] Generally speaking, offering various examples, Kombos notices that "The willingness of the Supreme Court to engage with other legal systems could also be seen in the strong and frequent use of the comparative method."[155]

The existence of vertical dialogues depends on the existence of a more complex institutional setting, where national and international or supranational laws interact. From this perspective, the European Union constitutes a remarkable field of enquiry.

In Cyprus, vertical dialogues between domestic courts and the ECJ, especially thanks to the procedure for preliminary reference provided for in Article 267 of the Treaty on the Functioning of the European Union, have been possible in spite of a somewhat unstable domestic legislation that made it complicated. Overall, the judiciary has first been reluctant to use the preliminary reference. But the *Alpha*

---

148 Psygkas, Accommodating Legal Pluralism and 'Pluralizing' the Constitution: The Example of the United Kingdom, § 2.4.

149 De Barcelos, Brazil and Its Many Realities. Courts and State-Centrism; Administrative Agencies and International Cooperation, § 3.

150 De Barcelos, Brazil and Its Many Realities. Courts and State-Centrism; Administrative Agencies and International Cooperation, § 3.

151 Viellechner, 'Friendliness' Towards Others: How the German Constitution Deals with Legal Pluralism, § 2.3.1.

152 De Savigny (1855), pp. 206–208.

153 Viellechner, 'Friendliness' Towards Others: How the German Constitution Deals with Legal Pluralism, § 2.3.1.

154 Kombos, Legal Pluralism and Constitutionalism in the Cypriot Example, § 3.3.2.2.

155 Kombos, Legal Pluralism and Constitutionalism in the Cypriot Example, § 3.3.2.2.

*Bank Cyprus Ltd* case[156] testified to the adoption of a more cooperative standpoint and of greater deference to the interpretation of EU law by the ECJ.[157]

The Greek report offers a detailed presentation of an interesting case study. In this country, one example of transconstitutional dialogue is the reference that the Council of State decided to submit to the European Court of Justice.[158] What can be regarded as an example of cooperative attitude—similar to what has been witnessed in Austria,[159] Italy,[160] France,[161] and Germany[162]—cannot hide the very heated discussion regarding the relationship between domestic and supranational legal systems that took place in Greece. There are two opposed conceptions of the European Union: one based on supranationalism and favouring integration, the other based on States' sovereignty and insisting on the national character of democracy. Whereas some judges considered that the Constitution needed to be interpreted in conformity with EU law, as imposed by the ECJ, others refused to let the Constitution give way. Among the arguments of the latter were the principle of national sovereignty, the fact that nothing in the Constitution allows Greek judges to set aside the basic norm, and the fact that the binding nature of the EU legal order depends on a statute that is valid precisely because it has been adopted pursuant to constitutional provisions, especially Article 28, which does not enjoy any paramount status among constitutional norms. The difficulty appears to have been solved by giving up any reasoning in terms of formal normative hierarchies:

> When the CJEU ruled that the irrebuttable presumption regarding the capacity of major shareholders in both media enterprises and public work contractors, imposed by GRC art. 14.9, violated the principle of proportionality, the CS changed course in 3470/2011 (in pleno). The Court abandoned the strict construction of GRC art. 14.9 and adopted a teleogical and evolutionary interpretation, accepting that it should be harmonized and construed in conformity with EU law, which must be upheld in the domestic legal order, as required by the Constitution itself, establishing the principle of proportionality (art. 25.1).[163]

[156]Alpha Bank Cyprus v. Si Senh Dau and others, Joint Civil Appeals 23-29/2013, Decision of 13 September 2013, quoted by Kombos, Legal Pluralism and Constitutionalism in the Cypriot Example, § 3.3.2.1.

[157]On the remaining limitations, see Kombos, Legal Pluralism and Constitutionalism in the Cypriot Example, § 3.4.1.

[158]Council of State 3670/2006, quoted by Tassopoulos, Between Constitutionalism and Legal Pluralism: Perspectives from Greece, § 2.

[159]VfGH, 10 March 1999, B 2251/97, B 2594/97.

[160]Corte costituzionale, ord. 102/2008, 103/2008, 207/2013.

[161]Decision n° 2013-314P QPC, 4 April 2013, M. Jeremy F. [Absence de recours en cas d'extension des effets du mandat d'arrêt européen - question préjudicielle à la Cour de justice de l'Union européenne]. See generally Drigo (2013).

[162]BVerfG, 2 BvR 2728/13.

[163]Tassopoulos, Between Constitutionalism and Legal Pluralism: Perspectives from Greece, § 2.

The principle of proportionality, which is common to both legal systems, offered a substantive common ground to accommodate the "metaconstitutional claims"[164] of both regarding the other. As Tassopoulos puts it,

> That EU law is upheld over domestic law, including the Constitution, is the legal consequence of the federal principle, which can operate without a federal constitution, or a federal State. In the supranational European structure of dual sovereignties, i.e. of the EU and of the member-States, one may think, not in terms of hierarchy, but of a relation of priority, or precedence, of EU law *vis-à-vis* the domestic legal order, resulting from the federal principle. The latter makes necessary, at least for functional purposes of coordination, the prevalence of EU law. More important than figures of speech about vertical or horizontal relations, are the functional aspects and the underlying normative considerations.[165]

As will be explained in greater detail below,[166] because of the lack of any formal hierarchical authority to solve the conflict, the solution has to be found by means of common dialogical efforts and by reference to shared substantive principles.[167] Only such principles, understood as underlying each legal system's claims, can provide common ground for dialogue and accommodation. From this perspective, the notion of a "constitution" cannot be understood in purely formal, hierarchical terms, but also necessarily in substantive terms (values, social ideals, goals, etc.). The convergence of the values that underlay both European and national constitutionalisms is the major building block for a peaceful solution to more or less problematic interactions. A sort of common constitutional patrimony, based on values such as human dignity, freedom, equality, etc., helps offer a shared grammar for dialogue. That is why, for example, Edouard Dubout and Sébastien Touzé regard fundamental rights as the major "hinges" between legal orders and systems.[168]

Nevertheless, there appears to be some limits to the possibilities of accommodation. In Italy, they have taken the form of "controlimiti".[169] In France and Germany, they are related to "constitutional identities".[170] In Greece, the unamendable provisions of Article 110.1 of the Constitution deal with the form of the government as a parliamentary republic, and proclaim human dignity, legal equality, the free development of personality, religious freedom, and the separation of powers. Article 28 also sets limits to international integration, by insisting on the rights of man, the foundations of a democratic government and reciprocity. That is why the priority of EU law is acknowledged because it is based on a domestic provision, and because it is conditional on the protection of fundamental values. As presented by Tassopoulos, this debate perfectly reflects what has become the grammar of transconstitutional interaction in Europe, whereby "Constitution and EU law [need

---

[164]Cruz Villalón (2004), p. 73.

[165]Tassopoulos, Between Constitutionalism and Legal Pluralism: Perspectives from Greece, § 2.

[166]See infra, §§ 4 and 6.

[167]See e.g. Dubout (2015).

[168]Dubout and Touzé (2010).

[169]Bernardi (2017).

[170]See infra, § 4.

to be interpreted] in a spirit of mutual deference and consideration, so as to achieve harmony and to avoid conflicts"[171]: "Were the European integration process to take a different route (e.g. imposing restrictions on voting rights in the Council for indebted countries), anti-democratic, scornful of reciprocity, and forgetful of respect for fundamental rights, the [Council of State] would certainly react to the violation of the fundamental principles, which set the material limits to the amendment of the Greek Constitution, following a rationale similar to the German Solange decisions."[172] The Greek report also points to the case of the Public Sector Involvement, leading to the replacement of Greek bonds with new ones in the context of the Greek financial crisis, where three constitutional systems interfered with one another: the Greek domestic one, the ECHR, and the ECJ.[173]

As is clear from the last remarks, and will also appear later,[174] Germany indeed seems to be the focal point of European transconstitutional dialogues. Viellechner underlines the paradoxical situation of the German constitutional order. Although it expresses an unprecedented external openness, the Basic Law simultaneously insists in a very idiosyncratic way on the domestic protection of fundamental rights. That is why friendliness "towards other normative orders, arising both beyond the State through international or transnational cooperation and within the State through migration [do] not mean unconditional recognition",[175] let alone submission. This attitude is obvious in the case of EU law. Regarding European Union secondary law, the German Federal Constitutional Court generally accepts the principle of primacy, but it sets three limits to this openness. First, the Court retains a competence to control secondary norms in case the European supranational level does not offer sufficient guarantees in terms of human rights protection.[176] Secondly, supranational acts that are manifestly *ultra vires*, i.e. go beyond the express conferrals, can be left unapplied on the domestic soil. Thirdly, as is the case in France,[177] the constitutional identity of the German legal order offers a last limit to international openness.[178]

Until recently, that sort of reminder of more or less outspoken threat was hardly regarded as serious, because "the dog appeared to bark more than to bite".[179] Things

---

[171]Tassopoulos, Between Constitutionalism and Legal Pluralism: Perspectives from Greece, § 3.

[172]Tassopoulos, Between Constitutionalism and Legal Pluralism: Perspectives from Greece, § 2.

[173]Tassopoulos, Between Constitutionalism and Legal Pluralism: Perspectives from Greece, § 4.

[174]See infra, § 4.

[175]Viellechner, 'Friendliness' Towards Others: How the German Constitution Deals with Legal Pluralism, § 1.

[176]BVerfGE 37, 217 (1973); BVerfGE 73, 339 (1986); BVerfGE 102, 147 (2000), quoted by Viellechner, 'Friendliness' Towards Others: How the German Constitution Deals with Legal Pluralism, § 3.1.4.

[177]French Conseil constitutionnel, Decision n° 2006-540 DC, 27 July 2006 Loi relative au droit d'auteur et aux droits voisins dans la société de l'information.

[178]German Federal Constitutional Court, Judgment on Lisbon Treaty, June 30, 2009 (BVerfG, 2 BvE 2/08). On the doctrine of "constitutional identity", see infra, §§ 4 and 6.

[179]See e.g. Schmid (2001).

have changed however because the hostile move was actually made by the Czech Constitutional Court in 2012 in the "Slovak Pensions" case.[180]

In its ruling of January 31st, 2012, the Czech Constitutional Court directly and brutally jeopardized the ECJ's authority. In that case, the Court quashed several decisions of administrative courts regarding the old-age benefits of the litigant. The applicant was a Czech citizen, a permanent resident in the current territory of the Czech Republic, who had spent part of his career in the Czechoslovak railways, on the present territory of the Slovak Republic, and then, after the partition of the country, in the Czech railways. The Social Security Administration granted him a pension without taking into account the interpretation by the Constitutional Court of the treaty between the Czech Republic and the Slovak Republic concerning social security of 29th October 1992, which required the administration to increase the pension so as to reach the amount to which one would have been eligible if one had spent one's entire career on Czech territory with a Czech employer and under the Czech pension system.

Since it appeared to be contrary to EU law, such a reading of the Treaty was submitted by the Supreme Administrative Court to the European Court of Justice by way of a reference for a preliminary ruling. The European Court considered that granting a social benefit supplement only to Czech nationals residing on the territory of the Czech Republic violated the rules of European Union law, in particular the principle of equality (Article 12 of the Treaty establishing the European Community; Council Regulation (EEC) No 1408/71 of 14th June 1971 on the application of social security schemes to employed persons, to self-employed persons and to members of their families moving within the Community). Freedom of movement was also undermined, as the scheme did not benefit those residing outside the Czech Republic. According to the ECJ,

> As regards the requirement of residence in the territory of the Czech Republic, it must be recalled that the principle of equality of treatment, as referred to in Article 3(1) of Regulation No 1408/71, prohibits not only overt discrimination based on the nationality of the beneficiaries of social security schemes but also all covert forms of discrimination which, through the application of other distinguishing criteria, lead in fact to the same result [...]. Accordingly, conditions imposed by national law must be regarded as indirectly discriminatory where, although applicable irrespective of nationality, they affect essentially migrant workers or the great majority of those affected are migrant workers, where they are applicable without distinction but can more easily be satisfied by national workers than by migrant workers, or where there is a risk that they may operate to the particular detriment of the latter [...]. That applies to a condition of residence, such as that at issue in the main

[180] This case is also commented on by Kombos, Legal Pluralism and Constitutionalism in the Cypriot Example, § 2.4. For other examples of transconstitutional conflicts in Poland (where the Constitutional Tribunal was ready to ignore a EU Regulation if it had disregarded domestic fundamental rights (Polish Constitutional Tribunal, Decision SK 45/09), Venezuela (where the constitutional chamber of the Supreme Court decided by Expediente n° 11-1130 du 17 octobre 2011, not to abide by a ruling of the Inter-American Court of Human Rights), and Italy (where the Constitutional Court by Constitutional Court, sent. 238/2014, refused to abide by a ruling of the International Court of Justice), see Muir Watt and Tusseau (2016) and Tusseau (2012, 2013b, 2014a). See also Lavranos (2008).

proceedings, which essentially affects migrant workers who reside in the territory of Member States other than their State of origin.[181]

ECJ judges concluded that:

It follows from the foregoing that the Ústavní soud [Constitutional Court] judgment involves a direct discrimination based on nationality and indirect discrimination based on nationality, as a result of the residence test, against those who have made use of their freedom of movement.[182]

As a result of this decision, the Czech legislature prohibited the payment of the compensation required by the Constitutional Court's interpretation of the Treaty. The administrative judges therefore applied the ECJ ruling and its domestic legislative consequences, against the previous decisions of the Constitutional Court.

After recalling the decision of the judges in Luxembourg, the Brno Court summarized its own case-law on the relations between Czech law and supranational law.[183] Those relations are based on a principle of proper interpretation of national law governing Union law, which, in accordance with the *Solange I*, *Solange II* and *Maastricht* judgments of the German Federal Constitutional Court,[184] must ensure that national law is influenced by supranational law, provided principles such as that of the democratic State governed by the rule of law (Article 9 C) are preserved. From its judgments 19/08 and 29/09 it follows that:

The Constitutional Court remains the supreme protector of Czech constitutionality, including against possible excesses by Union bodies or European law, which also clearly answers the contested issue of the sovereignty of the Czech Republic; if the Constitutional Court is the supreme interpreter of the constitutional regulations of the Czech Republic, which have the highest legal force on Czech territory, it is obvious that Art. 1 par. 1 of the Constitution cannot be violated. if European bodies interpreted or developed EU law in a manner that would jeopardize the foundations of materially understood constitutionality and the essential requirements of a democratic, law-based State that are, under the Constitution of the Czech Republic, seen as inviolable (Art. 9 par. 2 of the Constitution), such legal acts could not be binding in the Czech Republic. In accordance with this, the Czech Constitutional Court also intends to review, as ultima ratio, whether the legal acts of European bodies remain within the bounds of the powers that were provided to them. In this regard the Constitutional Court basically agreed with certain conclusions of the German Federal Constitutional Court, stated in its Maastricht decision.

The Court identifies three main areas in which it is entitled on that basis to monitor the Union institutions' exercise of their powers:

the non-functioning of its institutions, the protection of the material core of the Constitution, not only in relation to European law but also to the particular application thereof, and, finally, the functioning as ultima ratio, i.e. the authority to review whether an act by European Union bodies exceeded the powers that the Czech Republic transferred to the

[181]ECJ, 22 June 2011, Marie Landtová c/ Česká správa socialního zabezpečení, C-399/09, §§ 44–46.

[182]ECJ, 22 June 2011, Marie Landtová c/ Česká správa socialního zabezpečení, C-399/09, § 49.

[183]Décisions Pl. ÚS 50/04, Pl. ÚS 66/04, Pl. ÚS 19/08, Pl. ÚS 29/09.

[184]BVerfGE 89, 155 (1993).

> European Union under Art. 10a of the Constitution; these could be, in particular, abandoning a value identity and exceeding the scope of the entrusted competences.[185]

In the case under study, the Constitutional Court had to determine the effects of the ECJ's ruling on the Czech territory. The purpose of the Constitutional Court's ruling on pensions has always been to ensure equality among Czech citizens, regardless of the place where, prior to the dissolution of the State, they worked in Czechoslovakia, and to guarantee the maximum level of social benefits. According to the constitutional judges, a period of employment in the Slovak territory before January 1st, 1993 could not be considered retroactively as a period of employment abroad. Therefore, the European regulation in question did not apply. From that point of view,

> Failure to distinguish the legal relationships arising from the dissolution of a State with a uniform social security system from the legal relationships arising for social security from the free movement of persons in the European Communities, or the European Union, is a failure to respect European history, it is comparing things that are not comparable.[186]

That is why, according to the Court, Regulation 1408/71 was not applicable:

> Due to the foregoing, European law, i.e. Regulation (EEC) No 1408/71 of the Council of 14 June 1971 on the application of social security schemes to employed persons, self-employed persons, and members of their families moving within the Community, cannot be applied to entitlements of citizens of the Czech Republic arising from social security until 31 December 1992; and, based on the principles explicitly stated by the Constitutional Court in judgment file no. Pl. ÚS 18/09, we cannot do otherwise than state, in connection with the effects of ECJ judgment of 22 June 2011, C-399/09 on analogous cases, that in that case there were excesses on the part of a European Union body, that a situation occurred in which an act by a European body exceeded the powers that the Czech Republic transferred to the European Union under Art. 10a of the Constitution; this exceeded the scope of the transferred powers, and was ultra vires.[187]

In particular, the Court of Luxembourg erred in the eyes of the domestic court by ignoring the specific features of the Czechoslovak situation. In severe terms, they considered that:

> the ECJ would familiarize itself with the arguments that respected the case-law of the Constitutional Court and the constitutional identity of the Czech Republic, which it draws from the common constitutional tradition with the Slovak Republic, that is from the over seventy years of the common State and its peaceful dissolution, i.e. from a completely idiosyncratic and historically created situation that has no parallel in Europe.[188]

This decision, which was also related to conflicts between the Administrative Supreme Court and the Constitutional Court, was revolutionary. Before it, no domestic judge had ever refused to comply with the rulings of the ECJ.

---

[185] Czech Constitutional Court, Pl. ÚS 5/12, § VII.

[186] Czech Constitutional Court, Pl. ÚS 5/12, § VII.

[187] Czech Constitutional Court, Pl. ÚS 5/12, § VII.

[188] Czech Constitutional Court, Pl. ÚS 5/12, § VII.

In Germany, such a decision could only be reached after prior reference to the European Court of Justice for a preliminary ruling.[189] This procedure was followed, for example, for the first reference the Constitutional Court submitted to the ECJ, in the OMT case.[190] Unlike what had happened in the Czech Republic however, no suspension of the applicability of EU secondary law ever took place.

As María Carlota Ucín makes clear, a similar controversy is going on between Argentina and the Inter-American Court of Human Rights. In the *Fontevechia* decision of November 29th, 2011, the Court declared that Argentina had violated freedom of speech (Art. 13 in connection with Art. 1.1. of the Convention) because of a judicial ruling awarding damages to former President Menem following the publication of an article regarding his private life in a magazine. The IACHR ordered the Argentinian State to "leave without effect" the aforementioned judicial ruling. But on February 14th, 2017, the Supreme Court decided that, pursuant to Article 27 of the Constitution, which imposes on the government "to strengthen its relationships of peace and trade with foreign powers, by means of treaties *in accordance with the principles of public law laid down by this Constitution*," it could not derogate "a decision that was already firm and with the *res judicata status*".[191] The Supreme Court also considered that the IACHR was exceeding its competences. In what is regarded as a dialogue, the IACHR replied to the Supreme Court's arguments on October 18th, 2017. Among other considerations, it underlined that:

> Internal dispositions cannot be alleged as reasons to avoid complying with international compromises;
>
> States must comply with International Law compromises in good faith;
>
> The Argentinian State should have identified the way in which [it] could comply with the given order. [It] must have adopted the measures oriented to leave without effect the analysed judicial decision; [. . .]
>
> Additionally, it argued that the Supreme Court cannot evaluate the IACHR remedial competence nor can [it] evaluate its competence as a condition to comply with those orders.[192]

The United Kingdom is also (for the moment) a member of the EU and a party to the European Convention on Human Rights. According to Psygkas, transconstitutional dialogues have developed with the ECJ and the ECtHR. In order to remain within a pattern reciprocal accommodation, British courts have refused the principle that they had to abide by the other courts' rulings. As the Supreme Court explained, "This court is not bound to follow every decision of the

---

[189]BVerfGE 126, 284 (2010), quoted by Viellechner, 'Friendliness' Towards Others: How the German Constitution Deals with Legal Pluralism, § 3.1.4.

[190]BVerfGE 134, 366 (2014), quoted by Viellechner, 'Friendliness' Towards Others: How the German Constitution Deals with Legal Pluralism, § 3.1.4. On this case, see e.g. Tusseau (2014b).

[191]Ucín, A Particular Dialogue Between Systems. The Argentinian Case, § 3.

[192]Ucín, A Particular Dialogue Between Systems. The Argentinian Case, § 3.

European court [of Human Rights]. Not only would it be impractical to do so: it would sometimes be inappropriate, as it would destroy the ability of the court to engage in the constructive dialogue with the European court which is of value to the development of Convention law... Of course, we should usually follow a clear and constant line of decisions by the European court... But we are not actually bound to do so or (in theory, at least) to follow a decision of the Grand Chamber."[193] Even though the principle of the primacy of EU law should lead to a more moderate position regarding the ECJ, UK judges refused this idea and preferred the idea of dialogue. This concept really seems to have displaced the more traditional legal concepts of authoritativeness, bindingness, obligatoriness, mandatoriness, etc. Could pluralism have favoured the emergence of a sort of new form of legal reasoning?

## 4 The Renewal of Legal Reasoning

This part of the report intends to tackle the following issues. Have the legal interactions that globalisation implies led to a change in both the form and substance of legal reasoning and arguments? Has legal reasoning undergone changes, either in litigation and cases related to the issue of pluralism, or because of some spillover effect in other domains? To give an example, has there been an important development of reasoning in terms of principles, proportionality control or balancing? Is there a strong opposition between syllogism and weighing? Have the "methods of interpretation" been modified depending on the multiplied audience which the different legal spheres now address? Have the concrete working methods of legal actors (constitutional courts, ordinary courts, legislative bodies, individual legislators, administrations, local authorities, companies and their legal services, arbitration courts, law firms, etc.) evolved (e.g. by setting up international relations services, comparative law services, etc.)? Is the idea of "dialogue" used in jurisprudence (and which jurisprudence: constitutionalist? internationalist, etc.?) and/or by legal actors (normative authorities, courts, law professionals, etc.) themselves? Have concepts or tools enabling the interconnection and limitation of the interconnection among legal spheres appeared (e.g. *controlimiti* in Italy or constitutional identity in France and Germany)? Do these concepts tend to replace arguments founded on sovereignty? Even more fundamentally, has it been necessary to think anew the concepts of "law", legal "system", or "order" (e.g. so as to take into account the multiplication of sources of law, soft law, the fragmentation of the law, etc., or to highlight the emergence of a law which has a less determining importance, is based on autonomy,

[193] Manchester City Council v Pinnock [2010] UKSC 45 [48] (Lord Neuberger), quoted by Psygkas, Accommodating Legal Pluralism and 'Pluralizing' the Constitution: The Example of the United Kingdom, § 2.4.

reflexivity, self-coordination, and operates in mobile and dynamic networks, and not according to the vertical model of the pyramid of norms)?

The main teachings of the national reports can once again be presented according to a scalar logic rather than by using clear-cut categories. It seems possible to start with the States where legal reasoning seems to have been impacted by a lower level of pluralisation and to go on studying those where major developments seem to have taken place, especially due to the dynamics of globalisation.

In Botswana, because of the colonial past, there has always been a double legal culture, especially among the judiciary. Depending on the specific background of the judge, this has led to using different precedents, different methodologies, and different techniques.[194] Fombad does not seem to regard this situation as a factor for the development of a more imaginative legal culture, nor does he seem to document the emergence of any original hybrid legal culture.

In Solomon Islands, one of the most important issues is related to the enforcement of human rights. As Corrin puts it, "The rights chapter is modelled on the *Universal Declaration of Human Rights* (1948) and the *European Convention for the Protection of Human Rights and Fundamental Freedoms* (1950)."[195] In spite however of this evident transplant and the original jurisdiction that is granted to the High Court for the enforcement of these provisions, uncertainties remain in case of conflict between human rights norms and customary norms. Especially regarding non-discrimination and freedom of movement, courts have adopted a narrow view of the application of human rights. As far as the right to life and religious freedom are concerned, international norms have had a greater influence.[196] In this respect, Corrin concludes that: "Overall, it cannot be said that there has been a 'reshuffle' of the interactions among norms imposed by globalisation. Where there has been some movement, it cannot be described as natural or chaotic or conflictive in Solomon Islands. Instead, the more appropriate descriptor is *'ad hoc'*. There is some evidence of international law operating as an influence on the law through its use by the courts as an aid to interpretation. [. . .] However, the courts do not take a uniform approach to application of the international norms encapsulated in the Constitution or to the use of international norms as a guide to interpretation."[197] The local institutions have not adopted any principled or systematic doctrine regarding the interconnection of domestic and international norms, as the review of cases which is offered by Corrin makes clear.[198] The courts have refused to let human rights override customary law several times.[199] That was for example the case in

[194]Fombad, Reconciling Legal Pluralism and Constitutionalism: New Trajectories for Legal Theory in the Age of Globalisation in Botswana, § 4.

[195]Corrin, Constitutionalism and Customary Law in Solomon Island, § 3.4.

[196]Corrin, Constitutionalism and Customary Law in Solomon Island, § 4.1.

[197]Corrin, Constitutionalism and Customary Law in Solomon Island, § 4.1.

[198]Corrin, Constitutionalism and Customary Law in Solomon Island, § 4.2.3.

[199]See also Corrin Care (1999).

*Taenavalu v. Tanavalu*,[200] where the court refused to ignore a discriminatory customary law. While it was clearly incompatible with the right to freedom from discrimination proclaimed in Article 15 of the Constitution, customary law was held to be exempt from this constitutional norm. Such an argument, according to which only laws made after the Constitution came into force are subject to this provision, leads to the conclusion that traditional customs cannot be subjected to this part of the Constitution. The rationale for that attitude may also be that, as opposed to a constructivist logic which is prevalent in contemporary legislation, some judges are prone to prefer the traditional wisdom that, according to a sort of Burkean logic, is internal to customary norms.[201]

The development of the Pacific Islands Forum, of which Solomon Islands is a member, may help improve the international integration of this country. Similarly, although "There is little opportunity for transconstitutional dialogue, as there are few avenues for external appeals or referral of disputes from Solomon Islands to supra-national bodies,"[202] the recent initiatives for a transnational Asian-Pacific regional rights protection system may change this situation in the future. International norms are used as interpretive aids, for example to guide the implementation of domestic human rights norms.[203] Sometimes, judges have even referred to international norms to which Solomon Islands had consented but which were not ratified, whereas in other cases they have outrightly refused to consider international instruments. No consistent judicial attitude thus emerges in terms of a formal hierarchy of norms.[204]

Conversely, "Legal borrowing and engagement has always been part of Singapore's legal tradition as part of the common law world."[205] However, Neo considers that this attitude is more obvious in the domain of private law than in the domain of constitutional law. In the latter, the judiciary developed a "four-wall doctrine". According to Chief Justice Yong Ping How, the constitution is "primarily to be interpreted within its own four walls and not in the light of analogies drawn from other countries such as Great Britain, the United States of America or Australia".[206] This attitude, which reminds one of Justice Scalia's claims of American exceptionalism, is nevertheless presented as somehow paradoxical by Neo, as it

[200] Quoted by Corrin, Constitutionalism and Customary Law in Solomon Island, § 4.2.3.

[201] See especially in this respect Muria CJ in Pusi v. Leni, quoted by Corrin, Constitutionalism and Customary Law in Solomon Island, § 6: "I have made these observations because it appears to the court that this case is a classic example of an attempt to use the Constitution to circumvent the lawful application of custom, a course of action that may well engender disharmony in society. Such a course must not be allowed to flourish in this country."

[202] Corrin, Constitutionalism and Customary Law in Solomon Island, § 4.3.

[203] Corrin, Constitutionalism and Customary Law in Solomon Island, § 4.3.

[204] Corrin, Constitutionalism and Customary Law in Solomon Island, § 4.3.

[205] Neo, Legal Pluralism in Centralist Singapore, § 4.

[206] Chan Hiang Leng Colin v Public Prosecutor [1994] 3 SLR(R) 209, quoted by Neo, Legal Pluralism in Centralist Singapore, § 4.

iself results from a borrowing from a Malaysian case.[207] As a consequence, parochialism precisely appears as a shared and transferable perspective. Singapore courts thus tend to resist one of the most important and widely operating devices of contemporary constitutionalism and transconstitutionalism: proportionality, because it involves too many risks of second-guessing what the political authorities have decided and infringing on the proper separation of powers. Another element of "global [constitutional] doctrine"[208] that has been rejected is the Basic structure doctrine that, following the Indian example,[209] allows courts to review the (supra) constitutionality of constitutional amendments.[210] Even though it is the object of judicial debates,[211] and although some mentions of this doctrine are made in order to highlight the importance of the principle of the separation of powers or the possibility of identifying unenumerated fundamental rights, it cannot be said to be in force in Singapore for the moment.

In Brazil, the dominant attitude among legal practitioners seems to be rather parochial. Nevertheless, De Barcellos notices some changes. According to her, "As mentioned above, national legal criteria continue to be used by Brazilian Courts to deal with norms from different sources, including international law, to grant them validity and define its hierarchical position in the national system. However, the way these tools are handled, understood and applied by lawyers, academics and Courts have received and continue to receive relevant influence from constitutional and legal globalization. The cross-fertilization of ideas globalization fosters [have given] birth to new tools, incorporated by the national system, and new subjects of interest and research. Globalization [has also] had an important impact [on] the organization of legal services and [on] the dynamic of academic work."[212] In the legal academy, a dynamics of internationalisation, which favours the development of new ideas, is visible: students and professors go abroad, foreign students and professors are welcome, international events, publications, and research projects are organised. The Brazilian report proves that the distinction between Sects. 3 and 4 of this report may be a little artificial.

A major change in Brazil has been the development of proportionality reasoning, balancing, and the weighing method used in decisions. It was important enough to lead some scholars to suggest less balancing and more subsumption[213] or

---

[207] Government of the State of Kelantan v Government of the Federation of Malaya [1963] MLJ 355, quoted by Neo, Legal Pluralism in Centralist Singapore, § 4. See further Tan (2017).

[208] See more precisely infra, § 6.

[209] Kesavananda Bharati v. State of Kerala (AIR 1973 SC 1461).

[210] Teo Soh Lung v Minister for Home Affairs & Ors. [1989] 2 MLJ 449 (High Court of Singapore), quoted by Neo, Legal Pluralism in Centralist Singapore, § 4.2.

[211] Mohammad Fiazal bin Sabtu v Public Prosecutor [2012] 4 SLR 947; Yong Vui Kong v Public Prosecutor [2015] 2 SLR 1129, quoted by Neo, Legal Pluralism in Centralist Singapore, § 4.2.

[212] De Barcelos, Brazil and Its Many Realities. Courts and State-Centrism; Administrative Agencies and International Cooperation, § 4.

[213] On the opposition between these two types of reasoning, see Alexy (2003).

syllogism.[214] The methodological change was indeed correlated to a general tendency to judicial activism, which drew on the techniques invented by other constitutional courts such as the German and the Colombian ones, and led to greater legal uncertainty.

The report on the UK and the report on Germany indeed seem to offer the two most important examples of recent changes in legal reasoning due to the impact of globalisation and internationalisation.

In the UK, the impact of the new transconstitutional dynamics seems to have been important. As Psygkas notices, "European law, broadly understood to cover both EU law and the ECHR, has considerably influenced the UK's approach to rights protection by enhancing the powers of courts."[215] The impact of supranational norms prompted a revival of the common law in order to protect fundamental rights, and helped to update the content of traditional principles. The general convergence of domestic and international norms towards a *pro homine* principle prompted legal actors at all levels to identify local principles that had their counterparts in supranational law. "The normative accommodation of external sources, such as the ECHR, does not replace but expands or 'pluralizes' the domestic constitutional sphere. The [Human Rights Act] has had a catalytic effect in creating new or expanding existing common law rights."[216] Regarding not the substance of rights but the methods of legal reasoning, a form of spillover effect can be observed in the UK. Proportionality analysis,[217] which was first introduced thanks to cases that had an EU law or a Human Rights Act/ECHR dimension, progressively came to be used in purely domestic cases. The methods that are crucial to contemporary transconstitutionalism thus permeate the legal systems in all respects. When compared with the tools that were used before, such as the reasonableness test in the classical practice of administrative judicial review, "the advantage of the terminology of proportionality is that it introduces an element of structure into the exercise, by directing attention to factors such as suitability or appropriateness, necessity and the balance or imbalance of benefits and disadvantages. There seems no reason why such factors should not be relevant in judicial review even outside the scope of [ECHR] and EU law."[218]

Because of its influence on European constitutionalism and because of the influence of German scholarship abroad, especially in Latin America, Germany deserves special notice. Not only does legal reasoning seem to have been

---

[214] De Barcelos, Brazil and Its Many Realities. Courts and State-Centrism; Administrative Agencies and International Cooperation, § 4.

[215] Psygkas, Accommodating Legal Pluralism and 'Pluralizing' the Constitution: The Example of the United Kingdom, § 3.1.

[216] Psygkas, Accommodating Legal Pluralism and 'Pluralizing' the Constitution: The Example of the United Kingdom, § 3.1.

[217] Psygkas, Accommodating Legal Pluralism and 'Pluralizing' the Constitution: The Example of the United Kingdom, § 3.1.

[218] Kennedy v The Charity Commission [2014] UKSC 20 at [54], quoted by Psygkas, Accommodating Legal Pluralism and 'Pluralizing' the Constitution: The Example of the United Kingdom, § 3.1.

considerably enriched over the past decades, but this country seems to have supplied Europe—if not the world—with the basic elements of the transconstitutional toolkit. Whereas transconstitutional interactions and pluralism seem to have been handled in a haphazard or at least unsystematic way in other jurisdictions, this does not seem to be the case in Germany. As Viellechner notices, "Notably the Federal Constitutional Court has demonstrated much creativity in dealing with the pluralisation of law. Some of its doctrinal constructions have meanwhile been adopted by other national and international courts. The famous 'Solange' rules, for example, have migrated into several other contexts to account for complementary fundamental rights protection between different legal orders."[219]

German courts and scholars have indeed greatly contributed to the emergence of a transconstitutional vernacular, not only by developing substantive values, but also by offering concepts and modes of reasoning. Such a common language is all the more necessary as one acknowledges the existence of a plurality of sites of authority which, because of inevitable interlocking and overlapping, are in need of some intellectual and practical devices to connect to one another while not renouncing their own specificities.[220] Regarding substantive values, one only needs to mention how influent the *Grundrechte* that are paradigmatically enshrined in the Basic Law have been. One can hardly imagine a contemporary constitution that would not devote several articles to fundamental rights. Similarly, the international law of human rights has considerably developed over the past decades. Universal instruments, regional instruments, instruments focusing on the fundamental rights of specific categories (women, children, first nations and native people, etc.) have been burgeoning, leading to the idea that human rights, as they qualify as common "constitutional goods,"[221] may have constitutionalised the world.[222] Values such as dignity, liberty, equality, and fraternity, each being both understood and combined in various ways depending on the circumstances, are among the core values of a worldwide legal and political project, which David M. Beatty regards as "The Ultimate Rule of Law".[223]

Regarding concepts and modes of reasoning, it is not surprising that the increasing importance of such abstract values has led to the necessity to reshuffle legal reasoning. This need has been expressed very clearly by a German scholar, Robert Alexy, whose influence on Latin American legal thinking is overwhelming. Regarding legal ontology and following what had already been remarked by Ronald Dworkin, Alexy first noticed the increasing importance of a new type of norms: principles. Principles, among which human rights, are considerably different from

---

[219]Viellechner, 'Friendliness' Towards Others: How the German Constitution Deals with Legal Pluralism, § 3.3.3.

[220]For a discussion from the viewpoint of the language (keywords) that is used by transconstitutional actors, see Bobić (2017).

[221]Brudner (2004).

[222]Hennette-Vauchez and Sorel (2011).

[223]Beatty (2004).

rules. The first criterion Ronald Dworkin uses to oppose principles and rules is their origin: "Rules can be identified and distinguished by specific criteria, by tests having to do not with their content but with their pedigree or the manner in which they were adopted or developed."[224] "But this test of pedigree will not work for the [...] principles. The origin of these as legal principles lies not in a particular decision of some legislature or court, but in a sense of appropriateness developed in the profession and the public over time. [...] Even though principles draw support from the official acts of legal institutions, they do not have a simple or direct enough connection with these acts to frame that connection in terms of criteria specified by some ultimate master rule of recognition."[225] The test is the following: "a principle is a principle of law if it figures in the soundest theory of law that can be provided as a justification for the explicit substantive and institutional rules of the jurisdiction in question."[226] Principles thus seem to be already there, implicit in the positive legal norms. They are claimed not to be the product of a decision. Identifying them is independent from any exercise of power that would create them, so that if a legal actor works hard enough, it may reach the "one right answer". Similarly, Robert Alexy considers that rules are applied in an all-or-nothing process of subsumption. On the contrary, the application of a principle to a given situation does not result in so clear a determination of the outcome: "principles are norms which require that something be realized to the greatest extent possible given the legal and factual possibilities. Principles are optimization requirements, characterized by the fact that they can be satisfied to varying degrees, and that the appropriate degree of satisfaction depends not only on what is factually possible but also on what is legally possible. The scope of the legally possible is determined by opposing principles and rules."[227]

Several principles which are formally on a par, for example because they all are constitutional, can be applied to a given situation, and point to conflicting outcomes. For example, the principle of the freedom of the press and the principle of the secrecy of private life may conflict. One is to choose between the two principles. Because every principle is a "mandate of optimisation", each one is always in competition with all the others. It can prevail (and the other principles be defeated) only for good reasons. Flexible proportionality-judgments and balancing, as opposed to strict logical deduction, are the proper methodology to assess which principle is to prevail *in casu.*[228]

The reasoning appears to be much more indeterminate than in the case of the application of rules. It is an important concern for example in Brazil.[229] Moreover, even though similar formulations of principles seem to be valid all around the world,

---

[224] Dworkin (1978), p. 17.

[225] Dworkin (1978), pp. 40–41.

[226] Dworkin (1978), p. 66.

[227] Alexy (2002), pp. 47–48.

[228] Alexy (2003), pp. 436–437.

[229] See supra, n° 40.

one must not forget the possibility of reasonable disagreements in moral, social, and political matters.[230] There will always be several conceptions of the same concept or principle, and several ways to accommodate various principles. Besides, the relative weight given to each principle, even though they are understood in the same way, depends on local circumstances. For example, freedom of expression in hate speech is much more protected in the US than in Canada or Germany.[231]

Lastly, the confrontation between two apparently identical principles in a single factual situation can very well result in opposite decisions. The *Caroline of Monaco* case illustrates this. Princess Caroline of Monaco was concerned about the publication of pictures of her in a newspaper. She filed a constitutional complaint with the German Federal Constitutional Court. In its ruling, the Court had to balance the right to privacy, which is protected by Article 2.1 in conjunction with Article 1.1 of the *Grundgesetz*, and freedom of the press, which is protected under Article 5.1(2) of the *Grundgesetz*. It decided that for the major part of the contested pictures, freedom of the press had to prevail.[232] Unsatisfied, the Princess decided to appear before another "constitutional court": the ECtHR. In 2004, just as the *Bundesverfassungsgericht* had, it had to balance the right to privacy, as guaranteed by Article 8 of the Convention, with freedom of the press, as protected by Article 10 of the Convention. The ECtHR eventually "consider[ed] that the German courts [had not struck] a fair balance between the competing interests",[233] and reached the opposite result.

German legal actors, and especially the Federal Constitutional Court, whose case-law was explained and conceptualised by legal scholars, offered the language that allowed to deal with these new legal instruments: proportionality reasoning. That is not to say that proportionality was ignored before,[234] but it was popularised then.[235] Two other important conceptual tools that were devised or developed by the German Federal Constitutional Court are related to the accommodation of legal claims coming from several legal systems. The first one is "*Solange* reasoning". For example, the ECJ relied on its constitutional dimension in order to affirm the primacy of EC law, including over national constitutional principles. In 1970, the ECJ stated that "The validity or a Community measure or its effect within a member State cannot be affected by allegations that it runs counter to either fundamental rights as formulated by the Constitution of that State or the principles of a national constitutional structure."[236] Thus, in no way could an internal norm, even of a constitutional nature, impair the application of supranational law. The Court also

230 McMahon (2009).

231 See for example Rosenfeld and Sajó (2006).

232 BVerfGE 101, 361 (1999).

233 ECtHR, 24 June 2004, Von Hannover v Germany (59320/00), §§ 76–79.

234 See especially in this respect Kombos, Legal Pluralism and Constitutionalism in the Cypriot Example, § 3.4.1.

235 See e.g. Barak (2012) and Bernal Pulido (2007).

236 ECJ, 17 December 1970, Internationale Handelsgesellschaft mbH v Einfuhr- und Vorratsstelle für Getreide und Futtermittel, 11-70, §§ 3–4.

affirmed the obligation for national institutions, and most of all for judges, to set aside internal norms that would contradict the content or the objectives of European norms. In the *Simmenthal* case, the Court concluded that "every national court must, in a case within its jurisdiction, apply Community law in its entirety and protect rights which the latter confers on individuals and must accordingly set aside any provision of national law which may conflict with it, whether prior or subsequent to the Community rule."[237] Nevertheless, this did not prevent national constitutional courts from relying on their own constitutional qualities to resist such an attitude. Though it admitted that national statutes should yield to EC law, the *Bundesverfassungsgericht* refused to give up constitutional primacy. It contended that "so long as" (*Solange*) the European protection for basic rights was not globally equivalent to that offered by the *Grundgesetz*, the Court would submit EC law to national constitutional review.[238] This reaction prompted the European institutions to reinforce their concern for human rights, presented as "principles", drawn from the respective traditions and international commitments of the member States, which underlay the whole European dynamics.[239] Later, the *Bundesverfassungsgericht* admitted that the ECJ's fundamental rights jurisprudence was good enough to be quite equivalent to that of the *Grundgesetz*. "So long as" this remains the case, the Court will no more review the constitutionality of EC law.[240] That episode, which may as well be regarded as a constitutional fight as a constitutional dialogue, has set a pattern of constitutional interlocking.[241] France has reached a similar position regarding the judicial review of administrative acts transposing EU law.[242] According to Daniel Halberstam, "The new accommodation on rights, then, may play out something like this: First, the member States will continue to refrain from reviewing fundamental rights violations involving European law as long as the ECJ generally provides an acceptable level of rights protection. [...] Second, and even more intriguing, the ECJ will refrain from aggressively reviewing all fundamental rights claims within its jurisdiction but only on the analogous terms."[243]

Following the ECtHR,[244] the ECJ embraced a similar method in the *Kadi* case.[245] It had to rule on the legality of a European regulation which was enforcing a UN Security Council resolution ordering the freezing of the financial resources of people

---

[237] ECJ, 9 March 1978, Amministrazione delle Finanze dello Stato v Simmenthal SpA, 106/77, § 21.

[238] BVerfGE 37, 271 (1974).

[239] See esp. ECJ, 14 May 1974, Nold, 4-73.

[240] BVerfGE 73, 339 (1986).

[241] See e.g. Lavranos (2008).

[242] Conseil d'Etat, 8 February 2007, Arcelor (287110).

[243] Halberstam (2009), pp. 352–353.

[244] See ECtHR, 30 June 2005, Bosphorus Hava Yollari Turizm ve Ticaret Anonim şirketi v Ireland (45036/98) concerning the respect of ECHR standards by EC law.

[245] ECJ, 3 September 2008, Yassin Abdullah Kadi and Al Barakaat International Foundation v Council of the European Union and Commission of the European Communities (C-402/05 P and C-415/05 P).

who were linked to terrorism. The appellant, whose funds had been frozen, claimed that the regulation breached his right to a fair hearing, his right to respect for property and the principle of proportionality, and his right to effective judicial review. The Court of First Instance granted primacy to the Security Council resolutions adopted under Chapter VII of the UN Charter. As a consequence, it refused to review the legality of the resolution and of the ensuing European regulation. On the contrary, the ECJ underlined the constitutional dimension of the EC. This reference was meant to suggest its autonomy, its commitment to the protection of fundamental rights, and its determination not to admit of any unconditional submission to any other legal order.[246] It consequently maintained that it was impossible to abandon the review of EC measures:

> Article 307 EC may in no circumstances permit any challenge to the principles that form part of the very foundations of the Community legal order, one of which is the protection of fundamental rights, including the review by the Community judicature of the lawfulness of Community measures as regards their consistency with those fundamental rights.
>
> Nor can an immunity from jurisdiction for the contested regulation with regard to the review of its compatibility with fundamental rights, arising from the alleged absolute primacy of the resolutions of the Security Council to which that measure is designed to give effect, find any basis in the place that obligations under the Charter of the United Nations would occupy in the hierarchy of norms within the Community legal order if those obligations were to be classified in that hierarchy. [. . .] [T]he reviews by the Court of the validity of any Community measure in the light of fundamental rights must be considered to be the expression, in a community based on the rule of law, of a constitutional guarantee stemming from the EC Treaty as an autonomous legal system which is not to be prejudiced by an international agreement.

According to the ECJ, the existence of a system of administrative review before the UNSC could not be regarded as a sufficient guarantee for fundamental rights, which could justify excluding review by the ECJ.[247] The ECJ thus set aside the judgment of the CPI and annulled the regulation. A *Solange* logic seems to permeate this reasoning, for an EC review of international norms will be in order so long as the UN does not comport a system of fundamental rights protection equivalent to that of the Communities.[248]

In the absence of any hierarchical way to monitor the potential for conflicts in transconstitutional dialogues, it appears that global constitutional actors converged towards the same method:

> By the Solange principles, each legal order accepts the decisions of the others, even if another decision would have been more consistent with the national constitutional tradition, 'so long as' those decisions do not systematically violate its own understanding of constitutional essentials. Solange thus commits each order to monitor the jurisprudential output of

[246] Ibid. § 288.

[247] Ibid. §§ 318–328, 365–371.

[248] See Opinion of Advocate General M Poiares Maduro §§ 54–55.

> the others, and to make acceptance of their deviations from national preferences contingent on a continuing finding of equivalence of fundamental results.[249]

As will also be discussed when the ideological dimension of this narrative is analysed,[250] the main rationale of this grammar for constitutional dialogue seems to be based on pressing every actor to do its best for human rights if it wants the others to defer to its decisions. In the end, the various actors will defer to one another's decisions provided all scrupulously enforce a homogeneous standard. They will only dare contradict one another—which they have many incentives not to do[251]—when one of them fails to achieve the purpose of constitutionalism. According to Jean L. Cohen, for example,

> If reference is to the highest level of protection of human rights that are acknowledged in the relevant legal orders, then the judicial suspension of an external legal obligation is not solipsistic but rather meant to trigger an equivalent level of protection among the relevant interconnected but not hierarchically related legal orders and to initiate dialogue among the respective judicial organs. [...] The focus is not on parochial understandings but on arriving at compatible interpretations of constitutionalist principles – an integrative not a dissociative logic.[252]

Conflicts which sometimes happen do not appear as rival pretensions of competing selfish actors, but as progressive and incremental deliberative adjustments towards the "one right global constitutional answer". Human rights as a shared set of values eventually benefit from the simultaneous, even though sometimes conflicting, efforts of the several actors. The overall system of social control which the global actors embody gains credit from the constitutional dialogues, be they smooth and congruent, or more chaotic.

The second tool that was invented to accommodate rival metaconstitutional claims is related to the more or less puzzling commitment to accept the mandates of another legal system, without renouncing the core principles that are mostly essential to one's legal system. This deals with the protection of elements that, in some of the jurisdictions covered by the report, would be included in the "basic structure" of the polity. As these elements where conceived of especially in France and in Germany, they are considered to be part of the "constitutional identity" of the State.[253] While this doctrine undoubtedly tends to protect substantive domestic values, it also offers a specific way to devise, organise, and manage the interactions between domestic and supranational constitutionalisms, especially the European Union's.

---

[249] Sabel and Gerstenberg (2010), pp. 512–513.

[250] See infra, § 6.

[251] See infra, § 6.1.

[252] Cohen (2010), p. 30. See also Cohen (2012).

[253] Tusseau G, "On a Constitutional 'Identity Movement' in Global Constitutionalism", Les matinées constitutionnelles du Regroupement stratégique Droit et Changement, McGill University, Montreal, May 6th, 2011; Marti (2011), Derosier (2015), Burgorgue-Larsen (2011), Millet (2013) and Saiz Arnaiz and Alcoberro Llivina (2013).

Two decisions by the French *Conseil Constitutionnel* are worth mentioning in this respect. They dealt with the constitutional review of statutes which transposed European Community directives. There are two major legal difficulties with such statutes. First, their transposition is mandatory under Article 88-1 of the Constitution. The problem is thus whether the *Conseil* must automatically rule in favour of the constitutionality of these statutes, the enactment of which is mandatory, and the content of which is to a large extent defined by EC authorities, or whether it can exercise any constitutional review on them (and of what type and vis-à-vis which norms). Second, the Court of Justice of the European Union holds a monopoly over the assessment of the validity of EU norms, among which directives. If a domestic constitutional review of transposition-statutes were admitted, this would amount to an indirect review of European directives, thus encroaching on the ECJ's jurisdiction.

In the Decision n° 2004-496 DC of June 10th, 2004 *Loi pour la confiance dans l'économie numérique*, the *Conseil* decided (Recital 7) that:

> Considering that under Article 88-1 of the Constitution: 'The Republic participates in the European Communities and in the European Union, constituted by States which have freely chosen, by virtue of the Treaties which established them, to exercise in common some of their skills'; In this way, the transposition into domestic law of a Community directive is the result of a constitutional requirement which can only be hindered by reason of a contrary express provision of the Constitution; that in the absence of such a provision, it is for the Community judicature, if necessary for a preliminary ruling, to check compliance by a Community directive with both the powers defined by the Treaties and the guaranteed fundamental rights Article 6 of the Treaty on European Union.

In the Decision n° 2006-540 DC of July 27th, 2006 *Loi relative au droit d'auteur et aux droits voisins dans la société de l'information*, the *Conseil Constitutionnel* maintained the principles of the previous ruling, rephrased the *ratio decidendi* of its previous ruling, and further explained the basic principles of the relations between European and national laws:

> - With respect to the obligations specific to a transposing statute
>
> 16. Title 1 of the statute referred for review is designed to transpose the abovementioned Directive of May 22nd 2001 on the harmonization of certain aspects of copyright and related rights in the information society;
> 17. Indent 1 of Article 88-1 of the Constitution provides: 'The Republic shall participate in the European Communities and the European Union constituted by States which have freely chosen, under the Treaties that established them, to exercise some of their powers in common'; the transposition of a Community Directive into domestic law thus complies with a constitutional requirement;
> 18. The Constitutional Council, to which referral has been made in the conditions provided for by Article 61 of the Constitution for review of a statute designed to transpose a Community Directive into domestic law, is under a duty to comply with this requirement; the review it carries out to this end is however subject to a twofold limitation;
> 19. Firstly, the transposition of a Directive cannot run counter to a rule or principle inherent to the constitutional identity of France, except when the constituting power consents thereto;
> 20. Secondly, insofar as it is required to give a ruling before the promulgation of the statute in the time allotted by Article 61 of the Constitution, the Constitutional Council cannot

request a preliminary ruling from the European Court of Justice under Article 234 of the Treaties setting up the European Communities; consequently it can only find a statutory provision unconstitutional under Article 88-1 of the Constitution if this provision is obviously incompatible with the Directive which it is intended to transpose; in all events it is incumbent upon national Courts of law, if need be, to refer a matter to the Court of Justice of the European Communities for a preliminary ruling.

In a nutshell, the *Conseil* will not bar the application of a European directive. It will even see to it that the French legislator complies with its duty (within the temporal framework imposed by Article 61 C), and it will not (even indirectly) review the constitutionality of a European directive through the review of the statute transposing it, unless it contradicts an "express provision" of the Constitution (2004 version) or a "principle inherent to the constitutional identity of France" (2006 version).

In the latest landmark case on the subject, regarding the Lisbon Treaty on June 30th, 2009,[254] the German Federal Constitutional Court confirmed the basic principles of its previous rulings.[255] Moreover, it insisted on the preservation of the identity of the Constitution, which it has to protect under Article 79.3[256] of the *Grundgesetz*. This provision limits the power of constitutional amendment. As a consequence, constitutional identity opposes a limit to European integration. From the Constitutional Court's very rich discussion, it results that:

Within the order of the Basic Law, the structural principles of the State laid down in Article 20 of the Basic Law, i.e. democracy, the rule of law, the principle of the social State, the republic, the federal State, as well as the substance of elementary fundamental rights indispensable for the respect of human dignity are, in any case, not amenable to any amendment because of their fundamental quality. [...] From the perspective of the principle of democracy, the violation of the constitutional identity codified in Article 79.3 of the Basic Law is at the same time an encroachment upon the constituent power of the people. [...] The empowerment to embark on European integration permits a different shaping of political opinion-forming than the one determined by the Basic Law for the German constitutional order. This applies as far as the limit of the inviolable constitutional identity (Article 79.3 of the Basic Law). [...] the powers are granted under the condition that the sovereign statehood of a constitutional State is maintained on the basis of an integration programme according to the principle of conferral and respecting the Member States' constitutional identity. [...] The Federal Constitutional Court has already opened up the way of the *ultra vires* review for this, which applies where Community and Union institutions transgress the boundaries of their competences. [...] Furthermore, the Federal Constitutional Court reviews whether the inviolable core content of the constitutional identity of the Basic Law pursuant to Article 23.1 third sentence in conjunction with Article 79.3 of the Basic Law is respected [...]. The

---

[254]BVerfG, 2 BvE 2/08, from which an immense literature has resulted. See for example Fischer-Lescano et al. (2010), Grimm (2009), Schorkopf (2009), von Bogdandy (2010), Terhechte (2009), Schönberger (2009) and Reestman (2009).

[255]See supra, n° 44.

[256]"Amendments to this Basic Law affecting the division of the Federation into Länder, their participation on principle in the legislative process, or the principles laid down in Articles 1 and 20 shall be inadmissible."

> *ultra vires* review as well as the identity review may result in Community law or, in future, Union law being declared inapplicable in Germany.[257]

The Court thus made a strong claim to limit the potential for European integration and the prospect of a disappearance of the German sovereign State. It also claimed not only to exercise a review which would ensure that the European institutions stick to their enumerated and limited conferred powers, such a review possibly leading to the inapplication of European law in Germany, but also to exercise an "identity review" (*Identitätskontrolle*) so as to protect fundamental principles which are so entrenched in the German *Grundgesetz* that they cannot even be altered by the *pouvoir constituant*. Similar rulings purporting to present the most crucial tenets of domestic constitutionalism, be they expressed in terms of "constitutional identity" or not, have been issued as a limit to supranational integration by several other constitutional courts in Europe, for example in Spain,[258] Poland,[259] or Italy.[260] This jurisprudence of constitutional identity appositely testifies to the current movements of the global age: Whereas its principles appear to set a limit to integration in order to preserve pluralism, they simultaneously illustrate the extent to which the major tools for the transystemic accommodation of legal sources result from borrowings and an active circulation and migration of constitutional ideas,[261] which greatly contributes to the renewal of global legal reasoning.

# 5 The Renewal of Legal Scholarship

This part of the report intends to tackle the following issues. Have specific teachings and works appeared following the emergence of new normative interactions? Are they related to foreign jurisprudence and law professionals? Have new theories emerged or has the dominant approach consisted in adapting traditional theories? Have elements of other subjects (and if so, which ones—social sciences [ethnology, sociology, etc.], logics, linguistics, systems theory, complexity theories, fuzzy logics, etc.) been called upon? In what proportion? Is this leading to a reorganisation of disciplinary boundaries (e.g. distinction between public and private law, constitutional and international law, etc.)? Is it possible to observe the development of research projects, journals, research centres that are specifically dedicated to the themes of global constitutionalism? Is there a meta-theoretical awareness of the very evolution of concepts and theories? Are there specific studies on that subject? Is the

[257] Lissabon Urteil, §§ 217–219, 240–241.

[258] Tribunal constitucional, DTC 1/2004, Fundamento jurídico 2.

[259] Constitutional Tribunal, K 18/04; K 32/09.

[260] See regarding European Union law: Corte costituzionale, sent. 183/1973; 170/1984; 232/1989, § 3.1. and very recently the "Tarrico Saga" (ord. 24/2017). Regarding the law of the United Nations, see sent. 238/2014.

[261] Choudhry (2006).

movement of identification of multiple constitutional or constitutionalised spheres admitted or is their constitutionalisation the object of debates, or is it even radically questioned as illegitimate from an intellectual point of view?

Have theories of legal pluralism been called upon to face the mutations that the globalisation imposes on legal systems? With what degree of precision (generic reference to pluralism, reference to a specific author, e.g. Santi Romano and his theory of the *rilevanza* of multiple legal systems, reinvention of new theories of pluralism, etc.)? What did the national tradition use to be in that respect (acknowledgment of pluralistic theories or theoretical centralism)? What representation of the theories and concepts that are being called upon is it possible to suggest to face "global normative disorder"?

Many national reports do not really provide in-depth discussion of this aspect of legal pluralism and constitutionalism, i.e. how both are perceived and how they contribute to reshaping legal scholarship. This proves that the problems or the issues of legal pluralism and new forms of constitutionalism and constitutionalisation are not perceived everywhere with the same intensity.[262]

For example, as the Brazilian reporter puts it, "The questions assume there is a potential legal tension that can be summarized in the following terms. The traditional conception of Constitution, State-originated rules and its claims of hierarchy upon all other norms *versus* the autonomy of many other non-State-originated [norms] that may not submit to the State's authority and may even impact the relevance and the construe of the Constitution itself."[263] But in that country, there is hardly any issue or discussion of that sort, to the point that "Despite isolated exceptions, legal pluralism is almost a non-topic in the country's constitutional discussions; there are important debates concerning constitutional pluralism, trans-constitutionalism and international human rights law, but not from the perspective of an insurmountable legal conflict."[264]

In Solomon Islands the impact of globalisation was apparently very limited. As Corrin analyses, "There is no sign that globalisation has had an impact on legal reasoning in Solomon Islands. Nor has a cohesive body of principles governing the relationship between different legal spheres emerged. The country remains protective of its sovereignty and determined to promote domestic culture and custom in preference to 'foreign' ideals."[265] She adds: "There is no discernible 'dialogue' in the jurisprudence driven by globalisation. Generally, there is an absence of discussion of these issues outside academic circles. Nor have concepts or tools appeared to assist in negotiating between the domestic and international legal spheres. This may be due to the lack of engagement by Solomon Islands government with international

[262]See especially infra, § 6.

[263]De Barcelos, Brazil and Its Many Realities. Courts and State-Centrism; Administrative Agencies and International Cooperation, § 1.

[264]De Barcelos, Brazil and Its Many Realities. Courts and State-Centrism; Administrative Agencies and International Cooperation, § 1.

[265]Corrin, Constitutionalism and Customary Law in Solomon Island, § 6.

law and failure to incorporate international laws into the domestic legal system."[266] Similarly in Cyprus, in spite of its interconnection with the supranational constitutional sphere, "Currently, there is no significant development of domestic research projects, journals or research centres that are specifically dedicated to the themes of constitutional pluralism and global constitutionalism."[267]

At first sight, this could be disappointing. On the contrary, however, one may feel that this allows for a very important conclusion. This is evidence that doctrinal questions such as those put forward in the questionnaire and in this report are highly dependent on contextual variables. Again, as Corrin puts it, "the country is still emerging from a tribal society and searching to find itself as a nation. Legal positivism and the theory of constitutionalism are themselves foreign concepts, far removed from the everyday experiences of Solomon Islanders. Traditional leaders often have more influence than government officials, and in this context customary law is far more relevant than State law. For many, international laws are not even on the horizon, and even constitutionally enshrined norms are at best aspirational concepts, rather than a reflection of practical reality."[268]

Ambitious projects such as a total overhaul of legal scholarship cannot be successful unless some very concrete, human, financial, and material conditions are met. Regarding the case of Botswana, Fombad accurately points to the material conditions of the emergence of a specific legal doctrine. In this respect, he underlines the fact that universities, which are the major institutions to train lawyers, have undergone considerable change since the adoption of the Constitution. "Whereas, a majority of the lecturers until the late 2000s were expatriates, today, most of them are [from] Botswana. The last decade has also seen more reliance on textbooks written on the different aspects of the law in Botswana in lieu of the previous reliance on South African textbooks."[269] How this could lead to the emergence of a more autochthonous legal doctrine remains to be seen. Fombad does not seem to be very optimistic. According to him, "with the departure of expatriate judges, the ideological conflicts that pitted English trained judges and their jurisprudential approach, against Roman-Dutch trained judges and their jurisprudential approach is likely going to reduce. However, given the limited scope for judicial independence and broad avenues for executive interference, the quality of jurisprudence is bound to diminish because of [the] arbitrary nature of many appointments to the bench."[270] On the contrary, before, it was not exceptional for Botswana precedents to be quoted

[266]Corrin, Constitutionalism and Customary Law in Solomon Island, § 6.

[267]Kombos, Legal Pluralism and Constitutionalism in the Cypriot Example, § 3.4.2.

[268]Corrin, Constitutionalism and Customary Law in Solomon Island, § 7.

[269]Fombad, Reconciling Legal Pluralism and Constitutionalism: New Trajectories for Legal Theory in the Age of Globalisation in Botswana, § 5.

[270]Fombad, Reconciling Legal Pluralism and Constitutionalism: New Trajectories for Legal Theory in the Age of Globalisation in Botswana, § 6.

by other Commonwealth jurisdictions.[271] Indeed, Fombad links his remarks on the academy to the current political situation in Botswana. According to him, the legal system as a whole suffers from a fundamental defect: the fact that the constitution is outdated as far as regards the requirements of contemporary constitutionalism, especially in terms of basic liberties. This seems to have prevented any obstacle from hindering the leadership of President Ian Khama, which resulted in severe limits on basic liberties. At a deeper level, most of the discriminatory aspects of customary law, especially regarding the situation of women, have been protected from change, whereas in most of the neighbouring countries—Kenya, Tanzania, Zambia, Zimbabwe—the recognition of customary law has been conditional on the elimination of what in it was incompatible with the basic values of contemporary constitutionalism.[272] As this in-built defect of the constitution gives huge powers to the presidency, Fombad seems to see no strong incentive for politicians to try and launch any important constitutional reform.[273] These reflections prove that constitutionalism, global constitutionalism, transconstitutionalism, etc. are not "machines that would go of themselves".[274] The emergence, development and engrafting onto a local legal reality depend on many contextual factors that are often too neglected. Although this might seem evident, these considerations are frequently overlooked—maybe for ideological reasons.[275]

The contrast with Germany is quite striking. Germany seems to be significant of the general situation of European countries. To a large extent however, this is due to the fact that German legal institutions and scholars have had a leading role in the creation of the transconstitutional conceptual apparatus.[276] According to Viellechner, "legal scholarship mainly focused on 'dogmatics', that is the systematic reconstruction of positive law [...]. Under the impact of globalisation, however, the so-called 'basic subjects', in particular legal history, sociology, theory and philosophy, are gaining fresh steam. Research on processes of norm-formation beyond the State, their legality and legitimacy has grown rapidly in recent years."[277] It seems that a new kind of literature has emerged about constitutionalism beyond the State or constitutionalisation as a process. Included in this trend are original and innovative works that "consciously depart from the statist tradition and try to establish novel

[271] Fombad, Reconciling Legal Pluralism and Constitutionalism: New Trajectories for Legal Theory in the Age of Globalisation in Botswana, § 3.

[272] Fombad, Reconciling Legal Pluralism and Constitutionalism: New Trajectories for Legal Theory in the Age of Globalisation in Botswana, §§ 5–6.

[273] Fombad, Reconciling Legal Pluralism and Constitutionalism: New Trajectories for Legal Theory in the Age of Globalisation in Botswana, § 6.

[274] Kammen (2006).

[275] See infra, § 6.

[276] See supra, § 4.

[277] Viellechner, 'Friendliness' Towards Others: How the German Constitution Deals with Legal Pluralism, § 3.3.1.

concepts of 'multilevel constitutionalism', which are highly contested."[278] There is evidence that, beyond authors, such as Robert Alexy and Peter Häberle, who have developed major theories to deal more broadly with new forms of constitutionalism, many among the leading scholars in this specific field belong to the German tradition, which is especially remarkable for Jürgen Habermas' seminal philosophical contribution to the debate about new forms of political communities. In the legal domain, Gunther Teubner has greatly contributed to offering new tools to confront new legal phenomena, such as the ideas of civil constitution, societal constitutionalism, and transnational constitutions, which he popularised.[279] These allow to conceive of forms of constitutionalism beyond the State, at the supranational level, at the international level, or at the transnational level (*lex mercatoria*,[280] *lex sportiva*,[281] *lex digitalis*, *lex petrolea*, etc.).

Taking into account the material conditions for the development of intellectual doctrines, Viellechner points to the fact that "In part, research in this field has been institutionalised,"[282] and mentions several initiatives by the Max Planck Institute for Comparative Public Law and International Law, the German Research Foundation, the Goethe University of Frankfurt, and the part German scholars take in the creation of specialised journals such as *Global Constitutionalism* and *Transnational Legal Theory*.

Offering a personal contribution to the identification of the lenses that should be resorted to, Viellechner suggests paying attention to the classical tools of private international law:

> Private international law usefully lends itself as an archetype here for two reasons. Firstly, it has always assumed that there are several valid legal orders coexisting with each other that might simultaneously claim application to cross-border situations. Secondly, since its inception, it has been built on a mechanism of horizontal coordination conceding that conflicts of norms may only be resolved from within a certain legal order, even though its intrinsic logic might strive for generalisation.[283]

Kombos offers his own tridimensional perspective, and "argues that in terms of the relational debate and the narratives of constitutional pluralism and global constitutionalism, there is an expression of *constitutionalism as 3-dimensional concept* that encompasses *a national, a post-national and a co-owned element.* Constitutional discussion cannot take place in isolation and on the basis of exclusively one of the three dimensions, especially in the case where the presence of a post-national

[278] Viellechner, 'Friendliness' Towards Others: How the German Constitution Deals with Legal Pluralism, § 3.3.1.

[279] Viellechner, 'Friendliness' Towards Others: How the German Constitution Deals with Legal Pluralism, § 3.3.1.

[280] See e.g. Goldman (1964) and Toth (2017).

[281] See e.g. Latty (2007), Siekmann and Soek (2012) and Leroy and Yboud (2017).

[282] Viellechner, 'Friendliness' Towards Others: How the German Constitution Deals with Legal Pluralism, § 3.3.1.

[283] Viellechner, 'Friendliness' Towards Others: How the German Constitution Deals with Legal Pluralism, § 3.3.3. See also Viellechner (2015).

setting is strong, as is the case in Europe."[284] He simultaneously points to the symbolic and cultural dimensions of contemporary constitutional interactions, and insists on the progressive consolidation of a meta-constitutionalism that encompasses both convergence and divergence between national and supranational legal systems, and leads to an ongoing symbiosis. He consequently proposes the following conceptual distinction:

> Constitutional pluralism is about constitutional symbiosis between legal orders and the mechanics of their co-existence and relation, whereas global constitutionalism forms a descriptive device for an even broader application of the 3-dimensional approach with stronger elements of localisation due to the lack of supranational framework systems, yet with the presence of a commonly shared *mentalité*. Therefore, the difference between pluralism and global constitutionalism is one about the lack of strong supranational framework systems within which the *mentalité* can operate. The more loose the framework systems, the slower and weaker becomes the dialogue element.[285]

## 6 The Ideological Dimensions of Legal Rationality

This part of the report intends to tackle the following issues. How important and numerous are debates on this report's topics? Is it possible to find a date or time division for the interest they have kindled? Are the different jurisprudential directions and practices thus described ideologically marked, in any way (right v. left; conservative v. progressive; nationalist v. internationalist; public v. private law supporters, etc.)? Is the issue of the impact of considerations on the factual power rather than the direct normative authority of legal norms being debated (e.g. for economic or social reasons, it is hard for national constitutionalism to resist sports constitutionalism, while EU constitutionalism, which does not participate in competitions, might be more likely to counter it by putting forward its own claims)? Is the current dynamics perceived as a multiplication of spheres of actors who are likely to promote universal human values or as a source of conflicts and a form of more or less hidden imperialism, related in particular to Western financial capitalism? Is the objective of giving birth to a new real pluralism which would lead to the enrichment of perspectives developed on either sides of the fundamental interests of political societies, or is it of hiding a form of covertly developing hegemony?

None of the national reports has addressed the foregoing topics straightforwardly and completely, nor has any of them intended to call into question the ideological dimensions of pluralism and constitutionalism, i.e. how these two major ways to address and frame the legal discussion about contemporary legal changes in the global age are involved in supporting specific forms of political power. Regarding the debates about global constitutionalism, global legal pluralism, constitutionalism beyond the State, etc., and the various versions of each of them that are competing

[284] Kombos, Legal Pluralism and Constitutionalism in the Cypriot Example, § 2.2.

[285] Kombos, Legal Pluralism and Constitutionalism in the Cypriot Example, § 2.2.

with one another, Viellechner accurately remarks that "it is unclear if and how far these theories are descriptive or prescriptive."[286] The almost constant lack of clarity between descriptive and normative approaches—i.e. between science and ideology—in itself deserves strong criticism.[287] It is not exceptional for many authors mainly to state their claims rather than provide strong arguments to support them.[288] As Kombos notices, there is high need for "*debating the constitutional debate*,"[289] and for trying to understand how embedded in "mentalités" the concepts we use or we devise to face contemporary phenomena are. This is not to say that some of the topics directly, indirectly, or implicitly addressed in the national reports do not call for such a "critical" examination,[290] as I will try and suggest by an examination of two of the main conceptual achievements of contemporary legal thought: the concept (s) of dialogue[291] (Sect. 6.1) and the concept of constitutionalisation (Sect. 6.2). Finally, looking back on the main teachings of this report and carefully paying attention to the fact that some of the initial issues the questionnaire tackled or suggested for consideration were not considered worth dealing at length, I will surmise that one of the most important teachings of our collective enterprise may be that it offers a lively example of the extent to which comparative legal research may help unveil the biases of comparative scholars themselves (Sect. 6.3).

## *6.1 Questioning Pluralist Dialogism*

Intense legal activity from so various national, international, transnational, societal and other spheres could well lead to widespread cacophony and instability. In the heterarchical paradigm, as Mattias Kumm puts it, "There is no one institution that is the final arbiter of constitutional claims. Constitutional conflicts get resolved by reference to underlying constitutional principles that determine which claims to constitutional authority have more weight under which circumstances."[292] There is no doubt at all as to the fact that each retains a final power of interpreting and reviewing the validity of the norms of its own legal order.[293] Formally this might very well lead to disorder, but the solution rests in substantive uniformity around a similar set of constitutional principles. In the absence of any supreme constitutional decision-maker, one could expect enduring conflicts and rivalries. Nevertheless, this

[286]Viellechner, 'Friendliness' Towards Others: How the German Constitution Deals with Legal Pluralism, § 3.3.2.

[287]See esp. Kammerhofer (2010) and Loughlin (2014).

[288]Loughlin (2014).

[289]Kombos, Legal Pluralism and Constitutionalism in the Cypriot Example, Introduction.

[290]See e.g. Muir Watt and Tusseau (2016).

[291]For a taxonomy of dialogues, see Poli (2016).

[292]Kumm (2010), p. 203. See also Kumm (1999).

[293]MacCormick (1995).

is hardly what is actually observed. Despite the potential sources of conflict that exist among the various constitutional spheres, the latter appear to be able to live in harmony, to the great benefit of the shared and universal values of human rights, democracy, the rule of law,[294] etc. According to what has become a conventional explanation, global constitutional actors have started a "dialogue".[295] According to Joseph Weiler, constitutional discourse in Europe is made of mutual learning and conversation among the actors of a united interpretative community. He thus praises "the current constitutional architecture, which [...] encapsulates one of Europe's most important constitutional innovations, the Principle of Constitutional Tolerance."[296] Every constitutional sphere seems to have renounced "narcissism"[297] and parochialism in order to open itself to the others and take part in a mutually fruitful discussion as to the best means to promote constitutional values. As illustrated for example by the growing importance and impact of a multilateral discursive practice of cross-quotation among constitutional actors,[298] this has resulted in a revival of the idea of *comitas gentium* and in the prospect of a new *jus commune*.[299] That is why constitutionalisation is not necessarily incompatible with the admission of an important degree of pluralistic autonomy.

According to Marcelo Neves' theory of transconstitutionalism, "the orders relate to one another on the reflexive plan of their normative structures which are self-binding and enjoy primacy. This is a 'constitutional conversation', which is incompatible with any 'constitutional diktat' from one order on another. [...] The reciprocal incorporation of contents implies a rereading of meaning in the light of the receptive order. There is a reconstruction of meaning, which induces a kind of deconstruction of the other and a self-deconstruction."[300] The fact that one and the same problem of human rights or limitation of power has to be dealt with at several constitutional levels induces cooperation. Everyone incorporates some of the manner in which the other is accustomed to dealing with legal problems, according to its own 'legal software'. A partly common and transversal, rationality emerges. It is made of cooperation, open-mindedness, experimentation and progressive harmonisation, to the benefit of shared values. In a similar vein, Viellechner considers that "Under

---

[294]See e.g. Rijpkema (2013).

[295]For a general overview of the use of the metaphore of dialogue in the literature, see Bateup (2006) and Rosas (2007). On this metaphor and its numerous illustrations see e.g. Fisher (1988), Hogg and Bushell (1997), Manfredi and Kelly (1999), Hogg and Thornton (1999), Hogg et al. (2007), Roach (2001a, b, 2004), Waldron (2004), Tremblay (2005), Petter (2003), Bernatchez and Russell (2008), Nogueira Alcalá (2012, 2013), Burgorgue-Larsen (2013), Friedman (1993), Webber (2002), AA VV (2009), Lichère et al. (2004), Meuwese and Snel (2013), Asociación de letrados del Tribunal constitucional (2013), Brandão (2011), Córdova Vinueza (2016), Fontanelli et al. (2010), Kenney et al. (1999) and Claes et al. (2012).

[296]Weiler (2001), p. 10.

[297]Neves (2009), p. 166.

[298]See e.g. Choudhry (2006) and Le Quinio (2011).

[299]McCrudden (2000) and Weiler (2000).

[300]Neves (2009), p. 118.

conditions of legal pluralism, the legitimacy and coherence of the law may only be guaranteed through a horizontal coordination among the different legal orders, taking each other into account by internally reflecting their mutual impact. The founding principle animating such practice, which could replace outdated notions of sovereignty, may be called 'responsivity'."[301] Although largely dominant, this analysis presents no less important limits.

Transconstitutional dialogues are presented as one of the major characteristics of the global age.[302] A journal, *Diálogo jurisprudencial*, is even devoted to this topic.[303] "It is increasingly *en vogue* to conceptualise relationships between constitutional courts on the one hand and legislatures and other courts, both at the domestic and the European level, on the other hand, as involving elements of communication and conversation. The notion of 'constitutional dialogues', in particular, has gained currency in Canadian and American scholarship to describe interactions between the political branches of government and the constitutional judiciary."[304] The idea is even so powerful that, notwithstanding its artificial or fictional aspect, some authors even go as far as to deploy the metaphor so that *hidden* or *implicit* dialogues take place.[305] As Claudia Escobar-García notices, "this broad and strong approach is conceived as a necessary and unavoidable process to which the entire legal system is submitted. This is not the result of a conscious and deliberate decision of certain agents or legal operators especially interested in carrying out exchanges, but the inexorable consequence of the contemporary dynamics of the production of the law. And through this note of spontaneity and naturalness, globalisation is understood as a peaceful, harmonious and fluid process, devoid of any backward step or any obstacle; sometimes this approach appears inadvertently, as when legal actors are influenced in their legal production by foreign cultural references. It is not by chance that the paradigmatic presentation of the phenomenon is characterised from the outset as 'inevitable'."[306]

From the outset, the very concept of dialogue may seem improper to the phenomena in question.[307] Indeed, the various authorities that "dialogue", and in particular the judges, are rarely in a situation in which they are likely to simultaneously exchange arguments in a disinterested manner about an object of common concern. On the contrary, each judge must make a decision that puts an end to the litigation before her. Any new "exchange" can take place only on the occasion of a new case. Thus, strictly speaking, the formula of "cross-jurisdictional

[301]Viellechner (2015), pp. 322–323.

[302]Yeh and Chang (2008), p. 95.

[303]Diálogo jurisprudencial. Derecho internacional de los derechos humanos. Tribunales nacionales. Corte interamericana de derechos humanos.

[304]De Visser (2014), p. 329.

[305]See esp. Fontanelli and Martinico (2008) and Martinico (2010).

[306]Escobar-García (2012), pp. 84–85.

[307]Criticizing the "dialogical literature" from a metalinguistic viewpoint, see Bateup (2006) and Meuwese and Snel (2013).

monologues"[308] or "sequential monologues"[309] is empirically more accurate. That is why it can very well be regarded as a misleading metaphor.[310] Therefore, the use of the term "dialogue" has all of a fictional process in the traditional sense, tending to act *as if* a form of conversation were taking place between these actors, but the term "dialogue" falls squarely within the category of laudatory (Bentham's "eulogistic") terms because of the image it suggests of a polished conversation between good people, willing to exchange and learn from each other. If the metaphor of dialogue is popular, it is as much because of its descriptive dimension, which allows to account for specific forms of institutional interactions, as for its normative dimension, which offers some sort of justification and legitimation of these practices.[311] Above all, while the old hierarchies are scrambled, this term cleverly suggests that none of the actors involved owes obedience to another and is imperatively obliged to submit to its decisions, and that all are likely to make a good contribution to a joint venture in good faith. This connotation of the term "dialogue" is undoubtedly one of the main reasons for its success, both in the doctrine and in the eyes of the actors themselves.[312]

Nevertheless, one needs to acknowledge that exchanges or dialogues are not always for the better. Even though this seems to be the dominant trend, one should not neglect the existence of somewhat regressive comparative jurisprudence. There is a very common assumption that transconstitutional dialogues among global legal actors is to the best of all ends: human rights and the rule of law. But this sounds very naive, as there are many examples of exchanges between global actors which mostly contribute to the opposite end. Such is for example the case of the great amount of exchanges and dialogues which took place between common law judges when they had to face coups d'Etat. In order to decide whether the new *de facto* legal order should be regarded as a valid legal power, many courts from countries such as Pakistan, Uganda, Southern Rhodesia, Ghana, Nigeria, Cyprus, Seychelles, Grenada, Lesotho, Transkei, and Bophuthatswana paid a great deal of attention to the ways the others had faced the conflicting claims of usurpation and treason of the pre-existing constitutional order, on the one hand, and of successful establishment of a new constitutional order, on the other hand.[313] Global transconstitutional dialogues do not necessarily and mechanically contribute to the advancement of basic rights and other fundamental values.

---

[308]Simon and Rigaux (2010).

[309]Paterson, quoted by Psygkas, Accommodating Legal Pluralism and 'Pluralizing' the Constitution: The Example of the United Kingdom, § 2.4. See also Law and Chang (2001).

[310]See Tushnet (2005).

[311]See e.g. Gibbs (2018).

[312]See e.g. De Visser (2014), pp. 330–331; Meuwese and Snel (2013).

[313]See e.g. Tayyab Mahmud (1994). See also Siems (2018).

In order to go beyond these general remarks, case studies are necessary.[314] Episodes from Poland, the Czech Republic,[315] Venezuela,[316] and Italy[317] show that the idea of dialogue does not always offer a convincing picture of what takes place, which might more appropriately be described openly in terms of conflicts. That is why the obsession with dialogue—i.e. in fact decisional convergence—may not only be descriptive, but also prescriptive. As such, what it convincingly describes may very well be accounted for by other theoretical means, while the logic of dialogues appears to be tied to the *ex ante* or *ex post* justification of specific forms of power in the global era.

First, any decision-maker purporting to direct someone's behaviour has an incentive to be consistent. If it were to decide strictly at random, past decisions would offer no reliable guide to their addressees. As a consequence, the subjects of the decisions would act without caring for what the decision-maker prefers, thus breaking down its power. From the point of view of the cooperative behaviour of global constitutional actors, if one of them departs from the logic of progressive consistency, others will too, and in the end all will lose their influence. Each can hardly afford to break the rhetorical instrument that is the guarantee of the power of the whole system of social control and its main source of legitimacy. As all use the same type of rhetoric, they all have an incentive to do so in similar ways and with similar results. The self-sustained dynamics of principled jurisprudence helps to progressively reach this objective.

Secondly, these actors all claim to be constitutional and, as such, to be independent from one another for their self-foundation. They cannot persist without being accepted by the others as members of the constitutional community. Horizontality induces cooperation, because in this generalised form of *Annerkenungstheorie*,[318] one's power depends on its being recognised by the others. No one can afford to isolate itself by systematically breaking away from the way the others solve constitutional problems.

Lastly, and more precisely, the interconnection of the different constitutional spheres operates primarily through norms that express fundamental rights, values, objectives, and so on. Their generality is likely to offer a shared language through which different actors belonging to discrete legal spheres are able to consider their mutual relations when they happen to govern similar facts. As a result, the discourse of global constitutionalism is very widely expressed in terms of "principles".[319] Because their identification does not depend on any test of pedigree but on their

---

[314]See Tusseau (2013a).

[315]See supra, § 4.

[316]Supreme Court of Venezuela, Constitutional Chamber, 17 October 2011, Expediente n° 11-1130.

[317]Corte costituzionale, sent 238/2014; ord. 24/2017.

[318]On this theory, see esp. Bierling (1894). For a discussion, see Bahlmann (1995) and Yoon (2009).

[319]See supra, § 4.

intrinsic substantive importance as values underlying the rules of a legal system, principles are conceived as if they were already implicitly present, in the positive legal system. They are not the product of a decision, so that their identification does not result from the exercise of a power the function of which would be to create them. By claiming to identify pre-existing principles, legal actors can thus conceal their power and suggest that they limit themselves to progress towards an ever more detailed knowledge of a political community and the fundamental morality that the principles embody.[320]

Two consequences follow. First, if there were no harmony, not even a minimal one, none of the actors could claim that the principles of institutional organisation or the fundamental rights that most of them use to justify their decisions are "already there", and waiting to be discovered by global Hercules,[321] nor could they claim that the way in which they interpret, confront and reconcile these constitutional principles is the product of some sort of rigorous "method" to discover a form of truth. Any discrepancy would prove how much a matter of decision resolving constitutional disputes is. On the contrary, the analysis in terms of dialogue is based on the "inarticulate major premise"[322] according to which the global constitutional enterprise is essentially cognitive in nature. Even if they are fundamentally at odds, the constitutional actors seem constrained to converge towards one another, through the type of legal reasoning they have adopted to justify their power. Secondly, the multiplication of constitutional spheres can be justified as an increase in the number of actors who will devote their efforts to the discovery of the harmonious global "one right constitutional answer". Consequently, according to this presentation, these actors cannot be considered as powers that fight or compete with each other. Each does not decide, in isolation, in consideration of its own objectives, but takes part in a collaborative and peaceful group, aiming to discover the same hidden object. That is why the possible skirmishes that punctuate the progression of the entire system of actors towards this goal are likely to be presented in a favourable light, and the image of dialogue preserved.

A last couple of remarks may be made regarding one of the major devices of dialogue in Europe, constitutional identity. One remarkable form of dialogism is that which follows from and depends on this concept, which has already been mentioned twice.[323] What is remarkable is the way reference to one's "identity" paves the way not for solipsism but for new forms of interaction. Indeed, Article 4 of the Treaty on European Union recites:

1. In accordance with Article 5, competences not conferred upon the Union in the Treaties remain with the Member States.

[320]Troper (1988) and Tusseau (2008).

[321]On this character, see Dworkin (1978).

[322]See Holmes J., dissent in Lochner v. People of State of New York 198 U.S. 45, 76 (1905).

[323]See supra, §§ 3 and 4.

2. The Union shall respect the equality of Member States before the Treaties as well as their national identities, inherent in their fundamental structures, political and constitutional, inclusive of regional and local self-government. It shall respect their essential State functions, including ensuring the territorial integrity of the State, maintaining law and order and safeguarding national security. In particular, national security remains the sole responsibility of each Member State.
3. Pursuant to the principle of sincere cooperation, the Union and the Member States shall, in full mutual respect, assist each other in carrying out tasks which flow from the Treaties.

   The Member States shall take any appropriate measure, general or particular, to ensure fulfilment of the obligations arising out of the Treaties or resulting from the acts of the institutions of the Union.

   The Member States shall facilitate the achievement of the Union's tasks and refrain from any measure which could jeopardize the attainment of the Union's objectives.

Pursuant to Article 6 of the Treaty on European Union,

1. The Union recognizes the rights, freedoms and principles set out in the Charter of Fundamental Rights of the European Union [. . .]
2. The Union shall accede to the European Convention for the Protection of Human Rights and Fundamental Freedoms. [. . .]
3. Fundamental rights, as guaranteed by the European Convention for the Protection of Human Rights and Fundamental Freedoms and as they result from the *constitutional traditions* common to the Member States, shall constitute general principles of the Union's law.[324]

As a consequence, the concept of "identity" simultaneously appears at the national and supranational levels.

In a series of cases, the ECJ had to face States that were invoking their constitutional identities in order not to comply fully with their European obligations. In the case *Omega Spielhallen*,[325] the problem was the following. The firm "Omega" operated a game of laserdrome, where people played at killing each other, in Germany. The German police authorities forbade this activity, contending that this game constituted a danger to public order, because simulated homicide and the trivialisation of violence contradicted the values prevailing in the public opinion. Omega contested this decision on the ground that it contradicted EC law, especially the freedom to provide services. The German *Bundesverwaltungsericht* considered that this game contradicted human dignity, which is protected by Article 1.1 GG. The following question was referred to the European Court:

> Is it compatible with the provisions on freedom to provide services and the free movement of goods contained in the Treaty establishing the European Community for a particular commercial activity – in this case the operation of a so-called "laserdrome" involving simulated killing action – to be prohibited under national law because it offends against the values enshrined in the constitution?'.

[324]Italics supplied.

[325]ECJ, 14 October 2004, Omega Spielhallen- und Automatenaufstellungs-GmbH v Oberbürgermeisterin der Bundesstadt Bonn (C-36/02).

In other words, the question was whether considerations of constitutional identity could preclude the full effect of crucial European norms. Though admitting that such a decision indeed violated the European freedoms, the ECJ considered it as legitimate. Nevertheless, the invocation of constitutional essential values by States in order to escape European obligations is no *carte blanche*.[326] As the Court put it (§§ 30–40),

> the possibility of a Member State relying on a derogation laid down by the Treaty does not prevent judicial review of measures applying that derogation [...]. In addition, the concept of 'public policy' in the Community context, particularly as justification for a derogation from the fundamental principle of the freedom to provide services, must be interpreted strictly, so that its scope cannot be determined unilaterally by each Member State without any control by the Community institutions [...]
>
> The fact remains, however, that the specific circumstances which may justify recourse to the concept of public policy may vary from one country to another and from one era to another. The competent national authorities must therefore be allowed a margin of discretion within the limits imposed by the Treaty [...].
>
> 32. In this case, the competent authorities took the view that the activity concerned by the prohibition order was a threat to public policy by reason of the fact that, in accordance with the conception prevailing in public opinion, the commercial exploitation of games involving the simulated killing of human beings infringed a fundamental value enshrined in the national constitution, namely human dignity. According to the Bundesverwaltungsgericht, the national courts which heard the case shared and confirmed the conception of the requirements for protecting human dignity on which the contested order is based, that conception therefore having to be regarded as in accordance with the stipulations of the German Basic Law.
>
> 33. It should be recalled in that context that, according to settled case-law, fundamental rights form an integral part of the general principles of law the observance of which the Court ensures, and that, for that purpose, the Court draws inspiration from the constitutional traditions common to the Member States and from the guidelines supplied by international treaties for the protection of human rights on which the Member States have collaborated or to which they are signatories. [...]
>
> As the Advocate General argues in paragraphs 82 to 91 of her Opinion, the Community legal order undeniably strives to ensure respect for human dignity as a general principle of law. There can therefore be no doubt that the objective of protecting human dignity is compatible with Community law, it being immaterial in that respect that, in Germany, the principle of respect for human dignity has a particular status as an independent fundamental right.
>
> [...] Since both the Community and its Member States are required to respect fundamental rights, the protection of those rights is a legitimate interest which, in principle, justifies a restriction of the obligations imposed by Community law, even under a fundamental freedom guaranteed by the Treaty such as the freedom to provide services [...].
>
> In this case, it should be noted, first, that, according to the referring court, the prohibition on the commercial exploitation of games involving the simulation of acts of violence against persons, in particular the representation of acts of homicide, corresponds to the level of protection of human dignity which the national constitution seeks to guarantee in the

[326]See Opinions of Advocate General Cruz Villalón in Case C-62/14 and of Advocate General Yves Bot in Case C-42/17.

> territory of the Federal Republic of Germany. It should also be noted that, by prohibiting only the variant of the laser game the object of which is to fire on human targets and thus 'play at killing' people, the contested order did not go beyond what is necessary in order to attain the objective pursued by the competent national authorities.
>
> [...] In those circumstances, the order of 14 September 1994 cannot be regarded as a measure unjustifiably undermining the freedom to provide services.

Thus an ECJ review on the invocation of constitutional identity by national authorities in inescapable. Similarly, in the case *Eugen Schmidberger, Internationale Transporte und Planzüge and Republik Österreich*,[327] the ECJ admitted after careful examination that the Austrian authorities could authorise a demonstration which impeded intra-Community trade for several days, relying on the preservation of the exercise of fundamental rights such as freedom of expression and of assembly which are guaranteed by the Austrian Constitution and the ECHR. Finally, in the case *Ilonka Sayn-Wittgenstein*,[328] the Court expressed in the clearest possible way its respect for the States' constitutional identity. The problem was that under Austrian constitutional law, titles of nobility have been abolished. The litigant was an Austrian citizen who had been adopted by a German national who had a title of nobility. In such cases, the Austrian Constitutional court considers that the claimant has no right to bear a title of nobility, even of a foreign origin. Was the fact that the applicant had to use different names according to where she was in the UE in contradiction with the right to travel within the European Member States? The question referred to the European Court was the following:

> Does Article [21 TFEU] preclude legislation pursuant to which the competent authorities of a Member State refuse to recognise the surname of an (adult) adoptee, determined in another Member State, in so far as it contains a title of nobility which is not permissible under the (constitutional) law of the former Member State?

One of the arguments of Austria was that these provisions are part of an effort to protect the constitutional identity of the Republic of Austria, and especially the principle of equality. After recalling the principles of *Omega*, the Court finally ruled in favour of Austria, considering that:

> The European Union legal system undeniably seeks to ensure the observance of the principle of equal treatment as a general principle of law. That principle is also enshrined in Article 20 of the Charter of Fundamental Rights. There can therefore be no doubt that the objective of observing the principle of equal treatment is compatible with European Union law.
>
> 90. Measures which restrict a fundamental freedom may be justified on public policy grounds only if they are necessary for the protection of the interests which they are intended to secure and only in so far as those objectives cannot be attained by less restrictive measures [...].

---

[327] ECJ, 12 June 12 2003, Case C-112/00, Eugen Schmidberger, Internationale Transporte und Planzüge and Republik Österreich.

[328] ECJ, 22 December 2010, C-208/09, Ilonka Sayn-Wittgenstein. See also the Runević-Vardyn case, C-391/09 (2011) regarding the protection of national language as an element of constitutional identity that can limit freedom of movement, provided it respects a standard of proportionality.

91. The Court has already explained in that regard that it is not indispensable for the restrictive measure issued by the authorities of a Member State to correspond to a conception shared by all Member States as regards the precise way in which the fundamental right or legitimate interest in question is to be protected and that, on the contrary, the need for, and proportionality of, the provisions adopted are not excluded merely because one Member State has chosen a system of protection different from that adopted by another State [...].
92. It must also be noted that, in accordance with Article 4(2) TEU, the European Union is to respect the national identities of its Member States, which include the status of the State as a Republic.
93. In the present case, it does not appear disproportionate for a Member State to seek to attain the objective of protecting the principle of equal treatment by prohibiting any acquisition, possession or use, by its nationals, of titles of nobility or noble elements which may create the impression that the bearer of the name is holder of such a rank. By refusing to recognise the noble elements of a name such as that of the applicant in the main proceedings, the Austrian authorities responsible for civil status matters do not appear to have gone further than is necessary in order to ensure the attainment of the fundamental constitutional objective pursued by them.

The transconstitutional interplay with the notion of constitutional identity shows how this notion can be used simultaneously by domestic and supranational constitutional actors and pave the way for specific forms of interaction. What needs to be highlighted is the extent to which this notion should, just like the substantive concepts of human dignity, freedom, equality, right to fair trial, etc. and the structural concepts of proportionality, margin of appreciation, subsidiarity, etc., be regarded as one of the building blocks of an emerging transconstitutional jurisprudence. At the same time a substantive and structural concept, constitutional identity also seems to be directly related to the ideological dimensions of constitutional pluralism.

First, as it appears in the discourses of legal actors, constitutional identity is composed of principles such as democracy, human rights, the rule of law, human dignity, etc. Several principles such as dignity, freedom, equality, etc. are included in the constitutional identity of Germany. In a later ruling, the Constitutional Court included basic rights into the constitutional identity of the country. In France, there is no detailed enumeration of what may be regarded as being part of constitutional identity. Some authors would include into it principles such as national sovereignty, *laïcité*, the unity and the indivisibility of the Republic, human rights, etc. In EU case-law, there is no precise idea of what constitutional identities may consist of. It seems that basic elements of national institutional architecture (horizontal and vertical separations of powers) and political organisation (political regime), as well as fundamental rights may be part of the constitutional identity.[329]

Second, constitutional identity appears as a text-free or a text-independent notion. Three consequences follow. As such, this argument is easy to handle, because none of the actors invoking it can be regarded as constrained by any specific enumeration of principles, rights or values. It can very well include under the notion of constitutional identity an unwritten principle, or a principle which is the implicit

[329] See Ritleng (2010).

presupposition or the implicit consequence of one or several written provisions. Thus legal actors invoking constitutional identity are more at liberty to invoke it, for it cannot conceptually be encapsulated in any definite and limitative formulation. Just as the identity of an individual cannot exclude some changes over time, constitutional identity can be enriched and modified. This is for example clearly evidenced by a Spanish *Tribunal constitucional*'s declaration, which mentions "material limits which are not expressly acknowledged in the constitutional text, but which can be implicitly inferred from the Constitution and from the essential meaning of this text."[330]

The second consequence is that while it uses that argument, the actor—especially the constitutional judge—can hardly be contradicted. Its appreciation of what belongs to the constitutional identity can hardly be overruled. This may account for the fact that the French *Conseil Constitutionnel* changed the way it expressed its reservation vis-à-vis European integration. In 2004, it spoke of an "express provision" of the Constitution, which would bar the principle of refusal of control for statutes transposing European directives. But an express provision can very well be changed by the *pouvoir constituant*. The *Conseil*'s appreciation could thus be overruled. In 2006, the *Conseil* talked about "constitutional identity", which of course cannot be located as such in any specific "express provision" of the Constitution. Thus its appreciation of what can be included in constitutional identity cannot be overruled so easily. That is similar to what the Indian Supreme Court did in the 1970s to quash constitutional amendments as unconstitutional. First it considered that they violated the provisions of the third part of the Constitution, regarding basic rights. But because they were expressly written provisions, they could be changed through constitutional amendment. Then, in a later decision, the Court resorted to the (necessarily unwritten and severed from any express formulation) idea of the constitutional "basic structure". Then the Court was not so much exposed to have its decisions overturned by the political power.[331] A limit to the analogy between France and India is the fact that the *Conseil Constitutionnel* expressly seems to keep the possibility for the *pouvoir constituant* to change the constitutional identity. But that decision may also be regarded as a first step towards a forthcoming new decision which would break with the former case-law and accept to review the constitutionality of constitutional amendments.

The third consequence consists in the fact that it is impossible to exhaust the argument of constitutional identity. Even if defeated several times in specific reasoning or controversies, the elements that are presented as belonging to the constitutional identity are not reducible to any exhaustive list. As a consequence of this open-endedness, the argument still remains available to legal actors, even if it is rejected from time to time with respect to the allegation that a specific item belongs to constitutional identity.

---

[330]Constitutional Tribunal, DTC 1/2004.

[331]*Kesavananda Bharati v. State of Kerala* AIR 1973 SC 1461.

The third aspect of the substantive character of constitutional identity is the specific flavour of the expression "constitutional identity". One should not neglect its eulogistic appeal, especially as compared with "national (or State) sovereignty". The former sounds "in" or legally fashionable, whereas the latter sounds old-fashioned and reactionary. As Joseph Weiler puts it, insisting on the power of the word, "National courts are no longer at the vanguard of the new European legal order, bringing the rule of law to transnational relations and empowering, through EC law, individuals vis-à-vis member-State authority. Instead they stand at the gate and defend national constitutions against illicit encroachment from Brussels. They have received a sympathetic hearing, since they are perceived as protecting fundamental human rights as well as protecting national identity. To protect national sovereignty is *passé*; to protect national identity by insisting on constitutional specificity is *à la mode*."[332]

It is possible that constitutional identity is no more than a new version of sovereignty, vital State interests, *raison d'Etat*, etc. That is for example what a study of the successive rulings of the *Bundesverfassungsgericht* since the 1970s suggests. The rulings are quite similar in substance. All purport to limit the power of the European legal order when what the Court regards as basic values is at stake. Nevertheless, the novelty is in the name, the linguistic apparel with which those considerations are vested. And it is no doubt more "bankable" or acceptable for other actors than a crude invocation of sovereignty.

As it is more substantive, constitutional identity appears as a less voluntaristic concept than sovereignty. It appears as something which it is not really possible to alter voluntarily. Somehow, identity is something one cannot escape from. There is a sort of necessity in it, which suggests that when a constitutional court invokes constitutional identity, it does not limit itself to the expression of a sovereign will or power devoid of any content, but somehow only gives expression to something which is, by its own strength, compelling for any legal actor of the legal order in question. There is thus a kind of "necessitarianism" in the invocation of constitutional identity. As Manuel Nuñez Poblete puts it, constitutional identity expresses some sort of metaconstitution, a set of preconstitutional norms and principles which define the very significance and meaning of the other constitutional norms, understood as formal instruments for the limitation of the political power. Strictly speaking, constitutional identity is inalienable and unavoidable. It strictly cannot be given up.[333] The invocation of constitutional identity can thus appear as a form of retreat for States' crude free will. The invocation of constitutional identity does not only promote the freedom of the legal order. It also demands it and constrains it.

Moreover, as we have seen before, it is made of several substantive principles (rule of law, human rights, etc.) which the conflicting levels of legal actors forcefully claim to promote. As a consequence, it does not appear only as a sort of rephrasing of the "national competence reservation" or "vital national interests". It does not appear

[332]Weiler (2005).

[333]Nuñez Poblete (2008).

as purely self-regarding. That is why it proves so convenient in transconstitutional dialogues. From this last viewpoint, the "constitutional identity argument" presents several advantages for continued transconstitutional dialogues.

First, identity can be considered as an element of selfness. It is a prerequisite to any discussion or dialogue, because there is no dialogue if the two partners are not able to retain their own identity. If they do not preserve their identities, they self-deny themselves. As a consequence, it is crucially useful for tranconstitutional dialogues to be maintained that each actor preserves its constitutional identity. Both partners in the dialogue have an interest in it.

Secondly, constitutional identity has been the dominant issue in a form of constitutional "hide-and-seek" game in the European context. When studying the interactions or dialogues between the ECJ and the domestic constitutional courts, it is possible to reconstruct some remarkable exchanges. They are the consequence of the fact that the expression "constitutional identity" simultaneously appears at both levels of the constitutional conflicts or dialogues.

Properly speaking and in the intentions of the Founding Fathers of Europe, European Communities had only strictly economic purposes and functions. But the European institutions were pressed to develop. In order to gain legitimacy, they especially resorted to the rhetoric of fundamental human rights, which in the end resulted in the Charter of Fundamental Rights of the European Union.[334] How did they make human rights part of the range of action of strictly economic institutions? The process may be reconstructed in the following way. The Court resorted to what it called "principles" of European law, thus benefiting (1) from the contention that those norms were already there, implicitly grounding the more detailed norms which were embodied in the treaties and secondary European law[335]; and (2) from the self-sustained dynamics principles implying both an increased action of the Communities leads to and the amount of litigation that could be expected as a consequence. But the ECJ made another very important move. In the *Nold* case,[336] it stated that:

> The applicant asserts finally that certain of its fundamental rights have been violated. The [EEC] decision is said to violate, in respect of the applicant, a right akin to a proprietary right, as well as its right to the free pursuit of business activity, as protected by the Grundgesetz of the Federal republic of Germany and by the constitutions of other Member States and various international treaties, including in particular the Convention for the protection of human rights and fundamental freedoms. [. . .] As the Court has already stated, fundamental rights form an integral part of the general principles of law, the observance of which it ensures.
>
> In safeguarding these rights, the Court is bound to draw inspiration from constitutional traditions common to the Member States, and it cannot therefore uphold measures which are

[334]For doubts as to the achievements of human rights protection by the ECJ, see Albi (2010).

[335]See supra, § 4.

[336]ECJ, 14 May 1974, J. Nold, Kohlen- und Baustoffgroßhandlung v Commission of the European Communities, Case 4-73.

> incompatible with fundamental rights recognized and protected by the constitutions of those States.
>
> Similarly, international treaties for the protection of human rights on which the Member States have collaborated or of which they are signatories, can supply guidelines which should be followed within the framework of Community law.

Thus the Court rooted those principles not only in European law, but claimed to infer them from the national constitutional traditions. It was then all the more difficult for States to criticise the revolution that was under way as the European institutions were opposing precisely *their own* ethos and telos, enshrined in *their* more fundamental norms: *their* constitutions and the deeper national traditions they were built upon, to the States. Of course, those traditions and their content are more or less freely interpreted by judges. Nevertheless, there was hardly any way out for the States from the rhetoric the European institutions had devised to promote human rights. How could a State criticise judicial activism (1) in the field of human rights, moreover (2) if such activism was the fruit of the State's political essence? As Miguel Poiares Maduro puts it,

> Where the Union encroached upon State's sovereignty, that construction of legitimacy was supplemented by the appeal to the protection of freedom and private autonomy in the face of power. European constitutionalism appeared, in this light, like an external but self-imposed constitutional constraint aimed at reinforcing the domestic constitutional limits imposed on the power of the State. In this case, European constitutionalism is, in effect, perceived like an instrument of State constitutional values.[337]

It appears however that whenever one constitutional actor tries to "trap" another, the other has enough imagination to escape it. In the Maastricht Treaty, both to release the States from the fear of a European federalism that would encroach on national constitutionalism and to legitimate the increased range of action of supra-national institutions, article F was inserted, which read:

1. The Union shall respect the *national identities* of its Member States, whose systems of government are founded on the principles of democracy.
2. The Union shall respect fundamental rights, as guaranteed by the European Convention for the Protection of Human Rights and Fundamental Freedoms signed in Rome on 4 November 1950 and as they result from the *constitutional traditions* common to the Member States, as general principles of Community law.[338]

Today, these principles appear in Article 6 of the Treaty on European Union. The Charter of Fundamental Rights of the European Union's preamble adds that:

> This Charter reaffirms, with due regard for the powers and tasks of the Community and the Union and the principle of subsidiarity, the rights as they result, in particular, from the *constitutional traditions* and international obligations common to the Member States, the Treaty on European Union, the Community Treaties, the European Convention for the Protection of Human Rights and Fundamental Freedoms, the Social Charters adopted by

[337]Poiares Maduro (2004), p. 16. See also Poiares Maduro (2012).

[338]Italics supplied.

the Community and by the Council of Europe and the case-law of the Court of Justice of the European Communities and of the European Court of Human Rights.

Article 53 reads:

Nothing in this Charter shall be interpreted as restricting or adversely affecting human rights and fundamental freedoms as recognised, in their respective fields of application, by Union law and international law and by international agreements to which the Union, the Community or all the Member States are party, including the European Convention for the Protection of Human Rights and Fundamental Freedoms, and by the *Member States' constitutions*.[339]

It appears that the States astutely managed to use the legitimising weapon of the EU law against EU law itself, thus ensuring that the dialogue among equals would continue and that none could be the final interpreter of basic national or European constitutional concepts.

The States can in apparent good faith claim that the European institutions are, under the Treaties, under an obligation to respect national identities. As a consequence, when seeing to it that domestic constitutional identities are respected, national judges can claim not to be displaying any kind of nationalism, but merely to be enforcing European obligations.[340] At the level of the member States, several constitutional judges decided that they would faithfully respect the supranational law, provided it did not imperil their constitutional identities.[341] A whole body of jurisprudence of "Identitätskontrolle"[342] has consequently emerged among the national constitutional actors. Thus States have managed to use what was part of a sort of reassuring discourse from the supranational actors, in order to maintain their own independence and autonomy. Nevertheless, as was mentioned before, the ECJ clearly maintained, for example in *Omega*, that the constitutional identity cannot be a *carte blanche* for States. As a consequence, the European institutions retain some power of review on how such a concept is to be interpreted and to what ends it can be used. As constitutional identity is mentioned in a European treaty, the authentic interpretation of this expression is the province of the ECJ, and not that of national courts.

As the duty to respect the member State's constitutional identity is contained in the Treaty, of which the Court of Justice is the ultimate interpreter, it plausibly might be argued that it is for this Court to interpret the notion. [...] There is however a most fundamental objection to the thesis: it simply seems incompatible with the very concept of constitutional identity, understood as specific to one member State (as opposed to constitutional principles which the member States have in common). Except when a constitutional provision explicitly States that it is part of a State's national identity, the qualification of a provision as belonging to a State's constitutional identity is always a matter of interpreting the national constitution. And this is the duty and province of national authorities, and more specifically that of the

[339]Italics supplied.

[340]See e.g. the insistence of the German Constitutional Court in the Lisbon ruling, §§ 57, 153, 234, 304, 339.

[341]See supra, § 4.

[342]BVerfG, 2 BvE 2/08 of 30th June 2009, § 240.

> national constitutional courts (if available. Would it not take the heart out of the Union's duty if it were otherwise? In short, the duty to respect the national constitutional identities seems to include the duty to respect the decisions of the relevant competent national authorities on these matters).[343]

There is therefore a sort of constitutional hide-and-seek game: (1) The ECJ begins by opposing the States their constitutional identities in order to broaden its scope of action; (2) the States impose the respect of constitutional identities upon the European institutions through a modification of the Treaties, thus making deference to national identities an EC law principle which it is the duty of European actors to enforce; (3) States constitutional courts threaten to disregard European law in case it violates their constitutional identities; (4) While sensitive to the argument, the ECJ maintains its power to review the invocation of constitutional identity.

The States have intended to gain protection from a tool which it is the province of the institution they wanted to be protected from to interpret. Each one opposes the other with considerations that belong to the latter's legal sphere. Each is trying to trap the other with the other's own weapons, in a renewed and iterative rhetoric that is playing national law against national sovereignty, and European law against European primacy, pursuant to a back-to-the-sender-and-back-again logic. The rhetoric of constitutional identity allows global constitutional actors to express the general principle of dialogue, while simultaneously saying that they keep some last-resort argument when what they would not imperil, even in cooperative dialogue, is at stake. The need for accommodation will then remain in the continuing discussions. In that way, while everyone takes advantage of one's own identities and specificities, one implicitly invokes elements that the other constitutional order intends to protect. Therefore, invoking one's own constitutional identity is not intended to deviate from the fundamental commitments of the other actor, but precisely to claim what the various parties have in common. Paradoxically, the national insistence on constitutional identity as irreducible "ipseity" frequently leads to underlining much more the elements the constitutionalisms share, that is to say the identity in the sense of "sameness". As Denys Simon notices, "In other words and in the final analysis, Article 6§1 TEU (now Article 4§2 TEU) guarantees respect for fundamental national constitutional values because they merge with the fundamental constitutional values of the Union."[344]

## 6.2 *Questioning Constitutionalism and Pluralism*

Like dialogism, constitutionalism and pluralism, understood as perspectives one uses to confront the current legal phenomena, are not neutral. That is why, understood not only as a group of empirical phenomena but also as a lens that more or less

[343]JHR and LB (2007), p. 180.

[344]Simon (2011), p. 41.

implicitly tends to conceal disagreement, violence, inequalities, oppressions, etc., global governance, pluralism, and constitutionalism spark criticism.[345] Despite the wide legal literature that has developed to account for changes in contemporary law, many authors remain sceptical about constitutional analysis as a model of intelligibility at the global level. According to them, transferring the language of constitutionalism to other spheres than the State remains illegitimate[346] or unsuccessful,[347] so that the global constitutional discourse is more a manipulation or pure play on words than an objective analysis. Similarly, one could as a matter of principle voice strong objections against the very idea of "pluralism". Resorting to this lens is a way to ensure a form of uniformisation, i.e. to ignore everybody's specificities, because an increasing number of social spheres can be analysed through this lens. One may very well contend that the metanarrative of pluralism is precisely one means to force the inclusion of different perspectives into a general perspective that encompasses all the others and implicitly conceals what makes them different. Paradoxically, pluralism would limit the resistance of otherness by purporting to make room for it in a more tolerant and accommodating scheme. Although Viellechner is able to distinguish between the constitutional and the pluralist orientation,[348] pluralism is not without its own ambiguities, and can hardly be distinguished from constitutionalism from a global perspective. Whereas constitutionalism would allow for a more centralising dynamics because of its insistence on common values, pluralism would be more adamant that the autonomy and specificities of the various legal spheres should be preserved. However, they are hardly distinguishable in the literature, where many theories of "constitutional pluralism", which combine both terms, also flourish. That is why both may be dealt with jointly without any important risk of misreading.

Global constitutionalists may be motivated by the generous desire to promote human rights around the world and in the private sphere. Similarly, pluralists may be sincerely motivated by the will to make room for various forms of legal life in the global era. However, from the point of view of reconstituting the dynamics of representations and legal ideologies, the development of these intellectual frameworks can also be the result of deeper tensions within the minds of jurists. Jerome Frank's legal realism[349] suggests analysing the use of the constitutional and pluralist paradigms as ways for legal doctrine and legal practice to relieve themselves of the anxiety of not being able to cope with what is changing today (fragmentation of

[345]See e.g. Stout and Love (2016), Gill (2008) and Diggelmann and Altwicker (2008).

[346]See e.g. Wahl (2010) and Tzanakopoulou (2018).

[347]Deplano (2013).

[348]Viellechner, 'Friendliness' Towards Others: How the German Constitution Deals with Legal Pluralism, § 3.3. See also Viellechner (2012) and Millet (2018).

[349]Frank (1949, 1950).

international law into a multiplicity of specialised regimes,[350] disintegration of the post-Westphalian order, collapse of pre-existing hierarchies, emergence and reinforcement of new transnational actors, etc.). The use of the constitutional or pluralist mental frameworks could, in such an analysis, prove to be a minimal way of dealing with a more unstable and disturbing reality. In the form of a simple extension of pre-existing, familiar and secure paradigms, the global constitutional or pluralist discourses would be tantamount to a kind of psychoanalytic compensation.[351] As Martti Koskenniemi puts it, "Much 20th century debate about Western modernity may be depicted as a succession of perceptions about breakdown, explosion, dispersal, fragmentation, followed by reassuring counter-narratives that explain the apparent chaos as mere complexity, healthy pluralism, dynamism, freedom."[352]

The idea of constitutional dialogues plays a decisive role in this reassuring project of conceptualising the theoretical and practical disturbances implied by international, supranational, transnational, national, and subnational constitutionalisms and their pluralisation. As Viellechner notices, "the concept of constitutionalism is currently no more than a reminiscence of a historical achievement as a benchmark. It serves as a cipher under which the reconstruction of law under conditions of globalisation has begun and will continue until more adequate concepts [have been] discovered."[353] From this point of view, rather than seizing the opportunity to experiment with new ways of analysing legal phenomena, global constitutionalism and pluralism would be mere avatars of the "rationalizing legal analysis"[354] criticized by Roberto M. Unger.[355] The analysis deserves to be extended however. The use of this constitutional or pluralist reading tool does not only illustrate the preservation or transfer of known concepts towards phenomena that are difficult to master. It takes, beyond what may seem only a theoretical or intellectual approach, a practical or political significance. Indeed, it is again important not to neglect the eulogistic dimension of the legal vocabulary.

In this respect, it seems difficult to criticise the idea of pluralism, which appears to be linked to those of freedom, tolerance, respect, diversity, etc. From this perspective, everyone has to renounce any claim for supremacy and embrace hybridity. No site of power is immune from being challenged, so that new spaces are created to resist forms of legal hegemony and promote freedom. Nevertheless, some authors highlight some of the possible drawbacks of pluralism. It may not equally expand the possibilities of choice for everyone: "Globally, legal particularism owes its rise to

350 International Law Commission, Report on the Fragmentation of International Law: Difficulties Arising from the Diversification and Expansion of International Law, UN Doc. A/CN/4/L.682, 13 avril 2006. See also Dupuy (2007) and Fischer-Lescano and Teubner (2013).

351 Peters (2006).

352 Koskenniemi (2005), p. 3.

353 Viellechner, 'Friendliness' Towards Others: How the German Constitution Deals with Legal Pluralism, § 3.3.2. See also Viellechner (2012).

354 Unger (1996).

355 More precisely, regarding the use of the concept of "federalism" in the analysis of the relations between member states and the EU, see Tusseau (2014c).

legal pluralism insofar as it entails the ability of pick and choose among multiple legal orders that allow business corporations to play different lawmakers against one another and thereby gain influence over law-making. It also enables global corporate actors to elude oversight by a shared common overarching legal order because it undermines the regulatory reach of existing public political forms while distorting new ones on regional or global levels."[356]

Similarly, constitutional language appears to be linked to concepts that tend to morally disqualify the opposite concepts.[357] According to Giovanni Sartori for example, "In our minds, constitution is a 'good word.' It has favourable emotive properties, like freedom, justice or democracy. Therefore, the word is retained, or adopted, even when the association between the utterance 'constitution' and the behavioural response that it elicits (*e.g.*, 'The constitution must be praised, for it protects my liberties') becomes entirely baseless."[358] It seems intrinsically linked to the struggle of freedom against oppression, and today to human rights and the rule of law, so that it has become extremely difficult for anyone to wish for a limitation of or a brake on constitutionalism. The idea of a constitution is associated with a rich network of ideas that are not confined to limiting the political power. They also participate in the establishment, rationalisation, stabilisation, and legitimisation of the political power. A constitution empowers authorities to achieve the goals it defines, and these goals in return justify their actions.[359] As Eduardo García de Enterría noted about the extent of the change the 1978 Constitution brought to the Spanish political society, "The legal constitution transforms the naked power into a legitimate legal power. The great lemma of the struggle for the Constitutional State was the requirement that the arbitrary *government by men* be replaced by the legal *government by laws*."[360] The constitutionalisation of any object confers upon it self-sufficiency and autonomy vis-à-vis other normative institutions. It is for that reason that this vocabulary is essential in the configuration of dialogic and heterarchical—and as a consequence pluralist—rather than hierarchical relationships between global legal actors. The mere application of the "constitutional label" to the least legal regime reinforces the perception of its importance. That is why Jörg Kammerhofer may very well wonder: "What, then, is the problem with constitutionalist scholarship? It is submitted that the use of language in this case has a mythological function."[361]

Everyone can accept the empirical finding that the global constitutional and pluralist discourses exist: claims, attitudes and institutional arrangements are described, expressed and justified using them. Knowing whether to enthusiastically

[356] Arato and Cohen (2018), p. 25.

[357] Neves (2009), p. 5.

[358] Sartori (1962), p. 855.

[359] Kuo (2010). See also Holmes (1995), pp. 161–166.

[360] García de Enterría (2006), p. 55.

[361] Kammerhofer (2010), p. 724.

welcome this approach or to be wary of it remains an open question.[362] For example, several authors have expressed fears about the inherent risk of conservatism that constitutionalism would carry. By concealing the dimension of power and ensuring the apparent control of disorder, constitutional discourse would strengthen existing situations. The constitutional label could thus prove to be an instrument intended to reinforce the pre-existing structures of power, notably non-State structures, and to favour the *status quo* and unchanged self-reproduction.[363] As they establish institutions apposite to the achievement of specific purposes, constitutional devices must be preserved and are defined as more permanent, entrenched, and difficult to change than ordinary law. According to Jeffrey L. Dunoff, who discusses the WTO's alleged constitutionalisation, "the constitutional turn in much trade scholarship can be understood as a mechanism for withdrawing controversial and potentially destabilizing issues from the parry and thrust of ordinary politics to a less inclusive constitutional domain."[364] The spread of constitution-talk with its reassuring tones is sometimes expressly regarded as a device to legitimate power-structures, make them immune from everyday political discussion, impair self-government and "enervate real political engagement".[365] Against the constitutional rigidity that is implied by legal constitutionalism, Richard Bellamy for example proposes to develop forms of "political constitutionalism."[366] In his views, constitutional rigidity limits the ability of a society to deliberate. The argument according to which at least the formal framework of deliberation and the rights to participate must be rigid does not hold, since this framework and these rights themselves are the subject of political debate.[367] The latter must be as open as possible, and ensure the construction of a public culture of collective definition of the just social order. As a result, constitutionalisation may appear as a fallacy designed to ensure that political issues such as fundamental rights or the limitation of the political power are removed from the political debate. The exclusion of these elements from the political debate, even though their content is the object of the most essential disagreements of any collectivity, risks being arbitrary and favouring a specific form of pre-established political domination.[368] According to this line of analysis, contemporary constitutional inflation, which is particularly illustrated in the field of global law, shows a disdain for the political energy of the people.[369]

As Third World approaches to international law suggest, we may also be witnessing the emergence of a "nascent imperial global State,"[370] which makes

[362]See esp. Scheiderman (2013).

[363]Kennedy (2008).

[364]Dunoff (2009), p. 179.

[365]Ward (2001), p. 29 and Sinclair (2012), pp. 1–8, 29.

[366]Bellamy (2007) and McGann (2004).

[367]Bellamy (2007), p. 178.

[368]Bellamy (2007), pp. 145–175.

[369]Parker (1994), pp. 66, 76, 98, 105, 107.

[370]Chimni (2004).

global constitutionalism an instrument of cultural and civilisational imperialism, with 20% of the globe claiming that their cognitive and normative patterns are valid for everyone.[371] Thus it is no surprise, for example, concerning the *Área de Libre Comercio de las Américas*, that Alberto J. Sosa considers that "As much as the WTO and the NAFTA, the ALCA project are market-oriented global constitutions. [. . .] Unlike traditional international treaties or to strictly interstate trade agreements, global constitutions regulate multiple aspects which modify and bear upon the ordinary life of the peoples of the member States. The rights that global constitutions confer are for corporations and not for citizens. This bestows in the hands of a privileged group of legislators which represent hegemonic States and/or of corporations the production of norms which will rule the life of present and future generations."[372] There is evidence of a link between "disciplinary neo-liberalism" which imposes structural reforms, liberalisation of exchanges, guarantee of property rights, free trade and freedom of contract upon the States, and the rights of investors, which secure a stable environment for capitalism and global constitutionalism.[373] Trying and identifying the main features of transnational constitutionalism, Jiunn-Rong Yeh and Wen-Chen Chang also notice that whereas it facilitates a global market, it undermines accountability, democracy and the rule of law at both domestic and transnational levels.[374] Similarly, pluralism could contribute to the maintenance of the pre-existing power structure by offering the picture of a sort of peaceful and respectful coexistence among various legal spheres.

However, just as much as the manifestation of the vigour of these spheres of power, their constitutionalisation could be interpreted as their swan song. As such, the insistence on constitutionalisation can be a symptom of the breakdown of endangered spheres of social power that use this rhetoric to maintain themselves. Such an attempt might appear hopeless, as suggested by Ferdinand Lassalle's analysis. According to him, the true constitution does not lie in a document or a speech, but in the actual situation of material and social forces on which the content of the laws of the society empirically depend. He draws the following consequence:

> whenever and wherever you come upon a party which has as its battle-cry the tremulous plea, 'Let us cling to the constitution!' – what can you deduce from this? [. . .] Well, gentlemen, without being prophets, you would say with certainty that this constitution is on its last legs; it is as good as dead; a few years more, and it will have ceased to exist.
>
> The reasons are simple. As long as a written constitution corresponds to the relation of forces in the nation, such cries will never be raised. Everyone stays three paces away from such a constitution and takes care not to approach closer. No one thinks of tangling with such a constitution; he will undoubtedly come away the worse for it if he does. Wherever the written constitution corresponds to the actually existing relation of forces, it will not occur to any party to take as its special battle-cry, "clinging" to it. When such a cry is heard, it is a certain and incontrovertible sign that it is a *cry of terror*; in other words, it is proof that there

[371]Yasuaki (2006).

[372]Sosa (2004).

[373]Gill (2000).

[374]Yeh and Chang (2008).

> is something in the written constitution which contradicts the real constitution, the existing relation of forces. And where-ever such a contradiction exists, the written constitution is inevitably doomed – neither God nor shrieks can help![375]

As well as a last resort of a doctrine hampered by the mutations of its object, the constitutional paradigm can be understood as depending on a form of strategy of political survival.

Unlike these sceptical analyses, and without necessarily embracing the prospect of global constitutionalism or repelling it, Anne Peters highlights some of its merits. The distance between traditional State constitutionalism and present-day global constitutionalism could lead to progress.[376] In Peters' views, the critical and empowering potential of constitutionalism is based on the fact that any claim of an actor to be "constitutional" necessarily prompts it to take a number of fundamental values seriously. It also invites communities that are subject to its power to question the "constitutionality" of the regime imposed on them.[377] As much as it strengthens a given institutional structure, its constitutionalisation would impose constraints on it, which would be commensurate with the ambition of the constitutionalist's project. Similarly, claims to respect "pluralism" may concretely lead to harmonious coexistence and learning from one another. Whatever the orientation or the concrete results, however, it remains that constitutionalism and pluralism understood as discourse and paradigms to frame the legal landscape and its analysis in today's global era fall short of being perfectly neutral. That is where the dominant concepts of legal analysis tend to have an ideological dimension, from which this general report is not totally immune.

## 6.3 *Questioning This General Report's Implicit Biases*

In itself, this comparative general report tends to prove that the very questioning about constitutional pluralism and what the global age implies for the considered legal systems says much about the relativity of legal rationality. Indeed, one may consider that many of the aspects that had been imagined in the questionnaire have been ignored or at most dealt with in a tangential way by several jurisdictions. That is by no means a defect or a disappointing result. It precisely offers one example of the fact that much in the comparative enterprise itself is driven by local interests, local perspectives, local ways to look at and to conceptualise objects, local ways to conceive, imagine and formulate problems. When the questionnaire was prepared, it was implicitly embedded in a specific paradigm. This conclusion is by no means

375 Lassalle (1862).

376 Peters (2009a).

377 Peters (2009b).

original, as this difficulty is nothing other than a version of very general hermeneutical problems, highlighted in particular by Hans-Georg Gadamer.[378] It is impossible to understand any cultural object in its "own" terms, that is, by freeing oneself from one's habits, beliefs, prejudices, expectations, interpretations, forms of life, and so on. Every observer is always placed in a certain intellectual disposition or situated in models and preconceptions, according to which she inevitably organises her perceptions and thoughts, and which necessarily condition them.[379] As Richard Rorty puts it, "We have not *got* a language which will serve as a permanent neutral matrix for formulating all good explanatory hypotheses, and we have not the foggiest notion of how to get one."[380]

The information gathered—or not gathered—thanks to the national reports empirically testifies to this fact, as each report implicitly or explicitly embodies one way to understand, frame, and address the topic "Debating legal pluralism and constitutionalism: new trajectories for legal theory in the global age." In this respect, any comparative study necessarily expresses a specific viewpoint. If ever one could somehow naively regret one's predicament, it cannot be avoided. Moreover, it is necessary to be conscious of it, and to take into account the fact that every comparative study speaks from somewhere.[381] By confronting the data offered by the national reports, this general reports exposes how dependent on local circumstances the initial questionnaire was.

Among comparatists, Pierre Legrand is the author who defends most vigorously the thesis according to which the compared legal systems are dependent on cultural, intellectual, linguistic, historical, social, psychological, etc., environments, which they incorporate to the point of being uneasily commensurable with each other.[382] From a methodological perspective, the transition from one culture to another that any satisfactory comparison implies can only be made from a given viewpoint, so that any pretension to conceive a totally neutral and detached comparative metalanguage is illusory. The bias induced by the author's original culture, and in particular the first legal culture in which she was trained, seems inevitable. As Legrand points out, "All otherness is gathered by a horizon of self-understanding – a precomprehension – which is part of a tradition, thus referring to a claim of truth emanating from a living context of convictions, habits and common value judgments. This means that what is, for the comparatist, only exists to the extent of the meaning, in fact culturally determined, that it takes for her."[383] In spite of the risk of what Joachim Matthes calls "Nostrifizierung", i.e. understanding someone else as if she were identical to ourselves, one needs to admit that any scheme of intelligibility

---

[378]Gadamer (2011).

[379]See also Skinner (1969), esp. p. 6; Dunn (1968).

[380]Rorty (1980), pp. 348–349.

[381]Tusseau (forthcoming).

[382]See e.g. Legrand (2011); Legrand (2009), pp. 209–244; Legrand (1999, 2003, 2013, 2014).

[383]Legrand (1999), p. 1058.

is embedded in its author's "cryptotypes".[384] As Günter Frankenberg puts it, "the fictitious neutrality stabilizes the influence and authority of the comparatist's own perspective, and nurtures the good conscience with which comparatists deploy their self-imposed dichotomies, distinctions and systemizations."[385] As Jack M. Balkin also observes, to postulate the existence of an impartial and detached observer, without any culture or legal history, amounts either to imagining an individual who does not have the skills to achieve an understanding of the phenomena, or to implicitly or even inadvertently elevating a particular culture to the level of an ideal. On the contrary, it is essential to highlight the active contribution of the knowing subject to the construction of the known object:

> Legal understanding is not the passive reception of an inert object by a consciousness untouched by the act of understanding. Rather, legal understanding, like all understanding, affects our beliefs and our lives. It is something that we do to the object of interpretation, and something that the constructed object does to us. [...] Ideological power is a special case of the power that derives from the tools of understanding that we use to express our values and make sense of the social world. The power of ideology is precisely the power that the tools of our understanding have over us. We need tools of understanding to make sense of the world, but, like our limbs and eyes, these tools become part of us. Those who shape or control the tools of our understanding have a certain power over us because we are, to a large degree, the tools of our own understanding.[386]

One of the main interests of comparative law is not to allow one to escape from who she is, but at least to be conscious of it. Achieving this operation of consciousness-raising paves the way for deeper comparisons. Geoffrey Samuel offers some important hints from this perspective. Because the method depends on contextual factors, there is no doubt that the conditions of this choice can themselves be the subject of a comparative study. As Samuel notes, "What comparative law should have as its primary object are the models which can be used for constructing facts,"[387] so as to "provide an opportunity to study the internal structures of legal knowledge."[388] If one understands comparative law as "the comparative study of the intellectual conceptions that underlie the principal institutions of one or more foreign legal systems,"[389] it points to a form of comparative study of legal reasoning, or even more deeply, of the comparative construction of legal consciences. At the same time, it opens the subject of comparative law studies to the legal mindsets and contextual determinisms that drive the development of comparative analysis methods, and argues for a form of "comparison of comparisons" aimed at understanding "how individuals enclosed in one culture are able to penetrate the thought of individuals

[384]On this concept, see Sacco (1991), esp. pp. 105–108.
[385]Frankenberg (1985), p. 425. See also Frankenberg (2016).
[386]Balkin (1993–1994), p. 166.
[387]Samuel (1988), p. 827.
[388]Samuel (1988), p. 833.
[389]Ewald (1995), p. 2114.

enclosed in another."[390] For this last activity, this general report cannot be an end but only a beginning.

## References

AA VV (2009) Le dialogue des juges. Mélanges en l'honneur du président Bruno Genevois. Dalloz, Paris
Acosta A (2013) El Buen Vivir. Sumak Kawsay, una oportunidad para imaginar otros mundos, Icaria, Barcelona
Albi A (2010) From the Banana saga to a sugar saga and beyond: could the post-communist constitutional courts teach the EU a lesson in the rule of law? Common Mark Law Rev 47:791–829
Alexy R (2002) A theory of constitutional rights. Oxford University Press, Oxford
Alexy R (2003) Constitutional rights, balancing, and rationality. Ratio Juris 16(2):131–140
Alkema E (2000) The European Convention as a constitution and its court as a constitutional court. In: Mahoney P et al (eds) Protecting human rights. The European perspective. Studies in memory of Rolv Ryssdal. Carl Heymans Verlag, Köln, p 41
Alston P (ed) (2005) Non state actors and human rights. Oxford University Press, Oxford
Andrade S, Grijalva A, Storini C (eds) (2009) La nueva Constitución de Ecuador. Corporación Editora Nacional, Quito
Arato A, Cohen JL (2018) Introduction. Forms of pluralism and democratic constitutionalism. In: Arato A, Cohen JL, Von Busekist A (eds) Forms of pluralism and democratic constitutionalism. Columbia University Press, New York, pp 1–30
Asociación de letrados del Tribunal constitucional (2013) Tribunal constitucional y diálogo entre tribunales. Tribunal constitucional, Madrid
Atienza M (2013) Podemos hacer más. Otra forma de pensar el derecho. Pasos perdidos, Madrid
Avbelj M, Komárek J (2008) Four visions of constitutional pluralism. Eur Constit Law Rev 4:524–527
Avbelj M, Komárek J (eds) (2012) Constitutional pluralism in Europe and beyond. Hart, Oxford
Ávila Santamaría R, Grijalva Jiménez A, Martínez Dalmau R (eds) (2008) Desafíos constitucionales. La Constitución ecuatoriana del 2008 en perspectiva. Ministerio de Justicia y Derechos Humanos Tribunal Constitucional del Ecuador, Quito
Ayala Corao C (2012) El diálogo jurisprudencial entre los tribunales internacionales de derechos humanos y los tribunales constitucionales. In: Barrios González B (ed) Temas de dercho procesal constitucional. Universal Books, Panamá, pp 127–185
Bachelard G (1967) La formation de l'esprit scientifique. Contribution à une psychanalyse de la connaissance objective. Vrin, Paris
Bagni S (ed) (2013) Dallo Stato del bienestar allo Stato del buen vivir. Innovazione e tradizione nel costituzionalismo latino-americano. Filodiritto, Bologna
Bahlmann C (1995) Die Rechtslehre Ernst Rudolf Bierlings unter besonderer Berücksichtigung seiner Anerkennungstheorie. Münster (Westfalen), Univ., Diss
Bailleux J (2014) Penser l'Europe par le droit. L'invention du droit communautaire en France. Dalloz, Paris
Balkin JM (1993–1994) Understanding legal understanding: the legal subject and the problem of legal coherence. Yale Law J 103:105–176
Barak A (2012) Proportionality. Constitutional rights and their limitations. Cambridge University Press, Cambridge

[390] Geertz (1993), p. 149.

Bastid P (1985) L'idée de constitution, [1962–1963]. Economica, Paris
Bateup C (2006) The dialogic promise: assessing the normative potential of theories of constitutional dialogue. Brooklyn Law Rev 71:1109–1180
Beatty DM (2004) The ultimate rule of law. Oxford University Press, Oxford
Bellamy R (2007) Political constitutionalism. A republican defence of the constitutionality of democracy. Cambridge University Press, Cambridge
Belov M (ed) (2018) Global constitutionalism and its challenges to Westphalian constitutional law. Hart, Oxford
Berman PS (2009) The new legal pluralism. Annu Rev Law Soc Sci 5:225–242
Bernal Pulido C (2007) El principio de proporcionalidad y los derechos fundamentales. El principio de proporcionalidad como criterio para determinar el contenido de los derechos fundamentales vinculante para el legislador. Centro de estudios políticos y constitucionales, Madrid
Bernardi A (ed) (2017) I controlimiti. Primato delle norme europee e difesa dei principi costituzionali. Jovene, Napoli
Bernatchez S, Russell M-A (2008) Grandeur et misère de la théorie du dialogue en droit constitutionnel canadien. http://dev.ulb.ac.be/droitpublic/fileadmin/telecharger/theme_2/contributions/BERNATCHEZ_et_RUSSELL-2-20081217.pdf
Besselink LFM (2006) National parliaments in the EU's composite constitution: a plea for a shift in paradigm. In: Kiiver P (ed) National and regional parliaments in the European constitutional order. Europa Law Publishing, Groningen, pp 117–131
Besselink LFM (2007) A composite European constitution. Kluwer, Groningen
Bierling ER (1894) Juristische Prinzipienlehre. JCB Mohr (Paul Siebeck), Freiburg i. B., Leipzig
Bobić A (2017) Constitutional pluralism is not dead: an analysis of interactions between constitutional courts of Member States and the European Court of Justice. German Law J 18 (6):1395–1428
Brandão R (2011) Supremacia judicial versus diálogos institucionais. Lumen Juris, Rio de Janeiro
Brudner A (2004) Constitutional goods. Oxford University Press, Oxford
Burgorgue-Larsen L (2009) De l'internationalisation du dialogue des juges. Missive doctrinale à l'attention de Bruno Genevois. In: Le dialogue des juges. Mélanges en l'honneur du président Bruno Genevois. Dalloz, Paris, pp 95–130
Burgorgue-Larsen L (ed) (2011) L'identité constitutionnelle saisie par les juges en Europe. A. Pedone, Paris
Burgorgue-Larsen L (2013) El diálogo judicial. Máximo desafío de los tiempos jurídicos modernos. Porrúa, México
Bustos Gisbert R (2005) La constitución red. Un estudio sobre supraestatalidad y constitución. Instituto Vasco de Administración Pública, Oñati
Cass DZ (2005) The constitutionalization of the World Trade Organization. Legitimacy, democracy and community in the international trading system. Oxford University Press, Oxford
Cerri A, Donnarumma MR (eds) (2014) Il costituzionalismo multilivello: profili sostanziali e processuali / Le constitutionnalisme à plusieurs niveaux : aspects de fond et de procedure. Atti del Convegno di Studi tenutosi all'Università di Napoli "Federico II" il 25 e 26 maggio 2010, sotto l'Alto Patronato del Presidente della Repubblica italiana e con il patrocinio della Repubblica francese. Aracne, Roma
Chemain R, Pellet A (eds) (2006) La Charte des Nations Unies, constitution mondiale ? Pedone, Paris
Chimni BS (2004) International institutions today: an imperial global state in the making. Eur J Int Law 15:1–37
Choudhry S (ed) (2006) The migration of constitutional ideas. Cambridge University Press, Cambridge
Claes M, De Visser M (2012) Reflections on comparative method in European constitutional law. In: Adams M, Bomhoff J (eds) Practice and theory in comparative law. Cambridge University Press, Cambridge, pp 143–169

Claes M, De Visser M, Popelier P, Van de Heyning C (eds) (2012) Constitutional conversations in Europe. Actors, topics and procedures. Intersentia, Cambridge
Clapham A (2006) Human rights obligations of non state actors. Oxford University Press, Oxford
Cohen JL (2010) Constitutionalism beyond the state. Myth or necessity? https://econpapers.repec.org/paper/erpreconx/p0072.htm
Cohen JL (2012) Globalization and sovereignty. Rethinking legality, legitimacy and constitutionalism. Cambridge University Press, Cambridge
Córdova Vinueza P (2016) Constitucionalismo dialógico y última palabra. Un agenda de políticas deliberativas para las cortes constitucionales. Anuario de derecho constitucional latinoamericano:253–270
Corrêa Souza de Oliveira F, Luiz Streck L (2014) El nuevo constitucionalismo latinoamericano: reflexiones sobre la posibilidad de construir un derecho constitucional común. Anuario iberoamericano de justicia constitucional 18:125–153
Corrin Care J (1999) Customary law and human rights in Solomon Islands. J Leg Pluralism Unoff Law 43:135–144
Cossalter P, Klement JH (2016) La place du droit international public dans l'ordre juridique allemande. In: Bonnet B (ed) Traité des rapports entre ordres juridiques. LGDJ, Paris, pp 1596–1629
Cossalter P, Giegrich T, Schlegel AE (2017) La Cour constitutionnelle allemande et les relatiosn entre ordre juridique national et ordre juridique international. Revue française de droit administratif:799–817
Cotterrell R (2006) Law, culture and society. Legal ideas in the mirror of social theory. Ashgate, Aldershot
Cover RM (1981) The uses of jurisdictional redundancy: interest, ideology, and innovation. William Mary Law Rev 22:639–682
Cruz Villalón P (2004) La constitucion inedita. Estudios ante la constitucionalización de Europa. Trotta, Madrid
Cutler AC (2003) Private power and global authority. Transnational merchant law in the global economy. Cambridge University Press, Cambridge
De Julios-Campuzano A (2009) La transición paradigmática de la teoría jurídica. El derecho ante la globalización. Dykinson, Madrid
De Savigny FC (1855) Traité de droit romain, vol 1. Firmin Didot, Paris
De Sousa Santos B (2002) Toward a new legal common sense. Law, globalization, and emancipation. Butterworths, LexisNexis, London
De Visser M (2014) Constitutional review in Europe. A comparative analysis. Hart, Oxford, xliii +484 p, p 329
Del Rosario-Rodríguez MF (2011) La supremacía constitucional: naturaleza y alcances. Díkaion 20 (1):97–117
Delmas-Marty M (2006) Le pluralisme ordonné. Editions du Seuil, Paris
Deplano R (2013) Fragmentation and constitutionalisation of international law: a theoretical inquiry. Eur J Leg Stud 6(1):67–89
Derosier J-P (2015) Les limites constitutionnelles à l'intégration européenne. Etude comparée: Allemagne, France, Italie. Lextenso, Issy-les-Moulineaux
Diggelmann O, Altwicker T (2008) Is there something like a constitution of international law? A critical analysis of the debate on world constitutionalism. Zeitschrift für ausländisches öffentliches Recht und Völkerrecht 68:623–650
Domingo R (2008) ¿Qué es el derecho global?, 2nd edn. Thomson, Aranzadi, Cizur Menor
Doyle MW (2009) The UN Charter – a global constitution? In: Dunoff JL, Trachtman JP (eds) Ruling the world. Constitutionalism, international law, and global governance. Cambridge University Press, Cambridge, pp 113–132
Drigo C (2013) Preliminary reference to the European court of justice and multilevel protection of human rights: the complex dialogue between the European court of justice and constitutional courts. Turk Yearb Int Rel 43:1–49

Du Plessis J (2006) Comparative law and the study of mixed legal systems. In: Reimann M, Zimmermann R (eds) The Oxford handbook of comparative law. Oxford University Press, Oxford, pp 477–512
Dubout E (2015) Droits fondamentaux et pluralisme constitutionnel dans l'Union européenne. In: Tinière R, Vial C (eds) La protection des droits fondamentaux dans l'Union européenne. Entre évolution et permanence. Bruylant, Bruxelles, pp 107–159
Dubout E, Touzé S (eds) (2010) Les droits fondamentaux : charnières entre ordres et systèmes juridiques. A. Pedone, Paris
Dunn J (1968) The identity of the history of ideas. Philosophy 43:85–104
Dunoff JL (2009) The politics of international constitutions: the curious case of the World Trade Organization. In: Dunoff JL, Trachtman JP (eds) Ruling the world. Constitutionalism, international law, and global governance. Cambridge University Press, Cambridge, pp 178–205
Dupuy P-M (1997) The constitutional dimension of the Charter of the United Nations revisited. Max Planck Yearb U N Law 1:1–33
Dupuy P-M (2007) A doctrinal debate in the globalisation era: on the "fragmentation" of international law. Eur J Leg Stud:1–19
Dworkin R (1978) Taking rights seriously. Harvard University Press, Cambridge
Ehrlich E (1913) Grundlegung der Soziologie des Rechts. Duncker & Humblot, Berlin
Escobar-García C (2012) ¿Constitucionalismo global? Vicisitudes y contingencias del proceso a partir de algunas experiencias en América Latina. Díkaion 21(1):79–118
Ewald W (1995) Comparative jurisprudence (I): what was it like to try a rat? Univ Pa Law Rev 143:1889–2149
Fassbender B (2009) The United Nations Charter as the constitution of the international community. Nijhoff, Leiden
Ferrarese MR (2012) Prima lezione di diritto globale. Laterza, Roma
Fioravanti M (1999) Costituzione. Il Mulino, Bologna
Fioravanti M (2009) Costituzionalismo. Percorsi della storia e tendenze attuali. Laterza, Roma
Fischer-Lescano A (2005) Globalverfassung. Die Geltungsbegründung der Menschenrechte. Velbrück Wissenschaft, Weilerswist
Fischer-Lescano A, Teubner G (2013) Collisions de régimes : la recherché vaine de l'unité juridique face à la framgmentation du droit mondial. Revue internationale de droit économique 27:187–228
Fischer-Lescano A, Joerges C, Wonka A (eds) (2010) The German Constitutional Court's Lisbon Ruling: legal and political science perspectives. http://www.mpifg.de/people/mh/paper/ZERP%20Discussion%20Paper%201.2010.pdf
Fisher L (1988) Constitutional dialogues. Interpretation as political process. Princeton University Press, Princeton
Flanders CW (2009) Toward a theory of persuasive authority. Oklahoma Law Rev 62:55–88
Fombad CM (2012) Internationalization of constitutional law and constitutionalism in Africa. Am J Comp Law 60:439–473
Fontanelli F, Martinico G (2008) Alla ricerca della coerenza: le tecniche del 'dialogo nascosto' fra i giudici nell'ordinamento costituzionale multi-livello. Rivista trimestrale di diritto pubblico:351–389
Fontanelli F, Martinico G, Carrozza P (eds) (2010) Shaping rule of law through dialogue. International and supranational experiences. Europa Law Publishing, Groningen
Frank J (1949) Law and the modern mind, 6th edn. Stevens & Sons, London
Frank J (1950) Courts on trial. Myth and reality in American justice. Princeton University Press, Princeton
Frankenberg G (1985) Critical comparisons: re-thinking comparative law. Harv Int Law J 26:411–455
Frankenberg G (2016) Comparative law as critique. Edward Elgar, Cheltenham
Freixes T, Remotti J-C, Marrani D, Bombin J, Vanin-Verna L (eds) (2012) La gouvernance multilevel : penser l'enchevêtrement. Editions Modulaires Européennes, Fernelmont

Friedman B (1993) Dialogue and judicial review. Mich Law Rev 91(4):577–682
Frishman M, Muller S (eds) (2010) The dynamics of constitutionalism in the age of globalisation. The Hague Academic Press, The Hague, xvii+205 p
Frydman B (2012) Comment penser le droit global ?, Working Papers du Centre Perelman de Philosophie du Droit. http://www.philodroit.be/IMG/pdf/comment_penser_le_droit_global_2011.pdf
Frydman B (2014) Petit manuel pratique de droit global. Académie royale de Belgique, Bruxelles
Gadamer HG (2011) Wahrheit und Methode, 2nd edn. Akademie Verl., Berlin
García de Enterría E (2006) La Constitución como norma y el Tribunal Constitucional, 4a edn. Thomson, Civitas, Madrid
Gatto A (2011) Multinational enterprises and human rights. Obligations under EU law and international law. E. Elgar, Cheltenham
Geertz C (1993) Local knowledge. Further essays in interpretative anthropology. Fontana Press, London
Gibbs A (2018) End of the conversation of recasting constitutional dialogue? Int J Semiotics Law 31:127–143
Gill S (2000) The constitution of global capitalism. http://www.theglobalsite.ac.uk/press/010gill.pdf
Gill S (2008) Power and resistance in the new world order, 2nd edn. Palgrave, MacMillan, Basingstoke
Glenn HP (1987) Persuasive authority. McGill Law J/Revue de droit de McGill 32:261–298
Goderis B, Versteeg M (2013) Transnational constitutionalism. In: Galligan D, Versteeg M (eds) The social and political foundations of constitutionalism. Cambridge University Press, Cambridge, pp 103–133
Goldman B (1964) Frontières du droit et "lex mercatoria". Archives de philosophie du droit:177–192
Gordillo Pérez LI (2014) Hacia la consolidación de un constitucionalismo interordinamental. Anuario iberoamericano de justicia constitucional 18:275–328
Griffiths J (1986) What is legal pluralism? J Leg Pluralism Unoff Law 24:1–55
Grimm D (1991) Die Zukunft der Verfassung. Suhrkamp, Frankfurt am Main
Grimm D (2009) Das Grundgesetz als Riegel vor einer Verstaatlichung der Europäischen Union. Der Staat 48:475–495
Grimm D (2016) Constitutionalism. Past, present, and future. Oxford University Press, Oxford
Grossi P (2007) Mitologie giuridiche della modernità, 3rd edn. Giuffrè, Milano
Halberstam D (2009) Constitutional heterarchy: the centrality of conflict in the European Union and the United States. In: Dunoff JL, Trachtman JP (eds) Ruling the world. Constitutionalism, international law, and global governance. Cambridge University Press, Cambridge, pp 326–355
Hall R, Biersteker T (eds) (2011) The emergence of private authority. Forms of private authority and their implications for international governance. Cambridge University Press, Cambridge
Hart HLA (2012) The concept of law, 3rd edn. Oxford University Press, Oxford
Helfer LR (2003) Constitutional analogies in the international legal system. Loyola Los Angeles Law Rev 37:193–237
Henkin L (1998) Elements of constitutionalism. International commission of jurists. Review 60:11–22
Hennette-Vauchez S, Sorel J-M (eds) (2011) Les droits de l'homme ont-ils constitutionnalisé le monde ? Bruylant, Bruxelles
Hogg PW, Bushell AA (1997) The charter dialogue between courts and legislatures (or perhaps the charter of rights isn't a bad thing after all). Osgoode Hall Law J 35:75–124
Hogg PW, Thornton AA (1999) Reply to "six degrees of dialogue". Osgoode Hall Law J 37:529–536
Hogg PW, Bushell Thornton AA, Wright WK (2007) Charter dialogue revisited – or "much ado about metaphors". Osgoode Hall Law J 45:1–65

Holmes S (1995) Passions and constraint. On the theory of liberal democracy. The University of Chicago Press, Chicago
Jackson VC (2010) Constitutional engagement in a transnational era. Oxford University Press, Oxford
JHR, LB (2007) Editorial. Eur Constit Law Rev 3:177–181
Kadelbach S, Kleinlein T (2006) Überstaatliches Verfassungsrecht. Archiv der Völkerrechts 44:235–266
Kammen M (2006) A machine that would go of itself. The constitution in American culture. Transaction Publishers, New Brunswick
Kammerhofer J (2010) Constitutionalism and the myth of practical reason: Kelsenian responses to methodological problems. Leiden J Int Law 23(4):723–740
Kelsen H (1962) Théorie pure du droit, 2nd edn. Dalloz, Paris
Kennedy DW (2008) The mystery of global governance. Ohio Northern Univ Law Rev 34:827–860
Kenney SJ, Reisinger WM, Reitz JC (eds) (1999) Constitutional dialogues in comparative perspective. MacMillan, London
Killander M (2017) The effects of international law norms on constitutional adjudication in Africa. In: Fombad CM (ed) Constitutional adjudication in Africa. Oxford Univeristy Press, Oxford, pp 209–224
Killander M, Adjolohoun H (2010) International law and domestic human rights litigation in Africa: an introduction. In: Killander M (ed) International law and domestic human rights litigation in Africa. Pretoria University Law Press, Pretoria, pp 3–22
Kjaer PF (2014) Constitutionalism in the global realm. A sociological approach. Routledge, Milton Park, New York
Klabbers J, Peters A, Ulfstein G (2009) The constitutionalization of international law. Oxford Univesity Press, Oxford
Kletzer C (2018) The idea of a pure theory of law. Hart Publishing, Oxford
Koskenniemi M (2005) Global legal pluralism: multiple regimes and multiple modes of thought. https://researchportal.helsinki.fi/en/activities/global-legal-pluralism-multiples-regimes-and-multiple-modes-of-th
Krisch N (2011) Beyond constitutionalism. The pluralist structure of postnational law. Oxford University Press, Oxford
Kumm M (1999) Who is the final arbiter of constitutionality in Europe? Common Mark Law Rev 36:351–386
Kumm M (2010) The best of times and the worst of times. Between triumphalism and nostalgia. In: Dobner P, Loughlin M (eds) The twilight of constitutionalism? Oxford University Press, Oxford, pp 201–219
Kuo M-S (2010) The end of constitutionalism as we know it? Boundaries and the state of global constitutional (dis)ordering. Transnatl Leg Theory 1:329–369
Lang AF, Wiener A (eds) (2017) Handbook on global constitutionalism. Edward Elgar, Cheltenham
Lassalle F (1862) On the essence of constitutions. https://www.marxists.org/history/etol/newspape/fi/vol03/no01/lassalle.htm
Latty F (2007) La lex sportiva. Recherche sur le droit transnational. M. Nijhoff, Leiden, Boston
Lavranos N (2008) The Solange-method as a tool for regulating competing jurisdictions among international courts and tribunals. Loyola Los Angeles Int Comp Law Rev 30:275–334
Law D, Chang W-C (2001) The limits of global judicial dialogue. Wash Law Rev 86:523–577
Le Quinio A (2011) Recherche sur la circulation des solutions juridiques. Le recours au droit comparé par les juridictions constitutionnelles. Fondation Varenne, Clermont-Ferrand
Legrand P (1999) Sur l'analyse différentielle des juriscultures. Revue internationale de droit compare 51:1053–1071
Legrand P (2003) The same and the different. In: Legrand P, Munday R (eds) Comparative legal studies: traditions and transitions. Cambridge University Press, Cambridge, pp 240–331

Legrand P (2009) La comparaison des droits expliquée à mes étudiants. In: Legrand P (ed) Comparer les droits, résolument. PUF, Paris, pp 209–244
Legrand P (2011) Le droit comparé, 4th edn. PUF, Paris
Legrand P (2013) What can you say, words it is, nothing else going. Int J Semiotics Law 26 (4):805–832
Legrand P (2014) Pour la relevance des droits étrangers. IRJS éd., Paris
Leroy C, Yboud L (eds) (2017) Le concept d'arbitrage. Regards croisés entre droit et sport. L'Harmattan, Paris
Letsas G (2012) Harmonic law. The case against pluralism. In: Dickson J, Eleftheriadis P (eds) Philosophical foundations of European Union law. Oxford University Press, Oxford, pp 77–108
Lichère F, Potvin-Salis L, Ragnouard A (eds) (2004) Le dialogue entre les juges européens et nationaux : incantation ou réalité ? Bruylant, Nemesis, Bruxelles
López Freire E et al (2009) La constitución ciudadana. Doce visiones sobre un documento revolucionario. Taurus, Ecuador
Loughlin M (2014) Constitutional pluralism: an oxymoron? Global Constitutionalism 3(1):9–30
MacCormick N (1995) The Maastricht Urteil: sovereignty now. Eur Law J 1:259–266
MacCormick N (1999) Questioning sovereignty. Law, state and nation in the European Commonwealth. Oxford University Press, Oxford
Maduro M, Tuori K, Sankari S (eds) (2014) Transnational law. Rethinking European law and legal thinking. Cambridge University Press, Cambridge
Mahmud T (1994) Jurisprudence of Successful Treason: Coup d'Etat & Common Law. Cornell Int Law J 49:49–140
Manfredi CP, Kelly JB (1999) Six degrees of dialogue: a response to Hogg and Bushell. Osgoode Hall Law J 37:513–527
Marti G (2011) Le statut contentieux du droit constitutionnel devant la Cour de justice de l'Union européenne. http://www.droitconstitutionnel.org/congresNancy/comN2/martiTD2.pdf
Martinico G (2010) Judging in the multilevel legal order: exploring the techniques of "hidden dialogue". King's Law J 21:257–281
McCrudden C (2000) A common law of human rights?: Transnational judicial conversations on constitutional rights. Oxford J Leg Stud 20:499–532
McGann AJ (2004) The tyranny of supermajority: how majority rule protects minorities. J Theor Polit 16:56–70
McGinnis JO, Movsesian ML (2000) The World Trade Constitution. Harv Law Rev 114:511–605
McIlwain CH (1940) Constitutionalism: ancient and modern. Cornell University Press, Ithaca
McMahon C (2009) Reasonable disagreement. A theory of political morality. Cambridge University Press, Cambridge
Merkl AJ (1962) Prolegomena einer Theorie des rechtlichen Stufenbaues, [1931]. In: Klecatsky H, Marcic R, Schambeck H (eds) Die Wiener rechtstheoretische Schule. Schriften von Hans Kelsen, Adolf Merkl, Alfred Verdross. Europa Verlag, Universitätsverlag Anton Pustet, Wien, Salzburg, Bd. 2, pp 1311–1361
Merry SE (1988) Legal pluralism. Law Soc Rev 22:869–896
Meuwese A, Snel M (2013) "Constitutional dialogue": an overview. Utrecht Law Rev 9 (2):123–140
Millet F-X (2013) L'Union européenne et l'identité constitutionnelle des Etats membres. LGDJ, Paris
Millet F-X (2018) Constitutional pluralism beyond monism and dualism. In: Davies G, Avbelj M (eds) Research handbook on legal pluralism and EU law. Edward Elgar, Cheltenham, pp 111–132
Mohnhaupt H, Grimm D (2002) Verfassung. Zur Geschichte des Begriffs von der Antike bis zur Gegenwart: zwei Studien, 2nd edn. Duncker & Humblot, Berlin
Muir Watt H (2004) New challenges in public and private international legal theory: can comparative scholarship help? In: Van Hoecke M (ed) Epistemology and methodology of comparative law. Hart, Oxford, pp 271–283

Muir Watt H, Tusseau G (2016) Repenser le dévoilement de l'idéologie juridique : une approche fictionnelle de la gouvernance globale. In: Bonnet B (ed) Traité des rapports entre ordres juridiques. LGDJ, Paris, pp 169–219

Navas Castillo A, Florentina Navas Castillo F (2016) El Estado constitucional multinivel. Dykinson, Madrid

Neo JL (2012) Incorporating human rights: mitigated dualism and interpretation in Malaysian courts. Asian Yearb Int Law 18:1–37

Neves M (2009) Transconstitucionalismo. W.M.F. Martins Fontes, São Paulo

Neves M (2015) From constitutionalism to transconstitutionalism: beyond constitutional nationalism, cosmopolitan constitutional unity and fragmentary constitutional pluralism. https://ssrn.com/abstract=3016498 or https://doi.org/10.2139/ssrn.3016498

Nogueira Alcala H (ed) (2012) El diálogo transjudicial de los tribunales constitucionales entre sí y con las cortes internacionales de derechos humanos. Librotecnia, Santiago

Nogueira Alcalá H (ed) (2013) Diálogo judicial multinivel y principios interpretativos favor persona y de proporcionalidad. Librotecnica, Santiago

Nolan J (2009) The nexus between human rights and business: defining the sphere of corporate responsibility. In: Ferrall J, Rubinstein K (eds) Sanctions, accountability and governance in a globalised world. Cambridge University Press, Cambridge, pp 223–224

Nuñez Poblete M (2008) Introducción al concepto de identidad constitucional y a su función frente al derecho supranacional e internacional de los derechos de la persona. Revista Ius et Praxis 14:331–372

Orakhelashvili A (2010) Peremptory norms as an aspect of constitutionalisation in the international legal system. In: Frishman M, Muller S (eds) The dynamics of constitutionalism in the age of globalisation. Hague Academic Press, The Hague, pp 153–180

Ost F, Van de Kerchove M (1988) De la "bipolarité des erreurs" ou de quelques paradigmes de la science du droit. Archives de philosophie du droit 33:177–206

Palandri L (2013) Theoretical reflections on legal pluralism and global constitutionalism: their possible reconciliation in an alternative model of plural constitutionalism. Acta Juridica Hungarica 54(1):58–72

Palmer VV (2012) Mixed jurisdictions worldwide. The third legal family, 2nd edn. Cambridge University Press, Cambridge

Palmer VV, Mattar MY (eds) (2015) Mixed legal systems, east and west. Ashgate, Farnham

Palombella G (2012) È possibile una legalità globale? Il Rule of law e la governance del mondo. Il Mulino, Bologna

Parker RD (1994) "Here the People Rule". A constitutional populist manifesto. Harvard University Press, Cambridge

Peczenik A (2009) On law and reason. Springer, New York

Pegoraro L, Figueroa Mejía GA (eds) (2017) Profesores y jueces. Influjos de la doctrina en la jurisprudencia constitucional de Iberoamérica, Suprema Corte de Justicia de la Nación, México

Pernice I (1999) Multilevel constitutionalism and the Treaty of Amsterdam: European constitution-making revisited? Common Mark Law Rev 36:703–750

Pernice I (2002) Multilevel constitutionalism in the European Union. Eur Law Rev:511–529

Pernice I, Mayer F (2000) De la constitution composée de l'Europe. Revue trimestrielle de droit européen 36:623–647

Peters A (2006) Compensatory constitutionalism: the function and potential of fundamental international norms and structures. Leiden J Int Law 19:579–610

Peters A (2009a) The merits of global constitutionalism. Indiana J Global Leg Stud 16:397–411

Peters A (2009b) Conclusions. In: Klabbers J, Peters A, Ulfstein G (eds) The constitutionalization of international law. Oxford University Press, Oxford, pp 342–352

Peters A, Koechlin L, Förster T, Fenner Zinkernagel G (eds) (2009) Non-state actors as standard setters. Cambridge University Press, Cambridge

Petersen H, Zahle H (1995) Legal polycentricity. Consequences of pluralism in law. Avebury, Aldershot

Petersmann EU (2000) The WTO constitution and human rights. J Int Econ Law 3:19–25
Petersmann EU (2011) Mutilevel trade governance in the WTO requires multilevel constitutionalism. In: Joerges C, Petersmann EU (eds) Constitutionalism, mutilevel trade governance and international economic law, 2nd edn. Hart, Oxford, pp 5–57
Petter A (2003) Twenty years of charter justification: from liberal legalism to dubious dialogue. Univ New Brunswick Law J 52:187–199
Piattoni S (2010) The theory of multi-level governance. Conceptual, empirical, and normative challenges. Oxford University Press, Oxford
Pigrau Solé A (eds) (2013) Pueblos indígenas, diversidad cultural y justicia ambiental. Un estudio de las nuevas constituciones de Ecuador y Bolivia. Tirant lo blanch, Valencia
Poiares Maduro M (2004) How constitutional can the European Union be? The tension between intergovernmentalism and constitutionalism in the European Union. www.jeanmonnetprogram.org/archive/papers/04/040501-18.rtf
Poiares Maduro M (2012) Three claims of constitutional pluralism. In: Avbelj M, Komárek J (eds) Constitutional pluralism in the European Union and beyond. Hart, Oxford, pp 67–84
Poli MD (2016) Der justizielle Pluralismus der Europäischen Verfassungsgemeinschaft : "Babylonische Gerichte" oder "Gerichte für Babylon" ? Der Staat 55:373–391
Ponthoreau M-C (2010) Droit(s) constitutionnel(s) comparé(s). Economica, Paris
Queiroz CMM (2011) Direito constitucional internacional. Coimbra editor, Coimbra
Ramadi Dinokopila B (2017) The impact of regional and sub-regional courts and tribunals on constitutional adjudication in Africa. In: Fombad CM (ed) Constitutional adjudication in Africa. Oxford Univeristy Press, Oxford, pp 225–243
Rasche A (ed) (2010) The United Nations global compact. Achievements, trends and challenges. Cambridge University Press, Cambridge
Reestman JH (2009) The Franco-German constitutional divide, reflections on national and constitutional identity. Eur Constit Law Rev 5:374–390
Reid KGC (2003) The idea of mixed legal systems. Tulane Law Rev 78:5–40
Rijpkema P (2013) The concept of a global rule of law. Transnatl Leg Theory 4(2):167–196
Ritleng S (2010) Le droit au respect de l'identité constitutionnelle nationale. In: Barbato JC, Mouton JD (eds) Vers la reconnaissance de droits fondamentaux aux Etats membres de l'UE? Réflexions à patir des notions d'identité et de solidarité. Bruylant, Bruxelles, pp 21–47
Roach K (2001a) Constitutional and common law dialogues between the Supreme Court and Canadian legislatures. Can Bar Rev 80:481–533
Roach K (2001b) The Supreme Court on trial. Judicial activism of democratic dialogue. Irwin Law, Toronto
Roach K (2004) Dialogic judicial review and its critics. Supreme Court Law Rev 23:49–104
Robé J-P (2012) L'entreprise et la constitutionnalisation du système-monde de pouvoir. In: Roger B (ed) L'entreprise, formes de la propriété et responsabilités sociales. Lethielleux, Collège des Bernardins, Paris, pp 273–344
Robé J-P (2013) Les multinationales, vecteur d'un nouveau constitutionnalisme. Archives de philosophie du droit 56:337–361
Romano S (2002) L'ordre juridique, 2nd edn. Dalloz, Paris
Rorty R (1980) Philosophy and the mirror of nature. Blackwell, Oxford
Rosas A (2007) The European Court of Justice in context: forms and patterns of judicial dialogue. Eur J Leg Stud 1(2):1–16
Rosas A, Armati L (2012) EU constitutional law. An introduction, 2nd edn. Hart, Oxford
Rosenfeld M, Sajó A (2006) Spreading the liberal constitutionalism: an inquiry into the fate of free speech rights in new democracies. In: Choudhry S (ed) The migration of constitutional ideas. Cambridge University Press, Cambridge, pp 142–177
Ross A (1946) Towards a realistic jurisprudence. A criticism of the dualism in law. E. Munksgaard, Copenhagen
Ross A (2004) Le problème des sources du droit à la lumière d'une théorie réaliste du droit [1934]. In: Ross A (ed) Introduction à l'empirisme juridique. Textes théoriques. LGDJ, Paris, pp 23–37

Sabel CF, Gerstenberg O (2010) Constitutionalising an overlapping consensus: the ECJ and the emergence of a co-ordinate constitutional order. Eur Law J 16:511–550
Sacco R (1991) La comparaison juridique au service de la connaissance du droit. Economica, Paris
Saiz Arnaiz A, Alcoberro Llivina C (eds) (2013) National constitutional identity and European integration. Intersentia, Cambridge
Samuel G (1988) Comparative law and jurisprudence. Int Comp Law Q 47:817–836
Samuel G (2003) Epistemology and method in law. Ashgate, Burlington
Samuel G (2013) A short introduction to the common law. E. Elgar, Cheltenham
Sartori G (1962) Constitutionalism: a preliminary discussion. Am Polit Sci Rev 56(4):853–864
Scalia-Breyer Debate on Constitutional relevance of foreign court decisions. http://www.freerepublic.com/focus/news/1352357/posts
Schauer F (2009) Thinking like a lawyer. A new introduction to legal reasoning. Harvard University Press, Cambridge
Scheiderman D (2013) A new global constitutional order? In: Ginsburg T, Dixon R (eds) Comparative constitutional law. E. Elgar, Cheltenham, pp 189–207
Schepel H (2004) Constituting private governance regimes: standards bodies in American law. In: Joerges C, Sand I-J, Teubner G (eds) Transnational governance and constitutionalism. Hart, Oxford, pp 161–188
Schepel H (2005) The constitution of private governance. Product standards in the regulation of integrated markets. Hart, Oxford
Schmid CU (2001) All bark and no bite: notes on the federal constitutional court's "Banana Decision". Eur Law J 7:95–113
Schneiderman D (2008) Constitutionalizing economic globalization. Investment rules and democracy's promise. Cambridge University Press, Cambridge
Schönberger C (2009) Lisbon in Karlsruhe: Maastricht's epigones at sea. German Law J 10:1201–1218
Schorkopf F (2009) The European Union as an association of sovereign states: Karlsruhe's ruling on the Treaty of Lisbon. German Law J 10:1219–1240
Schütze R (2012) European constitutional law. Cambridge University Press, New York
Schwöbel CEJ (2011) Global constitutionalism in international legal perspective. Martinus Nijhoff, Leiden
Scott C, Cafaggi F, Senden L (2011) The conceptual and constitutional challenge of transnational private regulation. J Law Soc 38(1):1–19
Shaw J (2011) Postnational constitutionalism in the European Union. J Eur Public Policy 6 (4):579–597
Shelton D (ed) (2011) International law and domestic legal systems. Oxford University Press, Oxford
Siekmann RCR, Soek J (eds) (2012) Lex Sportiva. What is sports law? TMC Asser Press, The Hague, Springer, Berlin
Siems M (2018) Malicious legal transplants. Leg Stud 38:103–119
Simma B (1994) From bilateralism to community interest in international law. Recueil des cours de l'Académie de droit international 250:217–384
Simon D (2011) L'identité constitutionnelle dans la jurisprudence de l'Union européenne. In: Burgorgue-Larsen L (ed) L'identité constitutionnelle saisie par les juges en Europe. Pédone, Paris, pp 27–44
Simon D, Rigaux A (2010) La priorité de la question prioritaire de constitutionnalité : harmonie (s) et dissonance(s) des monologues juridictionnels croisés. Cahiers du Conseil constitutionnel 29. https://www.conseil-constitutionnel.fr/nouveaux-cahiers-du-conseil-constitutionnel/la-priorite-de-la-qpc-harmonies-et-dissonances-des-monologues-juridictionnels-croises
Sinclair TJ (2012) Global governance. Polity, Cambridge
Skinner Q (1969) Meaning and understanding in the history of ideas. Hist Theory 8:3–53
Sosa AJ (2004) El ALCA como constitución global y su probable impacto sobre la sociedad argentina. https://www.rebelion.org/hemeroteca/economia/040316sosa.htm

St. John Macdonald R, Johnston DM (eds) (2005) Towards world constitutionalism. Issues in the legal ordering of the world community. M. Nijhoff, Leiden
Stein E (1981) Lawyers, judges and the making of a transnational constitution. Am J Int Law 75:1–27
Stone Sweet A (2009) On the constitutionalisation of the convention: the European Court of Human Rights as a constitutional court. Revue trimestrielle des droits de l'homme 80:923–944
Storini C, Alenza García JF (eds) (2012) Materiales sobre neoconstitucionalismo y nuevo constitucionalismo latinoamericano, Thomson, Reuters, Aranzadi, Cizur Menor
Stout M, Love JM (2016) A radically democratic response to global governance. Dystopian Utopias. Routlege, London
Tamanaha BZ (1993) The folly of the 'social scientific' concept of legal pluralism. J Law Soc 20:192–217
Tamanaha BZ (2008) Understanding legal pluralism: past to present, local to glocal. Sydn Law Rev 30(3):375–411
Tan EKB (2017) Much ado about nothing? The enigma of engagement of foreign constitutional law in Singapore. In: Neo JL (ed) Constitutional interpretation in Singapore. Routledge, London
Terhechte JP (2009) Souveränität, Dynamik und Integration – making up the rules as we go along? – Anmerkungen zum Lissabon-Urteil des Bundesverfassungsgerichts. Europäische Zeitschrift für Wirtschaftsrecht 20:724–731
Tetley W (2000) Mixed jurisdictions: Common Law v. Civil Law (codified and uncodified). La Law Rev 60:677–738
Teubner G (1992) The two faces of Janus: rethinking legal pluralism. Cardozo Law Rev 13:1443–1462
Teubner G (1997) "Global Bukowina": legal pluralism in the world society. In: Teubner G (ed) Global law without a state. Dartmouth, Aldershot, pp 3–28
Teubner G (2003) Globale Zivilverfassungen: Alternativen zur staatszentrierten Verfassungstheorie. Zeitschrift für ausländisches öffentliches Recht und Völkerrecht 63:1–28
Teubner G (2004) Societal constitutionalism: alternatives to state-centred constitutional theory? In: Joerges C, Sand I-J, Teubner G (eds) Transnational governance and constitutionalism. Hart, Oxford, pp 3–28
Teubner G (2010) Constitutionalising Polycontexturality. http://www.jura.uni-frankfurt.de/42852930/ConstitutionalisingPolycontexturality_eng.pdf
Teubner G (2011) Self-constitutionalizing TNCs? On the linkage of 'private' and 'public' corporate codes of conduct. http://www.jura.uni-frankfurt.de/42852833/CSR_conference_bremen.pdf
Teubner G (2012) Constitutional fragments. Societal constitutionalism and globalization. Oxford University Press, Oxford
Teubner G (2013) The project of constitutional sociology: irritating nation state constitutionalism. Transnatl Leg Theory 4(1):44–58
Teubner G (2016) Societal constitutionalism: nine variations on a theme by David Sciulli. https://www.jura.uni-frankfurt.de/59903648/Sciulli-VariationenENG-FINAL.pdf
Tomuschat C (1993) Obligations arising for states without or against their will. Recueil des cours de l'Académie de droit international 241:195–374
Toth O (2017) The lex mercatoria in theory and practice. Oxford University Press, Oxford
Trachtman JP (2006) The constitution of the WTO. Eur J Int Law 17:623–646
Tremblay LB (2005) The legitimacy of judicial review: the limits of dialogue between courts and legislatures. Int J Constit Law 3:617–648
Troper M (1988) Judges taken too seriously: Professor Dworkin's views on jurisprudence. Ratio Juris 1:162–175
Tsagourias N (ed) (2007) Transnational constitutionalism. International and European models. Cambridge University Press, Cambridge
Tshosa OB (2007) The status and role of international law in the national law of Botswana. In: Fombad CM (ed) Essays on the law of Botswana. Juta, Cape Town, pp 229–246

Tuori K (2013) Vers une théorie du droit transnational. Revue internationale de droit économique 27:9–36

Tuori K (2015) European constitutionalism. Cambridge University Press, Cambridge

Tuori K, Sankari S (eds) (2010) The many constitutions of Europe. Ashgate, Farnham, Burlington

Tushnet M (2005) Misleading metaphors in comparative constitutionalism: moments and enthusiasm. Int J Constit Law 3:262–268

Tusseau G (2008) Métathéorie de la notion de principe dans la théorie du droit contemporaine. Sur quelques écoles de définition des principes. In: Caudal S (ed) Les principes en droit. Economica, Paris, pp 75–112

Tusseau G (2012) Chronique de jurisprudence droit administratif et droit constitutionnel. Jurisprudence étrangère : Le financement politique vu de l'étranger (Cour constitutionnelle de Corée du Sud, Décisions n° 2009Hun-Ma170 du 25 mars 2010, 2008Hun-Ma491 du 27 mai 2010, 2008Hun-Ba89 du 28 décembre 2010, 2010Hun-Ma451 du 26 mai 2011) et Eligible... mais frappé par une incompatibilité en cas d'élection : le droit électoral aux prises avec le constitutionnalisme multiniveaux (Tribunal suprême de justice du Venezuela, Chambre constitutionnelle, Expediente n° 11-1130 du 17 octobre 2011). Revue française de droit administratif: 536–545

Tusseau G (2013a) A plea for a hint of empiricism in constitutional theory: a comment on Cesare Pinelli's "Constitutional Reasoning and Political Deliberation". German Law J 14 (8):1183–1194

Tusseau G (2013b) Chronique de jurisprudence droit administratif et droit constitutionnel. Jurisprudence étrangère : Le constitutionnalisme européen aux prises avec la « désobéissance institutionnelle » des juges nationaux (Tribunal constitutionnel polonais, Décision SK 45/09 du 16 novembre 2011 ; Cour constitutionnelle tchèque, Décision Pl. ÚS 5/12 du 31 janvier 2012, Pensions slovaques). Revue française de droit administrative: 149–157

Tusseau G (2014a) "Irregulare aliquod et (tantum non) monstro simile" : remarques sur les heurs et malheurs des dialogues juridictionnels transconstitutionnels. In: Brunet P, Hasegawa K, Yamamoto H (eds) Rencontre franco-japonaise autour des transferts de concepts juridiques. Mare & Martin, Paris, pp 97–140

Tusseau G (2014b) Chronique de jurisprudence droit administratif et droit constitutionnel. Jurisprudence étrangère : La gouvernance économique et monétaire européenne au prisme du constitutionnalisme allemand. Cour constitutionnelle fédérale allemande, 14 janvier 2014, 2 BvR 2728/13, et 18 mars 2014, 2 BvR 1390/12, 2 BvR 1421/12, 2 BvR 1438/12, 2 BvR 1439/12, 2 BvR 1440/12, 2 BvR 1824/12, 2 BvE 6/12. Revue française de droit administratif: 602–614

Tusseau G (2014c) Theoretical deflation: the EU order of competences and power-conferring norms theory. In: Azoulai L (ed) The question of competence in the European Union. Oxford University Press, Oxford, pp 39–62

Tusseau G (forthcoming) Droit comparé et théorie générale du droit. Remarques sur quelques allers-retours aporétiques

Twining W (2000) Globalisation and legal theory. Cambridge University Press, London

Twining W (2009) Elusive Ism: instrumentalism, pluralism, scientism, realism. Chapter 16 of Twining W, General jurisprudence. Understanding law from a global perspective. Cambridge UP, Cambridge, 2009. http://www.cambridge.org/fr/files/9713/6681/2547/6903_16_Some_elusive_-isms.pdf

Tzanakopoulou M (2018) Reclaiming constitutionalism. Democracy, power and the state. Hart, Oxford

Unger RM (1996) What should legal analysis become? Verso, London

Viellechner L (2012) Constitutionalism as a Cipher: on the convergence of constitutionalist and pluralist approaches to the globalization of law. Goettingen J Int Law 4:599–623

Viellechner L (2015) Responsive legal pluralism: the emergence of transnational conflicts of law. Transnatl Leg Theory 6(2):312–332

Von Bogdandy A (2010) Prinzipien der Rechtsfortbildung im europäischen Rechtsraum. Neue Juristische Wochenschrift 63:1–5

Von Bogdandy A, Bast J (eds) (2010) Principles of European constitutional law, 2nd edn. Hart, Oxford, C.H. Beck, München
Wahl R (2010) In defence of "constitution". In: Dobner P, Loughlin M (eds) The twilight of constitutionalism? Oxford University Press, Oxford, pp 220–242
Waldron J (2004) Some models of dialogue between judges and legislators. In: Huscroft G, Broadie I (eds) Constitutionalism in the charter era. Butterwroths, Markham, pp 7–47
Walker N (2002) The idea of constitutional pluralism. Mod Law Rev 65:317–359
Walker N (2012a) Le constitutionnalisme multiniveaux. In: Troper M, Chagnollaud D (eds) Traité international de droit constitutionnel, vol 1. Dalloz, Paris, pp 441–462
Walker N (2012b) Postnational constitutionalism and postnational public law: a tale of two neologisms. Transnatl Leg Theory 3(1):61–86
Walker N (2015) Intimations of global law. Cambridge University Press, Cambridge
Walker N (2016) Constitutional pluralism revisited. Eur Law J 22(3):333–355
Walter C (1999) Die Europäische Menschenrechtskonvention als Konstitutionalisierungsprozess. Zeitschrift für ausländisches öffentliches Recht und Völkerrecht 59:961–983
Ward I (2001) Beyond constitutionalism: the search for a European political imagination. Eur Law J 7:24–40
Webber J (2002) Institutional dialogue between courts and legislatures in the definition of fundamental rights: lessons from Canada (and elsewhere). In: Sadurski W (ed) Constitutional justice, east and west. Democratic legitimacy and constitutional courts in post-communist Europe in a comparative perspective. Kluwer Law International, The Hague, pp 61–99
Weiler JH (1999) The constitution of Europe. 'Do the New Clothes Have an Emperor?' and other essays on European Integration. Cambridge University Press, Cambridge
Weiler JHH (ed) (2000) The EU, the WTO and the NAFTA. Towards a common law of international trade. Oxford University Press, Oxford
Weiler JHH (2001) Federalism and constitutionalism: Europe Sonderweg. https://jeanmonnetprogram.org/archive/papers/00/001001.html
Weiler JHH (2005) On the power of the word: Europe's constitutional iconography. Int J Constit Law 3:173–190
Weiler JH, Wind H (eds) (2003) European constitutionalism beyond the state. Cambridge University Press, Cambridge
Wittgenstein L (2010) Le Cahier bleu et le Cahier brun. Gallimard, Paris
Wittgenstein L (2014) Recherches philosophiques. Gallimard, Paris
Wormuth FD (1949) The origins of modern constitutionalism. Harper & Row, New York
Yasuaki O (2006) A transcivilizational perspective on global legal order in the twenty-first century: a way to overcome west-centric and judiciary-centric deficits in international legal thoughts. Int Community Law Rev 8:29–63
Yeh J-R, Chang W-C (2008) The emergence of transnational constitutionalism: its features, challenges and solutions. Penn State Int Law Rev 27:89–124
Yoon Z-W (2009) Rechtsgeltung und Anerkennung. Probleme Der Anerkennungstheorie am Beispiel von Ernst Rudolf Bierling. Nomos, Baden-Baden
Zucca L (2018) Two conceptions of global constitutional order. https://www.academia.edu/36754624/Two_Conceptions_of_Global_Constitutional_Order
Zumbansen P (2010) Rough consensus and running code. A theory of transnational private law. Hart, Oxford
Zumbansen P (2011) Neither 'Public' nor 'Private', 'National' nor 'International': transnational corporate governance from a legal pluralist perspective. J Law Soc 38:50–75
Zumbansen P (2012a) Carving out typologies. Accounting for differences accross systems: towards a methodology of transnational constitutionalism. In: Rosenfeld M, Sajo A (eds) Oxford handbook of comparative constitutional law. Oxford University Press, Oxford, pp 75–97
Zumbansen P (2012b) Varieties of comparative and global constitutionalism: the emergence of a transnational legal-pluralist-order. Gobal Constitutionalism 1:16–52

# A Particular Dialogue Between Systems. The Argentinian Case

María Carlota Ucín

**Abstract** This report focuses on explaining the federal constitutional system in Argentina and how it interplays with Human Rights conventions and protective systems. For a better understanding I will divide the topic in the following three sub-sections: (i) the relationship among general treaties and the law; (ii) The constitutional hierarchy of Human rights treaties and declarations and (iii) Integration into supranational organizations and the hierarchy of the resulting norms. I will also illustrate some tensions in between these systems by referring to a recent case decided by the Supreme Court. Finally, I will also analyse the impact of constitutional law and rights in the recent reform of the Civil Code as another form of legal pluralism.

## 1 An Overview of Argentinean System

Argentina is a federal State, composed—since 1994—by 24 autonomous states. These states include 23 provinces and the autonomous city of Buenos Aires that is, at the same time, the place for the Federal government. The 23 provinces keep all the power that has not been delegated to the federation.

At its turn, Argentina is integrated into other supranational organizations. It is part of the MERCOSUR (Mercado Común del Sur) since 1991, the UNASUR (Unión de Naciones Sudamericanas), the CELAC (Comunidad de Estados Latinoamericanos y Caribeños) and the OEA (Organización de Estados Americanos).

This report is going to focus on the Federal Government as it is the one that may subscribe integration and Human Rights treaties. Consequently, it is in this domain where pluralism of legal sources may become more visible. The Federal Constitution, reformed in 1994, introduced several changes in relation to the way treaties may be incorporated into the legal system and in particular, which is the place they have

M. C. Ucín (✉)
National University of La Plata, Law Faculty, La Plata, Buenos Aires, Argentina

Palermo University, Law Faculty, La Plata, Buenos Aires, Argentina



G. Tusseau (ed.), *Debating Legal Pluralism and Constitutionalism*, Ius Comparatum – Global Studies in Comparative Law 41, https://doi.org/10.1007/978-3-030-34432-0_2

in the legal pyramid. As many authors agree, it established a moderated monism[1] in which Human Rights Conventions and integration Treaties (e.g. Mercosur resolutions) are in a superior range than laws.

For a better understanding of these reforms, I will divide the topic in the following three sub-sections: (i) the relationship among general treaties and the law; (ii) The constitutional hierarchy of Human rights treaties and declarations and (iii) Integration into supranational organizations and the hierarchy of the resulting norms.

## *1.1 The Relationship Among General Treaties and the Law*

It is the Article 75 the one that establishes the role of the Congress. In the following paragraphs, I'll analyze its sections 22 and 24.

> Article 75: corresponde al Congreso:
>
> Inc. 22: Aprobar o desechar tratados concluidos con las demás naciones y con las organizaciones internacionales y los concordatos con la Santa Sede. Los tratados y concordatos tienen jerarquía superior a las leyes.
>
> Article 75: corresponds to the Congress:
>
> Inc. 22: Approve or reject treaties concluded with other nations and with international organizations and concordats with the Holy See. The treaties and concordats have a higher hierarchy than the laws.

As it was already mentioned, this first paragraph introduces an important shift in our system since it implies that the treaties, once they are passed by the Congress, they are incorporated into the legal system and occupy a place that is above the law.

Before this reform, the Supreme Court had admitted that the law could derogate the prescriptions of a Treaty (in: "Compañía Azucarera", Fallos 150:157; "San Martín S.A.", Fallos 257:99 and "Esso S.A.", Fallos 271:7). The winds of change, however, made the Court change its criterion before the 1994 reform. In "Ekmekdjián" (Fallos: 315:1492), "Fibraca" (Fallos: 316:1669) and "Hagelin" (Fallos: 316:3176), the Supreme Court stated that because of the prescriptions contained in article 27 from Vienna Convention, in case of conflict between internal laws and treaties, the international law must prevail given the case that there is no compromise to internal public law principles. Consequently, the Court affirmed that the Conventions were in a superior level than the law, and that the latter should respect the former. The constitutional reform, then, consolidated this shift and clarified the place international convents occupy in the federal normative system.

Despite the deference to international law, it should be added that it is accepted as implicit in this norm that the Congress keeps the power to introduce modifications to

[1]Spota (2001).

any Treaty subscribed by the Executive Power. And this is coexistent with the President's veto power that could then exercise by derogating those changes.[2]

### *1.2 The Constitutional Hierarchy of Human Rights Conventions and Declarations*

In its second paragraph, the same section 22 of article 75 enumerates many *Human Rights treaties and declarations that have the same hierarchy as the Constitution.* These instruments are the following:

- Declaración Americana de los Derechos y Deberes del Hombre (Declaration of the Rights and Duties of Man);
- Declaración Universal de Derechos Humanos (Universal Declaration of Human Rights);
- Convención Americana sobre Derechos Humanos (American Convention On Human Rights "Pact Of San Jose, Costa Rica");
- Pacto Internacional de Derechos Civiles y Políticos y su Protocolo Facultativo (International Covenant on Civil and Political Rights and its Protocol);
- Convención sobre la prevención y la sanción del Delito de Genocidio (Convention on the Prevention and Punishment of the Crime of Genocide);
- Convención Internacional sobre la eliminación de todas las formas de discriminación racial (International Convention on the Elimination of All Forms of Racial Discrimination);
- Convención sobre la eliminación de todas las formas de discriminación contra la mujer (Convention on the Elimination of All Forms of Discrimination against Women);
- Convención contra la Tortura y otros tratados o penas crueles, inhumanos o degradantes (Convention against Torture and Other Cruel, Inhuman or Degrading Treatment or Punishment);
- Convención sobre los derechos del niño (Convention on the Rights of the Child).

As it is a logic corollary, all the treaties that are at this grade, are not only above the law but also above other treaties in case of normative conflict. It is thinkable that integration treaties may collide with Human Rights conventions. Then, the conclusion is that the former must respect Human Rights protective standards.

The norm explicitly says that these treaties are going to have constitutional hierarchy in "the conditions of its applicability" (this includes any reservations the State may have made and also the interpretative criteria provided by the application authorities of the system). The Supreme Court explicitly said in "Giroldi" (Fallos 318:514): that the Human Rights American Convention has constitutional hierarchy

[2]González (2001), p. 344.

in the terms it governs in the international law and considering the interpretative arguments given by the Interamerican Court.

This section 22, also provides an interpretative criterion. It mentions that the enumerated instruments must be considered as complementary of the rights and guarantees already included in the Constitution and that they do not abolish any of them. This topic is related to Constitutional supremacy (art. 31) and with prescriptions contained in article 27, related to the respect of Public Law principles that treaties may have.

More precisely, Article 27 says:

> El gobierno federal está obligado a afianzar sus relaciones de paz y comercio con las potencias extranjeras por medio de *tratados que estén en conformidad con los principios de derecho público establecidos en esta Constitución*
>
> The federal government is obliged to strengthen its relations of peace and trade with foreign powers through *treaties that are in accordance with the principles of public law established in this Constitution*

In the third paragraph, at its turn, section 22 of article 75, allows the Congress to incorporate new treaties to the Constitutional hierarchy. For this purpose, the Congress must obtain the particular majority there established (2/3 votes of both Chambers).

The norm prescribes:

> Los demás tratados y convenciones sobre derechos humanos, luego de ser aprobados por el Congreso, requerirán del voto de las dos terceras partes de la totalidad de los miembros de cada Cámara para gozar de la jerarquía Constitucional.
>
> The other treaties and conventions on human rights, after being approved by the Congress, will require the vote of two thirds of the totality of the members of each Chamber to enjoy the Constitutional hierarchy.

## *1.3 Integration into Supranational Organizations and the Hierarchy of the Resulting Norms*

The art. 75 inc 24 says (that the Congress is allowed to:

> Aprobar tratados de integración que deleguen competencias y jurisdicción a organizaciones supraestatales en condiciones de reciprocidad e igualdad, y que respeten el orden democrático y los derechos humanos. Las normas dictadas en su consecuencia tienen jerarquía superior a las leyes. (...)
>
> Approve integration treaties that delegate powers and jurisdiction to supranational organizations in conditions of reciprocity and equality, and that respect democratic order and human rights. The norms dictated in their consequence have hierarchy superior to the laws. (...)

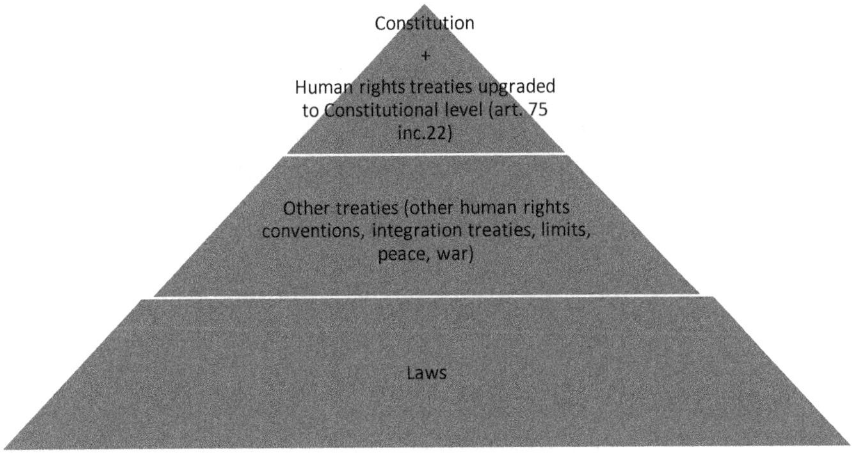


**Fig. 1** The pyramidal shape shows the constitutional hierarchy of treaties and the law

It is important to mention that is required a special majority to pass these treaties. But once approved, they may be delegating competences and jurisdiction in the supranational authorities. Therefore, it is a particular source of norms and the article prescribes that these norms, have a superior hierarchy than the internal laws.

As it was shown, our system is characterized by a moderated monistic position. By the explained procedures, the international law can become part of the legal system and in every case is going to be among our laws. The consequence of being in a superior level, implies that the law must adapt its contents to the Human Rights principles. In certain cases, additionally, they are going to have a constitutional hierarchy and consequently, some Human Rights treaties are above other treaties. According to constitutional supremacy and the diffuse constitutional control, every judge in Argentina must assure the enforcement of these instruments and the constitutional control then implies the conventional one.

The shape of the federal normative system could be outlined as follows (Fig. 1):

The illustrated hierarchy is mandatory and no citizen can choose to rule their controversies by changing the described superiority of treaties or laws (article 31, as mentioned, assures the Constitutional superiority and consequently, the above explained order). However, as regards commerce and in relation to contractual freedom, citizens may choose to solve their controversies by applying international law or the law of a particular State but if, and only if, this is not going against public order which may include the respect of Human Rights laws.

Normative pluralism may arise in Argentinian system especially from the impact of supranational entities activities (MERCOSUR, UNASUR and CELAC) and the Human Rights law and jurisprudence (Interamerican Court of Human Rights). In the following section I will focus on Human Rights conventions and the intertwined relationships among the Interamerican Court of Human Rights and the Federal Court.

Before ending this section, and though it is not the main topic of this report, I would like to state that in Argentina normative pluralism may also be configured by the recognition of aborigine's rights. The case in Patagonia, actually shows a conflict with an open ending, and the main problem arises when state legal institutions collide with aborigines" own institutions, in particular, with the general cosmovision, their own rules and their conception of communitarian property.

## 2 Argentina Among the Interamerican Human Rights Protection System

As a member of the OAS, Argentina ratified the Human Right Interamerican Convention in 1984. As it was detailed in previous sections, in 1994, the Constitutional reform gave this convention constitutional hierarchy. The convention has two competent organs: the **Interamerican Commission of Human Rights** and the **Interamerican Court of Human Rights (IACHR)**. Argentina has accepted the competence of this international court. Many cases were brought to the Interamerican system and Argentina has been condemned in many of them. This have been unproblematic but, last year there was a shift in the Supreme Court's jurisprudence. The "Fontevecchia" case is very interesting because it shows some limits in the implementation of the IACHR orders and a special dialogue that may be starting among Courts.

## 3 Tensions in Between Systems: The Fontevecchia Case

In Fontevechia decision (29-11-2011), the IACHR declared that Argentinian State had violated freedom of speech (art. 13 in connection with article 1.1 from the Interamerican Convention) in relation to Jorge Fontevecchia and Héctor D'Amico. These two journalists were condemned in a civil procedure as the Director and Editor of the Magazine called "Noticias". This lawsuit was sued by the former President, Carlos Menem, claiming for civil compensation for the legal injury he alleged. The condemnation was based on the release done by the Noticias Magazine in November 1995, informing about a sentimental affaire of the President Menem and about the birth of a child from that relationship.

The IACHR declared that the civil condemnation violated article 13 from the Convention and consequently, ordered the Argentinian State to "leave without effect this decision". This meant to leave without effect the civil responsibility attributed to Fontevecchia and D'Amico and also to reverse the condemnation to compensatory damages. The case should not have been a novelty if the Argentinian Supreme Court had not interpreted this order as it did. It was not the first time that the IACHR condemned our State and neither the first time that this international court ordered to reverse an internal decision that violated the Convention. But the Supreme Court found that this order implied a way of overruling a decision that was firm and had *"res iudicata"* status.

The Supreme Court then decided (14-2-2017),[3] in response to a requirement made by the Ministry of Foreign Affairs, that it was against our Public Law principles (art. 27 CN) to comply with that order of derogating a decision that was already firm and with the *res iudicata status,* as above mentioned. The Court argued that the Interamerican Human Rights System has a subsidiary role and consequently, it is not an additional instance of revision of judicial decisions. He considered that the *margin of appreciation* (or *margin of state discretion*) doctrine developed in the European Court of Human Rights was applicable to the case.

The Court added that "leaving without effect" the decision that he had previously confirmed in the "Menem" file, was like overruling or revoking that previous decision and this, was like admitting that the IACHR could act as a 4th instance by revoking internal decisions. The Court added that by this resolution the Interamerican Court was exceeding its competences. He claimed that article 63.1 only permits the Interamerican Court to guarantee the protection of Human Rights but not to revoke internal decisions. Finally, it concluded that it was juridically impossible to leave without effect a decision that was protected by the *res iudicata* status.

When supervising the compliance of the decision, the IACHR gave response to many of the Supreme Court's arguments. This was interpreted as a dialogue among these two Courts.[4] From a Dialogic Constitutionalism perspective, this experience has some valuable points though it is still far from becoming a fruitful conversation in which every part considers itself to be equal to the other and can cooperate in the construction of decisions that are respectful from the international compromises but also inside the democratic limits of legitimacy.

In the latter decision, the IACHR (18-10-2017) focused on the arguments of the Argentinean Court that denied the possibility of leaving without effect the civil condemnation to Fontevecchia and D'Amico, which was declared to be violating freedom of speech. The arguments could be summarized as follow:

- Internal dispositions cannot be alleged as reasons to avoid complying with international compromises;
- States must comply with International Law compromises in good faith;
- The Argentinian State should have identified the way in which he could comply with the given order. He must have adopted the measures oriented to leave without effect the analysed judicial decision (civil condemnation in Menem file);
- The Supreme Court interpreted, wrongly, that the order implied revoking that decision. However, this was not necessary, and many other alternatives were possible;

[3]CSJN, Fallos 340:47.

[4]Gargarella (2017).

- In many other cases, the IACHR had ordered that the States must leave without effect a decision that was violating the Convention. This was illustrated with examples of alternative ways of complying with the order;
- Additionally, it argued that the Supreme Court cannot evaluate the IACHR remedial competence nor can he evaluate its competence as a condition to comply with those orders;
- In this case, it was necessary to reverse the situation to the *statu quo ante*, so it was necessary to deprive effects to that decision and this does not mean that the IACHR is acting as a 4th instance;
- Consequently, he insisted that the Argentinian State must identify a way of complying with this order.

The Argentinean Supreme Court then decided, in December 2017[5] that the requirement of the Interamerican Court, consisting in writing down in the original decision that it was declared incompatible with the Interamerican Convention of Human Rights by the Interamerican Court, was legally possible under our public law principles (art. 27, CN). So, the Court ordered to write down that information in the primitive decision in Menem file.

## 4 Some Other Reflections of the Openness of the Normative System to Human Rights Protective Laws: The Renewal of Legal Reasoning

In some recent decisions, it is coming more visible the Human Rights perspective in a way that it incorporates international standards in order to judge the denounced violations. From this point of view, recent decisions start considering the obligations implied in the protection of Human Rights at the light of the normative standards given by International Courts or advisory bodies. Arguments based on the international obligations and their content are more common, specially based on the obligations like "taking measures" to assure the "progressive" development and respect of Human Rights. This kind of approach is very new; however, we find some theoretical development of this perspective, identified as "Rights perspective" or "*enfoque de derechos*".[6]

[5]Resolución 4015/2017, 5-12-2017.

[6]Pautassi (2010).

## 5 The Impact of the "Neoconstitutionalism" in the Recent Reform of the Civil Code and the Jurisprudence

The recent reform of the Civil Code, now unified with the Commercial one, has received the impact of the above explained importance of Human Rights treaties. The Doctrine agrees that this new code is a clear example of the incorporation of Constitutional Law into typical private domains. This shows that the limits that used to separate private and public law tend to disappear.

Additionally, the code incorporates the concept of reasonableness as a test for justifying judicial decisions. This concept is intrinsically linked to Proportionality principle developed in European Constitutional Courts and Doctrine.[7] The impact of the Proportionality Principle, applied in Constitutional Courts in European countries and the theoretical elaborations coming from European authors have probably lead to the new development of this concept in our legal practises.

However, it must be stated that the reasonability test was already part of our constitutional doctrine. Some authors as Linares have developed the concept in connection with the Substantive due process in U.S. Doctrine. This author pointed that the reasonable test emerges from the interpretation of article 14 and 28 in our Federal Constitution.[8] The Supreme Court indeed had also applied this test in order to evaluate the regulation power in relation to fundamental rights.

Even though the new Code insists on the importance of reasonableness and the concept is not new to our legal culture, it is still not so well developed in jurisprudence. The Supreme Court have mentioned the proportionality test, but it is still far from analysing in depth the different aspects that this analysis contains (necessity, adequacy and proportionality *stricto sensu*). For instance, in cases such as "Quisberth Castro" (Fallos 335:452) the Supreme Court appears to argue towards reasonableness, but it is not at all balancing or considering principles at stake.

Notwithstanding all these new changes in our system, there are not yet special research centres dedicated to the themes of global constitutionalism. Consequently, there is not much theoretical analysis of the mutations that legal pluralism may impose to our legal system.

## 6 The Ideological Dimension of Legal Rationality and Some Conclusions

The debates on the topic of the hierarchy of international treaties in our legal system took place even before the constitutional reform. However, the above-mentioned norms and the consolidated doctrine on the superiority of Human Rights treaties still

[7]Alexy (2008).

[8]Linares (1970).

have some aspects that must be determined. The recent change of the Supreme Court integration showed this, as the former composition appeared to be more deferent to international courts than the present appears to be.

The shift on the court's doctrine may be linked to a more conservative position. However, this does not impact on the consolidated doctrine about Human Rights respect. In particular, the new composition of the Court appears to be inspired by a need to preserve national sovereignty and to limit the intervention of Interamerican Court as a jurisdictional instance that may modify national decisions. The Court as it was explained above, highlighted the fact that she is the final instance in our legal system and that its decisions cannot be modified by any other court. However, it is pending the new decision after the didactic resolution of the IACHR.

## References

Alexy R (2008) Teoría de los derechos fundamentales, 2nd edn. Marcial Pons, Madrid

Gargarella R (2017) La ríspida conversación sigue. Consideraciones sobre el diálogo constituciona, a partir de la resolución de la Corte Interamericana de Derechos Humanos en "Fontevecchia". La Ley, 7

González J (2001) Manual de la Constitución Argentina (1853-1860). La Ley, Buenos Aires

Linares JF (1970) Razonabilidad de las leyes. Astrea, Buenos Aires

Pautassi L (2010) Perspectiva de derechos, políticas públicas e inclusión social. Debates actuales en la Argentina. Biblos, Buenos Aires

Spota AA (2001) Ensayo sobre la declinación de la supremacía constitucional y del federaliso como consecuencia de la globalización y de las grandes comunidades político económicas. In: Durante A (ed) La Constitución real. Enfoques multidisciplinarios. La Ley, Buenos Aires, pp 113–123

# Reconciling Legal Pluralism and Constitutionalism: New Trajectories for Legal Theory in the Age of Globalisation in Botswana

**Charles Manga Fombad**

**Abstract** This chapter examines developments in Botswana, which, like a few other countries in the Southern African region, is unique in that it received two entirely different and potentially conflicting legal traditions, the English common law and the Roman-Dutch law. The country has since its independence in 1966 made great strides in modernising its laws in a manner that incorporates and reflects its dual English law and Roman-Dutch legal heritage whilst also taking into account its customary law. Although Botswana is one of only two African countries that has not changed or substantially revised its independence Constitution, the other country being Mauritius, the discussion in this chapter shows that it has nevertheless adapted its laws to reflect contemporary legal developments. This is reflected not only in the country's approach to positive law but also in the manner of legal reasoning and the renewal of its jurisprudence.

## 1 Introduction

Most African legal systems are based on foreign laws received during the colonial era. In most cases, this is either the English common law or the French civil law received from the two most active colonial powers on the continent, Britain and France. This chapter examines developments in Botswana which, like a few other countries in the Southern African region, is unique in that it received two entirely different and potentially conflicting legal traditions, the English common law and the Roman-Dutch law.[1]

[1] The Southern African countries that share this legal heritage with Botswana are Lesotho, Namibia, South Africa, Swaziland and Zimbabwe.

C. M. Fombad (✉)
Institute for International and Comparative Law in Africa, Faculty of Law, University of Pretoria, Pretoria, South Africa
e-mail: Charles.fombad@up.ac.za



G. Tusseau (ed.), *Debating Legal Pluralism and Constitutionalism*, Ius Comparatum – Global Studies in Comparative Law 41, https://doi.org/10.1007/978-3-030-34432-0_3

Since independence in 1966, Botswana has made tremendous strides in its efforts to modernise its laws. Law reforms in such a complex legal system which does not only combine English and Roman-Dutch laws but also customary law is a fairly difficult matter. This is particularly so at a time of great change, brought about by globalisation and the post-1990 third wave of democratisation that led most African countries to revise their constitutions or write new ones.

Besides its complex mixed legal system, developments in Botswana deserve some attention because it is one of only two African countries that have not replaced their independence constitution in the light of post-1990 wave of constitutional reforms that swept through the continent.[2] Nevertheless, as the analysis below will show, there have been significant developments within its pluralistic legal system.

The discussion will proceed with section two which examines the balance among legal spheres in positive law. Section 3 reviews the dynamics of the relations among legal spheres in positive law. The renewal of legal reasoning is discussed in Sect. 4. The renewal of jurisprudence is considered in Sect. 5. Section 6 discusses the ideological dimension of legal rationality and Sect. 7 contains the closing remarks.

## 2 The Balance Among Legal Spheres in Positive Law

In many respects, Botswana, insofar as legal developments are concerned is an enigma. Although it has earned considerable praise and admiration for being probably the most politically stable African country since independence with a liberal multi-party democratic system, its politicians have largely ignored the fever of constitutional revision and rewriting that has taken place since 1990. As a result, its approach to international and transnational law has not evolved to reflect current legal developments as compared to most modern constitutions, especially in Anglophone Africa that expressly define the nature of the relationship between national and international law. In the absence of an express or implied constitutional provision dealing with the matter, Botswana has generally followed the English common law approach. Following this approach, there are three main ways in which international law and supranational legal norms can affect national law viz, by way of direct incorporation, as an aid to statutory interpretation and as part of the common law of Botswana.

As regards the first situation, it must be pointed out that Botswana is a dualist country. Treaties and other international instruments signed and ratified by Botswana only take effect at the domestic level after they have been incorporated into national law by an Act of Parliament.[3] The well established English common

[2]It is important to point out that there have been several amendments to the 1966 Constitution but none of them of a substantial manner. The other country is Mauritius that has retained its 1968 independence constitutions, with also insignificant amendments.

[3]See Tshosa (2007), pp. 229–246.

law principle, received in Botswana as part of the common law received in the country is that an international instrument does not become part of the national law unless and until it is formally incorporated by an Act of Parliament.

A second approach to dealing with an international treaties is in those instances where the treaty has been signed by the government. Regardless of whether it has been ratified, or ratified and domesticated, it may have important consequences in the interpretation of statutes. In dealing with this situation Amissah JP in the famous Botswana case of *Attorney-General v Dow,* cited with approval the following passage from the judge *a quo* in the same case:

> I bear in mind that signing the Convention [the OAU Convention] does not give it the power of law in Botswana but the effect of the adherence by Botswana to the Convention must show that a construction of the section which does not do violence to the language but is consistent with and in harmony with the Convention must be preferable to a 'narrow construction' which results in a finding that section 15 of the Constitution permits discrimination on the basis of sex.[4]

The Court basically followed the well-established common law presumption in statutory construction that courts will strive to interpret legislation in a manner that it will not conflict with international law. The judge went further to explain this:

> Botswana is a member of the community of civilised States which has undertaken to abide by certain standards of conduct, and, unless it is impossible to do otherwise, it would be wrong for its courts to interpret its legislation in a manner which conflicts with the international obligations Botswana has undertaken. This principle, used as an aid to construction as is quite permissible under section 24 of the Interpretation Act...[5]

Such an approach however must only be adopted when the domestic legislation in question is obscure. This caveat was explained by Diplock L.J., an English judge, in *Saloman v Commissioners of Custom & Excise*:

> If the terms of the legislation are clear and unambiguous, they must be given effect to whether or not they carry out Her Majesty's treaty obligations, for the sovereign power of the Queen in Parliament extends to breaking treaties, and any remedy for such a breach of an international obligation lies in a forum other than Her Majesty's own courts. If the terms of the legislation are not clear, however, but are reasonably capable of more than one meaning, the treaty itself becomes relevant, for there is a prima facie presumption that Parliament does not intend to act in breach of international law, including therein specific treaty obligations; and if one of the meanings which can reasonably be ascribed to the legislation is consonant with the treaty obligations and another and others are not, the meaning which is consonant is to be preferred. Thus, in case of lack of clarity in the words used in the legislation, the terms of the treaty are relevant to enable the court to make its choice between the possible meanings of these words by applying this presumption.[6]

Thus, in Botswana as in most of Anglophone Africa, international law indirectly exercises an influence on domestic constitutional law, even if the relevant international instrument on which it is based has not been formally domesticated. This will,

---

[4] [1992] BLR 119 (Botswana) at 154.

[5] *Id.*

[6] [1966] 3 All ER 875.

however, not apply to situations where it is absolutely clear that Parliament wanted to disregard or break its treaty obligations. Nevertheless, in this indirect manner, judges could in this creative and pragmatic manner adjust Botswana domestic law to reflect contemporary international standards.

The third situation deals with those instances where the government for whatever reason, has not signed or ratified an international treaty. This may deprive the citizens of the benefit of a very important international human rights treaty. Where however any such international treaty contains and codifies well established principles of customary international law or the principles contained in some of the treaties are so widely accepted and adopted that they may be considered as having crystallised into customary international law, these are considered differently. For although Botswana is a dualist state, insofar as international treaties are concerned, it follows a monist approach when it comes to customary international law once again, based on its general reception of the English common law during the colonial period. The basic English common law approach to this was explained by Ian Brownlie thus:

> The dominant principle, normally characterised as the doctrine of incorporation, is that customary rule are to be considered part of the law of the land and enforced as such, with qualification that they are incorporated only insofar as is not inconsistent with Acts of Parliament or prior judicial decisions of final authority. This principle is supported by a long line of authority and represents a practical rather than theoretical policy in the courts.[7]

The Botswana Constitution does not explicitly specify the hierarchy of norms in the country. It is again one of the matters dealt with by common law principles. In a number of cases, the highest court in the country, the Court of Appeal, has made it clear that the constitution is the supreme law of the land. For example, in the *Dow* case, Amissah JP said:

> A written Constitution is the legislation or compact which established the state itself. It paints in broad strokes on a large canvas the institutions of the state; defining relationships between such institutions and the institutions and the people within the jurisdiction of the state, and between the people themselves... The existence and powers of the institutions of state, therefore, depends on the terms. ...No institution can claim to be above the Constitution; no person can make any such claim.[8]

As a result of its common law legal heritage, an important source of the law is judicial precedents, not just of Botswana legal authorities but also of foreign legal material especially case law from foreign jurisdictions belonging to the same legal tradition. However, these legal authorities remain only persuasive authority.[9]

[7]In, Brownlie (2003), p. 41.

[8][1992] BLR 119 at p.129.

[9]See generally Fombad (2013), pp.74–91.

## 3 The Dynamics of the Relations Among Legal Spheres in Positive Law

A number of indicators can be used to gauge the dynamics within the different components of the pluralist system that operates in Botswana. One of these is the background of the judges that have manned the superior courts of the country since independence. Bojosi Othlogile, in *A history of the higher courts of Botswana 1912–1990*,[10] shows that knowledge of Roman-Dutch law was never a prerequisite for appointment to the bench in Botswana. In spite of the strong links between the Botswana and the South African legal systems, and the fact that the mixed system came in through South Africa, there was some reluctance to appoint South African judges to the Botswana bench. The author suggests that the apartheid system that was then entrenched in South Africa and the fact that the country also left the Commonwealth by 1961 led Botswana authorities to be reluctant about appointing South African judges. Nevertheless just less than half the judges that were appointed were from South Africa and most of the rest were British or British trained judges from other African countries. Until the early 2000s, just less than half the judges that manned the Botswana courts were trained in Roman-Dutch and the other half, in English law. This has had an effect on the dynamic Roman-Dutch/English common law mix.

Another factor which has influenced the positive law and which is certainly linked to the composition of the superior courts is the sources of precedents relied upon in interpreting and applying the law. A 2010 study investigated the sources of judicial precedents used in deciding cases by the superior courts (that is, the High Court and the Court of Appeal) and reported in the Botswana Law Report.[11] It showed a high frequency of reliance on South African precedents. This was surprising given the fact that because of apartheid, Botswana had from independence increasingly relied on English rather than South African law in developing its modern legislation in areas such as criminal law and the law of evidence. This was largely due to the fact that many of the judges had a Roman-Dutch background and the substratum of the legal system was Roman-Dutch law.

The demise of the apartheid system and the introduction of one of the most liberal constitutions in the world in South Africa in 1996 has in many respects provided more impetus for a reliance on South African precedents. It is a form of cross-judicial dialogue that is bound to change in dynamics but probably not in intensity. There are a number of reasons for this.

Firstly, there is a limit on the extent to which Botswana can rely on modern South African law because it has been substantially altered by the 1996 Constitution. For example, the scope of human rights protection under the Botswana Constitution is much narrower than the more liberal Bill of Rights that appears in the

---

[10] Othlogile (1995).

[11] See Fombad (2010).

South African Constitution. The South African approach to customary law is fundamentally different from that provided for under the Botswana Constitution. It is therefore not uncommon for some Botswana judges to erroneously try to interpret customary law by relying on the liberal human rights principles provided for in the South African Constitution rather than the more conservative approach which appears in section 15 of the Constitution which makes customary law an exception to the prohibition of discrimination.[12] Whereas the South African 1996 Constitution contains a general prohibition of discrimination, the Botswana Constitution which does same however makes customary law an exception to the rule.

A second factor that is likely to affect the dynamics of the Botswana mixed system is the fact that the bench is now almost entirely constituted of local judges. It is uncertain if they will be able to keep the high standards that were associated with the Botswana judiciary in the 1980s and 1990s when many of the judgments delivered by the Court of Appeal were cited with approval and as precedents in many Commonwealth jurisdictions. This is unlikely to happen due to so many questionable judicial appointments made since President Ian Khama came to power in 2008 and the frequent conflicts between the government and the judiciary. It is also possible that the localisation of the judiciary may lead to more inward-looking approach to dealing with issues. This, in itself is not necessarily bad but there is no evidence that sufficient good jurisprudence has been developed to warrant such an approach. By way of contrast, the South African Constitutional Court during the first 10 years of its existence relied extensively on foreign precedents but in the last few years has developed sufficient jurisprudence to such an extent that it relies more on its own precedents than foreign precedents.

## 4 The Renewal of Legal Reasoning

The Botswana legal system is in a transition. Gone are the days when high-level experienced judges were appointed from other Commonwealth countries. There was evidence that the particular background of the judge, whether Common law or Roman-Dutch law, influenced not only the precedents cited and relied upon but also the methodology and technique used in deciding cases and ultimately, the legal principles established. An example of this is the case of *Archibald v Attorney-General*.[13] The Court of Appeal was called upon to determine the method for assessing the quantum of damages in a dependant's claim for loss of future support resulting from unlawful and wrongful killing of the appellants' breadwinner. In the High Court, Livesey-Luke C.J., an English law-trained judge, after a careful examination of the evidence and a penetrating analysis of the relevant English and

[12]For an example of a case where a Botswana judge of the High Court was misled into relying on South African precedents, see Fombad (2014).

[13][1989] BLR 421.

Roman-Dutch legal authorities, observed that the actuarial method of assessment that the appellants' counsel had invited him to adopt was commonly used by the South African courts. After a review of the English law approach to this, and in terms evoking shades of English law insularity on the subject, rejected the actuarial method. In doing so, he recited many of the familiar reasons that English judges have used over the years to justify their misgivings of the actuarial technique. In his opinion, there was "nothing intrinsically Roman-Dutch common law about the use of the year-by-year method or of the actuarial calculations closely associated with it."[14] In the Court of Appeal, two of the three judges who wrote the majority judgment, Amissah J.P and Aguda J.A., both English-trained, whilst disagreeing with the Chief Justice's outright rejection of the actuarial method, as well as the amount he awarded as damages, adopted the English multiplier method that the latter had used. In doing so, they relied entirely on English law. Puckrin J.A., from a Roman-Dutch legal background dissented and saw no reason why the court should reject the use of the actuarial method and use in its stead, methods adopted *holus bolus* from other jurisdictions which may not be applicable to Southern Africa.[15] Whilst the three judges agreed that the amount awarded as damages for loss of support by the High Court was too low, the majority, using the English multiplier method arrived at a figure of P 582,211 as damages. Puckrin J.A., using the South African year-by-year method was ready to award P 1,076,342.00, that is, almost double the amount. Unlike the other two judges, Pukrin felt unconstrained in admitting legal writings as persuasive authorities. Whilst it is clear from this that judges by virtue of their legal training and culture are influenced by a certain *mentalié* this must often be tempered by legal rationality and the context within which they are operating.

Although there seems to be a shift in orientation in the legal system towards English law, the legal substratum of the system seems to be firmly civilian. The progressive injection of English law, principles, concepts and approaches has sometimes caused uncertainty and confusion. For example, the Botswana Penal Code of 1964, later replaced by the Penal Code of 1986 was based entirely on English law. But in drafting it, the civilian substratum was taken into account. Thus, in the part of the Code dealing with "offences relating to property" a special definition of property capable of being stolen had to accord with the general concept of property in Roman-Dutch law. By way of contrast, the substantial reforms of family law, whilst drawing heavily on several English statutes, such as the Matrimonial Causes Act, 1965, the Divorce Reform Act, 1999 and the Nullity of Marriage Act 1971, were hastily drafted and did not take into account the broader Roman-Dutch context in which these laws had to operate. This has sometimes led to contradictions, uncertainty and confusion.[16]

---

[14] *Ibid* at p. 420.

[15] [1991] BLR 169 at p. 183.

[16] See a discussion of these reforms by Himsworth (1974).

## 5 The Renewal of Jurisprudence

As explained in the preceding section, the legal system in Botswana is very much in transition. Perhaps the most significant change has been the wholesale localisation of the judiciary. There have been other changes as well. The Law Department of the University of Botswana, which for the last 37 years has trained most of the legal personnel in the country, has also undergone a large change.[17] Whereas, a majority of the lecturers until the late 2000s were expatriates, today, most of them are Batswana. The last decade has also seen more reliance on textbooks written on the different aspects of the law in Botswana in lieu of the previous reliance on South African textbooks. However, with little signs of any steps being taken to revise and update the 1966 Constitutions, Botswana's widely acclaimed reputation for good governance, respect for the rule of law and promoting constitutionalism will continue to depend, as it has done on the past, on the goodwill of its leaders. This has worked very well since independence but not so well under the leadership of present incumbent, President Ian Khama, a former army General and son of the first president, whose tenure has been marked by numerous restrictions on freedom of speech, intolerance of adverse views, especially from within his ruling Botswana Democratic Party (BDP) amidst signs of creeping authoritarianism. Some of the basic elements of modern constitutionalism which most African countries have constitutionally entrenched have been introduced in Botswana by way of ordinary legislation. This has several implications, two of which are worth noting here.

First, as pointed out earlier, the sustainability of its liberal democracy, respect for the rule of law and good governance will depend more on the good will of the president than on the democratic institutions set up to ensure that the constitution prevails. For instance, although the electoral commission has since independence been able to supervise elections in an independent manner, nothing prevents the incumbent president or his successor from appointing a partisan head of this body in order to ensure victory for the incumbent. It is also a fact that constitutionalism and democracy have so far thrived and flourished in Botswana because the opposition has been too weak, fractious and divided to pose any serious threat to the ruling BDP. The test of Botswana's constitutional democracy will come when there is a real threat of the opposition parties defeating the present BDP government.

The second point to note is that the failure to update the constitution and deal with the role of customary law in the modern pluralist system has left Botswana's much developed system of customary law, not only out of date with modern realities but also retarded its growth. For example, the inferior status of women under customary law sanctioned by the Botswana Constitution today is very similar to their position under other Anglophone independence Constitutions such as Kenya, Tanzania, Zambia and Zimbabwe. The post-1990 constitutional revisions whilst recognising customary law as part of the legal system have eliminated most of these

[17]It is worthwhile pointing out that this started as part of the University of Botswana, Lesotho and Swaziland, with the campus in Lesotho, before the University of Botswana was established in 1981.

discriminatory practices in accordance with the dictates of modern international human rights instruments. By contrast, in Botswana in spite of changing times women are yet to be fully released from dependence and lifelong subordination to men. The recent case of *Mmusi v Ramantele*[18] shows that this is not a matter that can be done stealthily by judicial legislation but rather by a clear amendment of the fundamental law of the land, the constitution.

## 6 The Ideological Dimension of Legal Rationality

There have been calls for a comprehensive review of the Botswana Constitution. In a recent opinion piece, Dithapelo Keorapetse in arguing that constitutional review is long overdue says:

> The 1963-1964 constitutional talks, held in Lobatse were between the then colonial masters, chiefs and representatives of few political parties existing at the time. At the time, most Batswana were illiterate, let alone politically developed (sic). The country was very poor.
>
> There was no intelligentsia and no professional bodies such as the Law Society of Botswana and other civil society organisations. There wasn't much consultation and even if there was, very few Batswana could understand what was required of them in terms of their contribution to the constitution. Consequently, few Batswana meaningfully participated towards the development of Botswana's Constitution.[19]

In July 2017, the ruling BDP used its parliamentary majority to defeat a motion calling for a comprehensive revision of the Botswana Constitution.[20] The motion stood little chance of being adopted, not just because the ruling BDP was firmly opposed to it and has the majority to defeat it but also the fact that the incumbent president has never supported the idea. The Constitution has suited his autocratic style of governance and given that he is due to leave office on 31 March 2018, having by then served the maximum 10 years allowed by the Constitution, any future constitutional review will depend on his successor. At present, there is no reason to think that a new president with such enormous powers will want to give them away voluntarily.

The decline in the quality of Botswana's democracy during the Ian Khama presidency has also affected the quality of its judiciary and as a result of this, the standards of legal pluralism. Whilst it is clear that the three elements of the pluralist system viz, customary law, English common law and Roman- Dutch law will continue to co-exist, the level and degree of interaction between the three is unlikely to change. Firstly, without the revision of the constitution to reflect contemporary

---

[18](MAHLB-000836-10)[2012] BWHCI (12 October 2012). Judgment delivered by the Honourable Justice Dr Dingake, and *Ramantele v Mmusi and Others*, CACGB-104-12 (Unreported) judgment of the Botswana Court of Appeal delivered on 3 September 2013. For a critical commentary on this case, see Fombad (2014).

[19]Keorapetse (2017).

[20]See Ramaphane (2017).

developments in global constitutionalism, rule of law and respect for human rights, the relationship between the three elements will remain the way it was in 1966. Nevertheless, there will be constant tension and conflicts because it will be increasingly difficult to enforce most of the customary laws which undermine modern fundamental principles of gender equality and non-discrimination. Although unlike most other countries, customary law and customary courts play a very important part in the Botswana legal system, the obsolete constitution does not provide much scope for it to develop and adapt to changing circumstances. Secondly, with the departure of expatriate judges, the ideological conflicts that pitted English trained judges and their jurisprudential approach, against Roman-Dutch trained judges and their jurisprudential approach is likely going to reduce. However, given the limited scope for judicial independence and broad avenues for executive interference, the quality of jurisprudence is bound to diminish because of arbitrary nature of many appointments to the bench. Finally, in spite of the increasing threats to Botswana's constitutionalism since President Ian Khama came to power, it can be argued that the culture and ethos of democracy is reasonably deep to withstand some of the challenges that the country has come under. Whilst there is no guarantee that things will not change, the added indirect pressure from regional organisations such as the South African Development Community (SADC) and the African Union (AU) may contribute to keep the country on the democratic course.

## 7 Concluding Remarks

Botswana's pluralistic legal system is complex because it combines a customary law system with two distinct modern legal traditions, the English common law and the Roman-Dutch law. Legal systems are constantly mixing, blending, melting and then solidifying into new shapes as they cool down.[21] Botswana is no exception. In the era of globalisation and internationalisation of legal standards, adapting to rapidly changing circumstances is not only unavoidable but also imperative. This chapter has tried to outline how Botswana is grappling with the different forces that impact on its three-layered legal system.

In spite of its impressive good governance record and being one of only two African countries that has since independence maintained an open, transparent, and multi-party democracy, all this has been achieved against a rather weak constitutional framework that has depended rather too much on the good will of the leaders. The third wave of global constitutionalism that blew through the African continent from the 1990s has largely left Botswana untouched. In spite of this, there have been other changes within its legal system. Two main conclusions can be drawn.

[21] Örürü (2008), p. 13.

Firstly, that at one level, the changes within the legal system have been rather inward than outward looking. These have entailed localisation of the bench. The exact impact of this is yet to be fully assessed.

Secondly, although the legal system is doing well, it can be argued that a revised constitution which entrenches most of the fundamentals of constitutionalism will ensure better harmony, coherence and consistency between the three main components of the pluralistic legal system viz, customary law, English common law and Roman –Dutch law. The future depends on how these three components of the legal system can operate in a manner that will provide effective solutions to the legal needs of the people.

## References


Brownlie I (2003) Principles of international law, 6th edn. Oxford University Press, Oxford

Fombad CM (2010) Mixed systems in Southern Africa: divergences and convergences. Tulane Eur Civil Law Forum 25:11–21

Fombad CM (2013) The Botswana legal system, 2nd edn. LexisNexis, Durban

Fombad CM (2014) Gender equality in African customary law: has the male ultimogeniture rule any future in Botswana? J Modern Afr Stud 52(3):475–494

Himsworth CMG (1974) Effects of matrimonial causes legislation in Botswana. J Afr Law 18:173–179

Keorapetse D (2017) Constitutional review overdue. http://www.mmegi.bw/index.php?aid=67663&dir=2017/march/24. Accessed in Feb 2019

Örürü E (2008) What is a mixed legal system: exclusion or expansion? Electronic J Comp Law 12 (1):10–17

Othlogile B (1995) A history of the higher courts of Botswana 1912-1990. Mmegi Publishing House, Gaborone

Ramaphane R (2017) Parliament throws out Keorapetse's constitution plea. http://www.weekendpost.co.bw/wp-news-details.php?nid=4097. Accessed in Nov 2017

Tshosa OB (2007) The status and role of international law in the national law of Botswana. In: Fombad CM (ed) Essays on the law of Botswana. Juta & Co, Cape Town, pp 229–246

# Brazil and Its Many Realities: Courts and State-Centrism; Administrative Agencies and International Cooperation

**Ana Paula de Barcellos**

**Abstract** The paper discusses how Constitutionalism and legal pluralism dialogue in Brazil in different environments as Judicial Courts, Administrative Agencies and law professors and lawyers' activities. For lawyers, and even more to law professors, it is crucial to be aware and engaged with foreign and international discussions and dynamics. In a similar way, international cooperation is a common trend and practice within Brazilian administrative agencies. The scenario is different for Judicial Courts. Most Brazilian Courts' rulings frame the legal order in a State-centered monistic perspective: hierarchical standards drawn from the Federal Constitution will measure and accommodate each any norm, from any source, into the national system. The paper also examines how other elements, as ideology, may influence this dialogue in Brazil.

## 1 Introduction: Brazil and Legal Pluralism

The Académie Internationale de Droit Comparé proposed to different countries a set of questions requiring an assessment of how constitutionalism and legal pluralism can reconcile in the globalization era. This paper tries to make this assessment from a Brazilian perspective. The questions assume there is a potential legal tension that can be summarized in the following terms. The traditional conception of Constitution, State-originated rules and its claims of hierarchy upon all other norms *versus* the autonomy of many other norms non-State-originated that may not submit to the State's authority and may even impact the relevance and the construe of the Constitution itself. The questions also assume a preferential point of view to discuss the phenomenon: the perspective of the legal constitutional theory and, inevitably, of Courts.

A. P. de Barcellos (✉)
State University of Rio de Janeiro (UERJ), Law School, Rio de Janeiro, Brazil
e-mail: abarcellos@bfbm.com.br

 
G. Tusseau (ed.), *Debating Legal Pluralism and Constitutionalism*, Ius Comparatum – Global Studies in Comparative Law 41, https://doi.org/10.1007/978-3-030-34432-0_4

Brazilian reality, though, poses some challenges to these two presuppositions. First, from a constitutional theory perspective, there is little recognition of the tension described above. Despite isolated exceptions,[1] legal pluralism is almost a non-topic in the country's constitutional discussions; there are important debates concerning constitutional pluralism, trans-constitutionalism and international human rights law, but not from the perspective of an insurmountable legal conflict.[2]

As the paper will discuss, the predominant view in Brazilian Constitutional theory is that any norm, from any source, will be measured and accommodated into the national system considering hierarchical standards drawn from the Constitution. International law in particular must be assimilated into Brazilian's legal system according to internalization proceedings, also provided for the Constitution, and then positioned according to those hierarchical standards.

Furthermore, the construe of all these norms will usually take into consideration much more the national system and its content than original systems of those norms. At the end of the day, the normativity key in Brazil continues to be the national legal system. In the same sense, Courts do not acknowledge the lack of legal criteria to deal with conflicts among norms from different sources. On the contrary, the hierarchical criteria resolves these kind of disputes.

Seemingly, the tension between constitutionalism and legal pluralism in Brazil may not exist in the same extent as in other countries or has not been noticed by constitutional legal scholars and Courts as a relevant legal issue, at least not for now: and it is possible that both ideas describe part of reality. There is no comprehensive explanation for that, but some features may distinguish Brazilian experience from other countries.

Differently from other countries around the globe, Brazil is not part of a supranational organization that has the power to enact legislation with autonomy, as happens, for instance, in Europe. Brazil is part of Mercosur, a free trade agreement among several Latin American countries, but Mercosur has never evolved in the direction of a source of autonomous normativity. Brazil, therefore, and so far, did not have to deal with this kind of alternative source of normativity.

In addition, differently from what has happened to Latin American countries as Bolivia, Ecuador and Venezuela, Brazilian Constitution does not deal with native communities from a legal pluralistic perspective, as the paper will show. Although indigenous communities received especial consideration from the Brazilian Constitution of 1988, it did not grant them autonomy or a particular *status* inside the country as a source of legal norms.

Moreover, from a theoretical point of view, Brazil relates to International Law basically from a monistic perspective, and the notion of Constitutional supremacy is very strict, both in legal theory and in Courts. The Constitution prevails over any other source and is the ultimate criteria to solve any legal conflict. Additionally, Brazilian Constitution of 1988 is rich in general principles that can be unfolded in

[1]Dellagnezze (2015), Wolkmer (2015) and Neves (2016a).

[2]de Carvalho Ramos (2012).

different directions and give grounds, at least from a rhetorical perspective, to different criteria in order to solve these conflicts. These two theoretical tools combined—monism and constitutional supremacy—seem to reduce the existence of conflicts between Constitutionalism and legal pluralism in Brazil, as the paper will try to explain.

On the other hand, it is true that legal constitutional theory and Courts deal with only a fraction—probably a small one—of the normative reality in Brazil. In other words, maybe Brazil has not dealt so far with some of the issues legal pluralism has confronted other countries with, but, at the same time, maybe a lot is happening in Brazil that is simply unseen by legal constitutional theory or Courts. Actually, the globalization impact and legal pluralism are probably much more real in the activity of the Administrative branch.

The roles of the Administrative branch, particularly the Federal one, have experience great growth and diversification in the last decades. This is a result of the growth of the Brazilian State itself, but also a legislative option as laws have granted Brazilian Federal Administration in general and agencies in particular discretionary powers to enact norms in many fields and implement them in order to pursue their regulatory aims. In the proceedings of designing regulations, Brazilian agencies engage frequently in direct international cooperation with foreign agencies with similar competencies precisely to standardize regulatory patterns. The paper will bring some examples on that.

This does not mean that, apart from the Administrative branch, Brazil is isolated. Congressional debates, for instance, mention frequently globalization and international and foreign normative realities. As the paper will show, Courts and legal constitutional theory are increasingly dealing with foreign academic materials and foreign and international jurisprudence, as well as norms from different non-State sources, internal and international. All this interaction has many consequences, as the paper will point out. However, when it comes to norms, Brazilian Courts have been able so far to assimilate and accommodate them in categories created and organized by the national legal system itself, with the Constitution at its top. The paper will try to clarify this dynamics.

That is to say: different realities and practices coexist in Brazilian normative landscape in what concerns globalization and legal pluralism, and this does not come as a surprise, considering Brazil's dimensions and social complexities.

Finally, it is worth mentioning an important discussion in Brazil around a slightly different kind of legal pluralism: the one that originates in areas of the territory due to the State's inability to exert its power. Although important to any legal theory, this debate has taken place mostly in political science and social studies research and literature. Slums in Brazilian's major cities are the textbook example of the issue: the vacuum created by the lack of State's authority leaves room to other kinds of norms, organized by the community itself and frequently defined and imposed by criminal groups. The work from Boaventura de Souza Santos on the reality of a Brazilian slum in Rio de Janeiro is an important landmark in the field.[3] Some literature around the globe is discussing a similar phenomenon under the title "hybrid governance".[4]

The paper will not discuss this particular kind of legal pluralism but the reference seems important to give the reader a better idea of Brazil. Despite the State-centered conception of normativity shared by many Courts, large groups of people and significant areas of the Brazilian territory are simply not under any sort of State's authority: they submit to a different kind of law in their daily routine. Notwithstanding that, Brazilian legal theory has still not fully acknowledge this reality and the legal challenges it poses, nor has developed an interdisciplinary exchange with other fields to start at least to understand it.

## 2 The Balance Among Legal Spheres in Positive Law

The first question we should try to answer in order to grasp the relationship between constitutional and legal pluralism in Brazil is the following: what statutory provisions have to say about it? Are there statutory rules dealing with the balance among legal spheres in Brazil? The answer is yes. Brazil legal system still belongs to the Civil Law tradition, so it is important to find out what statutory law has to say on the topic. Nevertheless, case law—particularly from the Brazilian Supreme Court—has become increasingly important in the country as many of the Brazilian Supreme Court decisions have now binding effects.

The relationship Brazilian law establishes with international and transnational law is a monistic one, as already mentioned. Brazilian Congress needs to approve any international legal document (Brazilian Federal Constitution of 1988, Article 49, I[5]), and constitutional custom requires additionally a Presidential decree after congressional approval: only then, the international law will come into force in Brazil. After internalized, international law may be subject to judicial review in the same fashion as domestic law.[6] Brazil adopts Constitutional supremacy and we have two systems in place to assure it. First, a judicial review system (similar to the US model) in which roughly any Court can declare a piece of legislation as unconstitutional and the Brazilian Supreme Court will have the final say on the matter. Second, the Brazilian Supreme Court hears cases directly (similar to what happens in the

---

[3]de Sousa Santos (1977).

[4]Reyntjens (2015).

[5]Brazilian Federal Constitution 1988: "Article 49. It is exclusively the competence of the National Congress: I – to decide conclusively on international treaties, agreements or acts which result in charges or commitments that go against the national property."

[6]Brazilian Federal Constitution 1988: "Article 102. The Supreme Federal Court is responsible, essentially, for safeguarding the Constitution, and it is within its competence: (CA No. 3, 1993; CA No. 22, 1999; CA No. 23, 1999; CA No. 45, 2004) (. . .) III – to judge, on extraordinary appeal, cases decided in a sole or last instance, when the decision appealed: (. . .) b) declares a treaty or a federal law unconstitutional."

Constitutional Court model adopted by many European and Asian Countries), producing binding rulings.

In 2004 the Brazilian Constitution was amended (Constitutional Amendment 45) to provide that international conventions and treaties on human rights approved by Congress according to the same proceedings required to approve constitutional amendments would be considered to be equivalent, in normative status, as constitutional amendments.[7] The proceeding requires approval by both houses of the National Congress, in two different voting sessions, by three-fifths votes of their respective members. So far, only the Convention on the Rights of Persons with Disabilities (CRPD) has this status in Brazil.

Some discussion arose among Brazilian international law scholars on the *status* of other human rights conventions and treaties approved by Congress before 2004, when the new proceeding still did not exist. For some, these norms from international human rights law should also receive the constitutional *status*.[8] The Brazilian Supreme Court decided otherwise. The Court's decisions on the subject held that they would not be equivalent to constitutional amendments, but would have supralegal *status,* meaning they are superior to national law, but inferior to the Constitution.[9] Other pieces of international law not related to human rights, after submitted to the internalization proceeding, will have the same *status* as national law in Brazil in general. Two additional comments on these general rules on the relationship with international law.

The Brazilian Supreme Court applied this hierarchical relationship between human rights treaties (the supralegal one) and national law at least once so far to invalidate national legislation. The Supreme Court considered non applicable anymore an internal provision that allowed some cases of debtor's prison, in the face of the general prohibition of his kind of prison provided for the American Convention on Human Rights, in force in Brazil since 1992.[10]

It is interesting to highlight that this Supreme Court ruling came after many years of resistance from Brazilian lower Courts that, despite the Convention, still considered the national law should prevail. The reasoning behind the lower Courts decisions was that the Convention could not limit the power granted by the Constitution to Congress to regulate the issue. In this sense, the national norm would still be in force as a special norm, besides the Convention general provision that prevented any kind of debtor's prison. The Supreme Court ruling recognizing supralegal *status* to the Convention precluded this sort of argument and the use of national law in this case.

---

[7]Brazilian Federal Constitution 1988: "Article 5°, §3° (Approved by the Constitutional Amendment 45, from 2004): International human rights treaties and conventions which are approved in each House of the National Congress, in two rounds of voting, by three fifths of the votes of the respective members shall be equivalent to constitutional amendments."

[8]Cançado Trindade (1996) and Piovesan (1997).

[9]STF, RE 349.703, Justice Rapporteur Gilmar Mendes, published in June 5, 2009.

[10]STF, RE 466.343, Justice Rapporteur Cezar Peluso, published in June 5, 2009.

The second comment has to do with a special rule on international transportation. Despite the general rule considering international law equivalent to national law—apart from human rights norms—Brazilian Constitution article 178 provides that national legislation "shall observe the agreements signed by the Union as to the organization of international transportation, in accordance with the principle of reciprocity."[11]

For many years, Courts in Brazil did not follow this guideline and considered Brazilian Consumer's Protection Code to apply instead of the Warsaw or the Montreal Conventions. The most frequent disputes involved damages claims for lost luggage, to which the two set of norms provided differently. The national Brazilian law has a broad provision allowing Courts to make a discretionary assessment of damages in each case, while the Conventions provide for a fixed amount of money as compensation to any case. Brazilian Court orders' discretionary assessment would frequently order transportation companies to pay much more for damages than the top values provided for the Conventions.

The Brazilian Supreme Court decided some appeals on cases discussing this issue in May, 2017, and ruled that the international conventions are to be applied to them, not national law.[12] The Court's reasoning developed from the notion of constitutional supremacy in this particular case, because of Article 178, and not from a general prevalence of international law.

Finally, there are no specific appeals to discuss international norms in Brazil, as they have no particular prevailing force. Once internalized, international norms will have the hierarchy the national systems attributes to them, may it be constitutional, supralegal or legal. Courts decide conflicts between international norms and the Constitution, or between them and the national law, in any sort of proceeding in order to solve the cases before them, as any other conflict that may arise among internal norms.

It is worth mentioning, however, that the same Constitutional Amendment 45 created a procedural figure that allows cases to be transferred from State Courts to Federal Courts when they involve "serious violation of human rights", in order to assure "compliance with obligations stemming from international human rights treaties to which Brazil is a party".[13]

In Brazil Federal State, most criminal persecution involving life-threating crimes is within State powers, not Federal ones. The history of some carnages that, after

[11]Brazilian Federal Constitution 1988: "Article 178. The law shall provide for the regulation of air, water and ground transportation, and it shall, in respect to the regulation of international transportation, comply with the agreements entered into by the Union, with due regard to the principle of reciprocity. (CA No. 7, 1995)."

[12]STF, RE 636.331, Rapporteur Justice Gilmar Mendes, published in November 13, 2017.

[13]Brazilian Constitution 1988, Article 109: "§5°. In cases of serious human rights violations, and with a view to ensuring compliance with obligations deriving from international human rights treaties to which Brazil is a party, the Attorney-General of the Republic may request, before the Superior Court of Justice, and in the course of any of the stages of the inquiry or judicial action, that jurisdiction on the matter be taken to Federal Justice."

many years, did not receive a proper response from the criminal justice system of the Brazilian State in charge of the investigation is clearly behind this new provision. The purpose of the Constitutional Amendment is to try to enhance the enforcement of the law in these cases, what is believed to happen better in Federal Courts, instead of State Courts. Although this new constitutional rule reveals a lot about the disparities inside Brazil and the challenges it's federalism faces, it also sheds light on the importance Brazil places on its image before international society, when it comes to be deemed as a country that complies with international human rights law.

Moving on to the existing relationships between Brazilian national legal system and other types of norms besides international ones, some distinctions are worthy noting. Firstly, one should consider those norms enacted by public entities. Brazil is a Federal State as already mentioned and both States and Municipalities have autonomy ensured and mapped by the Federal Constitution. This means that Brazil, at least in theory, has three different sources of legal norms. Notwithstanding, the Federal Constitution of 1988 concentrates most legislative powers in the Federal level: all Contracts law, Torts law, Family law, Commercial law, Labor law, Criminal law and Procedural law, for instance, are exclusively federal law.

Besides that, Brazilian Supreme Court traditionally construes States and Municipalities powers in a very narrow way, in order to ensure a national uniform regulation of topics. For instance, the Court considered void State legislation that provided for maximum waiting times for health insurance companies to make available lab tests to their customers, as the matter would be within Contracts Law, therefore only Federal Law could provide for it.[14] In another decision, the Court ruled as unconstitutional a State law providing for elections for principals in State public schools. The reasoning stated was the following: this provision would prevent Governors to appoint school principals, affecting separation of powers, a subject States could not regulate.[15]

More recently, it seems the Supreme Court's jurisprudence is showing some change on this respect, recognizing more legislative power to States and Municipalities. One example of this is the 2017 decision in which the Court considered valid State laws regulating the use of asbestos in a different manner than the provided for by the Federal law.[16]

According to the Brazilian Constitution, both States and National Congress can pass legislation on environmental law: national legislation ought to provide only guidelines or general provisions, to be followed by the State more specific legislation. The understanding of what "guidelines" or "general provisions" mean can design a wider or narrower space for States. In the case mentioned, the Supreme

---

[14]STF, ADI 4701, Justice Rapporteur Luís Roberto Barroso, published in August 25, 2014.

[15]STF, ADI 2997, Justice Rapporteur Cezar Peluzo, published in March 11, 2010.

[16]STF, ADIs 3356, 3357 and 3937 (Justice Rapporteur Dias Toffoli) and ADPF 109 (Justice Rapporteur Edson Fachin), all decided together on August 24, 2017, and all published in February 1st, 2019.

Court considered that the regulation of asbestos' use was not a guideline, so States could ordain in a different way.

A particular feature of this decision is that the construe of Federal powers received a clear influence from international law, particularly the Convention 162/1986, from the International Labor Organization, in force in Brazil since 1991. The Convention requires countries to revise their legislation on asbestos use in a periodic basis, to take into account new scientific knowledge available. Some Justices considered that as Congress did not revise the 1995 national law, States could regulate the issue in order to revise it, at least in the State level.

Notwithstanding this specific decision, and possibly a trend toward the recognition of more space for State and Municipalities, it is fair to say that Federal sources thrive in Brazilian legal system.

Leaving federal conflicts aside, but still dealing with norms from public entities, an interesting phenomenon develops in the federal regulatory realm, as already mentioned. Although Brazilian legal system is a monistic one, it is interesting to point out examples of regulatory international cooperation in Brazil below and out of legislative control. As referred to before, Brazilian legislation allows administrative agencies to issue norms and regulations in many fields, and some of these regulations result from an international effort among agencies from different countries to establish international uniform patterns.

Brazilian agencies joined, for instance, the International Coalition of Medicines Regulatory Authorities (ICMRA) and the International Cooperation on Cosmetics Regulation (ICCR). The first one intends to produce regulatory convergence in the regulation of any medicinal products.[17] The ICCR members state they work together to promote regulatory alignment, in order to maximize cosmetic consumer protection while minimizing barriers to trade.[18]

Brazil is also a member of the Financial Action Task Force (FATF), an intergovernmental body that aims "to set standards and promote effective implementation of legal, regulatory and operational measures for combating money laundering, terrorist financing and other related threats to the integrity of the international financial system."[19] Brazil administrative authorities also join an international group dealing with protocols of internet security.[20]

If the content of regulations enacted by these administrative agencies in Brazil violates legal or constitutional norms, they can be challenged as illegal and even as unconstitutional. This possibility, though, seems unlikely considering both the nature of the subject regulated and the fact the laws can be very broad when delegating powers to agencies. In any case, the interesting point is that these norms, whatever their content, are being framed through international cooperation

[17]http://www.ema.europa.eu/docs/en_GB/document_library/Other/2014/11/WC500177574.pdf.

[18]https://www.fda.gov/cosmetics/internationalactivities/iccr/default.htm.

[19]http://www.fatf-gafi.org/about/.

[20]https://www.cert.br/docs/palestras/certbr-caeat-camara2008.pdf.

in the administrative level without much control or even participation from Congress.

A particular situation in Brazil involves norms enacted by Councils for professional supervision, considered public institutions in Brazil. Some of the most important are those that oversee the activities of lawyers (Brazilian Bar Association), doctors (Medicine Federal Council), pharmaceuticals (Pharmaceutical Federal Council) and engineers (Engineering Federal Council). Eventually these councils try to regulate aspects of the professional activity they supervise through regulations. In many cases, however, Courts have struck down these norms.

The main reason for these rulings is that the regulation went beyond the council's competence because the provisions did not abide by statutory provisions. In other words, differently from what happens to Administrative agencies, Courts considered that Professional Councils can only apply existing legislation, but they cannot innovate or regulate issues not provided for by law.

Leaving the realm of public-entities originated law, another group of norms worth mentioning would be those originated from private spheres that received some sort of recognition from the Brazilian Federal Constitution of 1988. Article 7, XXVI, states as a worker's right the "recognition of collective bargaining agreements and covenants", and establishes that only workers' unions can negotiate and close deals in collective labor bargaining (Article 8, VI[21]).

For a long time Labor Courts have had the understanding that collective bargaining could only expand rights provided for by law and, because of that, Courts orders frequently considered void agreements if they provided in different and more restricted terms than legislation. Collective bargaining norms, therefore, could not undermine national law provisions.

In 2015, the Brazilian Supreme Court overruled Labor Courts decisions that considered void collective agreements, ruling that, according to the constitutional provision of article 7, XXVI, collective bargaining should prevail upon legislation generally, and the only limit would be the protection of basic workers right.[22] The Supreme Court highlighted the *status* the Federal Constitution of 1988 gave to the workers collective autonomy and their right to decide, via their unions, on the norms affecting their labor relations.

After these decisions from the Supreme Court, National Congress has passed legislation stating that collective bargaining should prevail upon legislation, even to limit legal rights. The new law establishes a list of exceptions to this general rule considered to encompass basic workers' rights, which collective bargaining could not restrict (Law 13.467/2017).

The Brazilian Federal Constitution of 1988 also gave some attention to traditional and native communities. Article 216 protects the cultural heritage of the various groups that form Brazilian society, including their "ways of creating, making and

---

[21]Brazilian Constitution of 1988: "Article 8, VI - the collective labor bargainings must be held with the participation of unions."

[22]STF, RE 590.415, Justice Rapporteur Luís Roberto Barroso, published in May 29, 2015.

living".[23] Although there is no explicit reference to norms, it seems reasonable to understand that the idea of "way of living" may include some sort of normative practices. In addition, Brazil has internalized the Indigenous and Tribal Peoples Convention from 1989 (International Labor Organization—C169).

Besides this general provision, the Brazilian Federal Constitution of 1988 recognizes particularly the social organization, customs, languages, creeds and traditions of indigenous peoples (Article 231).[24] So far, this recognition has been associated more to land rights than to some sort of respect for these peoples' normative practices. Some interesting Court decisions are worth mentioning.

In 2009, the Brazilian Supreme Court delivered a very important and controversial decision on the Raposa Serra do Sol Indigenous Reserve demarcation in the Brazilian State of Roraima, discussing mainly the validity of the criteria used for the demarcation.[25] The issue of normative practices of indigenous peoples was not directly relevant to the case and there was no ruling on the subject. However, in different moments Justices opinions revealed they do not think the Constitution recognizes an indigenous autonomous legal order and the final opinion states that the "indigenous lands provided for by the Federal Constitution of 1988 belong to

---

[23]Brazilian Federal Constitution 1988: "Article 216. The Brazilian cultural heritage consists of the assets of a material and immaterial nature, taken individually or as a whole, which bear reference to the identity, action and memory of the various groups that form the Brazilian society, therein included: (CA No. 42, 2003): I – forms of expression; II – ways of creating, making and living."

[24]Brazilian Federal Constitution 1988: "Article 231. Indians shall have their social organization, customs, languages, creeds and traditions recognized, as well as their original rights to the lands they traditionally occupy, it being incumbent upon the Union to demarcate them, protect and ensure respect for all of their property. Paragraph 1. Lands traditionally occupied by Indians are those on which they live on a permanent basis, those used for their productive activities, those indispensable to the preservation of the environmental resources necessary for their well-being and for their physical and cultural reproduction, according to their uses, customs and traditions. Paragraph 2. The lands traditionally occupied by Indians are intended for their permanent possession and they shall have the exclusive usufruct of the riches of the soil, the rivers and the lakes existing therein. Paragraph 3. Hydric resources, including energetic potentials, may only be exploited, and mineral riches in Indian land may only be prospected and mined with the authorization of the National Congress, after hearing the communities involved, and the participation in the results of such mining shall be ensured to them, as set forth by law. Paragraph 4. The lands referred to in this article are inalienable and indisposable and the rights thereto are not subject to limitation. Paragraph 5. The removal of Indian groups from their lands is forbidden, except ad referendum of the National Congress, in case of a catastrophe or an epidemic which represents a risk to their population, or in the interest of the sovereignty of the country, after decision by the National Congress, it being guaranteed that, under any circumstances, the return shall be immediate as soon as the risk ceases. Paragraph 6. Acts with a view to occupation, domain and possession of the lands referred to in this article or to the exploitation of the natural riches of the soil, rivers and lakes existing therein, are null and void, producing no legal effects, except in case of relevant public interest of the Union, as provided by a supplementary law and such nullity and voidness shall not create a right to indemnity or to sue the Union, except in what concerns improvements derived from occupation in good faith, in the manner prescribed by law. Paragraph 7. The provisions of article 174, paragraphs 3 and 4, shall not apply to Indian lands."

[25]STF, Pet 3388, Justice Rapporteur Carlos Brito, published on June 30, 2010.

Brazilian territory upon which Brazilian national law has exclusive authority". One cannot be sure whether this would be the opinion of the Court in a case dealing directly with a conflict among State-originated law and indigenous norms, by it at least signs out how Justices thought about the subject at that moment.

Courts in the State of Roraima, however, had to deal with this kind of conflict at least in two cases, and seemed to have taken a different approach. In one case, the Superior State Court dismissed criminal charges for murder against members of an indigenous people, because their community had already punished them.[26] In a similar ruling, the Federal Court in Roraima also dismissed criminal charges for stealing liquor because the tribal chief had already punished the defendants to clear off the area in which the stealing happened.[27]

Finally, the Brazilian Federal Constitution acknowledges the autonomy of sports controlling entities and associations (Article 217).[28] This has been understood as respect to these entities norms—FIFA's regulations, for instance—if they are not in conflict with national legislation. The standard here is similar to the one applied to voluntary associations internal regulations, even though the voluntary nature of these associations can be subject to discussion.

Finally, how Brazilian statutory law deals with norms from private origin with no specific connection with the Brazilian Constitution provisions? The Federal Constitution of 1988 has many general provisions protecting freedoms in general and these rules apply here. However, contractual freedom in Brazil is respected only to a certain extend and regulatory and judicial interventions are widely practiced. In some kinds of relationships—as labor and consumer contracts—in which may exist power and information asymmetry, many clauses are considered mandatory and some others are prohibited by law, despite the parties will.

Contracts law provides also that Courts can review seriously unbalanced contracts from a financial point of view. Courts are also sensible to arguments that contractual clauses are abusive, particularly when one of the parties is poor or uninformed.

Parties are free to establish binding arbitration clauses but not really because of contractual freedom alone. Law 9.307/1996 expressly provided for this possibility, and the Supreme Court decided the law did not hinder the constitutional guarantee of access to Justice and, thus, was valid.[29] Before the law was enacted, arbitration clauses were not considered binding just by the force of the parties agreement.

Brazil has one case of successful private self-regulatory council in the advertising industry named CONAR (Conselho Nacional de Autoregulamentação

---

[26]TJRR, proceeding n° 0090.10.000302-0/RR.

[27]JFRR, proceeding n° 0005735-10.2010.4.01.4200/RR.

[28]Brazilian Federal Constitution of 1988: "Article 217. It is the duty of the State to foster the practice of formal and informal sports, as a right of each individual, with due regard for: I – the autonomy of the directing sports entities and associations, as to their organization and operation."

[29]STF, SE 5.206, Justice Rapporteur Sepúlveda Pertence, published in April 30, 2004.

Publicitária).[30] The Council was created in 1979 as an instrument to prevent and avoid any kind of official censorship, and examines and decides on claims that basically anyone can brought against advertising pieces considered unethical on different grounds. CONAR can make different kinds of decisions and even decide the ad should be shut down or changed. Although CONAR decisions are not enforceable, agencies and advertisers usually comply with them.

Finally, a particularly relevant source of private norms in Brazil is condominium association bylaws. They may contain many regulations and even restrictions in the possible use of property units and common areas, as discipline on pets, noise, etc. Differently from what most frequently happens to professional council's norms, condominium association bylaws are usually considered valid when challenged in Courts. The standard in this case is not whether the condo regulations is supported by legal provisions, but whether the norm is reasonable considering the use of the property inside the condo's community. The room for autonomy in this environment seems to be much larger than in other settings.

## 3 The Dynamics of the Relations Among Legal Spheres in Positive Law

The second question to answer can be framed in this way: how the interactions among different norms develop in Brazil considering not only what statutory law provides for, but also the different players dealing with them and their relationships? This is a very complex question for many reasons and two must be pointed out upfront. Both private and public institutions deal with different legal spheres and are players in this sense, so the universe to consider is immense.

Just to give an idea of the dimensions of the Brazilian State institutions, for instance, the country has more than 17,000 Judges; Legislative bodies in 26 States, in all 5570 Municipalities and the Federal District, besides National Congress with the House of Representatives and Senate. The Federal government, States governments and Municipalities governments together hold thousands of administrative organizations, agencies and authorities. Private players would be even more difficult to categorize.

Second, specific research will be needed to identify and access the dynamics involving at least some of these players. In this context, it is important to disclose that the comments below are not grounded in any comprehensive quantitative research of Brazilian reality. Despite these limitations, some dynamics can be observed and are worth mentioning.

As mentioned above, legal pluralism is not really a central topic of discussion for constitutional legal scholars in Brazil or a pressing reality for Courts in the normative system so far. For the most part, Brazilian legal system adopts a very state-centered

[30] http://www.conar.org.br/.

conception of normativity and the interaction between norms from different sources is usually mediated by the national system of production of norms and by the Constitution. This does not mean, though, this mediation is simple or uniform. The Brazilian Constitution of 1988 broad provisions allow for many different understandings and this applies when it comes to deal with norms from different origins: Courts in Brazil can easily reach different conclusions when facing normative conflicts, all of them resourcing to constitutional provisions.

A first dynamic that can be observed establishes itself between lower Courts and the Brazilian Supreme Court. It seems some lower Courts tend to be more attached to norms from national origin and state-originated, instead of international norms or private ones. This pattern was observed in the Supreme Court overrule of Labor Courts decisions, mentioned before, that wouldn't recognize collective bargaining unless its content would grant more rights to workers than the ones provided for by law. Of course an important issue here was the ideological one—more rights or less rights to workers—and the reasoning behind it is that the Constitution protects workers' rights, so collective bargaining should be understood only as a mean to advance rights, and not as an autonomy. The last topic in this paper will deal with the ideological part of the discussion.

In a way, the same dynamic prevailed in the Brazilian Supreme Court decision that overruled State Courts orders on the international transportation disputes. Again, State Courts would apply the national-originated norm, instead of the international law. The Supreme Court, as mentioned, decided precisely the opposite but not on the grounds of any kind of general preference for the international law, but because of the specific Constitutional provision dealing with the subject (Article 178).

Finally, a similar logic underlined the Brazilian Supreme Court ruling on the supralegal *status* of the American Convention on Human Rights on the debtor's prison issue. More than 16 years had passed between the Convention entered in force in Brazil (1992) and the Supreme Court ruling (2009). Even ascribing only legal *status* to the Convention, it would be accurate to conclude that the Convention—as any new law—had repealed the previous national legislation that allowed for this kind of prison. Lower Courts, as described, did not follow this path, in a clear preference for norms State-originated, as discussed before.

A second dynamic relates to the tensions between State-originated law and community-originated normative practices. It seems the physical proximity a Court has with a native community plays an important role in the apprehension and understanding of this kind of conflict. The comparison one can make is between Courts that have a particular proximity with the indigenous communities—as the ones in the State of Roraima—and those—the Supreme Court, for instance—that do not have any real connection with this reality, and approach it only from a theoretical point of view. The State of Roraima is one of the Brazilian States that has a large indigenous peoples population.

In the cases mentioned above, Courts in the State of Roraima seemed more willing to consider indigenous peoples norms not only to be respected and considered, but also as enough reason to depart from what national criminal law would command them to do, in order to prevent double jeopardy. In this sense, to avoid two punishments for the same fact, the State law punishment was simply not applied.

A third dynamic one can observe emerge from the relationship between the Brazilian Supreme Court and foreign and supranational Courts. Some Justices are particularly prone to make references to foreign Courts (usually United States Supreme Court and European Constitutional Courts) and supranational Courts decisions, usually to reinforce a position already stated for other reasons. It seems this kind of argumentative resource has been used more frequently by Court members, but we still do not have enough research on that. It seems clear, though, that the Supreme Court refers much more frequently to foreign and international courts decisions than other Courts in Brazil.

A particular dynamic in this context is the one between the Brazilian Supreme Court and the Inter-American Court of Human Rights, that has been described as one of resistance or indifference from the national Court towards the international one.[31] In 2010, an interesting phenomenon took place involving them: both Courts processed and decided two claims on the same subject—the validity of the Brazilian Amnesty law and the possibility of criminal persecution of public officers for facts occurred during the dictatorship.

In April 28, 2010, the Brazilian Supreme Court decided the Amnesty Law was valid in a decision binding for Brazilian Courts and Administrative authorities (ADPF 153). In November 24, 2010, the Inter-American Court of Human Rights decided that Brazil should disregard its Amnesty Law in order to investigate and bring criminal charges against repression agents for acts committed during the dictatorship. No dialogue took place so far between the Courts on the topic and it seems Brazil simply ignored the Inter-American Court of Human Rights decision, as the Inter-American Court had ignored the Brazilian Supreme Court previous ruling.

This relative indifference to the Inter-American Court of Human Rights is observed in other contexts too, involving also the Administrative branch. In 2002 the Inter-American Court of Human Rights ordered Brazil to implement a series of measures to guarantee the life and physical integrity of the prisoners at one of the biggest prisons in the country's northern region (*Urso Branco* Prison in *Rondônia*). Little has been done since then. The orders of the Court were not complied with and in October 2009 Brazil was required to go before the Court once again to explain what was going on at that same prison.

It is worth mentioning that the conditions at the prisons in the state of *Espírito Santo* also resulted in Brazil being summoned by the UN to provide explanations in 2010. At a parallel session of the 13th Meeting of the UN's Council on Human Rights held in March 2010, Brazil's representatives had to respond to accusations received by that organization.

The challenges posed by the inmate's conditions in Brazil are much more complex than simply a matter of complying or not with international decisions.[32]

---

[31]Neves (2016b).

[32]de Barcellos (2010).

In any case, the truth is that, since those decisions, little has being done by the Executive branch. The National Council of Justice, however, has organized concentrated efforts to review cases in order to free inmates who could benefit from some sort of parole.[33] The Supreme Court has decided the Brazilian prisons system describes an "unconstitutional state of affairs",[34] although no real consequence derived from this decision.

As already mentioned, regulatory agencies more easily immerse in the globalization era through international cooperation in setting common standards globally. This is increasingly relevant once the Administrative Branch is now responsible for most of the regulation in many fields in Brazil, besides those mentioned in the examples above. Brazil has administrative agencies or similar administrative bodies with some sort of normative power, for instance, in areas such as environmental control, water, telecommunications, mining, energy, oil and gas, transportation (both inland and via water), aviation, among others.

Finally, we do not have research tracking the use of "global" arguments in debates within lawmaking processes in Brazil. We know, though, "global" arguments played an important role in Congressional discussions in at least two recent pieces of legislation: anticorruption law and labor reform. Law 12.846/2014, described as an Anticorruption Law, provides for penalties to companies—and not only individuals—engaged in or that profited from corruption. Before that, Brazilian law only allowed for natural persons to be punished according to their personal culpability, but not the companies for which these people work. This change was a direct response to the OCDE guidelines on the topic.

In the labor reform discussion, "global" arguments were dealt with in different perspectives. First, one recurrent point was the need for Brazil to have a less rigid labor legislation to be able to create more jobs and face both global competition and new realities in the workplace. In addition, foreign experiences in labor legislation reform were discussed in the House of Representatives and the Senate.

## 4 The Renewal of Legal Reasoning, Jurisprudence and Legal Practice

As mentioned above, national legal criteria continues to be used by Brazilian Courts to deal with norms from different sources, including international law, to grant them validity and define its hierarchical position in the national system. However, the way these tools are handled, understood and applied by lawyers, academics and Courts have received and continue to receive relevant influence from constitutional and legal globalization. The cross-fertilization of ideas globalization fosters gave birth to

[33]http://www.cnj.jus.br/sistemas/sistema-carcerario-e-execucao-penal/21236-sistema-do-mutirao-carcerario.

[34]STF, ADPF 347, Justice Rapporteur Marco Aurélio, published in February 19, 2016.

new tools, incorporated by the national system, and new subjects of interest and research. Globalization also has had an important impact in the organization of legal services and in the dynamic of academic work. Some examples may help to paint the picture.

A first notable sign of the globalization in the legal field in Brazil has been the growth of associations between national law firms and international ones. The interest of international law firms in Brazil is directly connected with the interest of foreign investors—their clients—in doing business in Brazil, usually in the privatizations operations. The market in Brazil for legal services is a regulated one, as in most countries, and international law firms cannot simply open a branch in Brazil. The most common path has been to use forms of association with local firms and the practice has trigged reaction from some of the larger Brazilian law firms.[35]

From another perspective, it has become much more frequent (from anecdotal evidence) to Brazilian young lawyers to go pursue a LLM or a Master degree abroad, after graduating in Law School, although this may be a general trend in all areas, not only in legal studies.[36] Even law school students are more interested in engaging in foreign exchange programs during their course. The Brazilian legal services market values these international experiences in job candidates.

Important changes are also happening in the legal academic work. Higher education in Brazil is a regulated activity subjected to federal governmental authorization and periodical evaluations by the Federal Ministry of Education, and there is a federal agency for higher education improvement (CAPES[37]). All these administrative systems are engaged in fostering the internationalization of Brazilian universities. Federal Government has announced that most grants for Brazilian Universities in the following years will focus on internationalization projects[38] and other initiatives will be initiated to try to foster a general movement of Brazilian higher education institutions towards internationalization.[39]

Internationalization means different things in this context: to send Brazilian professors and students abroad in some sort of academic international experience, to bring foreign professors and students, to provide classes in foreign languages to accommodate foreign students and develop language skills and national ones, to fund events, publications and research project that promote international cooperation and dialogue, etc.

From the perspective of the daily activity of professors, for instance, to publish in international journals became particularly encouraged by the evaluation system all

[35] https://esaoabsp.edu.br/Artigo?Art=73.

[36] https://prpi.ufg.br/up/680/o/Internacionalizacao_Programas_CAPES.pdf. See also http://www.capes.gov.br/plano-nacional-de-pos-graduacao.

[37] http://www.capes.gov.br/.

[38] http://portal.sbpcnet.org.br/noticias/presidente-da-capes-anuncia-edital-para-internacionalizacao-de-universidades-brasileiras/.

[39] https://prpi.ufg.br/up/680/o/Internacionalizacao_Programas_CAPES.pdf.

higher education institutions are submitted to, as well as to participate in international seminars and events. Brazilian journals are encouraged to establish a wider international dialogue. It is interesting to observe that many judges in Brazil are also involved in academic activities and are exposed to these international experiences and exchanges.

This environment is certainly at least partially responsible for the growing internationalization of issues being discussed in legal academia, which tend to be later reflect and tested in Court discussions and eventually also in Courts reasoning and orders. Some examples may explain the point.

One first change in legal reasoning for Courts in the last decades involves the detailed academic discussion on proportionality (and other similar concepts, as feasibility and equity) and the frequent use of proportionality in legal reasoning by Courts in general, not only by the Supreme Court. Actually, proportionality has become a very common standard of judicial review and Courts use it frequently to evaluate the constitutionality of laws and public acts in general. The influence of globalization on this process is very clear in Brazil: standards developed in Germany and the United States were expressly imported and used my Brazilian authors and Courts.

The same process happened with the balancing or weighting method of decision, that became extremely popular in academia and Courts: so much so that same Brazilian scholars, myself included, are proposing less balancing and more syllogism in Brazil adjudication.[40] It must be noticed that the rise of balancing in Brazil, although certainly fueled by foreign and international experiences in a global movement noted in many places,[41] is also connected with the features of the Federal Brazilian Constitutional of 1988.

As already mentioned, the Brazilian Constitution makes use of many general principles, as human dignity, equality, freedom, freedom of enterprise, solidarity, social justice, among others. Besides them, the Constitution provides also for goals for the State to pursue: environmental and consumer protection, guarantee of free markets, elimination of poverty, reduction of social and regional inequalities, promotion of the well-being of all, without any sort of prejudice, among others. The combination of the balancing tool, the Brazilian Constitution set of principles and goals, and a heterogeneous society has led to a real change in how Courts decide in Brazil. Syllogism is viewed by many Courts as same sort of inferior kind of legal reasoning, and balancing has spread enhancing the unpredictability from Courts jurisprudence.

Still in the context of decision-making methods, the Brazilian Supreme Court has incorporated different modes of decisions initially adopted by foreign national Constitutional Courts (the German Constitutional Court has been an important influence in this matter). Some examples, are decision that declare a piece of legislation unconstitutional but do not undo its effects; or decisions that

[40]de Barcellos (2005).

[41]Aleinikoff (1987).

acknowledges a law is in the process of becoming unconstitutional and calls Congress attention to correct it before it happens; or yet decisions that give an specific meaning to a law to prevent it from being declared void.

Examples of the incorporation of foreign experiences and discussions can be observed also in the procedural realm. Discussions on more participation in the decision making process, particularly in Courts and in Administrative adjudication, have become increasingly relevant and legislation has been enacted to deal with that.

Law 9.868/1999, that regulates some of the proceedings before the Brazilian Supreme Court, provides for the possibility of amicus curiae participation and allows the Justice Rapporteur to conduct a public hearing about the issues discussed in the case. These two participatory instruments were incorporated in a more broadly provision in the 2015 Federal Code for Rules of Civil Procedure, applicable to all State and Federal Civil Courts around the country. Law 9.784/1999, the Federal Administrative Procedure Act, provides for opportunities to those potentially affected by the Administrative authorities' decisions to participate in the process.

Brazilian legal theory and Courts are also testing some innovative kinds of procedures experienced first in other countries, as the structural injunction and the state of unconstitutional affairs. Structural injunctions are being used, for instance, in public interest lawsuits asking for the construction of sewage plants. The idea of a state of unconstitutional affairs has been used for the first time in Brazil before the Supreme Court in the case dealing with the prisons' system already mentioned.

Finally, from a more substantive perspective, it is important to mention the valuable cross-fertilization that constitutional globalization has brought to Brazilian discussions on fundamental rights. Topics as the objective dimension and insufficient protection of fundamental rights, and indirect discrimination are now discussed in Brazil directly because of the contact and dialogue with international authors and publications. Moreover, approaches to law from consequentialism and the discussions around law and economics are now themes discussed in Brazilian academia and even referred to by Courts that came into life directly from foreign sources.

## 5 The Ideological Dimension of Legal Rationality

A final note must be made on the ideological dimensions of the dynamics described above among legal spheres, the players who deal with them and decide over them, and the result of their work. At least two different ideological tensions can be noticed in the context of Brazilian legal rationality connected to globalization and legal pluralism: they will be presented in a very simplistic way, as it would be impossible to discuss the different trends and complexities of them here.

The first ideological axis that mediates many aspects of legal reasoning in Brazil is the one that opposes "progressive" and "conservative", and classifies norms and understanding's contents accordingly. There is no objective standard to describe what is "progressive" or "conservative", but as in Brazil "progressive" is usually valued, people and groups will usually try to describe their position as progressive.

In any case, legal scholars and Courts in Brazil will most commonly consider progressive any kind of solution (normative or adjudicative) that produces more benefits, for instance, for consumers, workers and minorities. Solutions providing for a higher level of environmental protection are also considered progressive by the legal elite.

The application of this ideological distinction to economic regulations has been particularly contentious in Brazil in recent years. Those defending less State participation and intervention in economic activities identify themselves as progressive, focusing on more efficiency and more jobs. Those who defend more State intervention, and less autonomy and less freedom to enterprises, claim the same label alleging that the State would run larger aspects of the economy in the benefit of the poor. It seems fair to say that this last State-centered ideology is still predominant in Brazil.

Another ideological key to Brazilian legal rationality in the context of pluralism confronts a particular conception that values above all social phenomenon the State, and other conceptions that place more value in society and social groups' norms and dynamics, and do not recognize the State as the sole or main player in social life.

This ideological dispute has deep roots in Brazilian history and cultural formation during which society and different social groups have established in various ways a relationship of dependency even to a paternalistic point with the State. This dependency can be observed not only within the worst off, who depend on social security benefits, but also in big companies, that seek public sources of finances and support, special permits, particular tax benefits, regulatory restrictions to competitors, etc.

In addition, under the influence of socialist theories, the State is understood by many groups as a central tool to promote wellbeing, to assure rights for the poor, to reduce inequalities and to create wealthy for all. Other groups will question the theoretical and historical correction of these assumptions about the State, and this authoritative top down ideology, to value more the autonomous organization of social groups and their ability to deal with their own problems and build solutions. These groups will usually value more social norms, instead of State-originated ones, or at least demand more participation. It seems reasonable to say the State-centered view of social life is still predominant in Brazil, but the country is going through deep changes so this may not be true in the near future.

## 6 Conclusion

The paper tried to paint a picture of the various realities that coexist in Brazil concerning Constitutionalism and legal pluralism. Constitutional supremacy and monism together organize a system in each any norm, from any source, will be measured and accommodated into the national system considering hierarchical standards drawn from the Constitution, in such a way State-centrism continues to be the main logic behind Courts rulings in most parts of the country. Administrative agencies, notwithstanding, work in a completely different environment, in which international cooperation is a common trend and practice. For Brazilian law professors and lawyers, the need to catch up constantly with foreign and international discussions and dynamics is very real and present. Finally, to be labeled as progressive or conservative is still a driving force of many discussions in Brazil that can lead to more State-centrism or less, depending on the outcome in each case. The picture described, I am aware, looks much more like a patchwork piece than any kind of homogenous or ordered scenario, which after all may resemble what real contemporary large societies really look like.

## References

Aleinikoff TA (1987) Constitutional law in the age of balancing. Yale Law J 96:943–1005

Cançado Trindade AA (1996) A interação entre o direito internacional e o direito interno na proteção dos direitos humanos. In: Cançado Trindade AA (ed) A incorporação das normas internacionais de proteção dos direitos humanos no direito brasileiro. Instituto Interamericano de Direitos Humanos, San José, Costa Rica, Brasília

CAPES - Coordenação de Aperfeiçoamento de Pessoal de Nível Superior, Brasil. http://www.capes.gov.br. Accessed 15 May 2019. http://www.capes.gov.br/plano-nacional-de-pos-graduacao. Accessed 15 May 2019. https://prpi.ufg.br/up/680/o/Internacionalizacao_Programas_CAPES.pdf. Accessed 15 May 2019. http://portal.sbpcnet.org.br/noticias/presidente-da-capes-anuncia-edital-para-internacionalizacao-de-universidades-brasileiras/. Accessed 15 May 2019

CERT.BR – Centro de Estudos, Resposta e Tratamento de Incidentes de Segurança no Brasil. (2008) HOEPERS, Cristine. Cooperação Internacional na Segurança da Internet e no Tratamento de Incidentes. https://www.cert.br/docs/palestras/certbr-caeat-camara2008.pdf. Accessed 15 May 2019

CNJ – Conselho Nacional de Justiça. http://www.cnj.jus.br/sistemas/sistema-carcerario-e-execucao-penal/21236-sistema-do-mutirao-carcerario. Accessed 15 May 2019

de Barcellos AP (2005) Ponderação, Racionalidade e atividade jurisdicional, Editora Renovar

de Barcellos AP (2010) Urban violence, prison conditions and human dignity. http://digitalcommons.law.yale.edu/yls_sela/87/. Accessed 10 May 2019

de Carvalho Ramos A (2011/2012) Pluralidade das ordens jurídicas: uma nova perspectiva na relação entre o Direito Internacional e o Direito Constitucional. Pluralism of legal orders: toward a new perspective of the relationship between international and constitutional law. R. Fac. Dir. Univ. São Paulo 106/107:497–524

de Sousa Santos B (1977) The law of the oppressed: the construction and reproduction of legality in Pasargada. Law Soc Rev 12(1)

Dellagnezze R (2015) O pluralismo jurídico. Âmbito Jurídico, Rio Grande XVIII, n. 138. http://ambito-juridico.com.br/site/?n_link=revista_artigos_leitura&artigo_id=16159. Accessed 10 May 2019

FATF – The Financial Action Task Force. http://www.fatf-gafi.org/about/. Accessed 15 May 2019

ICMRA - International Coalition of Medicines Regulatory Authorities – Fact Sheet. http://www.ema.europa.eu/docs/en_GB/document_library/Other/2014/11/WC500177574.pdf. Accessed 10 May 2019

Neves M (2016a) Transconstitucionalismo. Editora WMF Martins Fontes, São Paulo

Neves RTS (2016b) Por que resistir? A resistência do STF ao diálogo judicial com a Corte IDH. Why resist? The STF resistance to judicial dialogue with Corte IDH. Revista Brasileira de Direito Internacional 2(1):16–37

OAB/SP. https://esaoabsp.edu.br/Artigo?Art=73. Accessed 15 May 2019

Piovesan F (1997) Direitos humanos e o direito constitucional internacional. Max Limonad, São Paulo

Reyntjens F (2015) Legal pluralism and hybrid governance: bridging two research lines. Dev Change 47(2):347

Wolkmer AC (2015) Constitucionalismo e Pluralismo na trajetória do Direito Brasileiro. In: Baldi CA (ed) Aprender desde o sul: Novas constitucionalidades, pluralismo jurídico e plurinacionalidade. Aprendendo desde o Sul. Fórum, Belo Horizonte, p 254

# Legal Pluralism and Constitutionalism in the Cypriot Example

**Constantinos Kombos**

**Abstract** The Cypriot legal order represents an example of openness towards external influences, primarily in the form of case law development. That cosmopolitanism of Cypriot law has nonetheless appeared in an atypical, selective, non-structured and inconsistent manner. There is a notable differentiation between openness towards the ECHR system and certain foreign jurisdictions and relative caution and closeness towards the EU system, despite the hierarchical nature of that relationship. Cyprus is a mixed legal system, with constitutional idiosyncrasies, that has remained open to informal dialogue with other legal orders, yet in a manner that is circumstantial and asymmetric.

## 1 Introduction

Discourse about the conceptual nature of the Constitution as a complex legal object of study remains both contemporary and traditional.[1] The nature of that debate is characterised by a dynamic and ever-evolving set of constituent conceptual parameters,[2] thus reflecting the need for repositioning[3] existing argumentation and for creating new ratiocination schemes. New challenges originating from new social phenomena, like globalization,[4] cast doubt as to the scope of their impact on the constitutional discourse. Moreover, the emergence and actual function of atypical

[1]See for example the classic analysis on the meaning and origins of the Constitution by Sartori (1962).

[2]Kuo (2010) and Perju (2010).

[3]Loughlin (2015).

[4]Tushnet (2009), Rosenfeld (2008) and Rosenfeld (2011).

C. Kombos (✉)
University of Cyprus, Department of Law, Nicosia, Cyprus
e-mail: c.c.kombos@ucy.ac.cy



G. Tusseau (ed.), *Debating Legal Pluralism and Constitutionalism*, Ius Comparatum – Global Studies in Comparative Law 41, https://doi.org/10.1007/978-3-030-34432-0_5

legal constructs, like supranational organisations,[5] have had a growing and even dominating effect on our constitutional understanding.

*Constitutional pluralism* and *global constitutionalism* are two intertwined conceptual trends that offer descriptive and exegetical narratives about constitutionalism. Nonetheless, it is submitted that despite the unquestioned influence of the plethora of academic analyses that rest on constitutional pluralism and global constitutionalism, the debate often proceeded as if it refers to a unified object of study. Instead, it can be argued that there is an inherent need for *debating the constitutional debate* and for identifying its different aspects that quite often are overlapping.

In terms of structure, this paper is divided in two parts. The first part introduces the adopted theoretical rationale and the consequent delimitation between global constitutionalism and constitutional pluralism, with reference to their respective versions and critical responses. The second part examines the application that constitutional theoretical views find in the specific Cypriot context. More specifically, the second part will first elaborate on the balance among legal spheres in positive law, by examining the hierarchy of the rules of law in the Cypriot legal order and the approach of Cyprus law towards international and supranational law (with particular emphasis on the ECHR and EU law). Then the second part of this paper will turn to the dynamics of the relations among legal spheres, through the analysis of the unique mixed legal system of Cyprus and the external influences that the Cypriot system received.

The argument submitted states that the Cypriot legal order has indeed been affected by external influences mostly in the field of adjudication, yet in an atypical, selective, non-structured and inconsistent manner. There is a notable differentiation between openness towards the ECHR system and certain foreign jurisdictions and relative caution and closeness towards the EU system, despite the hierarchical nature of that relationship.

## 2 Theoretical Rationale: Concepts and Content, Accounts and Critique

### *2.1 The Three Facets of the Constitutional Debate*

As a matter of preliminary clarification, the approach adopted in this paper needs to be introduced and certain observations must be made. The constitutional debate is not unified and perceptions about the constitutional concept(s) vary.[6] The underlying

[5]Walker (2007), p. 247; Eleftheriades (2007).

[6]See for example the debate about pluralism and State constitutional notions: MacCormick (1999); Maduro (2012), p. 1; Kumm (1999); Walker (2011). Cf. Kelemen (2016); Loughlin (2014, 2015, 2017).

matter remains the implied and often presumed view that the constitutional debate relates to one single object that has a universal meaning and responds to pre-existing and inherent prototypical premises. Nonetheless, it is argued that if such an argument forms the foundation for the subsequent analysis, then the isolation of the object of study as a single, unitary and universal concept must be first stated and then justified. This would form part of establishing realizations before assuming their universality and objectivity. In other words, the debate seems to be assuming objectivity of perception about the object of study when in effect there are powerful clashing analyses that point to a diverse and subjective notion of 'the Constitution'. Furthermore, there is, as a result of the pre-established preference for 'a Constitution' rather than for 'Constitutions',[7] an implied adherence to the orthodox constitutional understanding that is deeply founded on national understandings of what a Constitution is or should be.[8] This has the outcome of projecting nationally oriented criteria for a Constitution when there is no unified national model.

Therefore, the debate about the Constitution remains at the epicentre of legal thought in a manner that is dynamic in nature and multifaceted in terms of its objectives, yet often predetermined by initial subconscious assumptions and preferences that are infrequently particularized. New phenomena and processes of thinking have repositioned the discourse that nonetheless remains fixated about *ontological, typological and relational aspects* of the object study. These three internal aspects of the constitutional debate are explained *infra* and with the important recognition that there are overlaps between them that nonetheless allow for relative content-based demarcation.

On that basis, there is within the constitutional discourse a debate that is *ontological* in nature and which focuses on whether a legal phenomenon qualifies as a Constitution.[9] This is perhaps the most traditional type of discussion because it examines the nature of the Constitution and the criteria that it must satisfy in order to be considered worthy of the constitutional denomination.[10] This classic discussion has found renewed vigour in relation to the assessment of the supranational entities and systems.[11] Such complex organizational structures have created a novel legal reality due their often normative competences, their vertically binding force and the subsequent reorientation of the key constitutional concept of sovereignty. The EU paradigm forms a classic preoccupation for the ontological analysis.[12] Similarly, the ontological yardstick applies to the ECHR example but to a lesser extent than the EU, because of the narrower thematic scope and norm-making capacity of the

[7]Seitzer (2007), pp. 57–166 on the typology and meaning of the Constitution.

[8]See the excellent analysis by Besselink (2008).

[9]On terminology and the distinction between ontology, epistemology and interlegality see Green (2018); Beaulac (2017), p. 867.

[10]Grimm (1991), pp. 11, 101, 397.

[11]Zumbansen (2012), p. 77; Teubner (1997), p. 3; Wet (2006a, b); Sweet (2009).

[12]Piris (2006); Walker (2007), p. 247; Barber (2006); Maduro (2007); Fabbrini (2015).

Convention system.[13] Overall, both supranational entities have been the focal point of the constitutional ontological discussion for some time.

The *typological* aspect of the debate has focused on the variations of constitutional examples, thus forming both an aftermath and a clarification of the ontological aspect. More specifically, the manner in which the Constitution is ontologically recognised and the criteria applicable to that determination, are both abstract and non-rigid due to the pragmatic existence of systems with constitutional qualities and characteristics of various types, degrees and density. Therefore, if supranational legal phenomena are *ab initio* considered to be lacking, *inter alia*, the 'essential statehood elements' of people, constitutive and constituent power, geographical borders where the power of the State entity is exercised, then one is simply projecting exclusively national/State features to supranational examples. It is consequently not surprising that the conclusion reached points to the nullity of constitutional existence for any legal construct that is not a nation-State. What such an approach presupposes is the unity of the constitutional entity and as a corollary it bypasses the reality that of having within the national constitutional example a plurality of constitutional examples.[14]

It can be reasonably argued that a constitutional prototype and archetype does not exist in a manner that forms a rule of recognition. For example, if the focus is placed on the genesis of a Constitution, the conclusion can be reached that there are various ways in which that process can materialise.[15] There is the more well-known *revolutionary constitutional genesis*, where the constitutional creation follows a significant political event that often manifests itself as a revolution and whereby the Constitution becomes the celebrated materialisation of the objectives of a movement.[16] The American and French Constitutions would qualify as such examples.[17] There is also the case of *treaty-based constitutional genesis*, where the Constitution results from a transfer of sovereignty or better by the prior acceptance of self-determination by 'others'.[18] Such an example could be the Dutch Constitution, the Indian Constitution and the German Basic Law. Furthermore, there can be a *visible exercise of the ultimate and unique power of the people as exclusive agent of popular sovereignty*, thus leading to the formation of the primordial Constitution or to its redefinition into another form.[19] For instance, the genesis of a Constitution and the definition of its contents can result from a formal process with a central role for a constituent assembly, as was the case with Pakistan and Greece.[20] The members can be elected or appointed, while there can be subsequent validation through a

[13]Repetto (2013) and Martinico (2012).

[14]Tuori (2010), p. 3; Kombos (2010c), p. 291.

[15]Klein and Sajó (2012), p. 419.

[16]Besselink (2008).

[17]Klein and Sajó (2012), p. 426.

[18]Grimm (2012), p. 98.

[19]Klein and Sajó (2012).

[20]On Greece see Tsatsos (1994), pp. 301–433.

referendum or even direct acceptance of the popular validity via the representation process. Moreover, there can be a subsequent reconstitution in terms of content; France is currently in the 5th Republic thus forming an example of reconstituting the initial revolutionary Constitution.[21] Furthermore, there can be *an evolving genesis* where the Constitution results from a longer process of adaptation, modification and then finality that is nonetheless relative and perhaps never-ending. The English constitutional example is a classic case of a historically growing organic constitutional setting that at the same time is not self-defined in a single document but which rather draws from multiple sources. The English constitution is in effect a puzzle that when put together then its content becomes visible to the observer, whereas formal, written and self-defined constitutions follow the reverse order regarding the identification of their content.[22] On this issue it can also be argued that there is a typical and prevailing trend of written constitutions yet there are examples of exceptions like Israel, New Zealand, Canada and England. Finally, there can even be *granted or imposed constitutional settings* that were quite common in the post-colonisation period. Cyprus is an example of this type of constitutional genesis, since the terms of the constitutional arrangements were determined by Greece, Turkey and the United Kingdom as part of an exercise of international diplomacy with normative effects. The outcome was then imposed on the Cypriot people without it having the power to either deviate from the detailed parameters that were externally determined or to approve the content through a direct exercise of the popular will.[23]

Surmising, there is an extensive typology of constitutional examples that do not adhere to a single production process or to even the type of expression of their content being necessarily in self-referential, conclusive and written form. In addition, there can be noticeable differences between the hierarchical position that the Constitution holds in different systems, the manner in which it can be amended or revised and also in terms of the way in which a system of government is established. Consequently, it can be argued that the absence of a unified rule of recognition that takes the form of a constitutional ontological criterion is documented from the variety of examples of constitutional frameworks. Ignoring constitutional practice and reality for the benefit of theoretical purity is unquestionably an error in theory. That is the case when other examples are clearly visible and bypassed due to their non-compliance with a rigid yardstick that is also not applicable even with reference to the national examples. Instead, it is argued that there is a *constitutional spectrum with shades of different types of constitutions* that share certain crucial constitutional qualities with different degrees of concentration. That can lead to a subjective assessment as to the *quality* of a constitutional example as regards the functional characteristics of attribution of powers, organisation of the exercise of power, separation of powers, protection of fundamental rights and presence of the rule of law. These do not form criteria for a Constitution to exist but evaluation tools as to

[21]Klein and Sajó (2012), p. 430.

[22]Martinez (2012), p. 548.

[23]Kombos (2015a), pp. 135–142.

the quality of a Constitution. One could also supplement the preceding evaluating criteria with other but that is an entirely different, yet important, discussion that for practical reasons is beyond the scope of the present paper.[24] Moreover, within such a spectrum, there is room for 'classic' revolutionary constitutions and for constitutionally different examples that are fluid, flexible and even partly unwritten, as well as for nation-State constitutions and supranational constitutional settings and also for 'bad' constitutions that are undemocratic or despotic.[25] It is within this framework that the present analysis proceeds when referring to a typological constitutional debate.

There is also the *relational aspect* of the constitutional debate that refers to the manner in which various constitutional entities are associated.[26] It is within this part of the constitutional discourse that the discussion about constitutional pluralism and global constitutionalism are to be placed since both narratives concentrate primarily on the way in which constitutional units interact and are affected. The EU and the ECHR frameworks have formed the fertile ground upon which the discussion has been founded, with the WTO and aspects of private action forming part of a broader and global setting. It is argued that within this cosmopolitan,[27] interdependent, mutually reflexive, multidimensional,[28] heterarchical[29] and dialogue-driven context,[30] the newest phase of the constitutional debate grows.

## 2.2 Adopted Theoretical Perspective

This paper argues that in terms of the relational debate and the narratives of constitutional pluralism and global constitutionalism, there is an expression of *constitutionalism as 3-dimensional concept* that encompasses *a national, a post-national and a co-owned element.* Constitutional discussion cannot take place in isolation and on the basis of exclusively one of the three dimensions, especially in the case where the presence of a post-national setting is strong, as is the case in Europe.

The approach adopted is founded on the acknowledgment and subsequent adoption of the concept of pluralism[31] in the European legal sphere that takes the form of

---

[24]Peters (2009), p. 405.

[25]Kombos (2010c).

[26]For example: Claes and Visser (2012); Voβkuhle (2010); Millet (2014); Bogdandy and Schill (2011); Wendel (2013); Goldmann (2016); Walker (2016); Kombos (2010b), pp. 1–42.

[27]Perju (2010); Tan (2004); Sweet (2012); Kumm (2009), p. 258.

[28]Scharpf (2009), Chowdhury and Wessel (2012) and Pernice (1999, 2009).

[29]Denoting lack of hierarchical position. See Bobić (2017), p. 1399.

[30]Kombos (2010b).

[31]On Pluralism, see Avbelj and Komárek (2008); Maduro (2003), p. 501; Kumm (1999); Komárek (2006); Walker (2002b).

coexistent and interdependent sources of law,[32] originating from formally independent legal orders.[33] Pluralism in the preceding form is resulting in a dynamic state of synergy that characterises the system of participating legal systems,[34] both national and supranational in origin, thus contributing to the establishment of a network of exchanging legal influences that are particularly present in the field of public law.[35] Pragmatism points to the interaction between different legal systems in the area of public law and that has as its founding premise the open character of an evolving public space/*topos* that exceeds rigid national boundaries. As explained elsewhere, "that openness is made possible through the actual formation of common legal frameworks like the EU's and the ECHR's and through the therein originating vertical and horizontal legal routes of the principles of primacy and direct effect of EU law, as well as the preliminary reference procedure and State liability. These principles operate as psychological icebreakers that enable and facilitate the observation of and coexistence with other legal systems at the same time as implementing a common core of principles that the framework systems create".[36]

Accordingly, in the second part of the paper, the Cypriot constitutional order is examined under the scope of the preceding methodological approach, thus perceived as another paradigm of a national constitutional order entangled with other national and supranational constitutional orders. Nonetheless, the field of constitutional law must be approached with caution given the significance that the national psyche and national values have and which define the essence of each constitutional system.[37] Therefore, the nationally specific symbolism[38] associated with each national constitutional order should not be side-lined for the benefit of the inherent tendency of a comparatist to identify points of convergence between comparable systems.[39]

In this sense, the approach adopted perceives *convergence and divergence as equally significant parameters of the symbiosis between national and supranational legal orders*,[40] with perhaps the role of divergence being even more influential for the stability of the pluralist system.[41]

---

[32]For the early accounts see Weiler (1993, 1994, 1999), Lenaerts (1990) and Burley and Mattli (1993).

[33]Formally refers to the insularity of each legal order that is nonetheless a formalistic approach that in Europe becomes a fiction. The participating legal orders are those of the European States that are members of the two regional organisations—European Union (EU) and Council of Europe (ECHR).

[34]Kombos (2010c), p. 291; Birkinshaw and Kombos (2009), p. 35.

[35]Kombos (2010b). For some classic accounts, see Snyder (2000); Jans et al. (2007); Schwarze (2006); Beaumont et al. (2002); Beatson and Tridimas (1998); Anthony (2000, 2002); Börzel (2002); Conant (2001), p. 97.

[36]Kombos (2010b), p. 8.

[37]Ibid, 7–43.

[38]Kombos (2010c), p. 291.

[39]Scott (2002), p. 19; Himsworth (2002), p. 99; Harlow (2002).

[40]Kombos (2010b), p. 8.

[41]See for instance the Primacy of EU law issue and the constructive disagreement between the CJEU and national courts: Aziz (2001) and Groussot (2005). For case law, see *Internationale*

Summarizing, the methodological approach adopted approaches the concept of public law especially at European level as a *mentalitè*[42] (state of mind) that is broader than the national one. Within this framework, the flow of legal ideas and approaches applies also between States and at a global level, thus leading to a version of global constitutional perception that is co-owned and which can become visible with different clarity depending on the area of public law, the national system and the period. Consequently, uniformity is not the objective. Instead, converging and diverging legal ideas are of equal importance, while at the same time there is a *meta-constitutionalism* in the sense that a legal concept is constantly adjusted and re-projected back in the system. The mere transplantation as a process is not feasible or viable in that sense. Constitutional content is redefined slowly and organically and depends on the space of application, the pre-existing content and perceptions and time. Constitutional pluralism is about constitutional symbiosis between legal orders and the mechanics of their co-existence and relation, whereas global constitutionalism forms a descriptive device for an even broader application of the 3-dimensional approach with stronger elements of localisation due to the lack of supranational framework systems, yet with the presence of a commonly shared *mentalitè*. Therefore, the difference between pluralism and global constitutionalism is one about the lack of strong supranational framework systems within which the *mentalitè* can operate. The more loose the framework systems, the slower and weaker becomes the dialogue element.

It is on this basis that the next section proceeds to focus on the two narratives of constitutional pluralism and global constitutionalism.

## 2.3 Global Constitutionalism

Anne Peters argues that "[g]lobal constitutionalism comprises different strands of thought most of which read (or reconstruct) some features of the status quo of global law and governance as "constitutional" and even "constitutionalist" (positive analysis), and which also seek to provide arguments for their further development in a specific direction (normative analysis)".[43] Furthermore, Peters has argued for "compensatory constitutionalism"[44] as "a strategy to compensate for the de-constitutionalization of domestic governance, which is caused by globalization

*Handelsgesellschaft* (1972) CMLR 177; *Solange I* (1974) 2 CMLR 540; *Solange II (Wunsche Handelsgesellschaft)* (1987) 3 CMLR 225; *Brűnner* (1994) 1 CMLR 57; *Lisbon Case, BVG 30 June 2009,* http://www.germanlawjournal.com/article.php?id=1160; *Frontini v. Ministero delle Finanze* (1974) 2 CMLR 372.

[42]Kombos (2010b), p. 9. See for the wider meaning Legrand (2002), p. 242; Walker (2002a), p. 258 *et seq.*

[43]Peters (2015), p. 1.

[44]Peters (2006).

and global governance",[45] given that "globalization and global governance have put the state and state constitutions under strain. Global problems have compelled states to transfer previously typically governmental functions, such as guaranteeing human security, freedom, and equality, to "higher" levels, and to non-state actors acting in a trans-boundary fashion. This has led to governance which is exercised beyond the states' constitutional confines".[46] Therefore, "national constitutions are, so to speak, hollowed out; traditional constitutional principles become dysfunctional or empty",[47] thus necessitating compensatory constitutionalization on the international plane.

Pallandri starts by referring to the component term of 'globalization' as inevitably bearing "a negative ideological connotation since it has been overused, too often associated to politics", but which nonetheless "is useful because it manages to evoke the idea of the demise of national borders, which become porous and allow a continuous osmosis of values, behaviours, rules, tastes, habits, customs, which characterizes the post-Westphalian age".[48] In that context, global is defined as "the most commonly used term to refer to the law of the current world society" and it is differentiated from the term international because "global encompasses the different types of law of the contemporary time...[and] international law... indicates the relationships between sovereign states".[49] On that basis, 'global' identifies the movement of communality and sharing of a pattern observed in national and post-national legal phenomena. In that sense, there is an inclination of globalising and spreading the originally internal, national idea of constitutionalism as a descriptive process that is applicable or discoverable in various legal constructions both national and post-national. Pallandri explains this point eloquently:

> Originally, global constitutionalism described the worldwide spreading of typically national circumstances, something deeply bound to the state model, but then it appeared less and less tied to national borders, and progressively ceased to identify a clear-cut phenomenon and became an empty box, a theoretical framework through which legal scholarship tried to interpret what was happening on the global field. A proper global constitutional project has now developed as a sort of umbrella notion which covers a broad range of theories seeking to observe and interpret the international dimension through constitutional lenses.[50]

In similar vein,[51] Emmerich-Fritsche has located the surfacing of a 'global constitution' in the formation of a basic order of principles in positive law, and has diagnosed a paradigm shift from a law of nations to global law.[52] Teubner has gone further and has emphasized that the field of application for contemporary

[45]Peters (2009), pp. 404–405.

[46]Ibid, 405.

[47]Peters (2007), pp. 270–277, 285–293.

[48]Palandri (2013), p. 58.

[49]Ibid, 59.

[50]Ibid, 65.

[51]Emmerich-Fritsche (2007), p. 1034.

[52]As quoted in Peters (2015), p. 1.

constitutional theory includes both privatization and globalization, thus requiring from the notion of constitutionalism a voluntary shift in focus towards post-state legal phenomena. It must examine both global phenomena and private entities with a global reach. Teubner stresses the need for realizing that new constitutional phenomena are emerging and they form the new challenge facing constitutional theory: "constitutional problems arising outside the borders of the nation state in transnational political processes and at the same time outside the institutionalized political sector, in the 'private' sectors of global society".[53]

Teubner thus states that the current theoretical debate over global constitutionalism suffers from "methodological nationalism"[54] and according to Kuo "urges a turn to constitutional sociology as an alternative",[55] with an aim for "overcom[ing] the obstinate state-and-politics-centricity of [the] positions' staked out by constitutional lawyers and political philosophers".[56] In that approach, societal constitutionalism takes relies on the adjustment of constitutionalism in a global and complex context with the axis being society and States. In other words, the society needs to readjust based on constitutionalism in a bottom-up manner that cannot nonetheless ignore state oriented notions of constitutionalism.

This is different from setting the state-oriented constitutionalism as a prototype that just needs to be transplanted to the global society.[57] What has been termed as "proper global constitutional approach",[58] highlights the need form uniformity in the form of an "overarching constitutional framework encompassing the entire global legal system, and assumes a high level of global consensus on shared ethical values".[59] Such accounts resting on uniformity and dominance of the national prototype suffer from the weakness of relying on the assumption that such a unitary national prototype exists. Therefore, such accounts repeat the ontological debate's underlying premises whereby nation-related principles are projected to phenomena that are not national.[60] It is at this point that global constitutionalism in the preceding unifying form crosses paths with constitutional pluralism. The latter is taken the basis upon which the existence of other types of supranational constitutional entities can exist, thus enabling the expansion of such factual findings to a global level and with reference to specific international organizations like the WTO, the EU and the UN. It has been argued that "the major objection to a global constitutional framework is that such a model does not reflect, least of all respect, the pluralistic nature of

[53]Teubner (2012), pp. 1–2.

[54]Ibid, 46.

[55]Kuo (2014), p. 161.

[56]Teubner (2012), p. 3.

[57]Palandri (2013), p. 65.

[58]Ibid.

[59]Ibid.

[60]Fassbender (1998), p. 573; Wet (2006b), p. 55; Sweet (2009), p. 630.

the reality, rather tends to neutralize and negate it, driven by the ambition of an utopian reduction to unity, claiming to re-impose order and re-establish hierarchy".[61]

In the quest for a description of the relational interplay between national and the global constitutional spheres, a discussion that is relation and typological perhaps but which should not be ontological in terms of its hierarchical prototypical sense, various accounts have offered useful narratives. Cottier and Hertig argued for "multilevel constitutionalism" as a descriptive device for stating that various level of governance exist and must be acknowledged as forming part of a wider constitutional example and with the task for ensuring that the constitutional functions are safeguarded.[62] In addition, Kumm has argued for a "cognitive framework" of "cosmopolitan constitutionalism" which is conceptually reflective of national constitutionalism since there cannot be a full dissociation and there is always the impossibility of starting from zero.[63]

On this point, it can be argued that Kumm relies on the pragmatic recognition that a rich constitutional vocabulary pre-exists and although it is primarily national in origin, it still forms the lingua franca for the constitutional discourse. This is an analytical premise that this paper adopts since it is not to be argued that the ontological discussion and its vocabulary are irrelevant or that the national paradigm is obsolete due to the lack of a unitary prototype. Rather, the constitutional vocabulary remains and must be used with the explicit acknowledgment and recognition that is often used and projected on post-national phenomena.

In summary, global constitutionalism must be approached with caution if it is to be perceived as another example or attempt to impose a single national constitutional paradigm to the global arena. Not all spheres of law can be constitutionalized and in a manner that is uniform. Constitutional vocabulary as part of a *mentalitè* is inevitably present and must be coupled with the realization of the different nature of the object phenomenon and the 'original' phenomenon. Moreover, *mentalitè* requires a space/topos that enables constitutionalization and that depends on structures and institutional settings that are not always present in all global legal phenomena. In any terms, any process of constitutionalism is gradual and organic by definition and the perception of an intellectually superior movement towards global constitutionalism that must take place because of its undoubted advantages, does not necessarily mean its application or the dictate the form that it can take. Such an approach would be hierarchical and external in origin.

It can therefore be argued that proponents of global constitutionalism are expanding the reach of constitutional pluralism in a way that is stretching the foundational premises of the relational debate, which is debate about the manner of symbiosis between constitutional orders in different state of development and with specific characteristics that are often divergent between them and not present in the same degree in all systems. Put differently, global constitutionalism can be

[61]Palandri (2013), p. 67.

[62]Cottier and Hertig (2003), p. 301.

[63]Kumm (2009), p. 258.

construed as resting on a tendency for convergence, when constitutional pluralism and the relational debate are based on the at least equal value of divergence with convergence and the organic growth of constitutional *mentalitè* subject to space/ topos and time. Moreover, the difference between pluralism and global constitutionalism is one about the lack of strong supranational framework systems within which the *mentalitè* can operate.

## 2.4 Constitutional Pluralism

The analysis that follows focuses on constitutional pluralism, its various versions and the manner in which this paper approaches them. Therefore, it is important to note certain specific characteristics of the pluralism narrative.

The underlying premise for constitutional pluralism is the idea that, especially in the European context, there is need for an exegetical interpretation of the mechanics for constitutional coexistence. The hypothesis is that pluralism as an exegetical narrative device, expresses and reflects the current state of constitutional affairs. That hypothesis starts from the rejection of the unitary and singular constitutional paradigm as an independent and insular entity; a recognition that singular and insulated constitutional orders are neither existing nor possible. Instead, the focal point is relational constitutionalism and the manner in which various types of constitutional examples can coexist and interact in a symbiotic manner. Finally, it is important to point out that a symbiotic relationship does not necessarily mean that a frictionless state of affairs exists.

In terms of offering a snapshot of pluralism, the work by MacCormick and by Walker form the stepping stone. MacCormick argues that "it is possible that each [constitutional order] acknowledge the legitimacy of every other within its own sphere, while none asserts or acknowledges the constitutional superiority over another".[64] Walker referred to the factual reality of pluralism and to its value.[65] The factual element refers to the reality of modern constitutionalism and is empirical in nature, thus extending to the point where "it becomes increasingly difficult if not impossible not to conceive of the environment of constitutionalism in non-unitary terms – as a place of heterarchically interlocking legal and political systems".[66] In terms of value, for Walker pluralism is justified because it enables "viewing this changing landscape not as a threat to the maintenance of the traditional template of constitutionalism but as a welcome opportunity to integrate what in conventional constitutional wisdom tend to be treated as contrasting and even opposing modalities of normative thought. The constitutional pluralist, in short, seeks to make a virtue out of necessity".[67]

---

[64]MacCormick (1999), p. 102 *et seq.*

[65]Walker (2012), p. 17.

[66]Ibid, p. 18.

[67]Ibid.

Pernice introduced his version of multilevel constitutionalism as part of the pluralism perspective and has argued that the EU Constitution is the result of coordination between national and supranational legal orders that are interdependent and dually-reflexive.[68] Moreover, Weiler argued for constitutional tolerance as the voluntary acceptance by peoples of a binding discipline that has a high mix of legal integration while respecting national diversities.[69] Ana Bobić has eloquently presented the core of the approach to pluralism:

> [t]he reading of interactions between the national and the EU legal system should not be conducted in hierarchical, but in heterarchical terms. Such an understanding waters down the importance of the competition for the ultimate judicial authority in the EU, because their interactions are taking place in a setting of mutual respect and are based on the principle of sincere cooperation. The constitutional jurisdictions are ultimate interpreters and arbiters in their respective areas of competence.[70]

Moreover, Kaarlo Tuori in an insightful and deep analysis, argued that constitutional pluralism is about the plurality of constitutional pluralities, thus placing constitutional pluralism as the interpretation of interrelationships and interpenetrations between coexisting constitutional units.[71] This argument is founded on the premise that there is a numerical variety of interpretations/exegeses of pluralism all seeking to explain the manner of constitutional symbiosis. Therefore, pluralism is a *polysemous* concept, *id est* with multiple meanings,[72] while both pluralism and its derivatives were utilised as a popular device for both the polemics and the zealots of the pluralism narrative. In that sense, the anti-pluralism rhetoric is formed with reference to pluralism, thus being partly the result of *hetero-determination rather than auto-determination.*

Consequently, it can be argued that the terminology and vocabulary of constitutional pluralism have formed the common denominator for both proponents and opponents of that specific narrative, to the point that it has formed the internal point of reference for the theoretical debate. The dominance, popularity and influence of the preceding approaches led Kelemen[73] to argue that the impact factor of pluralism has been enormous and to the point that allowed Weiler to claim that "constitutional pluralism is today the only party membership card which will guarantee a seat at the high table of the public law professoriate".[74]

Therefore, the pluralism versus anti-pluralism debate has been structured with the latter referring to the former and with a common vocabulary. The argumentation of anti-pluralism[75] has targeted pluralism in an antithetical manner. It can be further

---

[68]Pernice (1999, 2002).

[69]Weiler (2005).

[70]Bobić (2017), p. 1399.

[71]Tuori (2010), p. 3.

[72]Kombos (2010c), p. 291.

[73]In a critical appraisement, Kelemen (2016).

[74]As quoted in Kelemen (2016), p. 145: Weiler (2011), p. 8.

[75]Sarmiento (2015), Fabbrini (2015), Loughlin (2014) and Davies (2010).

argued that anti-pluralism has failed to provide a self-standing account, that is a narrative that can stand without reference to the premises of pluralism. In specific, one can categorise the anti-pluralism claims as falling in three loosely defined categories. *Level One Critique (ontological)* focuses on whether the EU has or can ever have a Constitution. The typical response from the perspective of pluralism is that a rigid prototype is theoretically and pragmatically unstable, that the constitutional phenomenon is much more complex and flexible and that overall the EU has a Constitution of its own type, with the emphasis on the EU part (perhaps a *Grundgesetz* rather than a *Verfassung*).[76] Moreover, the critique rests on State/national concepts, perceptions and criteria of constitutionalism that are then projected on a supranational entity. *Level Two Critique (relational)* emphasises the claim stating that a hierarchical rule is needed if the pluralism analysis is to be complete and coherent.[77] Namely, the mere description of a system that has no hierarchical rule results in specific situations to a dead-end because of conflicts about sovereignty and has as a result the lack of a response to the need to identify the final power holder in cases of conflict. To this type of attack, the response normally is that the described system rests on the lack of hierarchy and it has so far functioned effectively,[78] thus the critique stems from a very different and dogmatic standpoint that sees hierarchy, as is found in national constitutional examples, as essential.[79] Connected to that point is the *level 2 1/2 critique (crisis and examples of dead end)* where the anti-pluralism perception refers to specific and recent examples of constitutional conflict that brought to the surface the lack of hierarchy issue and the sovereignty gap in the pluralism narrative.[80] In specific, reference has been made to the economic crisis, the Outright Monetary Transactions (OMT) saga,[81] to the Czech Constitutional Court's defiance and triggering of the *ultra vires* rule in *Slovak Pensions*,[82] to Brexit and to the one point ominous Grexit. The founding premise for such examples remained the claim that the sovereignty question needs an answer both for theoretical and for substantive reasons. In the alternative, the permission to differentiate one's stand would create inequality vis-à-vis the other participating

---

[76]Kombos (2010c).

[77]E.g. Kelemen (2016).

[78]Avbelj (2006) and von Bodgandy (2008).

[79]Bobić (2017), p. 1399.

[80]Kelemen (2016), Sarmiento (2015), Fabbrini (2015), Loughlin (2014) and Davies (2010).

[81]Bundesverfassungsgericht, Jan. 14, 2014, 2 BVR 2728/13, *Gauweiler I*; CJEU, Case C-62/14, *Gauweiler et al. v. Deutscher Bundestag*, ECLI:EU:C:2015:400; Bundesverfassungsgericht, June 21, 2016, Case No. 2 BvR 2728/13, 2 BvR 2729/13, 2 BvR 2730/13, 2 BvR 2731/13, 2 BvE 13/13, *Gauweiler II*. For analysis of the case law detached from the pluralism and anti-pluralism approach, see: Tridimas and Xanthoulis (2016) and Craig and Markakis (2016).

[82]Decision of the Czech Constitutional Court of Dec. 31, 2012, Pl. ÚS 5/12, *Slovak Pensions Case*. The judgment declared as ultra vires the earlier decision by the CJEU in Case C-399/09, *Marie Landtová*. For analysis of the internal conflicts between Czech courts see: Komárek (2012), Bobek (2014) and Zbíral (2012).

systems that continue to comply without clash. Put differently, the power to disagree and not comply is at the expense of the others that agree and comply.

Nonetheless, the argument in response sees those examples as exaggerated misrepresentations and actual evidence of the continuity of the pluralism approach.[83] This paper focuses only on this last type of critique and examines the validity of the claims made; analysis of level one and two critique has already been attempted *supra*.[84]

The nucleus of the sovereignty argument is that pluralism fails to answer the fundamental question: Where does ultimately lie the Sovereignty? In that context, pluralism is perceived to be a pacifist/appeasement narrative device that manages to mask the lack of an answer at times of minimal conflict between participating units.[85] The argument states that recent developments, with the OMT saga being at the forefront, have ended the pluralist narrative in the same way that *Brunner* created it.[86] The anti-pluralism argument also refers to the Czech Constitutional Court's triggering of the *ultra vires* rule, to the impact of the economic crisis and to Brexit as further evidence for the theoretical gap in the pluralism argument. Therefore, the argument goes, the *Sovereignty Question* needs an answer: conflict cannot be a footnote anymore since it became an urgent reality. To that effect, the anti-pluralism argumentation makes an interesting claim based on the principle that is fundamental to the EU's design, namely *national constitutional identity*: acceptance of the primacy of EU law rests on the respect for national constitutional identity and to the equality in treatment for all Member States.[87] Accordingly, Member States are obliged both under national and EU law to take position when the national constitutional identity and equality of treatment are directly undermined. They must select either acceptance of the EU perspective or exit from the system[88]; fundamental and structural disagreements going at the heart of the protection of national constitutional identity are not just disagreements about semantics but existential.[89]

In response at a general level, the pluralism narrative argues that the opposing view places disproportionate and overstated emphasis on judicial supremacy at the expense of the political dimension.[90] The judicial level of pluralism can only go so far and with the economic crisis this came to the surface as an expression of the need for deeper reflection about the EU project at the political level. Moreover, the

---

[83]See the thorough response by Bobić (2017), p. 1399.

[84]See, Sect. 2.1.

[85]Loughlin (2014), Kelemen (2016) and Fabbrini (2015).

[86]Bundesverfassungsgericht, *Brunner v The European Union Treaty* (Cases 2 BvR 2134/ 92 & 2159/92) (Maastricht Judgment) [1994] 1 CMLR 57. See on German approach: See BVerfG, Case No. 2 BvL 52/71, 37 271 Judgment of May 29, 1974 (Solange I); BVerfGE 73, 339 judgment of October 22, 1986 (Solange II); BVerfG, Case No. 2 BvE 2/08.

[87]Fabbrini (2015).

[88]Kelemen (2016).

[89]Kelemen (2016), Fabbrini (2015) and Loughlin (2014).

[90]Bobić (2017).

economic crisis was about something more complex since it encompasses conflicts not only between the EU and Member States but also between Member States. One can simply refer to the chasm between Member States as creditors and Member States as debtors; their position, needs, constitutional impact is different and polar. Therefore, the issue is the "harmonious co-existence of national constitutionalisms without hierarchy".[91] Finally, the anti-pluralism view is suggesting that divorce is the only solution to a marriage, thus opting for the extreme tools with questionable ease.

The pluralism response on a more specific level and with reference to the examples of conflict that the anti-pluralism view sees as necessitating hierarchy and a response to the sovereignty question, is far more interesting because it deconstructs the basis for the claims.[92] The OMT decision is an example not of conflict but of the limits of disagreement through judicial engagement. The German Federal Constitutional Court (FCC) at the end tested the limits of the CJEU's jurisdiction by correctly proposing its view on the matter referred under article 267 TFEU. The response by the CJEU took into account those arguments and carefully responded in disagreement, while the FCC finally and reluctantly complied with cautious reservations. Therefore, the disagreement was aired, discussed and concluded, thus the OMT can be seen as an example of the manner that pluralism can work in instances where sensitive issues are examined and where different initial views were established. In effect, there was no clash but initial disagreement channelled through the dialogue procedure of the preliminary reference.

As regards the *Slovak Pensions* decision by the Czech Constitutional Court, there was a clear disagreement that resulted in a clash.[93] Nonetheless, it is necessary to place that disagreement and clash in context: how it was produced and what was its impact. As to the former, the case concerned the export of domestic constitutional conflict between the Constitutional and the Administrative Court that pre-existed and was on-going. The Constitutional Court exercised the *Brunner ultra vires* jurisdiction but in a manner that ignored the pre-conditions that the German jurisprudence requires to be satisfied (*Atlanta Bananas, Lisbon Treaty Case, Mangold*). Therefore, the triggering of the nuclear option leading to the 'invalidation' of the CJEU's *Landtova* judgment was erroneous, ill-conceived and motivated by internal constitutional disagreements. The impact of the *Slovak Pensions* ruling has been subsequently minimal, with no further reference to it and with a gradual streamlining with the CJEU's approach. It has rightly been described as a footnote in the relationship between national courts and the CJEU, thus enabling the argument that even such conflicts can be circumvented.[94] At the end of the day, the system can withstand conflicts of such nature and can moreover call into account national orders if their disagreement goes at the heart of the structure of the EU system. One such example

[91] Wilkinson (2017).

[92] Bobić (2017), p. 1404 *et seq*; Wilkinson (2017), pp. 217–219.

[93] Bobić (2017), pp. 1422–1423.

[94] Ibid, 1422–1423.

relates to Poland and Hungary and the presently ongoing saga about violating judicial independence. These types of constitutional clashes can and will get a political dimension when resolution at the judicial level is not possible.

A much more problematic challenge arises out of the Danish Supreme Court's *Ajos Decision*,[95] where the answers given by the CJEU in a preliminary reference[96] on the application of the general principle of prohibition of age discrimination in horizontal situations prior to the entry into force of the EU Charter were expressly disregarded by the national court as being *ultra vires*.[97] The Danish Supreme Court held that the effect of EU norms on the Danish system is governed by the Act of Accession 1972 with later amendments.[98] Therefore, the amendment introduced in 1993 for the purpose of ratifying the Maastricht Treaty did not expressly confer powers to the EU in terms of the creation of general principles of law, including the principle of non-discrimination on the grounds of age. Consequently, such competence remained with the national system and the formulation of such general principles by the CJEU was an expression of competence that was not attributed. This is a challenge far more important than the *Slovak Pensions* case but it can be explained in terms of three factors. Firstly, the Danish Court failed to follow the preliminary reference rules that dictate the sending of a new reference, thus showing a remarkable unwillingness to utilize dialogue as a tool for resolving differences. That remains problematic and its impact is to be assessed in the future, yet it can be argued that the fault is shared given that the CJEU's reasoning in *Mangold* contributed to such an outcome. Secondly, the issue of age discrimination has been controversial,[99] primarily due to the poor justification by the CJEU that erroneously stated that "the source of the actual principle underlying the prohibition of those forms of discrimination being found, as is clear from the third and fourth recitals in the preamble to the directive, in various international instruments and in the *constitutional traditions common to the Member States*".[100] It has been argued that such a statement was inaccurate,[101] even though subsequently two Advocate Generals of the CJEU provided additional justification.[102] Nevertheless, it has been argued that

[95]Danish Supreme Court, Case no. 15/2014, *Dansk Industri (DI) acting for Ajos A/S,* Judgment of 6th December 2016, available in Danish at the Supreme Court's website www.hoejesteret.dk.

[96]CJEU, Case C-441/14, *Dansk Industri v Rasmussen* [2016], EU:C:2016:278.

[97]For analysis see: Neergaard and Sørensen (2017).

[98]Danish Supreme Court, Case no. 15/2014, *Dansk Industri (DI) acting for Ajos A/S,* Judgment of 6th December 2016, available in Danish at the Supreme Court's website www.hoejesteret.dk, p. 40.

[99]CJEU, Case C-144/04, *Mangold*, EU:C:2005:709; CJEU, Case C-555/07, *Kücükdeveci*, EU: C:2010:21. See difficulty of German Courts in *Honeywell* (BVerfG, 06 Juli 2010, – 2 BvR 2661/ 06 – Rn. (1-116)). For an English example see: *X v Mid Sussex Citizens Advice Bureau* [2011] EWCA Civ 28.

[100]CJEU, Case C-144/04, *Mangold*, para. 74, emphasis added. At the time, only Finland and Portugal could be cited as examples.

[101]de Mol (2011), p. 133; Papadopoulos (2011).

[102]Opinion of Advocate General Bot in Case C-555/07 Kücükdeveci, end of footnote 49 referring to the judgment of the European Court of Human Rights of 13 July 2004, *Pla and Puncernau*

"Only the Finnish Constitution (Article 6) and – if at all – the Portuguese Constitution (Article 59) contain such a provision. That is by no means enough for a 'common tradition'."[103] Thirdly, the matter is perhaps chronologically bypassed by the coming into force of the EU Charter and article 21(1) that expressly refers to the prohibition of age discrimination. Admittedly, the matter of horizontal application of the Charter remains, thus leaving room for reemergence of the issue. Consequently, the *Ajos* example offers a paradigm of break-up in communication that nonetheless has to be construed in the broader context, namely as one instance where the disagreement got out of hand and not as a rule.[104] To that point also the willingness of the CJEU to even alter its earlier position when national courts express clear reservations after using for a second time the preliminary reference procedure. One such example can be found in the *Taricco I* and *Taricco II* cases.[105]

Finally, a comment is needed about exit as the only solution when clashes arise. The Brexit negotiations and their complexity is a vivid example why the exit option is overstated and exaggerated. One can only imagine what would be the result of triggering such option available to Member States whenever courts express divergent opinions. The answer that is preferable is to give time to courts to reach an accommodating solution and only if they fail in a matter that is crucial to the stability of the system, one can trigger the political involvement as an auxiliary medium. If that also fails, then the procedures for ensuring that Member States comply with their EU obligations can be enforced (Articles 258-260 TFEU, Article 7 TEU) and only and if those also fail one can consider how important the matter is for the Member State in order for it to trigger Article 50 TEU. Proposing a mutually destructive course instead of mutually assured trust based on dialogue is not the solution.

Consequently, the primacy of EU law should not be regarded as subordination; it depends on competences as the examples of Article I-6 of Constitutional Treaty, Declaration 17 Lisbon Treaty and Opinion of the Legal Service of the Council (11197/07 (JUR 260), 22 June 2007) show. Moreover, the application of primacy of EU law is an endothermic matter, where external heat and disagreement is absorbed internally by the participating units, thus resulting to the release of pressure and stability. As regards EU law's respect for national identity, that is equally important as it encompasses and enables national perceptions to coexist with the CJEU's narrative. The unconditional primacy of EU law would render the national

---

*v. Andorra*, no. 69498/01, ECHR 2004-VIII, in which the European Court of Human Rights seems to accept that the prohibition of discrimination contained in Article 14 of the European Convention for the Protection of Human Rights and Fundamental Freedoms, signed in Rome on 4 November 1950, is to be applied to relations between private persons, thereby opening the way to review of the compatibility of purely private acts in the light of that article. Also, Opinion of Advocate General Trstenjak in Case C-80/06 Carp [2007] ECR I-4473, para. 69–70, 75–79.

[103]Stein (2011), p. 225.

[104]For example, see: CJEU, Case C-399/11, *Melloni* and the Spanish Constitutional Court Decision, *Melloni*, STC 26/2014, 13 February 2014.

[105]Case C-105/14, *Taricco I* and Case C-42/17, *Taricco II*.

identity clause (Article 4(2) TEU) redundant,[106] thus the Treaties prescribe a balanced system of cooperation and not conflict, that is founded on the formation of common principles of understanding and of a common constitutional space occupied by both the national and the post-national examples. It is in that regard that this paper presents constitutional discourse as a 3-dimensional concept: comprising national(s), post-national(s) and co-owned spaces. Accordingly, the full picture is possible only if one can view the 3-dimensions; otherwise a distorted and flat picture would result. What is proposed is a *Penrose type of relation*, i.e. one where the view is three dimensional and not flat and bi-dimensional. The discourse should be about the debate and about the process of constitutionalism as a fluid and never-ending phenomenon rather than about constitutions as rigid and insulated entities. What remains contentious is arguably the sovereignty issue as the origin of constitutionalism, namely who is the final decision-maker in the 3-dimensional state of affairs. That is a matter based in a bi-dimensional view and prone to conflict resolution, thus bypassing the reaching of consensus as part of the common space. Put differently, the sovereignty question is one that is better left unanswered.

# 3 Application of the Theoretical Views in the Cypriot Context

The paper now turns to the manner in which the Cypriot constitutional order has applied constitutional pluralism and global constitutionalism in practice.[107]

## *3.1 Cypriot Constitutional Context: A Snapshot*

In terms of substantive issues that need to be clarified, it is useful to offer a brief exegesis of the development of the legal order of the Republic of Cyprus. The classic distinction between 'Constitution' and 'constitutional law' is especially relevant to the Cypriot context given the fact that the Constitution of 1960 must be read in the light of the doctrine of necessity that, since 1964, offers the pillar on which the Constitution relies for its preservation.

As to the 1960 Constitution *per se*, it proved to be overly rigid and has been accurately described by De Smith as being conceived "by a constitutionalist and a mathematician in nightmarish dialogue".[108] It is exactly this mathematical logic

[106] Bobić (2017), p. 1397.

[107] On the legal system of the Republic of Cyprus, see in general: Papasavvas (1998); Tornaritis (1980); Kyriakides (1969); Polyviou (1975); Kombos (2010d), pp. 81–113; Loizou (2001); Nicolaou (2000); Evriviades (1975).

[108] De Smith (1964), p. 284.

combined with the assumed absolute mistrust between the two communities (Greek and Turkish) that the drafters of the Constitution highlighted, that resulted in a lengthy, detailed, rigid and permanent Constitution that has at its epicentre two principles: protected bi-communalism and a system of multiple checks and balances to ensure that the *status quo* remains intact and that minority rule is safeguarded. Therefore, the Constitution "attempted to insure that both communities would participate fully in the political decision-making process of the island".[109] Moreover, the Constitution stipulates in Article 182 that the Constitution can only by amended with a separate 2/3 majority in the House of Representatives, while in Annex III there is a list of 48 articles (out of the 199 and of which only Article 23 relates to a fundamental human right, that of property) that cannot be amended, thus creating a crucial bulk that can be seen as eternal clauses and which include naturally every article embedded on bi-communalism. This deadlock led President Makarios to *propose*[110] 13 amendments to the constitution that the Turkish community never managed to reject, given the immediate rejection by Turkey.

After a period of rising tensions and extensive armed confrontations between the two communities, the Turkish Cypriots withdrew from participation in the government, thus rendering the executive, legislative and judicial branch incapable to take any decision whatsoever. Therefore, the emerging *cul-de-sac* was such that rendered constitutional amendment impossible, excluded resort to the people's *pouvoir constituent*, since the majority rule could not apply, thus creating an existential dilemma: follow the letter of the Constitution having as a corollary the collapse of the State or resorting to the only constitutional alternative that would enable the functioning of the State until a political compromise could be reached. These dangerous for the existence of the Republic developments resulted in the introduction of legislation (Law 33/64) adopted by the House of Representatives in the absence of Turkish-Cypriots members that created a new Supreme Court that merged the jurisdictions of the constitutionally provided Supreme Constitutional Court and the High Court. In assessing the constitutionality of that legislation (Law 33/64), the doctrine of necessity emerged as the cornerstone of the legal order in the decision in *Mustafa Ibrahim.*[111] For the economy of space, the ruling approved as constitutional the exceptional departure from constitutional provisions when compliance with them was rendered impossible due to the withdrawal of the Turkish community. In terms of the requirements that *Ibrahim* established, those included: the existence of an urgent and unavoidable need or exceptional circumstances endangering the existence of the State that can be objectively established; no other alternative exists; the measures adopted are proportionate to the need; the measures are temporary in duration and are to apply for as long as the emergency exists; the legality of such

[109]Stavsky (1983), p. 356.

[110]Emphasis added. Note that the amendment proposals were just invitation to negotiation and was not a unilateral act of imposed amendment. See Tornaritis (1980), pp. 67–73.

[111]*The Attorney General of the Republic v. Mustafa Ibrahim* (1964) CLR 195.

measures is subject to judicial scrutiny; the burden of proof is placed on the side invoking the doctrine of necessity.

## 3.2 *The Balance Among Legal Spheres in Positive Law*

### 3.2.1 Hierarchy of the Rules of Law

In general, the Cypriot legal order has a clear hierarchy of sources of law, as its rules of law form a pyramid.[112] The Constitution used to lie at the top of the pyramid, as per Article 179(1) which declared the Constitution the "supreme law of the Republic". This provision had been characterized as "the cardinal and all pervasive norm of the Constitution; the bedrock of constitutional order".[113] Consequently, no law or decision could be repugnant to, or inconsistent with, any of the provisions of the Constitution.[114]

However, following the 2006 fifth amendment of the Constitution,[115] the *acquis communautaire* acquired precedence over the Constitution. More specifically, the fifth amendment inserted a new provision, namely Article 1A which envisages that "[n]o provision of the Constitution shall be deemed to annul laws enacted, acts done or measures taken by the Republic which become necessary by reason of its obligations as a member state of the European Union, nor does it prevent Regulations, Directives or other acts or binding measures of a legislative character, adopted by the European Union or the European Communities or by their institutions or competent bodies thereof on the basis of the Treaties establishing the European Communities or the Treaty of the European Union, from having legal effect in the Republic". The fifth amendment modified Article 179 of the Constitution as well, and now reads: "*[s]ubject to the provisions of Article 1A*, this Constitution shall be the supreme law of the Republic".[116]

At the third tier of the pyramid lie international treaties, conventions and agreements that have been ratified in accordance with the internal procedures, as found in Article 169 of the Constitution. Particularly, Article 169(3) provides that as from their publication in the official gazette of the Republic, such international instruments have superior force to any municipal law. However, such instruments do not enjoy supremacy over the Constitution (or EU law).

At the fourth tier of the pyramid are ordinary laws, either enacted by the House of Representatives after the independence of the Republic of Cyprus in 1960, or

[112] Markides (2006), pp. I–25. See also, *Malachtou v. Armefti* (1987) 1 CLR 207, p. 217.

[113] Pikis (2006), p. 9.

[114] See *Solomos Stylianou v. The Police* (1962) CLR 152; *Pantelis Petrides v. The Greek Communal Chamber* (1963) 2 CLR 417.

[115] Law relating to the Fifth Amendment of the Constitution, (Law No. 127(I)/2006).

[116] Emphasis added.

enacted during the colonial era by the British administration and maintained in force thereafter.[117] It is thus evident that, if a national court identifies an inconsistency between any law of the Republic and a ratified international treaty or the Constitution, it is obliged to refuse to implement the domestic law, but if possible, the Court should interpret the legislative act in conformity with the relevant international treaty and/or the Constitution.[118]

### 3.2.2 Cyprus: A Monist or a Dualist State?

It has been supported that Cyprus adopts the monist theory of incorporation of international treaties into its domestic legal order; thus, the provisions of international treaties that have been ratified according to Article 169(3) are directly applicable within Cypriot legal order and before national courts.[119] Similarly, Kyriakou argues that "Article 169(3) of the Constitution resolves the monism – dualism distinction in favour of the first".[120]

Nonetheless, the adoption of monism is not absolute, since Article 179 grants superiority to the Constitution over all other sources of law, thus the superiority of international norms of law resulting from ratified international treaties does not extend when there is a direct conflict with a constitutional provision.[121] On this point, Paraskeva argues that "the relationship between domestic and international law in Cyprus is characterized by its dualist character".[122]

The differences in opinion regarding the characterization of the system as either monist or dualist result from the approach towards the legal formality of Article 169 (2) of the Constitution which requires "the approval by law" of the international treaty, whereupon it shall be concluded. One view places the emphasis on Article 169(2) and the other on Article 169(3) that places treaties hierarchically above conflicting national laws and under the Constitution.[123] The issue is merely semantic given that "the difference between monistic systems and non-monistic systems [...] may have lost some of its impact as in most cases as in most European states

[117]See generally, Constitution of Cyprus, Articles 61-85 and 188.

[118]*Xenios Larkos v. Attorney General* (1995) 1 CLR 510, 515. See also, Article 179(2) of the Constitution, according to which "[n]o law or decision of the House of Representatives or of any of the Communal Chambers and no act or decision of any organ, authority or person in the Republic exercising executive power or any administrative function shall in any way be repugnant to, or inconsistent with, any of the provisions of this Constitution or any obligation imposed on the Republic as a result of its participation as a member state of the European Union".

[119]Pikis (2006), p. 44.

[120]Kyriakou (2010), p. 3.

[121]See Kombos (2015b), pp. 38–40.

[122]Paraskeva (2010), p. 121.

[123]Pikis (2006), p. 44; Emiliou (2006), p. 304; Loizou (2001), p. 220.

compliance with rules of international law can be achieved by interpreting rule of national law in the light of the particular treaty".[124]

### 3.2.3 The Special Position of International Human Rights Law and EU Law in the Cypriot Legal Order

The Cypriot system follows a very interesting approach towards human rights protection, especially in relation to the European Convention on Human Rights (ECHR), due to its particular constitutional framework regarding human rights. More specifically, Article 5 of the Treaty of Establishment of the Republic states that:

> [t]he Republic of Cyprus shall secure to everyone within its jurisdiction human rights and fundamental freedoms comparable to those set out in Section I of the European Convention for the Protection of Human Rights and Fundamental Freedoms signed at Rome on the 4th of November, 1950, and the Protocol to that Convention signed at Paris on the 20th of March.

However, the Constitution of Cyprus—following the example of many post-war constitutions—opted for a holistic approach, guaranteeing civil and political rights, as well as social rights.[125] Thus, Part II of the Constitution (Articles 6 to 35), is dedicated to the protection of human rights, and is substantially based on Articles 2 to 14 of the ECHR and its First Protocol, which served as the prototypes for drafting the relevant constitutional provisions.[126] In addition to these provisions, and after a proposal by Professor Marcel Bridel of the University of Lausanne at the Joint Constitutional Committee, social and economic rights were also included in the constitutional text.[127] In effect, Part II provides a catalogue of human rights that reflects those provided by the ECHR, which in "certain instances are wider in scope and substance compared to their counterparts found in the [ECHR]".[128]

Due to this special relation between the Cypriot Constitution and the ECHR, the general approach of the Supreme Court towards the ECHR and the European Court of Human Rights (ECtHR), that has been extremely extrovert.[129] The adoption of

---

[124]Thomassen (2009), p. 115 as cited in Kyriakou (2010), p. 3.

[125]*Dinos Kontos v. Republic (Permits Authority)* (1974) 3 CLR 112; *Apostolou and others v. Republic* (1984) 3 CLR 509; *Georghios Hadjisavva v. Republic (Council of Ministers)* (1972) 3 CLR 174.

[126]Report of Cyprus under Art. 40 of the International Covenant on Civil and Political Rights to the Human Rights Committee, UN Doc. CCPR/C/1/Add. 6, 6 April 1977; *Christou v. Christou* (1964) CLR 336, at 346. See also, Article 5 of the Treaty concerning the Establishment of the Republic of Cyprus between the United Kingdom Greece, Turkey and Cyprus, Cmnd 1252; UNTS vol. 382, 16 August 1960.

[127]See Tornaritis (1968), Chapter 1.

[128]Kyriakou (2010), p. 2.

[129]See for instance, *Attorney-General v. Afamis* 1 RSCC 121, *Pilavachi and Co v. International Chemical Co Ltd* (1965) 1 CLR 97, *Tsirides v. The Police* (1973) 2 CLR 204, *Kannas (Pombas) v. Police* (1968) 2 CLR 29, *Police v. Yiallourou* (1992) 2 CLR 147.

that approach resulted in attributing to the ECHR and to the relevant jurisprudence a status of a source of inspiration for the interpretation of the identical or parallel provisions of the Constitution.[130] In some instances, the Supreme Court did not merely adopt the jurisprudence of the ECtHR but it has on occasions discussed it and found it to be limited in scope.[131] In the case that the standard of protection applied by the Supreme Court is lower than that of the ECtHR, then the Supreme Court modifies its position; if on the other hand, the Cypriot standard is higher than that of the Strasbourg court, then the Supreme Court proceeds to apply its higher standard.

In regard to EU law, it has already been stated that its supremacy over Cypriot law was achieved through the fifth amendment of the Constitution and the subsequent introduction of new Article 1A. The introduction of Article 1A may be considered as the most comprehensive accommodation of the principle of supremacy of EU law when compared with the legal orders of other Member States. In relation to the fifth amendment, serious constitutional questions arise relating to procedure, structure, scope and substance.[132] Yet, the Supreme Court has never commented on those issues and proceeds to apply the letter of the requirements of the fifth amendment.[133]

The only notable exception to the lack of a comprehensive elaboration as to the status of the relationship between national constitutional law and EU law is the dissenting opinion of Judge Erotokritou in the *Myrto Christodolou* case, concerning the legality of the measures adopted to impose the 'bail-in' (i.e. the haircut of uninsured deposits).[134] There one can detect very interesting and advanced legal arguments that nonetheless fell short from developing a concrete and holistic approach towards the principle of supremacy of EU law. In his dissenting opinion, Judge Erotokritou stated:

> [w]here conflict is found and there is no ambiguity, Union law is to be applied, as it takes precedence and is directly applicable. Where conflict is found, but the requisite clarity as to the content and validity of the provisions of Union law is not present, then the national court has the power under Article 267 TFEU to apply with a preliminary question to the CJEU calling either for the interpretation of certain provisions of EU law, e.g. free movement of capital (Article 63 TEU), or for a ruling on the validity of specific legal instruments of the EU institutions. With this assistance, the national court may now proceed to examine the compatibility of national law with EU law.

Judge Erotokritou further specified:

> [n]ational sovereignty undoubtedly gives way to the supremacy of European law and rightly so I would say. But it seems that the further erosion of that national sovereignty and the parallel erosion of fundamental rights, often through informal procedures should at some

[130]Drzemczewski (1983), p. 279.

[131]See Kombos (2015b), pp. 44–46.

[132]For a critical assessment of the fifth amendment of the Constitution, see *infra*, Sect. 3.3.2.3. See also, Kombos (2015b), pp. 81–84.

[133]For an extensive analysis of the application of the principle of supremacy of EU law by Cypriot courts, see Kombos (2015b), pp. 93–105.

[134]*Myrto Christodoulou a.o. v. Central Bank of Cyprus a.o* (2013) 3 CLR 427.

stage be scrutinized by the CJEU, albeit indirectly through Article 267, as to whether it is compatible with the primary law of the European Union.

This is perhaps the centre of gravity for the approach of Judge Erotokritou. The judge adopts a realistic approach that accepts the limitation of national sovereignty as a logical consequence of the need to apply the principle of supremacy of EU law. This indirectly refers to the nature of the EU system as being founded on the principle of conferred powers that the Member States voluntarily transferred to the EU. It is respectfully submitted that if this point was explicitly included in Judge Erotokritou's dissenting opinion, then that would acquire a more holistic theoretical and substantial character in relation to the way that the national constitutional system sees the Union. This would therefore form an opportunity for starting to express the inherent reservations as regards the principle of supremacy of EU law and for starting to set potential limits to the acceptance of the principle. In any case, the *Myrto Christodoulou* judgment remains the point of reference and the reserve for the national constitutional system and it is argued that the Supreme Court must in the near future revisit the issue with that point of reference directly in mind.

### 3.2.4 The Establishment of Norm Combination in Specific Areas of Law

Contract Law

Contractual freedom in Cyprus is, to a certain extent, constitutionally regulated. In particular, Article 26(1) of the Constitution of Cyprus safeguards the right of every person "to enter freely into any contract subject to such conditions, limitations or restrictions as are laid down by the general principles of the law of contract". The prevailing view today holds that Article 26(1) guarantees the right to enter into legal contracts, subject to conditions and qualifications therein; it does not refer to the rights created under such contracts.[135] Contracts are regulated under the Law concerning Contracts (Cap. 149), which entered into force in 1931. Cap. 149 does not contain any limitations as to the choice of applicable law or provisions regarding litigation resolution. However, it is a fundamental principle that a term or provision of a law must be interpreted in such way that it is not incompatible with the Constitution.[136]

Cyprus, as a Member State to the EU, is bound by Regulation (EU) No 1215/2012 on jurisdiction and the recognition and enforcement of judgments in civil and commercial matters.[137] As a result, if the parties to a contract, regardless of their

[135] *Chimonides v. Manglis* (1967) 1 CLR 125; *Harvest Capital Management Ltd v. Georgios Tamasiou* (2003) 1C CLR 1683.

[136] Polyviou (2014), p. 18.

[137] Regulation (EU) No 1215/2012 of the European Parliament and of the Council of 12 December 2012 on jurisdiction and the recognition and enforcement of judgments in civil and commercial matters.

domicile, have agreed that a court (or courts) of a Member State are to have jurisdiction to settle any disputes which have arisen or which may arise in connection with a particular legal relationship, that court(s) shall have jurisdiction.[138] Additionally, Cyprus is bound by Regulation (EC) No 593/2008 on the law applicable to contractual obligations (Rome I).[139] Rome I provides that the parties to a contract can choose the applicable law; the applicable law may be applied to only a part or the whole of the contract and it can be changed at any time as long as all parties agree.[140]

### Collective Bargaining

Furthermore, Article 26(2) of the Constitution provides that "[a] law may provide for collective labour contracts of obligatory fulfilment by employers and workers with adequate protection of the rights of any person, whether or not represented at the conclusion of such contract". Such obligatory collective bargaining contracts have never entered into force. Instead, there are non-legally binding collective labour contracts, which are concluded between employers and trade unions.[141] Consequently, any rights or interests envisaged in these non-binding instruments are not justiciable, unless they are included in the employment contract between an employer and an employee.[142] In any case, it should be noted that despite the non-binding nature of these collective labour contracts, Cyprus is a party to a number of International Labour Organisation (ILO) conventions concerning collective bargaining; for instance, it is a party to the 1949 Right to Organise and Collective Bargaining Convention (No. 98) and to the 1981 Collective Bargaining Convention (No. 154). Both conventions have been ratified in accordance with Article 169(3) of the Constitution, and thus they enjoy superior force to any municipal law.[143]

### Regulation of Native Communities and Churches

Another interesting feature of the Cypriot Constitution is the delegation of specific legislative powers to the Greek communal chamber and to the Turkish communal chamber, regarding educational, cultural, religious and other matters of purely

[138] Ibid, Article 25.

[139] Regulation (EC) No 593/2008 of the European Parliament and of the Council of 17 June 2008 on the law applicable to contractual obligations (Rome I).

[140] Ibid, Article 3.

[141] Polyviou (2016), p. 121.

[142] *Michalis Soteriou v. Cyprus Airways Ltd* (Civil App. 210/2007, Decision of 21 May 2012).

[143] The 1949 Right to Organise and Collective Bargaining Convention (No. 98) was ratified by the Ratification Law concerning the Right to Organise and Collective Bargaining Convention (No. 98) (Law 18/1966); the 1981 Collective Bargaining Convention (No. 154) has been ratified by the Convention (No. 154) for the Promotion of Collective Bargaining (Ratification) Law (Law 241/1988).

communal nature.[144] Nonetheless, since the withdrawal of all members of the Turkish community from all state organs in 1964 and the 1965 self-dissolution of the Greek communal chamber, these provisions have become obsolete.[145]

As regards religious groups, there are five main religions that enjoy special constitutional status; the Orthodox Christian religion, the Islamic religion, the Maronites, the Roman Catholics (Latins) and the Armenians.[146] Other religions or religious groups are not considered to be religious groups in the constitutional sense, however they enjoy the right of freedom of religion under Article 18 of the Constitution, thus, no legislative, executive or administrative act of the state can discriminate against them.

Article 110 of the Constitution asserts special treatment to two of the main religious groups on the island. Article 110(1) provides that "[t]he Autocephalous Greek-Orthodox Church of Cyprus shall continue to have the exclusive right of regulating and administering its own internal affairs and property in accordance with the Holy Canons and its Charter in force [. . .]". Similarly, Article 110(2) envisages that "[a]ll matters relating to or in any way affecting the institution or foundation of Vakf or the vakfs or any vakf properties, [. . .] shall be governed solely by and under the Laws and Principles of Vakfs and the laws and regulations enacted or made by the Turkish Communal Chamber [. . .]". In terms of assessment, it has been argued that "the model prevailing in Cyprus is essentially a pluralistic model, which recognizes and embraces the public dimension to religion, while at the same time attempting co-operation with all religions. The significance of faith in people's lives is considered as worthy of protection by the state and where the function of the state overlaps with religious concerns, the state seeks to accommodate religious views, in so far as they are not inconsistent with state's interests."[147] As a result, the notion of religious pluralism is engraved in the constitutional structure "through the recognition that the state and the various religions occupy in principle different societal structures; religious neutrality is not, however, achieved simply because there is religious autonomy, but also through positive measures on behalf of the state, which aim at the protection of religions. Other religions and rites, such as the Jews, the Jehovah's Witnesses, the Buddhists, or the Protestants, or the Orthodox Christians who follow the Old Calendar, enjoy religious freedom according to Article 18 of the Constitution, and are equal before the law, so that no legislative, executive or administrative act should discriminate against them. However, such religions are not considered as religious groups in the constitutional sense and therefore, do not enjoy the special constitutional status of the five main religions of the island; difference in treatment between the five constitutionally recognized religions and

---

[144]See Part V of the Constitution (Articles 86–111).

[145]It should be noted that in regard to the provisions concerning the Greek communal chamber, its powers have been conferred (and are exercised) by the House of Representatives, as well as the Ministry of Education and Culture.

[146]See Article 2 of the Constitution.

[147]Emilianides (2011), p. 74.

other religions of the island principally occur with respect to religious education, direct financing and family law matters."[148]

Moreover, Article 111 of the Constitution, prior to its amendment, provided for the adjudication of issues relevant to marriage and divorce of members of the Greek-Orthodox Church. However, after the first amendment of the Constitution in 1989,[149] any matter relating to divorce, judicial separation or restitution of conjugal rights or to family relations of the members of the Greek-Orthodox Church are cognizable by family courts.[150] The case law of the Supreme Court indicates that the Greek-Orthodox church does not constitute organ or authority of the Republic; it is a private entity enjoying exclusive competence with respect to its internal affairs.[151]

## *3.3 The Dynamics of the Relations Among Legal Spheres in Positive Law*

### 3.3.1 A Mixity of Systems and External Influences

Cyprus gained its independence from the British Empire in 1960 and the English common law plays an important role in the domestic legal order until today. Article 29(1) of the Law concerning the Courts of Justice (Law 14 of 1960), which provides the applicable law in the Cypriot order, in subparagraph 1(c) encompasses that "the common law and the principles of equity shall apply, save where they do not coincide with or where they are in conflict with the Constitution of the Republic of Cyprus or where any law provides differently". Put differently, the courts do not apply common law and equity in a mechanical manner but on condition that it is suitable for Cyprus.[152]

Another prime example of such influence of the English legal system in Cyprus is the use of the English language in all governmental sectors, including judicial proceedings, despite gaining its independence from the British Empire in 1960. For instance, Article 3 of the Constitution clearly provides that the official languages of the Republic are Greek and Turkish and all legislative, executive and administrative acts and documents shall be drawn up in both official languages.[153] What is more, judicial proceedings shall be conducted or made and judgments shall be drawn

[148]Ibid, 75.

[149]Law concerning the First Amendment of the Constitution (Law 95/1989).

[150]Emilianides (2006).

[151]*Autocephalous and Apostolic Orthodox Church of Cyprus v. House of Representatives* (1990) 3 CLR 338.

[152]Symeonides (2003), p. 451.

[153]The publication of laws solely in the Greek language was held to be a justified diversion from the Constitution due to the 1964 bi-communal crisis; see *Mamas Koumi v. Mikkos Kortari* (1983) 1 CLR 856; *Al Shark Undwearwear Manufacturing v. Sunnydays Shipping* (1990) 1 CLR 270; *Kamal Hassanein v. Hellenic Island and/or Island* (1994) 1 CLR 303.

up in the Greek language if the parties are Greek, in the Turkish language if the parties are Turkish, and in both the Greek and the Turkish languages if the parties are Greek and Turkish.[154] Yet, Article 189 of the Constitution envisages a transitional provision according to which, notwithstanding Article 3, all laws which would continue to be in force (as per the provisions of Article 188) could continue to be in the English language and the English language could be used in any proceedings before any court in the Republic for a period of 5 years after the date of the entry into operation of the Constitution.

After the elapse of the transitional 5-year period, the House of Representatives passed the 1965 Laws and Courts (Text and Proceedings) Law, which extended the usage of any language other than the official until the governmental machinery was in a position to comply with Article 3 of the Constitution.[155] This legislation was in force until 1988, when the House of Representatives repealed the 1965 Laws and Courts (Text and Proceedings) Law, by virtue of Article 3 of Law concerning the Official Languages of the Republic.[156] The 1988 Law restored the constitutional order (i.e. the provisions of Articles 3 and 189) through the re-establishment of the Greek and Turkish languages as the official languages of the Republic.

Indeed, the influence of English common law is such that Cyprus is frequently regarded as a common law jurisdiction.[157] However, this is not the case. The Cypriot legal system is a *unique mixed legal system* in which (most disciplines of) private law and criminal law follow the common law, whereas public law follows a continental orientation.[158] In specific, the three main Codes of the Cypriot legal system—the Criminal Code (Cap. 154), enacted as Law 8/30, the Contract Law (Cap. 149), enacted as Law 24/30 and the Civil Wrongs Law (Cap. 148) enacted as Law 35/32—directly derived from common law (especially from the Nigerian Criminal Code, the Indian Contract Code and the Indian Civil Wrongs Code). These Codes "constituted an effective codification of common law principles in their respective fields; the statutes in question are still in force today, often with little modification".[159] On the other hand, in the field of public law, there is strong presence of the influence of the Greek *droit administratif*,[160] both in terms of the normative framework and of the case law of the Supreme Court. The presence of that influence is evident in the form of frequent reliance on Greek academic works and on

[154] Constitution, Article 3(4).

[155] The Laws and Courts (Text and Proceedings) Law (Law 51 of 1965). The constitutionality of this law was affirmed by the Supreme Court in *Mamas Koumi v. Mikkos Kortari* (1983) 1 CLR 856.

[156] Law concerning the Official Languages of the Republic (Law 67/1988).

[157] Hatzimihail (2015), p. 84.

[158] Ibid, 75.

[159] Hatzimihail (2013), p. 75.

[160] Ibid, 79 where it is rightly argued that the Law concerning the Codification of the General Principles of Administrative Law (Law 158(I)/1999) reflects "the definitions of from the treatises of Professor Prodromos Dagtoglou on administrative law and procedure".

the case law of the Greek *Conseil d' Etat*,[161] to the point where it is reasonable to argue that it is rare to find a decision in the area of administrative law where reference is not made either directly or indirectly to Greek academic works and/or to Greek jurisprudence.

### 3.3.2 Vertical and Horizontal Trans-Constitutional (Judicial) Dialogues

Because of the abovementioned mixed legal tradition of the Cypriot system and its particular connection with the ECHR, the Cypriot courts draw substantial influence from the case law of the ECtHR and significant guidance from the case law of foreign legal orders. Therefore, it is argued that there exists some kind of a horizontal type of dialogue between Cypriot courts and the ECtHR, as well as between the national courts (especially the Supreme Court) and foreign legal orders (i.e. foreign case law), as they have a persuasive rather than a legally binding effect in the Cypriot legal order. On the other hand, it seems to exist (or could exist) a vertical type of dialogue between the Cypriot court and the CJEU, in the sense that in case of an ambiguity regarding EU law, the national courts can always enable the procedure for preliminary references.

#### Vertical Dialogue with the CJEU

In an attempt to achieve uniformity of interpretation and implementation of EU law between EU member states (and their national courts), the Treaty on the Functioning of the EU (TFEU) created a mechanism for a multilevel and continuous dialogue[162] between the CJEU and national courts; the procedure for preliminary references (Article 267 of the TFEU, ex Article 234 of the Treaty establishing the European Community). The judgment of the CJEU on a preliminary reference binds the national court that made the reference and in subsequent cases where the same point of EU law arises, national courts may either follow the existing judgment or make a fresh reference.[163] Consequently, such dialogue between the national legal orders and the Luxembourg Court is vertical.

---

[161]There is a plethora of case law on this point. See, for instance, *Cypriot Dental Association v. Competition Commission* (2003) 4 CLR 921; *Drousiotis v. The Cyprus Broadcasting Corporation* (1984) 3 CLR 546; *Tasmi Trading v. Republic* (1988) 3 CLR 782; *Tamassos Tobacco Suppliers and Co. v. Republic* (1992) 3 CLR 60; *Director of Customs v. Grecian Hotel* (1985) 1 CLR 476; *P. Makrides Ltd* (1997) 1 CLR 1424; *Golden Trans Ltd*, Case 537/2002, 25 September 2002.

[162]Timmermas (2004), p. 399.

[163]Case 28-30/62, *Da Costa* (1963) ECR 31.

On an internal level,[164] the procedural issue of creating the legal route for submitting a preliminary reference to the CJEU was resolved by the Courts (Amendment) Law of 2007[165] that added a subsection to Article 25 of the Courts Law of 1960.[166] The effect of the amendment was that where a first instance court decides after request by one of the parties to submit or not to submit a preliminary reference to the CJEU, that decision of the lower court could within 15 days be appealed against to the Supreme Court. In 2008 a further amendment was introduced to the Courts Law that provided for an appeal only against decisions to submit a reference, thus removing the possibility of appeal where the lower court decided not to make a reference.[167]

This amendment rendered the system even more rigid than it already was and the justification was that in that way unnecessary delays would be avoided. Put differently, the legislative framework was problematic and established a concentrated supervisory system that was unnecessarily restrictive. The Courts Law was once again amended in 2009 to remove the appeal right for all situations,[168] thus streamlining the approach of the Cypriot legal order with those of the majority of Member States and more importantly with the case law of the CJEU. Finally, it must also be noted that in March 2008 the Supreme Court adopted a procedural regulation providing for basic general rules to be followed by Cypriot courts when referring a matter to the CJEU.[169]

The Cypriot paradigm has been examined some time ago and was found to be unnecessarily reserved towards the preliminary reference procedure.[170] Initially, the Supreme Court was reluctant regarding the use of the preliminary reference procedure,[171] leading to the bypass of its treaty obligations.[172] Yet, the Supreme Court's decision in *Alpha Bank Cyprus Ltd*[173] marks the stage of maturity of the Court's cooperation and dialogue with the CJEU. Through a careful and methodical approach, the Supreme Court in *Alpha Bank Cyprus Ltd*, first "established that the application of a provision of EU law was necessary for deciding the case and that there was at least some uncertainty as to the way this provision must be interpreted"; and second "while not adjudicating the case, it decided on all issues other than those

[164]For an analysis of the applicable national legislative framework and the EU rules on preliminary references, see Kombos (2015b), pp. 129–172.

[165]Law 99(I)/2007.

[166]Law 14/1960, as amended.

[167]The Courts (Amendment) (No. 4) Law of 2008 (Law 119(I)/2008).

[168]The Courts (Amendment) (No. 2) Law of 2009 (Law 129(I)/2009).

[169]The Preliminary Reference to the Court of Justice of the European Communities Procedural Regulation (No. 1) of 2008.

[170]Kombos (2010a).

[171]See for instance, *Cresencia Cabotaje Motilla v. Republic* (2008) 3 CLR 29.

[172]For a detailed analysis of the relevant case law, see Kombos (2015b), pp. 140–156.

[173]*Alpha Bank Cyprus v. Si Senh Dau and others*, Joint Civil Appeals 23-29/2013, Decision of 13 September 2013.

of EU law, thus allowing its final decision to be handed down shortly after the ruling of the ECJ, without any further loss of time".[174] Surmising, it is argued that today all conditions exist for national courts to take a more proactive role in this vertical dialogue, as it has acquired sufficient experience in its approach towards the procedure of preliminary references.[175]

### Horizontal Dialogue with the ECHR/ECtHR and Foreign Jurisdictions

It is argued that the Supreme Court of Cyprus has engaged in a long-standing dialogue with external legal sources and has shown great willingness to define ambiguous constitutional concepts with direct reference to decisions originating in foreign jurisdictions.[176] One of the most interesting examples of reference to foreign jurisdictions as regards due process is the decision in *Republic of Cyprus (Minister of Finance and Another) v. Demetrios Demetriades*[177] where the Supreme Court in a lengthy judgment examined the constitutionality of a tax law[178] and the taxing, thereunder, of the husband on the combined total of his and his wife's income derived from sources other than from her own labour. The Supreme Court examined the alleged violation through the tax law of Articles 24 and 28 of the Constitution guaranteeing proportionate taxation and equality, through the lens of US jurisprudence.[179] The Court engaged in perhaps the most expansive use of comparative law and foreign jurisprudence, thus analysing in considerable depth the US case law on due process as well as that of India, Germany and Greece.

In a different context, the judicial approach to the fundamental rights has been extremely favourable and often forward looking, with the Supreme Court resorting to the use of the comparative method to construe ambiguities in the constitutional provisions. Moreover, and as already mentioned, the ECHR has proved instrumental in that process, with the Supreme Court illustrating a remarkable willingness to use the ECHR and the jurisprudence of the ECtHR as a *complementary interpretative guide* for national constitutional provisions. In effect, the Cypriot standard of protection is an amalgam of national constitutional law and ECHR principles.

The willingness of the Supreme Court to engage with other legal systems could also be seen in the strong and frequent use of the comparative method. Such an example is the case before the Supreme Court in *Police v. Ekdotiki Eteria*[180] that

---

[174]Lycourgos (2016), pp. 632–633.

[175]Ibid, p. 637.

[176]See Kombos (2015b), pp. 33–46.

[177]*Republic of Cyprus (Minister of Finance and Another) v. Demetrios Demetriades* (1977) 3 CLR 213.

[178]Article 21 of the Income Tax Law (Law 58/1961).

[179]From a real plethora of US decisions, particular emphasis was placed on *Hoeper v. Tax Commission of Wisconsin*, 284 US 206 (1931).

[180]*Police v. Ekdotiki Eteria* (1982) 2 CLR 63.

concerned whether Article 50(1) of the Criminal Code contravened Article 19 of the Constitution on the freedom of speech. The relevant provision introduced a criminal offence for publishing in any form false news or information which may impair public order or the confidence of the public in the State or its organs. Therefore, the issue was whether the freedom of speech extends to publishing false news and information. The Supreme Court held that the right safeguarded by Article 19 (1) and (2) of the Constitution is not limited by reference to the truth or falsity of a statement made in the exercise of such right; therefore, it extends to false as well as to true statements. Moreover, the Court found that Article 50(1) of the Criminal Code is constitutional, in view of Article 19(3) of the Constitution, provided the expression "impairing public confidence in the State and its organs" is interpreted as referring to the organs of the State as institutions of Government. Therefore, it was held that publications containing false information which had the capacity to shake the public's confidence into the public order or to the State or its agents constituted an acceptable limitation to the right to free speech in accordance with Article 19 of the Constitution of the Republic, as long as the information related to the State and its organs and not to individual persons carrying executive power.

The interesting point in *Police v. Ekdotiki Eteria* is that the Supreme Court reached the above conclusions after citing and analysing three decisions from the USA,[181] one from the UK,[182] one from India[183] and four from the ECtHR.[184] In specific, the Court stated that:

> The decisions of the USA courts on the legitimacy of limitations to freedom of expression, are of limited assistance because unlike Article 19 of our Constitution, the limitations are not ingrained in the Constitution but are the product of case law evolved in the context of the judicial doctrine acknowledging residual powers to the State to legislate 'police powers' as a concomitant of sovereignty. Also, decisions of the European Commission and European Court of Human Rights, though instructive, offer only indirect assistance to the solution of the problem in hand for they concentrate primarily on the definition of the outer limits of State power to enact restrictions not inconsistent with the Convention, leaving a wide margin of appreciation to member States as to the need to limit the right guaranteed by Article 10 (2) of the Convention.[185]

## The Adaptation of the Constitution to Globalisation and Supranational Obligations

The interaction of the domestic system with external legal spheres has not really affected the Cypriot legal order, as the imposition of norms by globalisation

[181] *Whitney v. California* (1926) 274 US 357; *Schenck v. United States* (1919) 249 US 47 (52).

[182] See *Attorney-General v. the BBC* (1980) 3 AllER 161.

[183] Basu (1961), p. 658, and the decision in *Kedermath*, cited therein, per *Police v. Ekdotiki Eteria* (1982) 2 CLR 63, p. 75.

[184] *The Handyside* (1976) Vol. 24 Publications of the European Courts of Human Rights, p. 2.

[185] *Police v. Ekdotiki Eteria* (1982) 2 CLR 63, p. 72.

happened in a rather natural way based on consensus. Article 179 of the Constitution and the supremacy of the Constitution over any other norm (subject, of course, to the provisions of EU law) serve as the test according to which conflicts between legal norms are resolved. Due to Article 179 and the insistence and adherence to the pyramid of norms as described above,[186] the Cypriot legislator felt the need to proceed to constitutional amendments so as to accommodate norms that emerged from globalisation as well as supranational legal orders. Thus far, the House of Representatives introduced ten constitutional amendments.[187]

The Constitution can be validly described as a living instrument that is designed to regulate the lives of present and future generations. As a result, it must evolve in order to accommodate contemporary aspirations, interests and desires, to embody the modern needs of society, to reflect political realities and to achieve a more efficient functioning of democratic government as dictated by contemporary norms which emerged from globalisation. This view seems to have been embraced by the Cypriot legislator, in the sense that a number of amendments have been implemented for this exact purpose.

For instance, the first constitutional amendment (which modernized family law), was deemed necessary in order to revise and adapt state laws regulating family relations in accordance with contemporary legal principles and social perceptions.[188] The second amendment (which extended the right of citizens to vote from the minimum age of 21–18) was deemed absolutely necessary for adapting to modern facts and perceptions for a more efficient functioning of democratic government.[189] Similarly, the sixth constitutional amendment (which enabled authorities to intervene with the right to privacy on specific grounds) was considered necessary for the security of the Republic, public safety, the prevention and suppression of crime, as well as the protection of constitutionally safeguarded rights and freedoms of every person.[190]

The Constitution was not only amended in order to adapt its text to modern facts and perception, but it was further amended in order to meet Cyprus's human rights obligations undertaken by virtue of international treaties and to harmonize Cyprus law with EU law. For instance, the need to ensure transparency in public life and to

---

[186] See Sect. 3.2.1.

[187] See, Law concerning the First Amendment of the Constitution (Law 95/1989); Law concerning the Second Amendment of the Constitution (Law 106(I)/1996); Law concerning the Third Amendment of the Constitution (Law 115(I)/1996); Law concerning the Fourth Amendment of the Constitution (Law 104(I)/2002); Law concerning the Fifth Amendment of the Constitution (Law 127(I)/2006); Law concerning the Sixth Amendment of the Constitution (Law 51(I)/2010); Law concerning the Seventh Amendment of the Constitution (Law 68(I)/2013); Law concerning the Eighth Amendment of the Constitution (Law 130(I)/2015); Law concerning the Ninth Amendment of the Constitution (Law 69(I)/2016); Law concerning the Tenth Amendment of the Constitution (Law 93(I)/2016).

[188] See the preamble of the Law concerning the First Amendment of the Constitution, ibid.

[189] See the preamble of the Law concerning the Second Amendment of the Constitution, ibid.

[190] See the preamble of the Law concerning the Sixth Amendment of the Constitution, ibid.

enact anti-corruption measures for the prevention of criminal offences, as per Article 8(2) of the ECHR, led to the ninth constitutional amendment in regard to Article 15. Most recently the House of Representatives introduced the tenth amendment (deletion of any reference to the death penalty) with the view of harmonizing the text of the Constitution with the obligation of abolishing the death penalty, as envisaged in binding international human rights instruments, such as the Charter of Fundamental Rights of the European Union, the ECHR and its Additional Protocols Nos. 6 and 13 and the International Covenant on Civil and Political Rights and Additional Protocol No. 2. It should be noted that the amended provisions were already inactive, as the death penalty had been *de facto* abolished, since 1962.

As to the interaction of EU law with the Constitution, the fifth amendment and the introduction of new Article 1A are of great significance. Cyprus acceded to the EU in 2004, however the supremacy of EU was not introduced until 2006. A constitutional amendment was deemed necessary by the House of Representatives and the executive branch following the Supreme Court's decision in *Attorney General v. Costas Constantinou.*[191] The case concerned the implementation of the relevant EC Framework Decision relating to the European arrest warrant[192] by Law 133(1)/2004 and the issuing of an order of surrender and extradition of the Respondent (Mr. Constantinou), a citizen of both Cyprus and the UK, to the UK. The main argument was based on the fact that Cyprus had an obligation to implement the Framework Decision, yet EU law enabled its Member State to select the way for doing so. Therefore, it was questioned whether the selected way for complying with the obligations arising from the membership to the EU was compatible with Article 11(2) of the Constitution, which prohibits the extradition of Cypriot citizens.[193] Therefore, the constitutionality of Law 133(1)/2004 was questioned, with the first instance judge finding that the Law in question was unconstitutional. Subsequently, the Republic appealed against that judgment and the case went before the Supreme Court.

One of the main arguments of the Republic was that the principle of supremacy of EU law clearly states that EU law is superior even against national constitutional provisions. Therefore, because Law 133(1)/2004 implements the EU Framework Decision as part of complying with the Republic's obligations arising from membership to the Union, then the national implementing measure becomes an extension of EU law. The consequence is that the relevant law acquires the protection of the supremacy of EU law even against the Constitution.

The Supreme Court rejected this argument on the basis that the Framework Decision could not prevail over Article 11 of the Constitution, which does not allow the extradition of Cypriot nationals. More precisely, as Lycourgos argues:

---

[191] *Attorney General of the Republic v. Costas Constantinou* (2005) 1 CLR 1356.

[192] Council Framework Decision 2002/584/JHA of 13 June 2002 on the European arrest warrant and the surrender procedures between Member States (EEL 190, 18.7.2002, p. 1).

[193] On the matter see the earlier decision in *Attorney-General v. Afamis* 1 RSCC 121.

> the Court held that the provisions of a framework decision in order to apply in a Member State need to be transposed into national legislation. This, according to the Court, had not been properly done in the Republic of Cyprus, given that, even if a transposing law had been enacted[194] which allowed Cypriot nationals to be surrendered as a result of the execution of a European arrest warrant, this law was unconstitutional. Therefore, the proper transposition of the framework decision would have required an amendment of the Constitution.[195]

As a result, the House of Representatives enacted the Law concerning the Fifth Amendment of the Constitution, which provided, *inter alia*, for the supremacy of EU law vis-à-vis the Constitution, via new Article 1A; a single article that would then function as the point of reference for any arising incompatibility of EU law with national constitutional law. Nonetheless, it is submitted that there is a crucial problem with Article 1A of the Constitution and that problem has both formal and substantial aspects.[196] Formally, Article 1 of the Constitution is included in the list of Annex III of the Constitution as an unamendable provision.[197] The addition of paragraph A to Article 1 is only indirectly justified in the Preamble of the Law concerning the Fifth Amendment of the Constitution as not amounting to a constitutional amendment of a basic constitutional provision. It is submitted that this approach is not correct and is at best playing with formalism, because the addition to any article of the Constitution cannot be construed as anything other than a constitutional amendment. Strictly speaking, the rest of Article 1 of the Constitution remains unaltered yet the content of Article 1 after the addition of paragraph A has changed. The issue has also a substantial aspect since the content of Article 1A of the Constitution in effect incorporates the supremacy of EU law, while at the same time the insertion to Article 1 of the Constitution was deliberate in order to pre-empt any future constitutional amendment. That is circular, because even if one accepts that Article 1A does not amount to a constitutional amendment of a basic article of the Constitution, then this would mean that with the same ease and on the same logic paragraph A can be removed at any point.

In addition, there is also another serious issue with Article 1A of the Constitution since the Supreme Court and the legal community in general has been extremely cautious with constitutional amendments. There has never before or since been any amendment of a basic constitutional provision. This is significant given what has been cited previously about the need to protect the Republic from any problems arising from constitutional amendments of basic provisions.[198] There seems to be an antithesis with the classic judicial approach towards constitutional amendments which might have shifted towards accepting constitutional amendments but only where those do not affect basic provisions.

---

[194]Law 133(I)/2004.

[195]Lycourgos (2010), p. 104.

[196]For an analysis of the problems of the fifth amendment of the Constitution, see Kombos (2015b), pp. 81–84.

[197]See *supra*, Sect. 3.1.

[198]*President of the Republic v. House of Representatives* (1986) 3 CLR 1439.

Lastly, it would have been expected that the Supreme Court would have at least examined even as obiter the nature of Article 1A of the Constitution; this has never happened so far. It is not argued that the Supreme Court should now find the constitutional amendment as unconstitutional since it is perhaps too late, but it would be expected at least to clarify that the addition of a paragraph to a basic constitutional provision does not amount to a constitutional amendment. The implications from such an acceptance would be dramatic for the Cypriot legal order as it offers a way for complementing the doctrine of necessity with this new rationale. Nonetheless, this would be unwise in terms of constitutional propriety, yet it is imperative that the Supreme Court takes a position on the matter as the issue exceeds by far the matter of supremacy of EU law raised above.

## The Power of Judicial Review of the Compliance with International and Transnational Law

The Cypriot courts have the authority to assess the constitutionality of laws and executive orders and decisions under Articles 144 and 146 of the Constitution. In other words, the procedures codified therein allow the courts to assess whether a public person or organ adhered to the principle of legality, in the sense that the law or order/decision under scrutiny is compatible with hierarchically superior norms (i.e. international treaties ratified as per Article 169, EU law and constitutional law).

More specifically, Article 144 reads:

> [a] party to any judicial proceedings, including proceedings on appeal, may, at any stage thereof, raise the question of the unconstitutionality of any law or decision or any provision thereof material for the determination of any matter at issue in such proceedings and thereupon the Court before which such question is raised shall reserve the question for the decision of the Supreme Constitutional Court and stay further proceedings until such question is determined by the Supreme Constitutional Court.

Due to the events of 1964 and the withdrawal of Turkish Cypriots from their participation in public offices, the House of Representatives enacted the abovementioned Law 33/64, which created a new Supreme Court that merged the jurisdictions of the constitutionally provided Supreme Constitutional Court and the High Court. It further established that whenever the parties raise a question of the unconstitutionality of any law, the procedure will not be referred before the Supreme Court but will be decided by the court before which the issue of unconstitutionality was raised.[199] Nonetheless, Article 144(1) has not become completely obsolete, but rather its provisions are applicable in the case of questions of unconstitutionality

[199]This approach was confirmed in the landmark decision of *Ibrahim*, were the Supreme Court indicated that: "[w]e unanimously now hold that the procedure for reference under Article 144(1) of the Constitution, by any court, to the Supreme Constitutional Court, is no longer applicable or necessary; and all questions of alleged unconstitutionality should be treated as issues of law in the proceedings, subject to revision on appeal, in due course. The procedure for reference introduced into our legal system by the Constitution, has caused in actual practice during the four-year period

before family law courts. In other words, a family law court refers question of the unconstitutionality of any law or decision or any provision material for the determination of any matter at issue in such proceedings to the Supreme Court.[200]

Article 146, on the other hand, establishes the right of an aggrieved person to file a recourse before the Administrative Court, against decisions of the state. More specifically, Article 146 of the Constitution, as amended,[201] provides that the Administrative Court has "exclusive jurisdiction to decide in the first instance on a recourse made to it on a complaint that a decision, an act or omission of any organ, authority or person, exercising any executive or administrative authority is contrary to any of the provisions of this Constitution or of any law or is made in excess or in abuse of powers vested in such organ or authority or person". Upon such recourse, the Administrative Court has the authority to: (a) confirm, either in whole or in part, such administrative decision or act or omission, (b) declare, either in whole or in part, such decision or act to be null and void and of no effect whatsoever, (c) declare that such omission, either in whole or in part, ought not to have been made and that whatever has been omitted should have been performed, or (d) amend, either in whole or in part, such decision or act, in the event that the issue before the Court concerns tax issues or it is a decision relating to an international protection procedure in accordance with EU law.[202]

Finally, the Court's stance towards the intervention with fundamental rights, such as the contractual freedom, that exceed the limits imposed by the constitutional text for reasons of public order is of particular interest.[203] In *Chimonides v. Manglis*,[204] the leading case on the matter, the issue at hand was the constitutionality of Law 19/65 that enabled the Council of Ministers to declare certain areas as 'depressed areas', thus placing any applicable contractual relationships under the control of the Court especially in relation to rent control. The rationale was that, because of the events of 1964, certain business premises were in dangerous proximity to areas of conflict which in turn affected in a negative way their ability to conduct business, thus meriting their protection by the State. In terms of facts, the case concerned an application under Article 3(1) of Law 19/65 for the determination of rent payable in respect of a shop situated in an area declared to be a depressed zone. The decision of the Supreme Court, on appeal from a first instance judgment that had dismissed the application for rent control, was split as regards the origins for intervening with Article 26(1) of the Constitution and the freedom to enter into legal contracts.

---

of its life, obstruction, delay and expense in ordinary litigation, of which parties are now relieved by the new Law".

[200] *Nikolaou a.o. v. Nikolaou a.o.* (1992) 1 CLR 1338.

[201] Law relating to the Eighth Amendment of the Constitution.

[202] Article 146(4) of the Constitution of Cyprus.

[203] For a further analysis, see Kombos (2015a), pp. 216–228.

[204] *Chimonides v. Manglis* (1967) 1 CLR 125.

On the one hand, the first view was expressed by Judge Josephides[205] and the alternative view was expressed by Judge Triantafyllides.[206] In relation to Article 26 of the Constitution, Josephides J. relied primarily on case law of the Supreme Court of the United States[207] and concluded that:

> [c]onsidering the circumstances under which the Law of 1965 came to be enacted, I am satisfied that severe economic conditions, arising out of the well-known recent events since December, 1963, created a public economic emergency, calling for the exercise of the State's police power. I am further satisfied that relief is justified by the economic emergency, that it is of an appropriate character and is granted upon reasonable conditions. I, therefore, hold that the aforesaid Law of 1965 is a reasonable and valid exercise of the State's reserved power to protect the vital interests of the public during the emergency and that it does not violate Article 26(1) of our Constitution.[208]

Therefore, it was held that the intervention with the freedom of contract can be justified by reference to the concept of 'State's police powers' which can apply to both the formation of contracts and also to their content but within specific and restrictive conditions. It was also held that this concept is of a special nature and forms part of the reserve powers of the State, thus is impliedly contained in the Constitution. The main supporting premise is that the freedom of contract is not absolute and can be restricted, while in situations of extreme economic emergency those restrictions can be expanded in order to maintain that "contractual relations are worthwhile".[209]

Put differently, a variation of 'necessity' justifies the intervention of the State in order to preserve the essence of contractual obligations that is the continuity of the worthwhile of having them. Judge Josephides opted for the application of an alternative concept, that of reserve police powers that is nonetheless also dependent on economic emergency. The importance of this argument is that it facilitates the limitation of the specific right through the deployment of an implied power of the State. Consequently, this finding enables the imposition of such limitations that are not expressly provided in the Constitution and creates a potential threat to the safeguarding of fundamental rights and also to the legal certainty.

Judge Triantafyllides adopted a different approach and was critical of the reserve police powers approach. In specific, it was stated that the constitutional provision is clear in allowing only specific limitations to rights[210] and moreover it was stated that there is also the possibility of declaring a state of emergency under Article 183 of the Constitution.[211] That provides an alternative route for addressing a public emergency that could not have been dealt with under the normal restrictions that the

---

[205]Judge Hadjianastassiou partly concurred.

[206]Judges Vassiliades, Stavrinides and Loizou concurred.

[207]*Chimonides v. Manglis* (1967) 1 CLR 125, pp. 148–151.

[208]Ibid, p. 153.

[209]Ibid, (quoting from John H. Blaisdell (1933) 290 US 398 at p. 434, per Chief Justice Hughes).

[210]Ibid, pp. 156–157.

[211]Ibid, pp. 158 and 162.

Constitution provides. Finally, the provisions in Part II of the Constitution (with the exception of article 23) are not basic provisions thus they can be amended at any time and this creates an additional solution that is of a last resort nature.[212]

Furthermore, Judge Triantafyllides was sceptical about the persuasiveness of the American jurisprudence on the matter and after a brief analysis concluded that "[i]t is not possible to rely on the aforementioned United States case law – decided in a different constitutional context than our own".[213] The foundation of the approach was the lack of any reference to public interest in Article 26 of the Constitution as a ground for restricting the freedom of contract, while Article 33(1) expressly stated that limitations can only include those stated in the Constitution. The invocation of the concept of 'State's police powers' was therefore dangerous and in clear conflict with the constitutional provisions and intent. Moreover, Judge Triantafyllides held that Article 26 of the Constitution guarantees only the freedom to form contractual relationships and not their content, which can thus be limited by legislative intervention.[214] Therefore, the conclusion was that Law 19/65 was not contrary to Article 26 of the Constitution.

To conclude, in *Chimonides v. Manglis* the concept of reserve police powers was discussed in detail and it was argued that it has a nature that is inherently connected with emergency situations and as such could provide an alternative to the doctrine of necessity. The case law that followed *Chimonides v. Manglis* created a confusion,[215] as it inconsistently endorsed the concept of reserve police powers with no clear justification and, moreover, that concept was without clear justification equated with the doctrine of necessity. As a result, a more cautious approach was required when in exceptional circumstances the expansion of the application of the doctrine of necessity to fundamental rights was to be applied. That serious in effect expansion should have taken place in separation from the concept of reserve police powers or with a cleared analysis about the nature of the two legal concepts.

## Cypriot Case Law Breakthrough: Exceeding the Strict Letter of the Constitution

The third-party effect of the fundamental rights (or the doctrine of *drittwirkung*) can be considered as an important evolutionary approach by the Courts of the constitutional text. In specific, the scope-setting provision of Article 35 of the Constitution creates an obligation to all branches of the Republic—the legislative, the executive

[212]Ibid, p. 158.

[213]Ibid, p. 161.

[214]Ibid, p. 162.

[215]See *Apostolides a.o. v. the Republic* (1982) 3 CLR 928; *Omiros Aristides v. Republic* (1983) 3 CLR 1507; *Aloupas and Another v. National Bank of Greece* (1983) 1 CLR 55; *Loukis Kritiotis v. Municipality of Paphos a.o.* (1986) 3 CLR 322.

and the judicial[216]—to secure, within the limits of their respective competences, the efficient application of the provisions of Part II of the Constitution regarding fundamental human rights.[217] The Supreme Court fulfilled its obligation under Article 35 in its leading judgment of *Takis Giallourou v. Evgeniou Nikolaou*,[218] heard by the full bench, by holding that the individual is protected not only from State interference, but also from interference by private persons. In more detail, the case concerned the award of damages in favour of an individual and against another, due to the violation of the right to private life (protected under Article 15 of the Constitution) and the right to respect for, and to the secrecy of, his or her correspondence and other communication (protected under Article 17 of the Constitution).

The Supreme Court held that the violation of any human right protected under Part II of the Constitution, vests to the victims the right to invoke legal remedies for the vindication of their rights.[219] Thus, the Court awarded compensation to the victim for moral damages resulting from the violation of his constitutional right to private life due to the tapping and monitoring of his telephone conversations for a year. As a result of this judgment, the violation of constitutional rights is directly actionable before the Cypriot district courts.

It is noteworthy that the Supreme Court in *Giallourou v. Nikolaou*, did not refer directly to the concept of *drittwirkung*, but based its reasoning on Article 35 of the Constitution. Yet, in later judgments the Supreme Court held that the notion of *drittwirkung* and the protection of constitutional human rights in the context of a private dispute was indeed endorsed in *Giallourou v. Nikolaou*.[220] Furthermore, it is submitted that the concept of *drittwirkung* can be applied to cases relating to social rights violations, as in *Gregoriou v. Attorney-General* the Supreme Court noted that "we are not unwilling to apply the notion of *drittwirkung* in the field of Labour Law [...], if we were to find a violation of a human right".[221]

[216]The manner in which the Supreme Court implements Article 35 of the Constitution was elaborated in *Police v. Georghiades* (1983) 2 CLR 33.

[217]Kombos (2016), pp. 62–66.

[218]*Takis Yiallouros v. Eugeniou Nicolaou*, 2001) 1 CLR 558.

[219]Ibid, at p. 576.

[220]*Costas Gregoriou v. Attorney General a.o.*, Civil App. 204/2011, 24/5/2016; *Montanios Michael v. Administrative Board of the Lawyers' Pension Fund* (2003) 1 CLR 610; *the Republic v. Vasos Vasileiou*, Civil Appeal 381/2010, 26/5/2016.

[221]*Costas Gregoriou v. Attorney General a.o.*, Civil App. 204/2011, 24/5/2016.

## 3.4 The Renewal of Legal Reasoning and Jurisprudence

### 3.4.1 The Influence of Globalization and Supranational Entities in Legal Reasoning

The influence of the norms imposed by globalisation have already been discussed above. What remains to be examined is the way in which such norms (including international human rights rules and EU rules) have influenced legal reasoning. Strictly speaking, globalization is not a distinct phenomenon in the case of Cyprus. However, the answer is different if the issue of the impact from legal interactions is approached from a supranational entities perspective. It has been clearly established that the Cypriot courts rely heavily and substantially on ECtHR judgments for reaching their conclusions in regard to alleged human rights violations. Both litigants and judges tend to refer to more and more cases from the ECtHR, as its relevance has been clearly established by the Supreme Court from its early judgments.[222]

The same does not apply with the same frequency to norms deriving from EU law or from the case law of the CJEU. While there has been a noticeable willingness to accommodate EU law rules at the normative level, the Supreme Court has not yet enabled the full influence of the jurisprudence of the Luxemburg Court. One may argue that this lack of significant influence is attributable to lawyers/litigants appearing before the Cypriot courts, in the sense that the courts depend primarily on the argumentation that the parties present to it and that the parties avoid presenting argumentation based on EU law. Yet, such argument does not exclude the possibility of the Supreme Court taking the initiative, for two reasons. Firstly, the Cypriot legal system and the Cypriot judiciary have shown remarkable boldness in the past; the decision in *Ibrahim* is the clearest example to that effect. Secondly, 14 years have passed since accession and if the legal community is yet to endorse the CJEU's jurisprudence then that unfortunate situation is partly to be blamed on the guidance that the Supreme Court offers.

As to "methods of interpretation", they have not been modified in favour of the multiplied audiences which the different legal spheres are now called to address. This attitude can be examined through, for instance, the principle of proportionality which remains the same for the past decades, without any development of reasoning. More specifically, the notion of proportionality is a constitutional principle in relation to the duty to pay taxes (Article 24 of the Constitution)[223] and to the right to life (a lawful deprivation of the right to life under Article 7 of the Constitution).[224]

---

[222]See for instance, *Vedat Ahmet Hasip v. the Police* (1964) 1 CLR 48; *the Attorney-General v. Ibrahim* (1964) 1 CLR 195.

[223]Article 24(1) of the Constitution provides: "[e]very person is bound to contribute according to his means towards the public burdens".

[224]Article 7(3) of the Constitution provides that "[d]eprivation of life shall not be regarded as inflicted in contravention of this Article when it results from the use of force which is no more than

The principle of proportionality was introduced and/or elevated as an autonomous and constitutionally integral principle in Cypriot legal order through the landmark decision in *Ibrahim*. One of the requirements that *Ibrahim* established is that required that "no other remedy applies and that the measure taken must be proportionate to the necessity".[225] Therefore, the classic elements of proportionality must form part of the assessing criterion, thus requiring that any action taken under the doctrine of necessity: (a) must be suitable to achieve the relevant aim, (b) must be necessary in the sense that no other measure can be identified that could have achieved the same objective with less detrimental impact and, (c) that the measure in question is proportionate *sensu stricto*.

Similarly, the case law of the Cypriot courts rely on the principle of proportionality in connection with human rights cases. For example, in the *President of the Republic v. House of Representatives*,[226] the President referred five different laws to the Supreme Court, as per Article 140 of the Constitution, requesting its opinion on their constitutionality. The Supreme Court issued one decision on all five references, as it decided that the contested issues were identical, in the sense that they all focused on the scope of Article 15(2) of the Constitution, as amended by the Law concerning the Ninth Amendment of the Constitution.[227] The President argued that the referred laws were unconstitutional, as they introduced obligations on certain state officials and civil servants to disclose their assets and source of funds, as well as to disclose the assets of their spouses and children. The petitioner argued, *inter alia*, that the protection of personal data is directly related to the fundamental right to respect private and family life (Article 15 of the Constitution) and, as a result, the disclosure of information as per the aforementioned laws constituted an interference with the right.

The Supreme Court noted that the assets are part of a person's private life. The disclosure and check of the assets constitute an interference with the exercise of the right. The rights enshrined in the Constitution are vested to the person; kinship does not provide a basis for interfering with the right to privacy nor restricts its limits.

absolutely necessary: (a) in defence of person or property against the infliction of a proportionate and otherwise unavoidable and irreparable evil [...]".

[225] *Ibrahim*, p. 265.

[226] References Nos. 11/2016, 12/2016, 14/2016, 15/2016 and 16/2016, decision of 16 March 2017.

[227] The referrals related to the Public Education Office (Amending) Law of 2016, which introduced new Articles 53A and 53B (Reference No. 11/2016) created such obligations on certain educational officers, their spouse and children; the Public Service (Amending) Law of 2016, which introduced new Articles 66A and 66B (Reference No. 12/2016) created such obligations on certain civil servants, their spouse and children; the Army of the Republic (Amending) Law of 2016, which introduced new Article 63A and 63B (Reference No. 14/2016) created such obligations on certain members of the Army of the Republic of Cyprus, their spouse and children; the Law concerning Legal Entities of Public Law (Disclosure and Assets Check) of 2016, and in particular Articles 3 and 4 (Reference No. 15/2016) created such obligations on certain officials of legal entities of public law, their spouse and children; and the Police (Amending) (No.2) Law of 2016, which introduced new Articles 23A and 23B (Reference No. 16/2016) created such obligations on certain police officials, their spouse and children.

Consequently, the Supreme Court held that the laws imposed a limitation to the right protected under Article 15(1) of the Constitution. Subsequently, the Court examined whether such limitation can be justified under Article 15(2) which provides that a limitation may be imposed by law "in the interests of transparency in public life or for the purpose of taking measures against corruption in public life", in the light of the principle of proportionality. The Supreme Court unanimously found the referred laws unconstitutional. The interference to the privacy of certain state officials and civil servants and their families were particularly drastic, without sufficient reasoning and justification as to the need sought and without adhering to the proportionality principle.

### 3.4.2 The Influence of Globalization and Supranational Entities in Jurisprudence

Currently, there is no significant development of domestic research projects, journals or research centres that are specifically dedicated to the themes of constitutional pluralism and global constitutionalism. The courts in Cyprus appear willing to draw guidance from the case law of foreign jurisdictions, as well as writings in jurisprudence (especially Greek jurisprudence in the field of administrative law); yet there seems to be a lack of theoretical explanation regarding new normative interactions. Moreover, there is a number of academic literature dealing with the relationship between international law/(European) human rights law and the Cypriot law.[228] However, much less has been written on the relationship between EU law and Cypriot law.[229]

As a matter of fact, the academic discourse in Cyprus on pluralism and on the relationship between EU law and Cypriot law, has been limited.[230] As a result, no new theories have emerged apart from the view that sees Cypriot public law as a selectively open system towards external jurisdictions and the ECHR, but no so much so in relation to the EU system. In that sense, meta theoretical awareness of the very evolution of concepts and theories has been absent but for the preceding analysis. There is currently an ongoing attempt to bring to the surface the debate and there is first hand empirical evidence of a growing interest that will remain to be seen if it will materialise in the publication of new approaches. It can be also argued that the present study represents an attempt to re-introduce the debate with reference to a plethora of sources and authors. Finally, the traditional openness of the Cypriot public law system to external sources represents in its own specific way an endorsement of the pluralism rationale, yet in an empirical manner and without a specific and direct justification basis. The theoretical dimension has been in absent during the practical reliance on foreign authorities and precedents. Given that the discussion

[228]See for instance, Paraskeva (2010) and Polyviou (2015).

[229]See for instance, Kombos (2010b).

[230]Kombos (2015b) is the main, if not the sole source on the matter.

remains at an infant stage, it is argued that elements of other subjects (e.g. social sciences, logistics, linguistics, etc.) have not been called upon, and therefore, there is no re-organisation of disciplinary boundaries (e.g. a distinction between public and private law or a distinction between constitutional and international law).

### *3.5 The Ideological Dimension of Legal Rationality*

While it can be argued that there is a conservative approach which is interconnected with rigid positivism, there are instances where the Supreme Court (surprisingly) adopted a progressive approach; for instance, the notion of the doctrine of necessity in *Ibrahim* and the doctrine of *drittwirkung* in *Giallourou v. Nikolaou*. In general, however, there is no specific jurisprudential direction towards an ideological stigma in respect with legal rationality, no "right vs. left", "conservative vs. progressive", "nationalist vs. internationalist", "public law supporter vs. private law supporter".

## 4 Conclusion

The Supreme Court of Cyprus has shown a remarkable willingness to embrace influences and approaches originating from external legal sources (national and supranational), even in the field of public law that is normally regarded to be nation-specific. Furthermore, the Supreme Court engages in constructive and extensive use of the methodology of comparative law and adopts an extrovert position towards external sources of law and towards foreign approaches to law. The ECHR has been at the core of the preceding approach, as have the jurisprudence of various courts from foreign jurisdictions and academic writings. The same openness or cosmopolitanism has not been witnessed in relation to the EU system. The main characteristic of the aforementioned openness has been the lack of a theoretical foundation and of a specific theoretical justification. Rather, the Court has been practical in recognising gaps in the national system and the usefulness of external interacting sources. In that sense, pluralism has been present in pragmatic and empirical terms and for the purpose of problem solving rather than as the corollary of theoretical reasoning. That can also explain the absence of global constitutionalism from the internal debate. Times are changing, as is the nature of the debate, thus it remains to be seen whether the courts shift from specific problem solving, to problem solving with theoretical grounding.

## References

Anthony G (2000) The Europeanization of United Kingdom public law. Yearb Eur Stud 14:83–104
Anthony G (2002) UK public law and European law. Hart, Oxford
Avbelj M (2006) The EU and the many faces of legal pluralism. Croatian Yearb Eur Law Policy 2:377–391
Avbelj M, Komárek J (2008) Four visions of constitutional pluralism. Eur Constit Law Rev 4:524–527
Aziz M (2001) Sovereignty lost, sovereignty regained? The European Integration Project and the Bundesverfassungsgericht. EUI Working Paper RSC No. 2001/31, Florence
Barber N (2006) Legal pluralism and the European Union. Eur Law J 12:306–329
Basu D (1961) Commentary of Indian constitution, 5th edn. Sarkar, Calcutta
Beatson J, Tridimas T (eds) (1998) New directions in European Public Law. Hart, Oxford
Beaulac S (2017) Constitutional interpretation: on issues of ontology and of interlegality. In: Oxford handbook of the Canadian Constitution. Oxford University Press, Oxford
Beaumont P, Lyons C, Walker N (eds) (2002) Convergence and divergence in European Public Law. Hart, Oxford
Besselink LFM (2008) The notion and nature of the European Constitution after the Reform Treaty. SSRN Electronic Journal. https://doi.org/10.2139/ssrn.1086189
Birkinshaw P, Kombos C (2009) The UK approach to the emergence of European Constitutionalism - repositioning the debate: departure from constitutional ontology and the introduction of the typological discussion. Electronic J Comp Law 10
Bobek M (2014) Landtová, Holubec, and the problem of an uncooperative court: implications for the preliminary ruling procedure. Eur Constit Law Rev 10:54–89
Bobić A (2017) Constitutional pluralism is not dead: an analysis of interactions between the European Court of Justice and constitutional courts of Member States. German Law Rev 18:1395–1428
Bogdandy AV, Schill S (2011) Overcoming absolute primacy: respect for national identity under the Lisbon Treaty. Common Market Law Rev 48:1417–1453
Börzel TA (2002) Member state responses to Europeanization. J Common Market Stud 40 (2):193–214
Burley AM, Mattli W (1993) Europe before the Court: a political theory of legal integration. Int Organ 47:41–76
Chowdhury N, Wessel R (2012) Conceptualising multilevel regulation in the EU: a legal translation of multilevel Governance? Eur Law J 18:335–357
Claes M, Visser MD (2012) Are you networked yet? On dialogues in European judicial networks. Utrecht Law Rev 8:100–114
Conant L (2001) Europeanization and the Courts: variable patterns of adaptation among National judiciaries. In: Cowles MG, Caporaso JA, Risse T (eds) Transforming Europe: Europeanization and domestic change. Cornell University Press, Ithaca, pp 97–115
Cottier T, Hertig M (2003) The prospects of 21st century constitutionalism. Max Planck Yearb United Nations Law 7(1):261–328
Craig P, Markakis M (2016) Gauweiler and the legality of outright monetary transactions. Eur Law Rev 41:1–24
Davies G (2010) Constitutional disagreement in Europe and the search for pluralism. Eric Stein Working Paper at the Czech Society of European and Comparative Law 1/2010. http://ssrn.com/abstract=1559323
de Mol M (2011) The novel approach of the CJEU on the horizontal direct effect of the EU principle of non-discrimination: (Unbridled) expansionism of EU law? Maastricht J Eur Comp Law 18:109–135
De Smith SA (1964) The new commonwealth and its constitutions. Stevens, London
Drzemczewski AZ (1983) European human rights convention in domestic law: a comparative study. Clarendon, Oxford

Eleftheriades P (2007) The idea of a European Constitution. Oxf J Legal Stud 27:1–22
Emilianides AC (2006) The cypriot law of marriage and divorce. Sakkoulas, Athens. (in Greek)
Emilianides AC (2011) Religion and law in Cyprus. Kluwer, Alphen aan den Rijn
Emiliou M (2006) Cyprus. In: Kellerman JCA (ed) The impact of EU accession on the legal orders of new EU member states and (pre-) Candidate Countries, hopes and fears. TMC Asser Press, The Hague, pp 303–312
Emmerich-Fritsche A (2007) Vom Völkerrecht zum Weltrecht. Duncker and Humblot, Berlin
Evriviades M (1975) The legal dimension of the Cyprus conflict. Texas Int Law J 10:227–264
Fabbrini F (2015) After the OMT Case: the supremacy of EU law as the guarantee of the equality of the Member States. German Law J 16:1003–1024
Fassbender B (1998) The United Nations charter as the constitution of the international community. Columbia J Int Law 36:529–619
Goldmann M (2016) Constitutional pluralism as mutually assured discretion: the Court of Justice, the German Federal Constitutional Court, and the ECB. Maastricht J Eur Comp Law 23:119–135
Green CR (2018) Constitutional truthmakers. Notre Dame J Law Ethics Public Policy 32:497–529
Grimm D (1991) Die Zukunft der Verfassung, 3rd edn. Suhrkamp, Frankfurt am Main
Grimm D (2012) Types of constitutions. In: Rosenfeld M, Sajó A (eds) The Oxford handbook of comparative constitutional law. Oxford University Press, Oxford, pp 98–132
Groussot X (2005) The Role of the National Courts in the European Union: a future perspective. Svenska Institutet för Europapolitiska Studier, Lund
Harlow C (2002) Voices of difference in a plural community. Am J Comp Law 50:339–367
Hatzimihail NE (2013) Cyprus as a mixed legal system. J Civil Law Stud 6:37–96
Hatzimihail NE (2015) Reconstructing mixity: sources of law and legal method in Cyprus. In: Palmer V, Mattar M, Koppel A (eds) Mixed legal systems: East and West. Routledge, London, pp 75–100
Himsworth C (2002) Convergence and divergence in administrative law. In: Beaumont P, Lyons C, Walker N (eds) Convergence and divergence in European public law. Hart, Oxford, pp 99–110
Jans JH, Lange R, Prechal S, Widdershoven RJ (2007) Europeanisation of public law. Europa Law Publishing, Groningen
Kelemen D (2016) On the unsustainability of constitutional pluralism: European supremacy and the survival of the Eurozone. Maastricht J Eur Comp Law 23:136–150
Klein C, Sajó A (2012) Constitution-making: process and substance. In: Rosenfeld M, Sajó A (eds) The Oxford handbook of comparative constitutional law. Oxford University Press, Oxford, pp 419–441
Komárek J (2006) European Constitutional pluralism and the European Arrest Warrant: contrapunctual principles in disharmony. SSRN Electronic Journal. doi: https://doi.org/10.2139/ssrn.934067
Komárek J (2012) Playing with matches: the Czech Constitutional Court's Ultra Vires Revolution. Available via Vergassungsblog on Matters Constitutional. http://verfassungsblog.de/playing-matches-czech-constitutional-courts-ultra-vires-revolution/
Kombos C (2010a) Report on European Public Law in Cyprus: the Supreme Court's of Cyprus approach to standing for judicial review and to the preliminary reference procedure. Eur Public Law 16:327–355
Kombos C (2010b) Studies in European Public Law. Sakkoulas, Athens
Kombos C (2010c) The Esoteric dimension of constitutional pluralism: EU's internal constitutional sub-units and the non-symbolic cumulative constitution. In: Birkinshaw P, Varney M (eds) The European Union legal order after Lisbon. Kluwer Law International, Alphen Aan Den Rijn
Kombos C (2010d) The judiciary in federal systems. In: Samara-Krispi A, Constantinides A (eds) The Cypriot problem in evolution. Sakkoulas, Athens, pp 81–113
Kombos C (2015a) The Doctrine of necessity in constitutional law. Sakkoulas, Athens
Kombos C (2015b) The impact of EU law on Cypriot public law. Sakkoulas, Athens

Kombos C (2016) Social rights in the Republic of Cyprus. In: Wojtyczek K (ed) Social and economic rights as fundamental rights. Eleven International Publishing, New York, pp 57–86
Kumm M (1999) Who is the final arbiter of constitutionality in Europe? Three conceptions of the relationship between the German Federal Constitutional Court and the European Court of Justice. Common Market Law Rev 36:351–386
Kumm M (2009) The cosmopolitan turn in constitutionalism: on the relationship between National Constitutional Law and Constitutionalism beyond the state. In: Dunoff JL, Trachtman JP (eds) Ruling the world? International law, global Governance, Constitutionalism. Cambridge University Press, Cambridge, pp 258–325
Kuo M-S (2010) The end of constitutionalism as we know it? Boundaries and the State of Global Constitutional (Dis)Ordering. Transnational Legal Theory 1(1):329–369
Kuo M-S (2014) Semantic Constitutionalism at the Fin de Siècle. Transnational Legal Theory 5 (1):158–175
Kyriakides S (1969) Cyprus: constitutionalism and crisis Government. University of Pennsylvania Press, Philadelphia
Kyriakou N (2010) National judges and supranational laws on the effective application of the EC law and the ECHR: the case of Cyprus. Available via SSRN. http://ssrn.com/abstract=1623560
Legrand P (2002) Public law, Europeanisation, and convergence: can comparatists contribute? In: Beaumont P, Lyons C, Walker N (eds) Convergence and divergence in European public law. Hart, Oxford, pp 225–256
Lenaerts K (1990) Constitutionalism and the many faces of federalism. Am J Comp Law 38:205–263
Loizou A (2001) The Constitution of the Republic of Cyprus, (in Greek). Nicosia
Loughlin M (2014) Constitutional pluralism: an oxymoron? Global Constitutionalism 3:9–30
Loughlin M (2015) The constitutional imagination. Modern Law Rev 78:1–25
Loughlin M (2017) The misconceived search for global law. Transnational Legal Theory 8:353–359
Lycourgos C (2010) Cyprus public law as affected by accession to the EU. In: Kombos C (ed) Studies in European public law: thematic, national and post-national perspectives. Sakkoulas, Athens, pp 101–114
Lycourgos C (2016) Building intra-judicial dialogue: the relationship between the ECJ and Cypriot national courts. Eur Law Rev 41:623–637
MacCormick N (1999) Questioning sovereignty: law, state and Nation in the European commonwealth. Oxford University Press, Oxford
Maduro MP (2003) Contrapunctual law: Europe's constitutional pluralism in action. In: Walker N (ed) Sovereignty in transition. Hart Publishing, Oxford, pp 501–538
Maduro MP (2007) Interpreting European Law: judicial adjudication in a context of constitutional pluralism. Eur J Legal Stud 1:137–152
Maduro MP (2012) Three claims of constitutional pluralism. In: Avbelj M, Komárek J (eds) Constitutional pluralism in the European Union and beyond. Hart Publishing, Oxford, pp 67–84
Markides A (2006) The Republic of Cyprus. In: Kortmann C, Fleuren J, Voermans W (eds) Constitutional Law of 10 EU Member States: the 2004 enlargement. Kluwer, Alphen aan den Rijn, pp I3–I77
Martinez JS (2012) Horizontal structuring. In: Rosenfeld M, Sajó A (eds) The Oxford handbook of comparative constitutional law. Oxford University Press, Oxford, pp 547–575
Martinico G (2012) Is the European Convention going to be 'Supreme'? A comparative-constitutional overview of ECHR and EU law before National Courts. Eur J Int Law 23:401–424
Millet FX (2014) How much lenience for how much cooperation? On the first preliminary reference of the French Constitutional Council to the Court of Justice. Common Market Law Rev 51 (1):195–218
Neergaard U, Sørensen KE (2017) Activist infighting among courts and breakdown of mutual trust? The Danish Supreme Court, the CJEU, and the Ajos Case. Yearb Eur Law 36:275–313

Nicolaou I (2000) The control of the constitutionality of the laws and the separation of powers of the State Institutions of Cyprus - Constitutional regulation and the evolution of the law of necessity (in Greek). Sakkoulas, Athens

Palandri L (2013) Theoretical reflections on legal pluralism and global constitutionalism: their possible reconciliation in an alternative model of plural constitutionalism. Acta Juridica Hungarica 54(1):58–72

Papadopoulos T (2011) Criticizing the horizontal direct effect of the EU general principle of equality. Eur Human Rights Law Rev 4:437–447

Papasavvas S (1998) La justice constitutionnelle à Chypre. Economica, Paris

Paraskeva C (2010) The relationship between the domestic implementation of the European Convention on human rights and the ongoing reforms of the European Court of human rights (with a Case Study on Cyprus and Turkey). Intersentia, Cambridge

Perju V (2010) Cosmopolitanism and constitutional self-Government. Int J Constit Law 8:326–353

Pernice I (1999) Multilevel constitutionalism and the Treaty of Amsterdam: European Constitution making revisited? Common Market Law Rev 36:703–750

Pernice I (2002) Multilevel constitutionalism in the European Union. Eur Law Rev 27:511–529

Pernice I (2009) The Treaty of Lisbon: multilevel constitutionalism in action. Columbia J Eur Law 15:349–407

Peters A (2006) Compensatory constitutionalism: the function and potential of fundamental international norms and structures. Leiden J Int Law 19:579–610

Peters A (2007) The globalization of state constitutions. In: Nijman J, Nollkaemper A (eds) New perspectives on the divide between national and international law. Oxford University Press, Oxford, pp 251–308

Peters A (2009) The merits of global constitutionalism. Indiana J Global Legal Stud 16:397–411

Peters A (2015) Global constitutionalism. In: Gibbons MT (ed) The encyclopaedia of political thought. John Wiley & Sons, Ltd., Hoboken. Available via http://www.mpil.de/files/pdf5/Peters_Global_Constitutionalism__Encyclopedia_of_Political_Thought_20151.pdf

Pikis G (2006) Constitutionalism – human rights – separation of powers: the Cyprus Precedent. Brill, Leiden

Piris JC (2006) The Constitution for Europe a legal analysis. Cambridge University Press, Cambridge

Polyviou PG (1975) Cyprus: the tragedy and the challenge. J. Swain and Son, London

Polyviou PG (2014) The law of contract, vol A. Chrisafinis and Polyviou, Nicosia. (in Greek)

Polyviou PG (2015) Cyprus: a study in the theory, structure and method of the legal system of the Republic of Cyprus. Chryssafinis and Polyviou, Nicosia

Polyviou PG (2016) Employment contract in Cypriot law, vol A. Chrisafinis and Polyviou, Nicosia. (in Greek)

Repetto G (2013) The constitutional relevance of the ECHR in domestic and European Law: an Italian perspective. Intersentia, Mortsel

Rosenfeld M (2008) Rethinking constitutional ordering in an era of legal and ideological pluralism. Int J Constit Law 6:415–455

Rosenfeld M (2011) Constitutional versus administrative ordering in an era of globalization and privatization: reflections on sources of legitimation in the post-Westphalian polity. Cardozo Law Rev 32:2339–2368

Sarmiento D (2015) The OMT case and the demise of the pluralist movement. Available via Despite Our Differences https://despiteourdifferencesblog.wordpress.com/2015/09/21/the-omt-case-and-the-demise-of-the-pluralist-movement/

Sartori G (1962) Constitutionalism: a preliminary discussion. Am Polit Sci Rev 56:853–864

Scharpf F (2009) Legitimacy in the multilevel European polity. Eur Polit Sci Rev 1:173–204

Schwarze J (2006) European administrative law, Revised First Edition. Sweet and Maxwell, London

Scott J (2002) Member states and regions in community law: convergence and divergence. In: Beaumont P, Lyons C, Walker N (eds) Convergence and divergence in European public law. Hart, Oxford, pp 19–36

Seitzer J (ed) (2007) Carl Schmitt: constitutional theory. Duke University Press, Durham

Snyder F (ed) (2000) The Europeanisation of law: the legal effects of European integration. Hart, Oxford

Stavsky MM (1983) The doctrine of state necessity in Pakistan. Cornell Int Law J 16:341–394

Stein T (2011) Always steering a straight course? The German Federal Constitutional Court and European integration. ERA Forum 12:219–228

Sweet AS (2009) Constitutionalism, legal pluralism, and international regime. Indiana J Global Legal Stud 16:621–645

Sweet AS (2012) A cosmopolitan legal order: constitutional pluralism and rights adjudication in Europe. Global Constitutionalism 1:53–90

Symeonides SC (2003) The mixed legal system of the Republic of Cyprus. Tulane Law Rev 78:441–455

Tan KC (2004) Justice without borders: cosmopolitanism, nationalism, and patriotism. Cambridge University Press, Cambridge

Teubner G (1997) 'Global Bukowina': legal pluralism in the World Society. In: Teubner G (ed) Global law without a state. Dartmouth, Aldershot, pp 3–30

Teubner G (2012) Constitutional fragments: societal constitutionalism and globalization. Oxford University Press, Oxford

Thomassen W (2009) Highest courts and the internationalisation of law. In: Muler A, Loth M (eds) Highest Courts and the Internationalisation of Law. Hague Academic Press, The Hague

Timmermas C (2004) The European Union's judicial system. Common Market Law Rev 41:393–405

Tornaritis C (1968) The social and economic rights under the law of the Republic of Cyprus. Mélanges Bridel, Lausanne

Tornaritis C (1980) Cyprus and its constitutional and other problems, 2nd edn. Tornaritis Law Firm, Nicosia

Tridimas T, Xanthoulis N (2016) A legal analysis of the gauweiler case: between monetary policy and constitutional conflict. Maastricht J Eur Comp Law 23:17–39

Tsatsos D (1994) Constitutional law, Volume A, 4th edn. Sakkoulas, Athens. (in Greek)

Tuori K (2010) The many constitutions of Europe. In: Tuori K, Sankari S (eds) The many constitutions of Europe. Routledge, London, pp 3–30

Tushnet MV (2009) The inevitable globalization of constitutional law. Va J Int Law 49:985–1006

von Bodgandy A (2008) Pluralism, direct effect, and the ultimate say: on the relationship between international and domestic constitutional law. Int J Constit Law 6:397–413

Voβkuhle A (2010) Multilevel cooperation of the European Constitutional Courts: Der Europäische Verfassungsgerichtsverbund. Eur Constit Law Rev 6:175–198

Walker N (2002a) Culture, democracy and the convergence of public law: some scepticisms about scepticism. In: Beaumont P, Lyons C, Walker N (eds) Convergence and divergence in European public law. Hart, Oxford, pp 257–272

Walker N (2002b) The idea of constitutional pluralism. Modern Law Rev 65:317–359

Walker N (2007) Post-constituent constitutionalism? The case of the European Union. In: Loughlin M, Walker N (eds) The paradox of constitutionalism: constituent power and constitutional form. Oxford University Press, Oxford, pp 247–267

Walker N (2011) Reconciling MacCormick: constitutional pluralism and the unity of practical reason. Ratio Juris 24:369–385

Walker N (2012) Constitutionalism and pluralism in global context. In: Avbelj M, Komarek J (eds) Constitutional pluralism in the European Union and beyond. Hart, Oxford, pp 17–38

Walker N (2016) Constitutional pluralism revisited. Eur Law J 22:333–355

Weiler J (1993) Journey to an unknown destination: a retrospective and prospective of the European Court of justice in the arena of political integration. J Common Market Stud 31:417–446

Weiler J (1994) A quiet revolution: the European Court of justice and its interlocutors. Comp Polit Stud 26:510–534

Weiler J (1999) The Constitution of Europe: do new clothes have an Emperor? And other essays on European integration. Cambridge University Press, Cambridge

Weiler J (2005) On the power of the Word: Europe's constitutional iconography. Int J Constit Law 3:173–190

Weiler J (2011) Prologue: global and pluralist constitutionalism – some doubts. In: de Búrca G, Weiler J (eds) The Worlds of European Constitutionalism. Cambridge University Press, Cambridge, pp 8–18

Wendel M (2013) Judicial restraint and the return to openness: the decision of the German Federal Constitutional Court on the ESM and the Fiscal Treaty of 12 September 2012. German Law J 14:21–52

Wet ED (2006a) The Emergence of international and regional value systems as a manifestation of the emerging international constitutional order. Leiden J Int Law 19:611–632

Wet ED (2006b) The international constitutional order. Int Comp Law Q 55:51–76

Wilkinson M (2017) Constitutional pluralism: chronicle of a death foretold? Eur Law J 23:213–233

Zbíral R (2012) Czech Constitutional Court, judgment of 31 January 2012, Pl. ÚS 5/12. Common Market Law Rev 49:1–18

Zumbansen P (2012) Carving out typologies and accounting for differences across systems: towards a methodology of transnational constitutionalism. In: Rosenfeld M, Sajó A (eds) The Oxford handbook of comparative constitutional law. Oxford University Press, Oxford, pp 75–97

# "Friendliness" Towards Others: How the German Constitution Deals with Legal Pluralism

**Lars Viellechner**

**Abstract** The tension between universalism and particularism, which characterises the modern concept of constitutionalism in general, is significantly more pronounced in the Basic Law [*Grundgesetz*] for the Federal Republic of Germany. On the one hand, the Basic Law not only provides for internal diversity by establishing a federal state and granting much leeway to societal self-regulation, but it also shows an unprecedented external openness. On the other hand, however, the strong commitment of the Basic Law to fundamental rights paradoxically entails distinct nationalist tendencies both internally and externally. This ambivalence is expressed by a peculiar principle of 'friendliness' towards other normative orders, arising both within and beyond the state. Arguably, the principle may best be captured and operationalised in a logic known from private international law, that is general recognition with a reservation of public order, which may vary depending on the trustworthiness of the norms to be recognised. The private law analogy appears as an attractive instrument for reconciling overlapping legal orders under conditions of globalisation. Indeed, it may be regarded as an adequate reformulation of modern constitutionalism for the current context. On the one hand, the rule of law in its aspects of legal certainty and equality presses for the mutual recognition of the various legal orders and hence for avoiding norm conflicts as far as possible. On the other hand, however, democracy allows for the self-determination of the various legal orders, at least as long as they do not affect the fundamental rights of outsiders.

Reprinted with permission from M. Schmidt-Kessel (ed.), German National Reports on the 20th International Congress of Comparative Law (Mohr Siebeck, Tübingen, 2018), pp. 511–545. Slightly revised and updated version.

L. Viellechner (✉)
University of Bremen, Law Department, Bremen, Germany
e-mail: lars.viellechner@uni-bremen.de



G. Tusseau (ed.), *Debating Legal Pluralism and Constitutionalism*, Ius Comparatum – Global Studies in Comparative Law 41, https://doi.org/10.1007/978-3-030-34432-0_6

# 1 Introduction

Despite its name, the Basic Law [*Grundgesetz*] for the Federal Republic of Germany is a constitution in the full sense of the term. When it came into effect in 1949, it was regarded as an interim arrangement for the West German state only, at that time still occupied by the allied powers and hence not fully sovereign. It had been drafted by a parliamentary council and adopted by the parliaments of the individual states.[1] Since their accession in 1990, it also applies to the Eastern parts of Germany, but it has never been directly ratified by the German people.[2]

These circumstances notwithstanding, the Basic Law has always displayed the essential elements of modern constitutionalism. In both structure and contents, it follows the model that emerged in the wake of the American and French revolutions at the end of the eighteenth century.[3] Hence it combines democracy with the rule of law, including fundamental rights protection. With its essential elements, the Basic Law also shares the inherent tension between universalism and particularism that characterises modern constitutionalism: The concept calls for generalisation, albeit in a pluriversum of states. Notably its fundamental rights element strives for worldwide dissemination, while its democratic element allows for variation in its implementation.[4]

The tension between universalism and particularism is significantly more pronounced in the Basic Law because of some special features that are predominantly owed to the historical experience of National Socialist dictatorship. On the one hand, the Basic law not only provides for internal diversity by establishing a federal state,[5] but it also shows an unprecedented external openness.[6] Its preamble declares an intention 'to promote world peace as an equal partner in a united Europe'. Moreover, Article 1 paragraph 2 of the Basic Law acknowledges 'inviolable and inalienable human rights as the basis of every community, of peace and of justice in the world'. On the other hand, however, the strong commitment of the Basic Law to fundamental rights paradoxically entails distinct nationalist tendencies both internally and externally. According to Article 1 paragraph 3 of the Basic Law, the federal charter of fundamental rights binds all state authorities, even those of the individual states, which does not leave much room for federal variation. Furthermore, Article 1 paragraph 1 of the Basic Law grounds the entire legal order on a principle of human dignity[7] the core of which, pursuant to the 'eternity clause' in Article 79

[1]See Weber (1949) and Ipsen (1950).

[2]For the debate on the various constitutional options in the process of unification, see Guggenberger and Stein (1991).

[3]For this model, see Grimm (1987). See also Brugger (2001).

[4]Cf. Holmes (1988) and Rosenfeld (1994).

[5]See Isensee (1990) and Grzeszick (1996).

[6]See Hobe (1998) and Giegerich (2010).

[7]See Dürig (1956) and Baldus (2016).

paragraph 3 of the Basic Law, may not even be altered by constitutional amendment. This construction also puts limits on European integration.

A similar ambivalence determines the attitude of the German constitution towards the further pluralisation of law under the influence of what is called 'globalisation'[8] or emergence of 'world society'[9] in the social sciences. The Basic Law presents itself as 'responsive'[10] or, metaphorically speaking, 'friendly'[11] towards other normative orders, arising both beyond the state through international or transnational cooperation and within the state through migration. This does not mean unconditional recognition. Rather, deference to other normative orders is usually placed under certain reservations of public order. To some extent, the mechanism reflects and generalises the logic of private international law. Although it had been engrained in the Basic Law from the outset (Sect. 2), it was expanded and refined in cooperation between legal practice and scholarship later on (Sect. 3). Thoroughly thought through, it might even amount to a new variant of constitutionalism for a globalised context (Sect. 4).

## 2 Foundations

In order to understand the attitude of German law towards other normative orders, it seems helpful to distinguish between law within the state (Sect. 2.1), law beyond the state (Sect. 2.2) and law across the state (Sect. 2.3).

### *2.1 Law Within the State*

Law within the state refers to federal state law (Sect. 2.1.1), private law (Sect. 2.1.2) and social norms (Sect. 2.1.3).

[8] Giddens (1990), pp. 63–78; Sassen (2007), pp. 11–44.

[9] Luhmann (1997), pp. 145–171.

[10] Viellechner (2012b). The term is borrowed from political theory where it denotes the attentiveness of the representatives to the interests of the represented, see Pitkin (1967), p. 209. For a usage of the term in a philosophical phenomenology of the other, see Waldenfels (1987), pp. 46–49. For a usage of the term in legal sociology, see Nonet and Selznick (1978), pp. 14–15: 'law as a facilitator of response to social needs and aspirations'. For a related concept with regard to European Union law, see Wendel (2011), pp. 5–45: 'permeability'.

[11] The notion was first employed with regard to international law, see Bleckmann (1996); Payandeh (2009).

### 2.1.1 Federal State Law

As its name suggests and as Article 20 paragraph 1 of the Basic Law distinctly declares, the Federal Republic of Germany is a federal state. It consists of several individual states with their own constitutions. Some of the states have even established their own constitutional courts. According to the prevailing doctrine, the individual states are states in their own right, disposing of original competences, and hence of constitutional autonomy, but not of sovereignty in the sense of competence-competence, that is the power to allocate competences.[12]

The relationship between the federation and the states is therefore regulated by the Basic Law as the federal constitution, which at first glance seems to leave the states in a strong position. Pursuant to Article 30 of the Basic Law, 'the exercise of state powers and the discharge of state functions is a matter for the states' except as otherwise provided or permitted. Moreover, pursuant to Article 83 of the Basic Law, as a general rule, the states even 'execute federal laws in their own right'.

Nevertheless, the autonomy of the states is curbed in several ways. The 'homogeneity clause' in Article 28 paragraph 1 of the Basic Law, which imposes an obligation on the states 'to conform to the principles of a republican, democratic and social state governed by the rule of law within the meaning of this Basic Law', still grants considerable leeway to the states for variation.[13] The rules on the allocation of legislative powers in Articles 70–74 of the Basic Law, by contrast, provide for many exceptions in favour of the federation.[14] Yet most significantly, the comprehensive applicability of the federal charter of fundamental rights according to Article 1 paragraph 3 of the Basic Law has a strongly unifying effect, which at the same time marginalises the constitutional courts of the individual states.[15] Therefore, it has been claimed that the Federal Republic of Germany is a 'unitarian federal state'[16] that does not leave much room for internal diversity.

### 2.1.2 Private Law

While the German legal order clearly distinguishes between public and private law, the divide does not refer to the source, but only to the subject matter of the law.[17] Therefore, it remains purely technical, relevant only for the jurisdiction of the courts

[12]BVerfGE 1, 14, 34—*Südweststaat* (1951); 36, 342, 360–361—*Niedersächsisches Landesbesoldungsgesetz* (1974). For the traditional understanding of sovereignty as competence-competence, see Laband (1911), pp. 55–88; Jellinek (1882), pp. 36–58.

[13]BVerfGE 9, 268, 279—*Bremer Personalvertretung* (1959); 24, 367, 390—*Hamburgisches Deichordnungsgesetz* (1968). See also Kersten (1993).

[14]See Degenhart (2006) and Ipsen (2006).

[15]See Grawert (1987) and Dreier (2000).

[16]Hesse (1962).

[17]See Molitor (1949), pp. 25–35 and Bullinger (1968), pp. 75–80.

according to Section 13 of the Courts Constitution Act [*Gerichtsverfassungsgesetz*] and Section 40 paragraph 1 of the Code of Administrative Court Procedure [*Verwaltungsgerichtsordnung*]. Private law for these purposes is that which regulates the relationships between individuals, whereas public law entitles or obliges the state.[18]

The Basic Law consequently does not know any notion of privately made law.[19] Certainly, some provisions of private law might have been generated in earlier times or outside of the legislative procedures of the state, but it is assumed that they derive their validity from the constitution, as Article 123 paragraph 1 of the Basic Law expressly states for pre-constitutional law, such as the German Civil Code [*Bürgerliches Gesetzbuch*] of 1896. Contract, then, is no source of law in its own right. Rather, it is only brought to bear through the mandatory provisions of private law on the formation and limits of contract, which shape freedom of contract as an aspect of private autonomy and thus fulfil a constitutional function in the horizontal relation between individuals.[20] On this account, all law in Germany is essentially public, that is state law.

Just because private persons are not authorised to make law, the distinction between public and private actors is still a crucial reference point for the constitution that, as a matter of principle, only obliges the state. Private persons, in contrast, enjoy freedom of action.[21] It should be noted, however, that the Federal Constitutional Court [*Bundesverfassungsgericht*] has early acknowledged an indirect horizontal effect of fundamental rights between individuals. According to its jurisprudence, the fundamental rights enshrined in the Basic Law are to be regarded as objective principles that have a 'radiating effect'[22] on all fields of law. Notably the general clauses and indeterminate legal concepts of ordinary law, such as 'good faith' in Section 242 of the German Civil Code, may therefore serve as 'points of entry'[23] for fundamental rights and must be construed in their spirit. The pervasive influence of fundamental rights has resulted in a 'constitutionalisation'[24] of the entire legal order.

### 2.1.3 Social Norms

The rejection of any notion of privately enacted law entails a strict separation of law and social norms as non-law. To be sure, the German legal order is cognitively open so as to stay in touch with social reality and to keep pace with technological

---

[18]See Wolff (1950) and Menger (1973).

[19]See Kirchhof (1987), pp. 48–53; Bachmann (2006), pp. 20–22.

[20]See Flume (1992), pp. 1–22; Hesse (1988), pp. 27–30.

[21]See Böckenförde (1972). For a critique, see Ehmke (1962).

[22]BVerfGE 7, 198, 207—*Lüth* (1958).

[23]BVerfGE 7, 198, 206—*Lüth* (1958).

[24]Schuppert and Bumke (2000).

progress.[25] For this reason, both public and private law occasionally refer to social norms. Thus, Section 138 paragraph 1 of the German Civil Code declares void a contract that violates the 'good morals'.[26] Similarly, environmental as well as technology law frequently point to the 'state of the art' or 'best available technology'.[27] Yet the relevant social norms and technical standards acquire a legal character only insofar as the legislator includes them in the statutory provisions.[28] It is still disputed under which conditions such incorporation is democratically legitimate[29] and yet another issue if a direct transfer of extra-legal knowledge to the law is possible from an epistemological point of view.[30]

Even in those fields in which German law does not formally recognise social norms as legal, it nevertheless enables and promotes societal self-regulation, not least because the legislator is unable to provide comprehensive regulation. Indeed, fundamental rights may be construed so as to implying an additional transsubjective dimension that supports and protects autonomous rule-making because it brings about innovation, knowledge and forces of social cohesion beneficial to all.[31] While this is a common feature, it is generally acknowledged only for those fundamental rights that explicitly comprise an institutional guarantee, such as freedom of the press, broadcasting or religion.[32]

Regarding the relationship between state and religion, the constitution even contains a more specific provision. According to Article 140 of the Basic Law that refers to Article 137 paragraph 3 of the previous Weimar Constitution of 1919, religious societies may 'regulate and administer their affairs independently within the limits of the law that applies to all'. Although this provision allows for autonomous regulation and adjudication in religious matters, it reserves for the state the last say in cases of conflict. It is nevertheless regarded as expressing a distinctive 'friendliness'[33] towards religion, which is reinforced through an extensive interpretation by the Federal Constitutional Court. Not only does the definition of what constitutes a religion or a religiously motivated behaviour have to take into account the 'self-conception'[34] of the religious communities, but state law that restricts

---

[25]See Ladeur (1995), pp. 118–140; Wielsch (2009).

[26]For the relationship between law and social norms in this provision, see Teubner (1971), pp. 65–115; Auer (2005), pp. 101–179.

[27]For the relationship between law and technical standards, see Breuer (1976); Marburger (1979), pp. 279–426.

[28]See Nicklisch (1986); Koch (1986), pp. 10–15.

[29]See Denninger (1990), pp. 141–147; Lübbe-Wolff (1991).

[30]See Augsberg (2014), pp. 283–305.

[31]See Ladeur (2000) and Vesting (2001).

[32]See Ridder (1975), pp. 85–93; Mager (2003), pp. 232–311.

[33]Czermak and Hilgendorf (2018), p. 34; Unruh (2018), p. 101.

[34]BVerfGE 24, 236, 247–248—*Aktion Rumpelkammer* (1968). See also Morlok (1993), pp. 78–83; Augsberg (2012).

religious rules has to be interpreted in the light of religious freedom on its part.[35] As a consequence, the provisions of labour law, for example, may be modified when applied to the churches as employers. Thus, even when the churches expand their religious activities to other spheres of social life by running hospitals or nursing homes, they may expect loyalty of their employees to their confession and prohibit strike in assuming not an antagonistic relationship between employer and employees, but a common commitment to charity.[36]

## 2.2 *Law Beyond the State*

The term law beyond the state as employed here comprises international law (Sect. 2.2.1) and European Union law (Sect. 2.2.2).

### 2.2.1 International Law

Regarding international law, the German constitution assumes a moderate dualist position.[37] While it insists that national and international law are separate legal orders originating from different sources, it acknowledges that they may overlap in their subject matters. Therefore, international law may take effect within the state, but only if it is incorporated by a provision of national law.

Such a provision can be found in Article 25 of the Basic Law. It recognises the 'general rules of international law', widely understood as comprising both customary international law and the general principles of law in the sense of Article 38 paragraph 1 letters b and c of the Statute of the International Court of Justice,[38] as 'an integral part of federal law' and determines that they 'take precedence of the laws'. According to the prevailing jurisprudence and doctrine, this part of international law is thereby as such adopted by national law and ranks in between the constitution and ordinary statutes.[39]

For international treaties, there is no similar provision. The procedural rule in Article 59 paragraph 2 of the Basic Law only requires that such treaties obtain 'the

[35] BVerfGE 53, 366, 401—*Konfessionelle Krankenhäuser* (1980); 83, 341, 356—*Bahá'í* (1991).

[36] BVerfGE 70, 138, 167—*Loyalitätspflicht* (1985); BAGE 143, 354—*Dritter Weg* (2012). See also Thüsing (2006). This view is now under attack by European courts, see ECtHR, Judgment of 23 September 2010, Application 1620/03, *Schüth v. Germany*; ECJ, Judgment of 17 April 2018, Case C-414/16, *Egenberger v. Evangelisches Werk für Diakonie und Entwicklung e.V.*, ECLI:EU:C:2018:257.

[37] BVerfGE 111, 307, 318—*Görgülü* (2004). See also Rudolf (1967), pp. 141–150.

[38] BVerfGE 23, 288, 317—*Kriegsfolgelasten II* (1968); 118, 124, 134—*Völkerrechtliche Notstandseinrede* (2007).

[39] BVerfGE 6, 309, 363—*Reichskonkordat* (1957); 46, 342, 363—*Philippinische Botschaft* (1977). See also Mosler (1957), pp. 43–45.

consent or participation, in the form of a federal law, of the bodies responsible in such a case for the enactment of federal law'. Nevertheless, it is generally assumed that the act of parliamentary approval not only authorises government to ratify the treaty, but also includes the treaty in the national legal order where the treaty shares its rank as an ordinary statute.[40] Consequently, all national authorities have to comply with the terms of the treaty if they meet the requirements of direct applicability, which means that they are sufficiently precise and unconditional and do not call for any implementing measure.[41] By contrast, the legislator is generally allowed to override its prior decisions at a later stage,[42] and the constitution retains its supremacy in any case of conflict. Despite these restrictions, commentators early acknowledged that the Basic Law had opted for erecting an 'open state'[43] that deviates from traditional notions of sovereignty.

### 2.2.2 European Union Law

The integration of the Federal Republic of Germany into the European Union follows special rules. Initially, it had rested upon Article 24 paragraph 1 of the Basic Law, which foresees that '[t]he Federation may by a law transfer sovereign powers to international organisations'.

After the German reunification and with a view to the ratification of the Maastricht Treaty establishing the European Union in 1992, a more detailed provision was inserted into Article 23 of the Basic Law.[44] This provision expressly considers European integration as a central goal of the state. At the same time, it contains several procedural and substantive safeguards regarding the transfer of powers to the European Union. Not only does it require an extensive participation of both parliament and the federal states through the Federal Council, but it also sets certain limits to European integration. On the one hand, the 'structure-securing clause' in Article 23 paragraph 1 clause 1 of the Basic Law expects the European Union to conform 'to democratic, social and federal principles, to the rule of law, and to the principle of subsidiarity'. On the other hand, the 'acquis-securing clause' in Article 23 paragraph 1 clause 3 of the Basic Law subjects the establishment of the European Union and further changes of its founding treaties that would alter the Basic Law to some of the rules on constitutional amendment. Notably, it refers to the majority requirement in Article 79 paragraph 2 and the eternity clause in Article 79 paragraph 3 of the Basic Law, which prohibits constitutional amendments affecting the principle of human dignity in Article 1 of the Basic Law and the essential structural principles of

[40] BVerfGE 1, 396, 411—*Deutschlandvertrag* (1952); 90, 286, 364—*Out-of-area-Einsätze* (1994). See also Partsch (1964), pp. 86–142.

[41] BVerwGE 80, 233, 235—*Mehrstaatigkeit* (1988). See also Bleckmann (1970).

[42] BVerfGE 6, 309, 362–363—*Reichskonkordat* (1957). For a critique, see Vogel (1997).

[43] Vogel (1964), p. 42.

[44] See Di Fabio (1993) and Schmalenbach (1996).

the state as enumerated in Article 20 of the Basic Law, in particular democracy and the rule of law. While the designation of the clause one-sidedly emphasises its limiting dimension, its empowering dimension should not be overlooked: The provision largely releases the ordinary constitutional restraints to state action und allows for constitutional amendment without changes to the text of the constitution.[45] Some commentators therefore regard the provisions on European integration as completing a 'second phase'[46] of legal development, turning the Basic Law from a domestically-focused to an outward-looking constitution.

## 2.3 *Law Across the State*

Law across the state not only alludes to the influence of foreign law (Sect. 2.3.1), but also to a newly emerging transnational law (Sect. 2.3.2).

### 2.3.1 Foreign Law

Foreign law, that is law of other states, may exceptionally find internal application in Germany. In this respect, the direct and indirect applications of foreign law need to be distinguished. Indirect application here means the interpretation of national law with the aid of foreign law.

The direct application of foreign law is provided for only in the realm of private law.[47] In matters of private law that imply a cross-border element, the provisions on private international law in Sections 3–46 of the Introductory Act of the Civil Code [*Einführungsgesetz zum Bürgerlichen Gesetzbuche*] generally permit the application of the law of other states. The guiding principle for referral is that of the 'closest connection'.[48] Although the courts, pursuant to Section 293 of the Code of Civil Procedure [*Zivilprozessordnung*], may take evidence on this issue, especially by seeking expert opinions, the applicable provisions of foreign law do not count as facts. Rather, they are recognised as valid law and must be applied as they are understood in the respective state.[49] The internal application of foreign private law only meets a reservation of public order. According to Section 6 of the Introductory Act to the Civil Code, the application is forbidden where it 'would lead to a result which is manifestly incompatible with the fundamental principles of German law', in particular fundamental rights.[50]

---

[45]See Hufeld (1997), pp. 114–138.

[46]Wahl (1999).

[47]See Schurig (1981), pp. 51–213; Schinkels (2007), pp. 11–31.

[48]See Kropholler (2006), pp. 25–28; Geisler (2001), pp. 59–81.

[49]See Jansen and Michaels (2003); Trautmann (2011), pp. 164–188.

[50]See Spickhoff (1989) and Helms (2017).

Foreign public law, contrary to foreign private law, is usually not applied internally since such referral would run counter to traditional notions of sovereignty.[51] Nevertheless, the Federal Constitutional Court has since its inception consulted foreign law for interpreting the Basic Law. In its famous '*Lüth*' judgment on the horizontal effect of fundamental rights, it even cited French and American authorities that stress the significance of freedom of speech for democracy in the original language.[52] While such recourse to comparative constitutionalism is highly disputed in some legal orders for reasons of democratic self-government, especially in the United States of America,[53] it has been practised recurrently, though not extensively, in German constitutional adjudication. Many decisions of the Federal Constitutional Court refer to provisions of other constitutions in the transatlantic Western tradition as a matter of course without further explanation and thus recognise a common idealist heritage on which the Basic Law rests.[54] Although some commentators have discovered a 'fifth approach to interpretation'[55] here, which supplements the four accepted canons of construction,[56] concise guidelines have not yet been developed. Frequently, the approach appears random and arbitrary. For this reason, other commentators consider it dispensable. In a more sympathetic appraisal, they detect mere decoration of a result already found. In a less favourable assessment, they insinuate that the judges conceal their actual motivation.[57]

### 2.3.2 Transnational Law

German law does not contain any provision that expressly deals with transnational law in the sense of private rules and agreements across borders enforced by arbitration.[58] It may well be argued, however, that such forms of self-regulation do not differ from any other private agreements or social norms and can hence be treated in the same way.[59]

From this perspective, private autonomy granted by the constitution allows for cross-border contracts within the limits of mandatory private law and fundamental

[51]See Vogel (1965), pp. 194–240; Ohler (2005), pp. 33–48.

[52]BVerfGE 7, 198, 208—*Lüth* (1958).

[53]The debate was triggered by *Lawrence v. Texas*, 539 U.S. 558 (2003); *Roper v. Simmons*, 543 U.S. 551 (2005). See Scalia and Breyer (2005).

[54]For an overview, see Hailbronner and Martini (2017).

[55]Häberle (1989).

[56]See von Savigny (1840), pp. 212–216: 'grammatical', 'logical', 'historical' and 'systematical' interpretation. Under modern constitutionalism, the 'teleological', or 'purposive', approach has replaced the 'logical' method, see Alexy (1978), pp. 295–299.

[57]See Hillgruber (2015).

[58]For this notion of transnational law, see Calliess (2004), pp. 254–255. For other conceptions of transnational law, see the overview in Viellechner (2013), pp. 165–185.

[59]See Michaels (2005) and Röthel (2007).

rights as far as their indirect horizontal effect is recognised.[60] Private autonomy also permits the parties to a dispute in matters of private law to subject themselves to arbitration. Sections 1025–1066 of the Code of Civil Procedure impose but certain limits on arbitration agreements. In particular, pursuant to Section 1030 paragraph 1 of the Code of Civil Procedure, only pecuniary claims are eligible for arbitration. Moreover, pursuant to Section 1059 paragraph 2 number 2 letter b of the Code of Civil Procedure, an arbitration award may be reversed especially if it leads 'to a result contrary to public order'.[61] Regarding foreign arbitration awards, Section 1061 paragraph 1 of the Code of Civil Procedure refers to the New York Convention on the Recognition and Enforcement of Foreign Arbitration Awards of 1958, which equally provides for a public order exception in Article V paragraph 2 letter b.[62]

Yet the question arises if it is appropriate to apply the rules of national private law to cases that imply a cross-border element and touch upon matters to be regulated by public law within the state. The distribution of domains on the Internet and the relating dispute settlement under the auspices of the Internet Corporation for Assigned Names and Numbers, a private corporation pursuant to Californian law, presents a difficult case of this kind.[63]

## 3 Transformations

In a dynamic process of interaction, courts (Sect. 3.1), legislator (Sect. 3.2) and legal scholarship (Sect. 3.3) have successively refined and readjusted the relationship of German law towards other normative orders.

### *3.1 Adjudication*

Frequently, problems arising from the collision of legal orders first confronted the judiciary. Especially the Federal Constitutional Court has taken the opportunity to specify the position of national law towards other normative orders, including federal state law (Sect. 3.1.1), social norms (Sect. 3.1.2), international law (Sect. 3.1.3), European Union Law (Sect. 3.1.4), foreign law (Sect. 3.1.5) and transnational law (Sect. 3.1.6).

---

[60] See notes 19–24 and accompanying text.

[61] See Kornblum (1987) and Geimer (2007).

[62] See Haas (1991) and Solomon (2007).

[63] See Viellechner (2013), pp. 293–300.

### 3.1.1 Federal State Law

In matters of federalism, the Federal Constitutional Court has taken an ambivalent stance, in part strengthening the constitutions of the individual states and their constitutional courts, but ultimately reinforcing the unitarian tendencies that are built into the Basic Law.[64] In particular, it has curbed the scope of application of the fundamental rights guaranteed by the state constitutions both indirectly and directly.

While Article 142 of the Basic Law declares that the fundamental rights guaranteed by the state constitutions remain in force insofar as they conform to the federal charter of fundamental rights, the Federal Constitutional Court has clarified that there may also be conformity when the state rights provide for less or more protection than the federal rights if the more narrowly defined right is to be understood as a minimum guarantee that does not exclude further protection.[65] Nevertheless, the elaborate jurisprudence of the Federal Constitutional Court on the federal charter of fundamental rights, which according to Article 1 paragraph 3 of the Basic Law also extends to the authorities of the individual states, in fact leaves little room for additional protection through state rights.[66]

While the fundamental rights of the states thus generally remain in force at least theoretically, it has long been contested whether they also extend to those acts of the individual states that apply or execute federal laws. A similar issue arises with regard to the implementation of European Union law by the member states.[67] The Federal Constitutional Court has affirmed the applicability of the state rights here, but only insofar as they are identical with the federal rights.[68] It has thereby only ostensibly bolstered the constitutions of the individual states and their constitutional courts for the purposes of reducing its own workload.[69]

### 3.1.2 Social Norms

The diversification of society through migration and the ensuing pluralisation of religions have brought about new conflicts between religious norms and state law. Especially the increasing importance of Islam and, to some extent, Judaism has challenged the constitutional law on religion, which, although generally formulated, was geared to the Christian churches.[70] Such conflicts soon gave rise to litigation

---

[64] See Möstl (2005) and Pohlreich (2014).

[65] BVerfGE 96, 346, 365—*Landesverfassungsgerichte* (1997).

[66] See Bryde (2005) and Badura (2007).

[67] See Kingreen (2013) and Masing (2015).

[68] BVerfGE 96, 345, 366–368—*Landesverfassungsgerichte* (1997).

[69] For a critique, see Menzel (1999).

[70] See Waldhoff (2010) and Walter (2010).

before state courts. For illustrative purposes two striking examples may be mentioned.

The first example concerns the slaughter of animals without stunning, practised in both Islam and Judaism. In this case, the courts had to answer the question in how far such a practice violates the legal provisions on animal protection that have meanwhile attained constitutional status in Article 20a of the Basic Law. The Federal Administrative Court [*Bundesverwaltungsgericht*] and the Federal Constitutional Court fundamentally disagreed on how to reconcile the opposing normative positions. In particular, it was highly disputed between them whether it could be expected of the respective religious communities to forego the consumption of meat, at least beyond ritual acts such as sacrificial ceremonies.[71]

The second example concerns the circumcision of male children, equally practised both in Islam and Judaism. While this practice has not provoked any litigation for a long time, certainly for lack of plaintiffs among the persons affected, the Regional Court of Cologne [*Landgericht Köln*] has recently qualified it as a criminal offence of personal injury, even if it is carried out in accordance with the rules of medical art and the consent of the parents or legal guardians.[72] The decision has provoked a public outcry, not only among the religious communities concerned.[73]

As both examples demonstrate, there is still a high degree of uncertainty about how to deal with the pluralisation of normative standards and the ensuing conflicts between state law and social norms. So far, the courts lack a consistent approach.

### 3.1.3 International Law

In several decisions, the Federal Constitutional Court has incrementally refined the rules on the relationship between national law and international law. From the ensemble of constitutional provisions on the status of international law within national law, notably Articles 1 paragraph 2, 23–26 and 59 of the Basic Law, it has induced a principle of 'friendliness'[74] towards international law [*Völkerrechtsfreundlichkeit*]. From this general principle, it has in turn derived several rules enhancing the internal position of international treaties that used to stand on par with ordinary statutes.

First of all, the Federal Constitutional Court has postulated an obligation of all national authorities to interpret statutes 'in conformity'[75] with the obligations following from international treaties, even if they were enacted afterwards. According to the reasoning of the court, there is a rebuttable presumption that the legislator does

---

[71]See BVerwGE 99, 1—*Schächten* (1995), on the one hand; BVerfGE 104, 337—*Schächten* (2002), on the other hand. For a discussion, see Oebbecke (2002).

[72]LG Köln, NJW 2012, 2128. For a critique, see Wiater (2012).

[73]See, e.g., Zypries (2012), p. 139.

[74]BVerfGE 6, 309, 362–363—*Reichskonkordat* (1957); 18, 112, 121—*Auslieferung I* (1964).

[75]BVerfGE 58, 1, 34—*Eurocontrol I* (1981); 64, 1, 20—*National Iranian Oil Company* (1983).

not intend to violate international law unless clearly stated otherwise. Moreover, the Federal Constitutional Court considers the stipulations of international human rights treaties as an 'interpretive aid'[76] for determining the contents and scope of the fundamental rights contained in the Basic Law because of their common intellectual heritage. These stipulations hence indirectly attain constitutional status. Finally and most importantly, the Federal Constitutional Court has recently imposed on all national authorities an obligation 'to take into account'[77] not only the stipulations of international treaties to which the Federal Republic of Germany is a party, but also the relating decisions of international courts when applying national law. While it has not yet become clear what this obligation precisely means and how it may be met in a methodologically compelling manner, it is certain that it sits in between the doctrines of merely persuasive authority and strictly binding effect.[78] Some authors suggest that the international requirements may be considered in weighting when assessing the proportionality of encroachments on fundamental rights, but it seems more convincing to treat them as authoritative unless they conflict with essential provisions of German law.[79] In any case, a violation of this obligation may be challenged by way of an individual constitutional complaint based on the fundamental right that should have been construed with reference to international law and jurisprudence.[80] Thus, the stipulations of international treaties, in particular those of the European Convention on Human Rights, become constitutionally entrenched.

In the field of tax law, however, the Federal Constitutional Court has lately underlined that the duty to take into account the stipulations of international treaties does not extend to the legislator. According to its reasoning, the principle of democracy requires that parliament be able to revoke the acts of its predecessors.[81] In this regard, it maintains a strictly dualist perspective.[82]

### 3.1.4 European Union Law

The jurisprudence of the Federal Constitutional Court has shaped even more profoundly the relationship between national law and European Union law. In a line of jurisprudence that includes several landmark decisions, it has spelt out the limits of

[76]BVerfGE 74, 358, 370—*Unschuldsvermutung* (1987); 128, 282, 306—*Zwangsbehandlung im Maßregelvollzug* (2011).

[77]BVerfGE 111, 307, 315—*Görgülü* (2004); BVerfGK 9, 174, 186—*Vienna Convention on Consular Relations* (2006).

[78]See Papier (2006) and Proelß (2009).

[79]See Viellechner (2012a).

[80]BVerfGE 111, 307, 329–330—*Görgülü* (2004); BVerfGK 9, 174, 186—*Vienna Convention on Consular Relations* (2006).

[81]BVerfGE 141, 1—*Treaty Override* (2015).

[82]For a critique, see Payandeh (2016).

European integration. Such limits extend to both primary and secondary law of the European Union.

Concerning the primary law contained in the founding treaties, notably the 'Maastricht' judgment of 1993 and the 'Lisbon' judgment of 2009 reviewing parliamentary approval to the founding treaties of the European Union and their revisions have accentuated the principle of democracy as a limit to European integration. With regard to the structure-securing clause of Article 23 paragraph 1 clause 1 of the Basic Law, which expects a commitment of the European Union to democratic principles, the Federal Constitutional Court clings to the democratic origins of European Union law in the parliaments of the member states as the primary and indispensable basis for legitimation, complemented by the European Parliament as a second strand only.[83] In correlation, with regard to the acquis-securing clause in Article 23 paragraph 1 clause 3 of the Basic Law, which prohibits alterations to the essence of the democratic principle within the state by reference to the eternity clause in Article 79 paragraph 3 of the Basic Law, it insists that the national parliament must retain competences of sufficient weight in both extent and substance so as to keep the scope of democratic action meaningful.[84] Additionally, the Federal Constitutional Court emphasises that the Basic Law precludes 'a loss of statehood'.[85] In its view, only the constituent power is entitled to release the state constituted by the Basic Law as set out in Article 146 of the Basic Law. Unless such a step is taken, the Federal Constitutional Court considers the European Union as a new form of organisation between a federal state and a federation of states, designated as 'association' or 'composition of states' [*Staatenverbund*].[86]

Concerning secondary law of the European Union, the Federal Constitutional Court generally accepts the primacy in application as postulated by the European Court of Justice, even though with a different reasoning. From the point of view of the Basic Law, it explains, this is a derived concept, which takes legal effect within the state only through the national order to apply European Union law given by the act approving the founding treaties.[87] At the same time, the Federal Constitutional Court has formulated three reservations for the application of European Union law in Germany.

The first reservation relates to the protection of fundamental rights. Initially, in its famous '*Solange I*'[88] decision of 1974, the Federal Constitutional Court had held that it would continue to exercise its jurisdiction on the application of European law in Germany as long as there is no adequate protection of fundamental rights at the

[83]BVerfGE 89, 155, 184–186—*Maastricht* (1993); 123, 267, 370–381—*Lisbon* (2009). For a critique, see Schönberger (2009).

[84]BVerfGE 89, 155, 172—*Maastricht* (1993); 123, 267, 330—*Lisbon* (2009).

[85]BVerfGE 123, 267, 352—*Lisbon* (2009).

[86]BVerfGE 89, 155, 181—*Maastricht* (1993); 123, 267, 348—*Lisbon* (2009). The term was coined by the former judge Kirchhof (1992), p. 881.

[87]BVerfGE 89, 155, 190—*Maastricht* (1993); 123, 267, 396–397—*Lisbon* (2009).

[88]BVerfGE 37, 271, 285—*Solange I* (1974).

European level. A few years later, in its '*Solange II*'[89] decision of 1986, it reversed this formula, abandoning its competence of control as long as the European Court of Justice guarantees in its case law a protection of fundamental rights that is to be regarded as substantially similar to that required by the Basic Law. In the aftermath, the Federal Constitutional Court has emphasised its 'cooperative relationship'[90] with the European Court of Justice in this matter and reactivated its competence of control only for the improbable case that a structural deficit of fundamental rights protection would reoccur at the European level.[91] Since the Charter of Fundamental Rights of the European Union entered into force with the Treaty of Lisbon in 2009, such a deficit is hardly conceivable.

The second reservation relates to '*ultra vires*'[92] acts that exceed the competences conferred to the European Union. As the Federal Constitutional Court has specified, however, a declaration of inapplicability in this case is subject to a double restriction. Procedurally, it requires a prior reference to the European Court of Justice for a preliminary ruling.[93] Substantially, the breach of competences must be manifest and highly significant.[94] Although it had long been suspected if such a case would appear, the Federal Constitutional Court has recently initiated a first procedure for a preliminary ruling to the European Court of Justice regarding certain acts of the European Central Bank during the Euro crisis,[95] shortly thereafter followed by a second one.[96] Nevertheless, the Federal Constitutional Court has not yet suspended the applicability of European Union law in Germany for transgression of competences, provoking some commentators to suggest that it follows a strategy of 'all bark, no bite'.[97] In a more positive appraisal, shared by some constitutional judges in extra-judicial statements, such a practice proves in an exemplary manner the well-functioning 'multilevel cooperation'[98] or 'network'[99] of European constitutional courts.

The third reservation relates to violations of 'constitutional identity'.[100] This concept has only recently emerged in the jurisprudence of the Federal Constitutional Court. It refers to the inviolable core content of the Basic Law as protected by the

[89]BVerfGE 73, 339, 387—*Solange II* (1986).

[90]BVerfGE 89, 155, 175—*Maastricht* (1993). See also Kirchhof (1998) and Limbach (2000).

[91]BVerfGE 102, 147, 164—*Bananenmarktordnung* (2000).

[92]BVerfGE 89, 155, 187–188—*Maastricht* (1993).

[93]BVerfGE 123, 267, 353–354—*Lisbon* (2009).

[94]BVerfGE 126, 286, 304—*Honeywell* (2010).

[95]BVerfGE 134, 366—*OMT* (2014).

[96]BVerfGE 146, 216—*Anleihenkauf* (2017).

[97]For trenchant critique from former judges of the Federal Constitutional Court, see Herzog and Gerken (2008) and Grimm (2010). The expression was used earlier with regard to the fundamental rights reservation by Schmid (2001).

[98]Voßkuhle (2010).

[99]Paulus (2013).

[100]BVerfGE 123, 267, 354—*Lisbon* (2009).

eternity clause in Article 79 paragraph 3 of the Basic Law, although it is not literally mentioned there. Neither its contours nor its relationship with Article 4 paragraph 2 of the Treaty on European Union, pursuant to which the European Union respects the 'national identities' of the member states, are beyond any doubt yet.[101] It adds to the confusion that the Federal Constitutional Court has lately dealt with both fundamental rights and competence issues under the title of constitutional identity. In 2015, it set aside an order of extradition to Italy on the basis of a European arrest warrant that had been issued for executing a criminal sentence rendered against the complainant in his absence by means of identity review for violation of human dignity.[102]

Apparently, the concept of constitutional identity is about to mutate into an umbrella concept that not only consumes both fundamental rights and competence review of secondary European Union law, but also extends to primary European Union law.[103] Still, the Federal Constitutional Court emphasises that the exercise of its review power corresponds with a principle of 'friendliness'[104] of the Basic Law towards European Union law [*Europarechtsfreundlichkeit*], calling for integration, though not unlimited subordination.

### 3.1.5 Foreign Law

The direct application of foreign law is provided for and regularly practised in matters of private international law.[105] The use of comparative argument, by contrast, although not generally contested even with regard to the interpretation of public law, seems to decrease in recent years. Especially in constitutional law, the case law has grown so complex and dense that it is almost self-supporting. As a consequence, the Federal Constitutional Court feels no longer inclined to extensively citing scholarship or foreign law. Instead it has taken up the habit of nearly exclusively referring to its own prior decisions.[106]

Recourse to foreign law hence occurs but rarely in current constitutional practice. When comparative arguments are advanced, methodology and status often remain obscure. An illustrative example can be found in a case raising the issue of whether the fundamental right to freedom of assembly may be invoked on the premises of an airport that is operated by a private corporation. The Federal Constitutional Court pointed to the doctrine of 'public forum'[107] as developed in U.S. American and Canadian jurisprudence, but finally followed a different line of argument. Apart from

[101] For some interpretations, see, e.g., Ingold (2015) and Wischmeyer (2015).

[102] BVerfGE 140, 317—*Europäischer Haftbefehl II* (2015). For a critique, see Schönberger (2016).

[103] See Dederer (2014).

[104] BVerfGE 123, 267, 354—*Lisbon* (2009). See also Kaiser and Schübel-Pfister (2010).

[105] See notes 47–50 and accompanying text.

[106] See Jestaedt (2009).

[107] BVerfGE 128, 226, 253—*Fraport* (2011).

that, the relevant decision of the U.S. Supreme Court had denied that an airport terminal is a public forum.[108]

Meanwhile, comparative reasoning seems to scale new heights with regard to European integration. The national constitutional courts increasingly engage and reassure with the jurisprudence of their counterparts in order to justify limits to the recognition of European Union law.[109] For example, the Federal Constitutional Court has selectively cited French and Czech decisions in its 'Lisbon' judgment.[110] Inversely and perhaps more extensively, other courts take the jurisprudence of the Federal Constitutional Court as a model.[111] Some observers claim that this judicial dialogue contributes to shaping a common constitutional law in Europe.[112]

### 3.1.6 Transnational Law

Phenomena of private self-regulation and arbitration across borders have rarely occurred before the German courts so far. Yet recently, the private law courts had to deal with a spectacular case in transnational sports law. An Olympic champion in speed skating challenged an award of the Court of Arbitration for Sports that confirmed a doping sanction imposed by the International Skating Union, a non-governmental organisation based in Switzerland.[113]

Because of the monopoly positions of the transnational sports federations, it is highly disputed whether the standard form submission of professional athletes to sports arbitration rests on voluntary consent. Moreover, there is doubt whether sports arbitration meets the rule of law requirements as established within the constitutional state.[114] In the case at hand, the Higher Regional Court of Munich [*Oberlandesgericht München*] found an abuse of a dominant market position as the arbitrators of the Court of Arbitration for Sports are predominantly nominated by the sports federations.[115] The Federal Supreme Court [*Bundesgerichtshof*], by contrast, held that sports federations and athletes may not be divided in opposing camps as regards the fight against doping. It also argued that the procedural rules of the Court of Arbitration for Sports offer sufficient guarantees for safeguarding the rights of the athletes. Therefore, it reversed the decision on appeal.[116]

[108] *International Society for Krishna Consciousness v. Lee*, 505 U.S. 672, 680 (1992).

[109] See Wendel (2013).

[110] BVerfGE 123, 267, 387/400—*Lisbon* (2009).

[111] See the references in Wendel (2013), pp. 344–353.

[112] See Wendel (2013), pp. 360–369.

[113] See Duve and Rösch (2014) and Prütting (2016).

[114] See Adolphsen (2003), pp. 484–704.

[115] OLG München, JZ 2015, 355—*Pechstein* (2015).

[116] BGHZ 210, 292—*Pechstein* (2016). For a critique, see Heermann (2016b).

## 3.2 *Legislation*

The legislator often lags behind the courts in responding to the challenges arising from the pluralisation of law. It has mainly taken action for two purposes. On the one hand, it has strived for clarification, confirming prior judicial decisions. On the other hand, it has tried to settle remaining disputes, in particular with regard to social norms (Sect. 3.2.1), European Union law (Sect. 3.2.2) and transnational law (Sect. 3.2.3).

### 3.2.1 Social Norms

Regarding conflicts between state law and religious norms, the legislator has approved the jurisprudence of the Federal Constitutional Court and tried to resolve remaining issues. In both respects, it has underlined the friendliness of the Basic Law to religion, granting far-reaching exemptions from general law.

Concerning the already familiar conflicts between labour law and religious norms, the legislator has clarified in Section 9 paragraph 1 of the General Act on Equal Treatment [*Allgemeines Gleichbehandlungsgesetz*] that discrimination against employees of religious communities on the grounds of religion may be permissible 'where such grounds constitute a justified occupational requirement for a particular religion or belief, having regard to the ethos of the religious community or organisation in question and by reason of their right to self-determination or by the nature of the particular activity'.[117] In the same vein, Section 9 paragraph 2 of the General Act on Equal Treatment acknowledges the right of religious communities 'to require individuals working for them to act in good faith and with loyalty to the ethos of the organisation'.[118]

Concerning the newly arising conflicts between state law and religious precepts especially from Islam and Judaism, the legislator has equally taken stand in favour of religious freedom. Thus, according to Section 4a paragraph 2 number 2 of the Animal Welfare Act [*Tierschutzgesetz*], an exemption from the prohibition to slaughter warm-blooded animals without stunning may be granted 'where necessary to meet the requirements of members of religious communities . . . whose mandatory rules require ritual slaughter and prohibit consumption of meat of animals not slaughtered in this way'.[119] To the same effect, the legislator has recently inserted a new Section 1631d in the provisions on parental custody of the German Civil Code, explicating not only that care for the person includes 'the right to give consent to the medically unnecessary circumcision of a male child', but also that such circumcision may, in the first six months after the child is born, be performed 'by persons designated by a religious group to perform this procedure if these persons

[117] *Allgemeines Gleichbehandlungsgesetz*, 14 August 2006, BGBl. 2006 I, 1897, 1899.

[118] *Allgemeines Gleichbehandlungsgesetz*, 14 August 2006, BGBl. 2006 I, 1897, 1899.

[119] *Neufassung des Tierschutzgesetzes*, 18 May 2006, BGBl. 2006 I, 1206, 1208–1209.

are specially trained to do so and, without being a physician, are comparably qualified to perform circumcisions'.[120] The legislative materials point out that this provision aims at reconciling the duty of the state to protect the physical integrity of the child with both individual religious freedom and the freedom of religious communities to regulate and administer their affairs independently.[121]

### 3.2.2 European Union Law

With a view to the establishment of the European Union by the Treaty of Maastricht in 1992, the constitution-amending legislator has introduced the complex and detailed new provision in Article 23 of the Basic Law that simultaneously aims at and limits European integration.[122] This provision and its implementing legislation also codify some of the guidelines on European integration that the Federal Constitutional Court had earlier developed in its jurisprudence.

For example, at the level of the constitution, the structure-securing clause in Article 23 paragraph 1 clause 1 of the Basic Law takes up the famous '*Solange II*'[123] formula of the Federal Constitutional Court, presupposing a European Union 'that guarantees a level of protection of fundamental rights essentially comparable to that afforded by this Basic Law'.[124] At the level of ordinary law, two new statutes, the Act on Cooperation between the Federal Government and Parliament in Matters concerning the European Union [*Gesetz über die Zusammenarbeit von Bundesregierung und Deutschem Bundestag in Angelegenheiten der Europäischen Union*][125] and the Act on Cooperation of the Federation and the Federal States in Matters concerning the European Union [*Gesetz über die Zusammenarbeit von Bund und Ländern in Angelegenheiten der Europäischen Union*],[126] specify the procedures for participation of parliament and the individual states through the Federal Council in European law-making. Due to the constitutional jurisprudence on the parliamentary 'responsibility for integration',[127] another statute strengthening the participatory rights of parliament, the Act on the Exercise by Parliament and the Federal Council of their Responsibility for Integration in Matters concerning the European Union [*Gesetz über die Wahrnehmung der Integrationsverantwortung des*

[120] *Gesetz über den Umfang der Personensorge bei einer Beschneidung des männlichen Kindes*, 20 December 2012, BGBl. 2012 I, 2749.

[121] *Entwurf eines Gesetzes über den Umfang der Personensorge bei einer Beschneidung des männlichen Kindes*, 5 November 2012, BT-Drs. 17/11295, 18–19.

[122] See notes 44–46 and accompanying text.

[123] BVerfGE 73, 339, 387—*Solange II* (1986).

[124] *Gesetz zur Änderung des Grundgesetzes*, 21 December 1992, BGBl. 1992 I, 2086.

[125] *Gesetz über die Zusammenarbeit von Bundesregierung und Deutschem Bundestag in Angelegenheiten der Europäischen Union*, 4 July 2013, BGBl. 2013 I, 2170.

[126] *Gesetz über die Zusammenarbeit von Bund und Ländern in Angelegenheiten der Europäischen Union*, 12 March 1993, BGBl. 1993 I, 313.

[127] BVerfGE 123, 267, 351—*Lisbon* (2009).

*Bundestages und des Bundesrates in Angelegenheiten der Europäischen Union*],[128] had to be enacted.

### 3.2.3 Transnational Law

Most recently, the legislator has also largely recognised autonomous regulation and arbitration in the field of transnational sports, especially in the fight against doping. Section 11 of the newly created Act against Doping in Sport [*Gesetz gegen Doping im Sport*] of 2015 reads: 'As a prerequisite for participating in organised sport, sports federations and athletes may conclude arbitration agreements on settling legal disputes arising from such participation if the arbitration agreements integrate sports federations and athletes into national and international sports organisations and if they facilitate, promote or ensure participation in organised sport overall. This is in particular the case if the arbitration agreements are intended to implement the provisions of the World Anti-Doping Code of the World Anti-Doping Agency.'[129]

The provision is remarkable because state law here defers to transnational self-regulation in two respects. Not only does it recognise the substantive private standards of the World-Anti Doping Code to which the Federal Republic of Germany has already committed itself by Article 4 paragraph 1 of the International Convention against Doping in Sport of 2005,[130] but it also declares arbitration agreements in the field of sports as valid. As an explanation, the legislator points to the need for uniform and prompt decisions as well as special expertise regarding the settlement of disputes in sports.[131]

It should be noted, however, that the scope of the provision is not quite clear yet. It appears that it still leaves room for a judicial review of both the conditions of conclusion and the content of the arbitration agreement.[132] Nevertheless, some commentators regard it as unconstitutional for unduly curtailing the freedom of occupation, the guarantee of access to justice and the right to a lawful judge.[133]

---

[128] *Gesetz über die Wahrnehmung der Integrationsverantwortung des Bundestages und des Bundesrates in Angelegenheiten der Europäischen Union*, 22 September 2009, BGBl. 2009 I, 3022.

[129] *Gesetz gegen Doping im Sport*, 10 December 2015, BGBl. 2015 I, 2210, 2212.

[130] *International Convention against Doping in Sport*, 19 October 2005, BGBl. 2007 II, 355, 360.

[131] *Entwurf eines Gesetzes zur Bekämpfung von Doping im Sport*, 13 May 2015, BT-Drs. 18/4898, 38–39.

[132] See Heermann (2016a).

[133] See Bleistein and Degenhart (2015) and Lehner (2015).

## 3.3 Legal Scholarship

Legal scholarship in Germany has played an ambivalent role in grasping issues relating to the pluralisation of law. While some theoretical contributions (Sect. 3.3.1), which are only little influenced by ideology (Sect. 3.3.2), have had a high impact on the international debate, they are hardly reflected in legal doctrine (Sect. 3.3.3) and education (Sect. 3.3.4).

### 3.3.1 Theory

After the enactment and consolidation of the Basic Law, the question of what is law and its relation to justice had lost significance in Germany. Therefore, legal scholarship mainly focused on 'dogmatics',[134] that is the systematic reconstruction of positive law, including the analysis and critique of supreme court jurisprudence. Legal theory and philosophy were only reactivated in extraordinary cases, such as the criminal trials against the border guards after the German unification, which the courts approached by reference to supra-positive law.[135] Under the impact of globalisation, however, the so-called 'basic subjects',[136] in particular legal history, sociology, theory and philosophy, are gaining fresh steam. Research on processes of norm-formation beyond the state, their legality and legitimacy has grown rapidly in recent years.

Perhaps due to the sustained success of the constitutional state, most of these efforts appear as constitutional theory. As a consequence, the concept of 'constitutionalism' beyond the state, or 'constitutionalisation'[137] as a process, has become popular. Broadly speaking, the concept takes the particular conjunction of democracy and the rule of law, including fundamental rights protection, which has evolved within the modern state, as a yardstick for other legal phenomena.[138] It is still an open question, however, if and in how far the notion of constitution and its elements may be detached from the state and transferred to different contexts. Some proponents consciously depart from the statist tradition and try to establish novel concepts of 'multilevel constitutionalism',[139] which are highly contested.[140] The debate started with regard to European law and accelerated at the beginning of the 1990s after the establishment of the European Union through the Treaty of

[134]Herberger (1981) and Bumke (2017).

[135]BGHSt 39, 1—*Mauerschützen I* (1992); 39, 168—*Mauerschützen II* (1993); 41, 101—*Mauerschützen III* (1995). See also Alexy (1993).

[136]Krüper (2017).

[137]Wahl (2002).

[138]Cf. Kadelbach and Kleinlein (2006) and Ley (2009).

[139]For the European Union, see Pernice (2001); for the global level, see Pernice (2006).

[140]See, e.g., Jestaedt (2004).

Maastricht.[141] When legal institutions beyond the state proliferated at the turn of the millennium, it was soon extended to other international organisations,[142] such as the World Trade Organisation[143] or the United Nations Organisation,[144] and international law in its entirety.[145] It was spurred not only by lawyers, but also by leading philosophers such as *Jürgen Habermas*. From the perspective of his discourse theory of law and democracy, he developed a notion of 'shared sovereignty', or 'dual legitimacy', residing in the citizens of the European Union and the peoples of the member states simultaneously.[146] By contrast, he remained sceptical regarding the chances for a democratic constitutionalisation of international law.[147]

Some observers claim that the debate on constitutionalisation originates from Germany, or Europe,[148] but it certainly came up elsewhere[149] and has meanwhile spread around the world.[150] It is true, though, that the debate was particularly pronounced in Germany and strongly influenced by German authors in the international arena.[151] At the same time, German scholarship has produced some of the fiercest opponents to the concept of constitutionalism beyond the state.[152] In this respect, it should also be noted that there had been a similar debate on the constitutionalisation of private associations and corporations that assume public tasks in Germany much earlier.[153]

A widely received approach from systems theory, mainly advanced by *Gunther Teubner* and his disciples, forcefully challenged and further developed the concept of constitutionalisation. Based on *Niklas Luhmann's* assumption of the functional differentiation of society[154] and *Eugen Ehrlich's* sociological theory of 'living law',[155] it identified 'legal pluralism',[156] or 'fragmentation',[157] in the global realm. At the same time, it supposed that the multiplicity of newly emerging legal orders

[141] See Pernice (1995) and Peters (2001).

[142] See Petersmann (1997) and Peters (2011).

[143] See Petersmann (2000) and Krajewski (2001).

[144] See Fassbender (1998).

[145] See Frowein (2000) and Kleinlein (2012).

[146] Habermas (2011), pp. 62–74.

[147] Habermas (2004).

[148] See Ruffert (2004), p. 41; Fassbender (2007), p. 74.

[149] See, e.g., Stein (1981) and Mancini (1989).

[150] See, e.g., Tsagourias (2007) and Dunoff and Trachtman (2009).

[151] See the overview in Schwöbel (2011).

[152] See, e.g., Grimm (2004) and Haltern (2003).

[153] See Teubner (1978).

[154] Luhmann (1984).

[155] Ehrlich (1913).

[156] Teubner (1996).

[157] Fischer-Lescano and Teubner (2006). The idea was taken up by the International Law Commission, Fragmentation of International Law: Difficulties Arising from the Diversification and Expansion of International Law, Report of the Study Group, 13 April 2006, A/CN.4/L.682, 11.

could incrementally bring about their own constitutions, including 'civil constitutions'[158] in the private sectors of world society, such as commerce, sports and the Internet, largely ignored by public law scholarship. An essential element of civil constitutions, in this view, is a 'horizontal effect'[159] of fundamental rights with regard to private actors as known in German constitutional law.

Subsequently, research on these questions has intensified and diversified. A number of authors have developed various competing approaches to the globalisation of law, notably federalist, pluralist and network theories. Almost all of these approaches show a pronounced interdisciplinary orientation and historical information. Some federalist theories of the European Union[160] draw on early conceptions of federalism in the United States of America. Others[161] try to adopt *Carl Schmitt's* little known theory of the federation in which the question of sovereignty 'always remains open'[162] so that it resides in 'an intermediary condition'[163] between unity and diversity. Elaborate theories of global legal pluralism[164] refer to the pluralist theory of the state that *Harold Laski* and others advocated in England at the beginning of the twentieth century,[165] for its part inspired by the theory of corporations that *Otto von Gierke* had earlier developed in Germany.[166] Concurring network theories[167] predominantly borrow from postmodern philosophy and transcend the conventional dichotomies of national and international as well as public and private law.

In part, research in this field has been institutionalised. For example, the Max Planck Institute for Comparative Public Law and International Law in Heidelberg conducted an extensive study on 'International Public Authority'[168] for several years. Its approach expressly turned away from the major concept of constitutionalism. At the same time, it dismissed theories of private ordering from a normative perspective. To this end, it tried to develop criteria for how to assess whether an international act is to be qualified as public and therefore needs democratic legitimation. In many respects, it closely relates to theories of 'global administrative law'[169] developed in the United States of America and Italy.

Large-scale research from a variety of perspectives including political science, philosophy, sociology, economics and history, was carried out in two other contexts.

---

[158]Teubner (2003). For more detail, see Teubner (2012).

[159]Teubner (2006). See also Viellechner (2014).

[160]Schütze (2009).

[161]Schönberger (2004). A related approach has been developed in France by Beaud (2007).

[162]Schmitt (1928), p. 372.

[163]Schmitt (1928), p. 371.

[164]Krisch (2010).

[165]Laski (1916). See also Barker (1915) and Cole (1920).

[166]Von Gierke (1868).

[167]Ladeur (1997, 2004).

[168]Von Bogdandy et al. (2010) and Goldmann (2015).

[169]Kingsbury et al. (2015) and Cassese (2005).

From 2003 to 2014, the German Research Foundation funded a collaborative research centre on 'Transformations of the State'[170] at the University of Bremen. From 2007 to 2017, the excellence initiative of the German federal and state governments supported a research cluster on 'The Formation of Normative Orders'[171] at Goethe University of Frankfurt. Besides, German researchers assumed leading positions in establishing specialised law journals with a theoretical and interdisciplinary focus, such as 'Global Constitutionalism'[172] and 'Transnational Legal Theory'.[173] As a matter of course, major collaborations of this kind do not produce any coherent approach, but support and promote multi-facetted research on the topic.

### 3.3.2 Ideology

Not only in Germany, the contemporary debate on the evolution of law is clearly dominated by theories of 'global constitutionalism'[174] and 'global legal pluralism',[175] which are often presented as opposing each other. Yet indeed, no unified school or movement acts in either line of thought. Rather, significant confusion and overlap occurs for two reasons. On the one hand, it is unclear if and in how far these theories are descriptive or prescriptive. Many of them oscillate between sociological observations and normative proposals to be realised in the future.[176] On the other hand, it is disputed if constitutionalism presupposes a unified and hierarchically structured legal order and a homogeneous social substratum. With regard to federalism and the pluralist immigrant society in the United States of America, this question may be denied.[177] Not surprisingly, then, some authors try to reconcile

[170]DFG-Sonderforschungsbereich 597 '*Staatlichkeit im Wandel*', Universität Bremen, http://www.sfb597.uni-bremen.de (last accessed 30 April 2019).

[171]Exzellenzcluster '*Die Herausbildung normativer Ordnungen*', Goethe-Universität Frankfurt am Main, http://www.normativeorders.net (last accessed 30 April 2019).

[172]Global Constitutionalism, Cambridge University Press, http://www.cambridge.org/core/journals/global-constitutionalism (last accessed 30 April 2019): *Mattias Kumm* (Wissenschaftszentrum Berlin für Sozialforschung, Humboldt University and New York University) and *Antje Wiener* (Universität Hamburg) among founding editors.

[173]Transnational Legal Theory, Routledge, http://www.tandfonline.com/loi/rtlt20 (last accessed 30 April 2019): *Peer Zumbansen* (King's College London, educated in Germany) as convening editor.

[174]For an overview, see Peters (2015).

[175]For an overview, see Michaels (2009). For a historical and conceptual inquiry, see Seinecke (2015).

[176]See Diggelmann and Altwicker (2008).

[177]See Halberstam (2009).

theories of global constitutionalism and global legal pluralism under the hybrid label of 'constitutional pluralism'.[178]

All variants of these approaches meet outright rejection by theories of 'national constitutionalism'[179] that uphold an inextricable link between constitutionalism and the modern nation-state. The essentialist strand of this position assumes that the state precedes the constitution and figures as its exclusive object.[180] The democratic strand of this position argues that the preconditions for collective self-determination, in particular a public sphere where political debate in a common language could take place, do not exist at the European and global levels.[181] Therefore, in this view, speaking of constitutionalism here generates a semblance of legitimacy that conceals the actual loss.[182]

Theories of national constitutionalism are sometimes regarded as conservative, while theories of global constitutionalism generally count as progressive.[183] Yet both theories share a common concern, that is upholding the aspirations of constitutionalism under changing social circumstances. They only disagree about the means to achieve this end. One approach pleads for preservation, the other for transfer of an established model, but none of them may prove to be sustainable, both from a factual and from a normative perspective. Neither national isolation nor global reproduction of the domestic ideal may be possible. Neither unilateral nor unitarian regulation of cross-border issues may be desirable. If this is true, the concept of constitutionalism is currently no more than a reminiscence of a historical achievement as a benchmark. It serves as a cipher under which the reconstruction of law under conditions of globalisation has begun and will continue until more adequate concepts will be discovered.[184]

### 3.3.3 Doctrine

Many theories of law and globalisation rest on a highly abstract level. Some of them lack empirical grounding, not relying on sufficient practical examples. Others fall short of doctrinal elaboration, not spelling out their consequences at the level of legal application.[185] Doctrinal innovation, therefore, is predominantly owed to legal

---

[178]The term was coined by MacCormick (1999), p. 104, and popularised by Walker (2002). For a German adaptation, see Mayer (2016), pp. 28–38. See also Kumm (2009).

[179]For a powerful statement of this antagonism, see Rubenfeld (2004).

[180]See Isensee (2004) and Kirchhof (2004).

[181]See Grimm (1995). For a critique, see Habermas (1995).

[182]See Grimm (2012).

[183]See Fassbender (2007), pp. 87–91. It should be noted, however, that some of the most fervent pleas for national constitutionalism are formulated by liberal constitutional thinkers, see Viellechner (2006), p. 14.

[184]See Viellechner (2015).

[185]For a remedy, see von Bogdandy (2009), p. 364: 'doctrinal constructivism'.

practice, in particular the judiciary, which for its part often lacks sound theoretical grounding.

Notably the Federal Constitutional Court has demonstrated much creativity in dealing with the pluralisation of law. Some of its doctrinal constructions have meanwhile been adopted by other national and international courts. The famous '*Solange*' rules, for example, have migrated into several other contexts to account for complementary fundamental rights protection between different legal orders. Thus, the European Court of Human Rights has adopted the '*Solange II*'[186] idea, transferring it to the relationship between the European Convention on Human Rights and the European Union.[187] Subsequently, the European Court of Justice has brought to bear the '*Solange I*'[188] logic to the relationship between the European Union and the United Nations in cases of individual sanctions against persons suspected of terrorism.[189] It appears likely that the formula will lend itself for application to other constellations as well,[190] including transnational private ordering.[191] Similarly, the idea of 'constitutional identity'[192] as an ultimate limit to European and global integration may well spread out. It is also employed in France, for instance.[193]

While these doctrinal constructions, taken separately, may be useful, the occasional interventions of the judiciary and its specific mode of operation do not allow for developing an overarching approach to the pluralisation of law. Apart from that, the opinions of the Federal Constitutional Court are at times ambiguous, at times even contradictory. For example, when the Federal Constitutional Court developed the far-reaching obligation of all state authorities to take into account the jurisprudence of international courts, in particular the European Court of Human Rights, it nevertheless insisted that the Basic Law 'does not waive the sovereignty contained in the last instance in the German constitution'.[194] Likewise, the tool of identity review has been perceived by some as a democratic variant of arguments founded on sovereignty.[195] Seen from a different angle, however, the doctrinal constructions developed by the Federal Constitutional Court in order to deal with legal pluralism may be considered as inducing a new form of horizontal coordination between the various legal orders that leaves earlier notions of sovereignty behind.[196]

[186]BVerfGE 73, 339, 387—*Solange II* (1986).

[187]ECtHR, Judgment of 30 June 2005, Application 45036/98, *Bosphorus v. Ireland*, § 155.

[188]BVerfGE 37, 271, 285—*Solange I* (1974).

[189]ECJ, Judgment of 3 September 2008, Joined Cases C-402/05 P and C-415/05 P, *Kadi and Al Barakaat v. Council and Commission*, (2008) ECR I-6351, § 322.

[190]See Lavranos (2008) and Tzanakopoulos (2012).

[191]See Viellechner (2013), pp. 285–300.

[192]BVerfGE 123, 267, 354—*Lisbon* (2009).

[193]See Millet (2013).

[194]BVerfGE 111, 307, 319—*Görgülü* (2004).

[195]See Schönberger (2015), p. 48.

[196]See Wendel (2011), pp. 14–45; Viellechner (2012b), pp. 569–574.

Unfortunately, mainstream legal scholarship does not offer much guidance in this regard. Here as elsewhere, it largely retreats to 'constitutional court positivism',[197] reconstructing rather than preparing doctrinal solutions to problems arising from the collision of legal orders. Most efforts dwell on commenting and criticising, systemising and refining the proposals of the constitutional court.

A remarkable exception stems from private law scholarship. Some authors suggest following the model of private international law, or conflict of laws as it is called in Anglo-American jurisprudence, here.[198] A viable form of horizontal coordination would correspondingly consist in the mutual recognition of the various legal orders with a reservation of public order. Indeed, the doctrinal constructions of the Federal Constitutional Court, including the '*Solange*' formulas, identity review and the obligation to take into account international law and jurisprudence, may be construed as different manifestations of public order reservations.[199]

Private international law usefully lends itself as an archetype here for two reasons. Firstly, it has always assumed that there are several valid legal orders coexisting with each other that might simultaneously claim application to cross-border situations.[200] Secondly, since its inception, it has been built on a mechanism of horizontal coordination conceding that conflicts of norms may only be resolved from within a certain legal order, even though its intrinsic logic might strive for generalisation.[201]

At the same time, classical conflict of laws theory suffers from two shortcomings that need to be overcome regarding the current context. Firstly, it is traditionally confined to the supposedly unpolitical realm of private law, which allegedly does not touch upon sovereignty.[202] Secondly, it is conventionally based on a principle of comity that grants recognition to foreign law as a courtesy only.[203]

A contemporary adaptation, by contrast, would under certain circumstances also require the internal application of foreign public law as well as international and non-state law. Inversely, it would expect to modify the standards of national law where it is exceptionally extended to cross-border situations. Thus, the Federal Constitutional Court has approved of restrictions to employment protection for foreign crew members on a sea-going vessel under the German flag, assuming an attenuated effect of the fundamental right to freedom of association in this constellation.[204] The doctrinal construction is not quite clear, but arguably a conflict of laws for the constitution itself would need to be developed for these purposes.[205]

---

[197] The term was coined by Schlink (1989), p. 163.

[198] See Teubner (2012), pp. 225–258; Joerges (2011). For a similar perspective on the relationship between state law and religious norms, see Janssen (2001).

[199] See Viellechner (2012b), pp. 575–577.

[200] See Kegel and Schurig (2004), p. 6.

[201] See Story (1834), pp. 19–38; von Savigny (1849), pp. 23–32.

[202] See Lowenfeld (1979) and Dodge (2008).

[203] See von Savigny (1849), p. 28; Yntema (1963).

[204] BVerfGE 92, 26, 41—*Zweitregister* (1995).

[205] See Bernstein (1965); Kronke (1998), pp. 47–49.

Furthermore, the friendliness of the constitution towards other normative orders would have to be turned into a legally actionable principle in order to make it meaningful, as already practised under the German Basic law with regard to the obligation to take into account international law and jurisprudence.[206]

### 3.3.4 Education

The German system of legal education mirrors the reluctant opening of German law towards other normative orders. Traditionally, studies of law in Germany are geared to obtaining two state examinations that qualify for a career as a judge, prosecutor, civil servant or attorney.[207] For this reason, the correct application of national law counts as the main object and purpose of instruction. Theoretical reflection and international aspects of the law have been marginalised in the past.[208]

Yet more recently, even the standard curriculum reflects the massive influence of external norms on German Law in a double way. On the one hand, course syllabi and textbooks on the core subjects of civil and public law have been supplemented by special sections on the transformation of national norms under the impact of European Union law.[209] On the other hand, courses on 'Constitutional Law III',[210] that is on the references of the constitution to international and European Union law, have grown both in importance and complexity. Nevertheless, a truly transnational legal education is far from being established. The German Science Council has therefore identified a need to strengthen the basic subjects as well as the interdisciplinary and international aspects of legal education in the future.[211]

At the level of graduate education, first steps in this direction have already been taken. From 2006 to 2015, the German Research Foundation supported a graduate college on 'Constitutionalism beyond the State'[212] at Humboldt University of Berlin. Three cohorts of 15 doctoral students und visiting researchers from the disciplines of law, political science, philosophy and history worked on individual dissertation projects relating to the main topic in a structured programme including

[206] See note 80 and accompanying text.

[207] For the state of Berlin as an example, see *Gesetz über die Ausbildung von Juristinnen und Juristen im Land Berlin*, Section 1 paragraph 3, 23 June 2003, GVBl. 2003, 232.

[208] See Hilgendorf (2008).

[209] See, e.g., Looschelders (2018), pp. 17–19; Maurer and Waldhoff (2017), pp. 28–39.

[210] Sauer (2018) and Schweitzer and Dederer (2016).

[211] Wissenschaftsrat, Perspektiven der Rechtswissenschaft in Deutschland: Situation, Analysen, Empfehlungen, Drs. 2558-12, 9 November 2012, http://www.wissenschaftsrat.de/download/archiv/2558-12.pdf (last accessed 30 April 2019).

[212] DFG-Graduiertenkolleg 1263 '*Verfassung jenseits des Staates: Von der europäischen zur globalen Rechtsgemeinschaft?*', http://www.rewi.hu-berlin.de/de/lf/oe/grakov (last accessed 30 April 2019).

methodological training and guest lectures from renowned external experts. So far, the programme has remained unique in kind. Successor institutions with a focus on the law have not yet been established.

## 4 Conclusion

In conclusion, 'friendliness' towards other normative orders can be identified as a characteristic feature of German law. This attitude not only extends to international and European law, but also to societal self-regulation both within and beyond the state. Arguably, it may best be captured and operationalised in a logic known from private international law, that is general recognition with a reservation of public order, which may vary depending on the trustworthiness of the norms to be recognised.

The private international law analogy appears as an attractive instrument for reconciling overlapping legal orders under conditions of globalisation. It combines several advantages. Firstly, from a methodological point of view, it is easy to implement. It can rely on a proven model, which, contrary to other approaches such as weighting, leads to clear-cut and predictable solutions for conflicts of norms. Moreover, due to its intellectual style as 'technique',[213] it may mitigate even highly politicised conflicts that otherwise appear unsolvable. Secondly, from a practical point of view, it is readily acceptable. As it only demands agreement on the terms of engagement, but not on substantive norms, the costs are low. At the same time, as the openness towards others in turn allows for exerting influence on external affairs, the gains are high.[214] Thirdly and finally, from a normative point of view, it is highly appealing. Indeed, it may be regarded as an adequate reformulation of modern constitutionalism in its inherent tension between universalism and particularism, democracy and the rule of law including fundamental rights protection, for the current context. On the one hand, the rule of law in its aspects of legal certainty and equality presses for the mutual recognition of the various legal orders and hence for avoiding norm conflicts as far as possible. On the other hand, however, democracy allows for the self-determination of the various legal orders, at least as long as they do not affect the fundamental rights of outsiders.[215] In between these poles, the processes of mutual recognition and contestation allow for articulating opposition, which may to some extent compensate for the lack of parliamentary law-making at the global scale.[216] The mechanism thus offers a promising fourth way to overcome both the outdated dualist doctrine of sovereigntism and the unattainable monist vision of universalism while avoiding the perils of radical legal pluralism.

---

[213]Knop et al. (2012).

[214]Cf. Resnik (2007).

[215]See Viellechner (2015), p. 256.

[216]Cf. Krisch (2010), pp. 264–276; Ley (2015).

## References

Adolphsen J (2003) Internationale Dopingstrafen. Mohr Siebeck, Tübingen
Alexy R (1978) Theorie der juristischen Argumentation: Die Theorie des rationalen Diskurses als Theorie der juristischen Begründung. Suhrkamp, Frankfurt am Main
Alexy R (1993) Mauerschützen: Zum Verhältnis von Recht, Moral und Strafbarkeit. Vandenhoeck & Ruprecht, Göttingen
Auer M (2005) Materialisierung, Flexibilisierung, Richterfreiheit: Generalklauseln im Spiegel der Antinomien des Privatrechtsdenkens. Mohr Siebeck, Tübingen
Augsberg I (2012) Taking religion seriously: on the legal relevance of religious self-concepts. J Law Rel State 1:291–308
Augsberg I (2014) Informationsverwaltungsrecht: Zur kognitiven Dimension der rechtlichen Steuerung von Verwaltungsentscheidungen. Mohr Siebeck, Tübingen
Bachmann G (2006) Private Ordnung: Grundlagen ziviler Regelsetzung. Mohr Siebeck, Tübingen
Badura P (2007) Stellenwert von Länderverfassungen und Verfassungskonflikten am bayerischen Beispiel. BayVBl 53:193–198
Baldus M (2016) Kämpfe um die Menschenwürde: Die Debatten seit 1949. Suhrkamp, Berlin
Barker E (1915) Political thought in England: from Herbert Spencer to the present day. Williams & Norgate, London
Beaud O (2007) Théorie de la fédération. PUF, Paris
Bernstein H (1965) Ein Kollisionsrecht für die Verfassung. NJW 18:2273–2276
Bleckmann A (1970) Begriff und Kriterien der innerstaatlichen Anwendbarkeit völkerrechtlicher Verträge: Versuch einer allgemeinen Theorie des self-executing treaty auf rechtsvergleichender Grundlage. Duncker & Humblot, Berlin
Bleckmann A (1996) Der Grundsatz der Völkerrechtsfreundlichkeit der deutschen Rechtsordnung. DÖV 49:137–145
Bleistein R, Degenhart C (2015) Sportschiedsgerichtsbarkeit und Verfassungsrecht: Schiedsvereinbarungen und Anti-Doping-Gesetzgebung auf dem Prüfstand. NJW 68:1353–1357
Böckenförde E-W (1972) Die Bedeutung der Unterscheidung von Staat und Gesellschaft im demokratischen Sozialstaat der Gegenwart. In: Böckenförde E-W, Knopp W (eds) Rechtsfragen der Gegenwart: Festgabe für Wolfgang Hefermehl zum 65. Geburtstag. Kohlhammer, Stuttgart, pp 11–36
Breuer R (1976) Direkte und indirekte Rezeption technischer Regeln durch die Rechtsordnung. AöR 101:46–88
Brugger W (2001) Der moderne Verfassungsstaat aus Sicht der amerikanischen Verfassung und des Grundgesetzes. AöR 126:337–402
Bryde B-O (2005) Bundesverfassungsgericht und Landesverfassungsgerichte. NdsVBl-Sonderheft:5–7
Bullinger M (1968) Öffentliches Recht und Privatrecht: Studien über Sinn und Funktionen der Unterscheidung. Kohlhammer, Stuttgart
Bumke C (2017) Rechtsdogmatik: Eine Disziplin und ihre Arbeitsweise. Zugleich eine Studie über das rechtsdogmatische Arbeiten Friedrich Carl von Savignys. Mohr Siebeck, Tübingen
Calliess G-P (2004) Transnationales Verbrauchervertragsrecht. RabelsZ 68:244–287
Cassese S (2005) Il diritto amministrativo globale: une introduzione. Riv trim dir pubbl 55:331–358
Cole GDH (1920) Social theory. Methuen, London
Czermak G, Hilgendorf E (2018) Religions- und Weltanschauungsrecht: Eine Einführung, 2nd edn. Springer, Berlin
Dederer H-G (2014) Die Grenzen des Vorrangs des Unionsrechts: Zur Vereinheitlichung von Grundrechts-, Ultra-vires- und Identitätskontrolle. JZ 69:313–322
Degenhart C (2006) Die Neuordnung der Gesetzgebungskompetenzen durch die Föderalismusreform. NVwZ 25:1209–1216

Denninger E (1990) Verfassungsrechtliche Anforderungen an die Normsetzung im Umwelt- und Technikrecht. Nomos, Baden-Baden
Di Fabio U (1993) Der neue Art. 23 des Grundgesetzes: Positivierung vollzogenen Verfassungswandels oder Verfassungsneuschöpfung? Der Staat 32:191–217
Diggelmann O, Altwicker T (2008) Is there something like a constitution of international law? A critical analysis of the debate on world constitutionalism. ZaöRV 68:623–650
Dodge WS (2008) The public-private distinction in the conflict of laws. Duke J Comp Int Law 18:371–394
Dreier H (2000) Grundrechtsschutz durch Landesverfassungsgerichte. De Gruyter, Berlin
Dunoff JL, Trachtman JP (eds) (2009) Ruling the world? Constitutionalism, international law, and global governance. Cambridge University Press, Cambridge
Dürig G (1956) Der Grundrechtssatz von der Menschenwürde: Entwurf eines praktikablen Wertsystems der Grundrechte aus Art. 1 Abs. 1 in Verbindung mit Art. 19 Abs. 2 des Grundgesetzes. AöR 81:117–157
Duve C, Rösch KÖ (2014) Der Fall Pechstein: Kein Startschuss für eine Neugestaltung der Sportschiedsgerichtsbarkeit. SchiedsVZ 12:216–227
Ehmke H (1962) 'Staat' und 'Gesellschaft' als verfassungstheoretisches Problem. In: Hesse K, Reicke S, Scheuner U (eds) Staatsverfassung und Kirchenordnung: Festgabe für Rudolf Smend zum 80. Geburtstag. Mohr Siebeck, Tübingen, pp 23–49
Ehrlich E (1913) Grundlegung der Soziologie des Rechts. Duncker & Humblot, München
Fassbender B (1998) The United Nations Charter as constitution of the international community. Colum J Transnat Law 36:529–619
Fassbender B (2007) Grund und Grenzen der konstitutionellen Idee im Völkerrecht. In: Depenheuer O, Heintzen M, Jestaedt M, Axer P (eds) Staat im Wort: Festschrift für Josef Isensee. CF Müller, Heidelberg, pp 73–91
Fischer-Lescano A, Teubner G (2006) Regime-Kollisionen: Zur Fragmentierung des globalen Rechts. Suhrkamp, Frankfurt am Main
Flume W (1992) Allgemeiner Teil des Bürgerlichen Rechts, vol 2: Das Rechtsgeschäft, 4th edn. Springer, Berlin
Frowein JA (2000) Konstitutionalisierung des Völkerrechts. BDGVR 39:427–447
Geimer R (2007) Der ordre public in der privaten Schiedsgerichtsbarkeit. In: Nikas NT et al (eds) Studia in honorem Pelayia Yessiou-Faltsi. Sakkoulas, Athens, pp 169–185
Geisler S (2001) Die engste Verbindung im Internationalen Privatrecht. Duncker & Humblot, Berlin
Giddens A (1990) The consequences of modernity. Polity Press, Cambridge
Giegerich T (ed) (2010) Der 'offene Verfassungsstaat' des Grundgesetzes nach 60 Jahren: Anspruch und Wirklichkeit einer großen Errungenschaft. Duncker & Humblot, Berlin
Goldmann M (2015) Internationale öffentliche Gewalt: Handlungsformen internationaler Institutionen im Zeitalter der Globalisierung. Springer, Heidelberg
Grawert R (1987) Die Bedeutung gliedstaatlichen Verfassungsrechts in der Gegenwart. NJW 40:2329–2338
Grimm D (1987) Entstehungs- und Wirkungsbedingungen des modernen Konstitutionalismus. In: Simon D (ed) Akten des 26. Deutschen Rechtshistorikertages. Klostermann, Frankfurt am Main, pp 45–76
Grimm D (1995) Braucht Europa eine Verfassung? JZ 50:581–591
Grimm D (2004) Die Verfassung im Prozess der Entstaatlichung. In: Brenner M, Huber PM, Möstl M (eds) Der Staat des Grundgesetzes: Kontinuität und Wandel. Festschrift für Peter Badura zum 70. Geburtstag. Mohr Siebeck, Tübingen, pp 145–167
Grimm D (2010) Die große Karlsruher Verschiebung: Das Bundesverfassungsgericht will nur noch Strukturveränderungen durch europäische Urteile prüfen – doch die geschehen schleichend. FAZ 9/9:8

Grimm D (2012) Die Errungenschaft des Konstitutionalismus und ihre Aussichten in einer veränderten Welt. In: Grimm D (ed) Die Zukunft der Verfassung II: Auswirkungen von Europäisierung und Globalisierung. Suhrkamp, Berlin, pp 315–344
Grzeszick B (1996) Vom Reich zur Bundesstaatsidee: Zur Herausbildung der Föderalismusidee als Element des modernen deutschen Staatsrechts. Duncker & Humblot, Berlin
Guggenberger B, Stein T (eds) (1991) Die Verfassungsdiskussion im Jahr der deutschen Einheit: Analysen, Hintergründe, Materialien. Hanser, München
Haas U (1991) Die Anerkennung und Vollstreckung ausländischer und internationaler Schiedssprüche. Duncker & Humblot, Berlin
Häberle P (1989) Grundrechtsgeltung und Grundrechtsinterpretation im Verfassungsstaat: Zugleich zur Rechtsvergleichung als ‘fünfter’ Auslegungsmethode. JZ 44:913–919
Habermas J (1995) Remarks on Dieter Grimm’s ‘Does Europe Need a Constitution?’. ELJ 1:303–307
Habermas J (2004) Hat die Konstitutionalisierung des Völkerrechts noch eine Chance? In: Habermas J (ed) Der gespaltene Westen: Kleine Politische Schriften X. Suhrkamp, Frankfurt am Main, pp 113–193
Habermas J (2011) Zur Verfassung Europas: Ein Essay. Suhrkamp, Berlin
Hailbronner M, Martini S (2017) The German Federal Constitutional Court. In: Jakab A, Dyevre A, Itzcovich G (eds) Comparative constitutional reasoning. Cambridge University Press, Cambridge, pp 356–393
Halberstam D (2009) Constitutional heterarchy: the centrality of conflict in the European Union and the United States. In: Dunoff JL, Trachtman JP (eds) Ruling the world? Constitutionalism, international law, and global governance. Cambridge University Press, Cambridge, pp 326–355
Haltern U (2003) Internationales Verfassungsrecht? Anmerkungen zu einer kopernikanischen Wende. AöR 128:511–557
Heermann PW (2016a) Auswirkungen von § 11 AntiDopG auf die deutsche Sportschiedsgerichtsbarkeit. CaS 13:108–117
Heermann PW (2016b) Die Sportschiedsgerichtsbarkeit nach dem Pechstein-Urteil des BGH. NJW 69:2224–2227
Helms T (2017) Ordre public: Der Einfluss der Grund- und Menschenrechte auf das IPR. IPRax 37:153–159
Herberger M (1981) Dogmatik: Zur Geschichte von Begriff und Methode in Medizin und Jurisprudenz. Klostermann, Frankfurt am Main
Herzog R, Gerken L (2008) Stoppt den Europäischen Gerichtshof: Die Kompetenzen der Mitgliedstaaten werden ausgehöhlt. FAZ 9/8:8
Hesse K (1962) Der unitarische Bundesstaat. CF Müller, Karlsruhe
Hesse K (1988) Verfassungsrecht und Privatrecht. CF Müller, Heidelberg
Hilgendorf E (2008) Zur Lage der juristischen Grundlagenforschung in Deutschland heute. In: Brugger W, Neumann U, Kirste S (eds) Rechtsphilosophie im 21. Jahrhundert. Suhrkamp, Frankfurt am Main, pp 111–133
Hillgruber C (2015) Die Bedeutung der Rechtsvergleichung für das deutsche Verfassungsrecht und die verfassungsgerichtliche Rechtsprechung in Deutschland. JöR NF 63:367–388
Hobe S (1998) Der offene Verfassungsstaat zwischen Souveränität und Interdependenz: Eine Studie zur Wandlung des Staatsbegriffs der deutschsprachigen Staatslehre im Kontext internationaler institutionalisierter Kooperation. Duncker & Humblot, Berlin
Holmes S (1988) Precommitment and the paradox of democracy. In: Elster J, Slagstad R (eds) Constitutionalism and democracy. Cambridge University Press, Cambridge, pp 195–240
Hufeld U (1997) Die Verfassungsdurchbrechung: Rechtsproblem der Deutschen Einheit und der europäischen Einigung. Duncker & Humblot, Berlin
Ingold A (2015) Die verfassungsrechtliche Identität der Bundesrepublik Deutschland: Karriere, Konzept, Kritik. AöR 140:1–30
Ipsen HP (1950) Über das Grundgesetz. Universitätsverlag, Hamburg

Ipsen J (2006) Die Kompetenzverteilung zwischen Bund und Ländern nach der Föderalismusnovelle. NJW 59:2801–2806
Isensee J (1990) Der Föderalismus und der Verfassungsstaat der Gegenwart. AöR 115:248–279
Isensee J (2004) Staat und Verfassung. In: Isensee J, Kirchhof P (eds) Handbuch des Staatsrechts der Bundesrepublik Deutschland, vol 2, 3rd edn. CF Müller, Heidelberg, pp 3–106
Jansen N, Michaels R (2003) Die Auslegung und Fortbildung ausländischen Rechts. ZZP 116:3–55
Janssen A (2001) Staatskirchenrecht als Kollisionsrecht: Überlegungen zur Auslegung der Artikel 140 GG/137 Abs. 5 WRV. In: Bohnert J, Gramm C, Kindhäuser U, Lege J, Rinken A, Robbers G (eds) Verfassung, Philosophie, Kirche: Festschrift für Alexander Hollerbach zum 70. Geburtstag. Duncker & Humblot, Berlin, pp 707–736
Jellinek G (1882) Die Lehre von den Staatenverbindungen. Hölder, Wien
Jestaedt M (2004) Der Europäische Verfassungsverbund: Verfassungstheoretischer Charme und rechtstheoretische Insuffizienz einer Unschärferelation. In: Krause R, Veelken W, Vieweg K (eds) Recht der Wirtschaft und der Arbeit in Europa: Gedächtnisschrift für Wolfgang Blomeyer. Duncker & Humblot, Berlin, pp 637–674
Jestaedt M (2009) Autorität und Zitat: Anmerkungen zur Zitierpraxis des Bundesverfassungsgerichts. In: Detterbeck S, Rozek J, von Coelln C (eds) Recht als Medium der Staatlichkeit: Festschrift für Herbert Bethge zum 70. Geburtstag. Duncker & Humblot, Berlin, pp 513–533
Joerges C (2011) A new type of conflicts law as the legal paradigm of the postnational constellation. In: Joerges C, Falke J (eds) Karl Polanyi, Globalisation and the potential of law in transnational markets. Hart, Oxford, pp 465–501
Kadelbach S, Kleinlein T (2006) Überstaatliches Verfassungsrecht: Zur Konstitutionalisierung im Völkerrecht. AVR 44:235–266
Kaiser K, Schübel-Pfister I (2010) Der ungeschriebene Verfassungsgrundsatz der Europarechtsfreundlichkeit: Trick or Treat? In: Emmenegger S, Wiedmann A (eds) Linien der Rechtsprechung des Bundesverfassungsgerichts: Erörtert von den wissenschaftlichen Mitarbeitern, vol 2. De Gruyter, Berlin, pp 545–572
Kegel G, Schurig K (2004) Internationales Privatrecht, 9th edn. CH Beck, München
Kersten J (1993) Homogenitätsgebot und Landesverfassungsrecht. DÖV 46:896–902
Kingreen T (2013) Die Grundrechte des Grundgesetzes im europäischen Grundrechtsföderalismus. JZ 68:801–811
Kingsbury B, Krisch N, Stewart RB (2015) The emergence of global administrative law. Law Contemp Probl 68:15–61
Kirchhof F (1987) Private Rechtsetzung. Duncker & Humblot, Berlin
Kirchhof P (1992) Der deutsche Staat im Prozeß der europäischen Integration. In: Isensee J, Kirchhof P (eds) Handbuch des Staatsrechts der Bundesrepublik Deutschland, vol 7. CF Müller, Heidelberg, pp 855–887
Kirchhof P (1998) Das Kooperationsverhältnis zwischen Bundesverfassungsgericht und Europäischem Gerichtshof. In: Müller-Graff P-C (ed) Perspektiven des Rechts in der Europäischen Union. CF Müller, Heidelberg, pp 163–182
Kirchhof P (2004) Die Identität der Verfassung. In: Isensee J, Kirchhof P (eds) Handbuch des Staatsrechts der Bundesrepublik Deutschland, vol 2, 3rd edn. CF Müller, Heidelberg, pp 261–316
Kleinlein T (2012) Konstitutionalisierung im Völkerrecht: Konstruktion und Elemente einer idealistischen Völkerrechtslehre. Springer, Heidelberg
Knop K, Michaels R, Riles A (2012) From multiculturalism to technique: feminism, culture, and the conflict of laws style. Stanford Law Rev 64:589–656
Koch H-J (1986) Grenzen der Rechtsverbindlichkeit technischer Regeln im öffentlichen Baurecht. Werner, Düsseldorf
Kornblum U (1987) 'Ordre public transnational', 'ordre public international' und 'ordre public interne' im Recht der privaten Schiedsgerichtsbarkeit. In: Habscheid WJ, Schwab KH (eds)

Beiträge zum internationalen Verfahrensrecht und zur Schiedsgerichtsbarkeit: Festschrift für Heinrich Nagel zum 75. Geburtstag. Aschendorff, Münster, pp 140–156
Krajewski M (2001) Verfassungsperspektiven und Legitimation des Rechts der Welthandelsorganisation. Duncker & Humblot, Berlin
Krisch N (2010) Beyond constitutionalism: the pluralist structure of postnational law. Oxford University Press, Oxford
Kronke H (1998) Die Wirkungskraft der Grundrechte bei Fällen mit Auslandsbezug. BDGVR 38:33–69
Kropholler J (2006) Internationales Privatrecht: Einschließlich der Grundbegriffe des Internationalen Zivilverfahrensrechts, 6th edn. Mohr Siebeck, Tübingen
Krüper J (ed) (2017) Grundlagen des Rechts, 3rd edn. Nomos, Baden-Baden
Kumm M (2009) The cosmopolitan turn in constitutionalism: on the relationship between constitutionalism in and beyond the state. In: Dunoff JL, Trachtman JP (eds) Ruling the world? Constitutionalism, international law, and global governance. Cambridge University Press, Cambridge, pp 258–324
Laband P (1911) Das Staatsrecht des Deutschen Reiches, vol 1, 5th edn. Mohr Siebeck, Tübingen
Ladeur K-H (1995) Das Umweltrecht der Wissensgesellschaft: Von der Gefahrenabwehr zum Risikomanagement. Duncker & Humblot, Berlin
Ladeur K-H (1997) Towards a legal theory of supranationality: the viability of the network concept. ELJ 3:33–54
Ladeur K-H (2000) Negative Freiheitsrechte und gesellschaftliche Selbstorganisation: Zur Erzeugung von Sozialkapital durch Institutionen. Mohr Siebeck, Tübingen
Ladeur K-H (2004) Globalization and the conversion of democracy to polycentric networks: can democracy survive the end of the nation-state? In: Ladeur K-H (ed) Public governance in the age of globalization. Ashgate, Aldershot, pp 89–118
Laski HJ (1916) The sovereignty of the state. J Phil 13:85–97
Lavranos N (2008) The Solange-method as a tool for regulating competing jurisdictions among international courts and tribunals. Loy Los Angel Int Comp Law Rev 30:275–334
Lehner M (2015) Fehlende Verfassungskonformität des geplanten Anti-Doping-Gesetzes. CaS 12:130–135
Ley I (2009) Kant versus Locke: Europarechtlicher und völkerrechtlicher Konstitutionalismus im Vergleich. ZaöRV 69:317–345
Ley I (2015) Opposition im Völkerrecht: Ein Beitrag zur Legitimation internationaler Rechtserzeugung. Springer, Heidelberg
Limbach J (2000) Die Kooperation der Gerichte in der zukünftigen europäischen Grundrechtsarchitektur: Ein Beitrag zur Neubestimmung des Verhältnisses von Bundesverfassungsgericht, Gerichtshof der Europäischen Gemeinschaften und Europäischem Gerichtshof für Menschenrechte. EuGRZ 27:417–420
Looschelders D (2018) Schuldrecht: Allgemeiner Teil, 16th edn. Vahlen, München
Lowenfeld AF (1979) Public law in the international arena: conflict of laws, international law, and some suggestions for their interaction. RdC 163:311–445
Lübbe-Wolff G (1991) Verfassungsrechtliche Fragen der Normsetzung und Normkonkretisierung im Umweltrecht. ZG 6:219–248
Luhmann N (1984) Soziale Systeme: Grundriß einer allgemeinen Theorie. Suhrkamp, Frankfurt am Main
Luhmann N (1997) Die Gesellschaft der Gesellschaft, vol 1. Suhrkamp, Frankfurt am Main
MacCormick N (1999) Juridical pluralism and the risk of constitutional conflict. In: MacCormick N (ed) Questioning sovereignty: law, state, and nation in the European commonwealth. Oxford University Press, Oxford, pp 97–121
Mager U (2003) Einrichtungsgarantien: Entstehung, Wurzeln, Wandlungen und grundgesetzgemäße Neubestimmung einer dogmatischen Figur des Verfassungsrechts. Mohr Siebeck, Tübingen
Mancini GF (1989) The making of a constitution for Europe. CMLR 26:595–614

Marburger P (1979) Die Regeln der Technik im Recht. Heymanns, Köln
Masing J (2015) Einheit und Vielfalt des Europäischen Grundrechtsschutzes. JZ 70:477–487
Maurer H, Waldhoff C (2017) Allgemeines Verwaltungsrecht, 19th edn. CH Beck, München
Mayer FC (2016) Verfassung im Nationalstaat: Von der Gesamtordnung zur europäischen Teilordnung? VVDStRL 75:7–64
Menger C-F (1973) Zum Stand der Meinungen über die Unterscheidung von öffentlichem und privatem Recht. In: Menger C-F (ed) Fortschritte des Verwaltungsrechts: Festschrift für Hans J. Wolff zum 75. Geburtstag. CH Beck, München, pp 149–166
Menzel J (1999) Verfahrensgrundrechte vor Landesverfassungsgerichten: Noch ein Kooperationsverhältnis? NVwZ 18:1314–1317
Michaels R (2005) The re-state-ment of non-state law: the state, choice of law, and the challenge from global legal pluralism. Wayne Law Rev 51:1209–1259
Michaels R (2009) Global legal pluralism. Annu Rev Law Soc Sci 5:243–262
Millet F-X (2013) L'Union européenne et l'identité constitutionnelle des États membres. LGDJ, Paris
Molitor E (1949) Über öffentliches Recht und Privatrecht: Eine rechtssystematische Studie. CF Müller, Karlsruhe
Morlok M (1993) Selbstverständnis als Rechtskriterium. Mohr Siebeck, Tübingen
Mosler H (1957) Das Völkerrecht in der Praxis der deutschen Gerichte. CF Müller, Karlsruhe
Möstl M (2005) Landesverfassungsrecht – zum Schattendasein verurteilt? Eine Positionsbestimmung im bundesstaatlichen und supranationalen Verfassungsverbund. AöR 130:350–391
Nicklisch F (1986) Technologierecht und Rechtsfortbildung. In: Hochschullehrer der Juristischen Fakultät der Universität Heidelberg (ed) Richterliche Rechtsfortbildung: Erscheinungsformen, Auftrag und Grenzen. Festschrift der Juristischen Fakultät zur 600-Jahr-Feier der Ruprechts-Karls-Universität Heidelberg. CF Müller, Heidelberg, pp 231–260
Nonet P, Selznick P (1978) Law and society in transition: toward responsive law. Harper & Row, New York
Oebbecke J (2002) Islamisches Schlachten und Tierschutz. NVwZ 21:302–303
Ohler C (2005) Die Kollisionsordnung des Allgemeinen Verwaltungsrechts: Strukturen des deutschen Internationalen Verwaltungsrechts. Mohr Siebeck, Tübingen
Papier H-J (2006) Umsetzung und Wirkung der Entscheidungen des Europäischen Gerichtshofes für Menschenrechte aus der Perspektive der nationalen deutschen Gerichte. EuGRZ 33:1–3
Partsch KJ (1964) Die Anwendung des Völkerrechts im innerstaatlichen Recht: Überprüfung der Transformationslehre. BDGVR 6:13–155
Paulus A (2013) Human rights protection in a European network of courts. Am Soc Int Law Proc 107:174–182
Payandeh M (2009) Völkerrechtsfreundlichkeit als Verfassungsprinzip: Ein Beitrag des Grundgesetzes zur Einheit von Völkerrecht und nationalem Recht. JöR NF 57:465–502
Payandeh M (2016) Grenzen der Völkerrechtsfreundlichkeit: Der Treaty Override-Beschluss des BVerfG. NJW 69:1279–1282
Pernice I (1995) Bestandssicherung der Verfassungen: Verfassungsrechtliche Mechanismen zur Wahrung der Verfassungsordnung. In: Bieber R, Widmer P (eds) L'espace constitutionnel européen. Schulthess, Zürich, pp 225–264
Pernice I (2001) Europäisches und nationales Verfassungsrecht. VVDStRL 60:148–193
Pernice I (2006) The global dimension of multilevel constitutionalism: a legal response to the challenges of globalisation. In: Dupuy P-M, Fassbender B, Shaw MN, Sommermann K-P (eds) Völkerrecht als Wertordnung: Festschrift für Christian Tomuschat. Engel, Kehl am Rhein, pp 973–1005
Peters A (2001) Elemente einer Theorie der Verfassung Europas. Duncker & Humblot, Berlin
Peters A (2011) The constitutionalisation of international organisations. In: Walker N, Shaw J, Tierney S (eds) Europe's Constitutional Mosaic. Hart, Oxford, pp 253–285
Peters A (2015) Global constitutionalism. In: Gibbons MT (ed) The encyclopedia of political thought, vol 3. Wiley-Blackwell, Chichester, pp 1484–1487

Petersmann EU (1997) Constitutionalism and international organizations. Northwest J Int Law Bus 17:398–469
Petersmann EU (2000) The WTO constitution and human rights. JIEL 3:19–25
Pitkin HF (1967) The concept of representation. University of California Press, Berkeley
Pohlreich E (2014) Die Rechtsprechung des Bundesverfassungsgerichts zu seinem Verhältnis zu den Landesverfassungsgerichten in Verfassungsbeschwerdeverfahren. In: Becker Y, Lange F (eds) Linien der Rechtsprechung des Bundesverfassungsgerichts: Erörtert von den wissenschaftlichen Mitarbeiterinnen und Mitarbeitern, vol 3. De Gruyter, Berlin, pp 37–62
Proelß A (2009) Der Grundsatz der völkerrechtsfreundlichen Auslegung im Lichte der Rechtsprechung des BVerfG. In: Rensen H, Brink S (eds) Linien der Rechtsprechung des Bundesverfassungsgerichts: Erörtert von den wissenschaftlichen Mitarbeitern, vol 1. De Gruyter, Berlin, pp 553–584
Prütting H (2016) Das Pechstein-Urteil des BGH und die Krise der Sport-Schiedsgerichtsbarkeit. SpuRt 23:143–148
Resnik J (2007) Foreign as domestic affairs: rethinking horizontal federalism and foreign affairs preemption in light of translocal internationalism. Emory Law J 57:31–92
Ridder H (1975) Die soziale Ordnung des Grundgesetzes: Leitfaden zu den Grundrechten einer demokratischen Verfassung. Westdeutscher Verlag, Opladen
Rosenfeld M (1994) Modern constitutionalism as interplay between identity and diversity. In: Rosenfeld M (ed) Constitutionalism, identity, difference, and legitimacy: theoretical perspectives. Duke University Press, Durham, pp 3–35
Röthel A (2007) Lex mercatoria, lex sportiva, lex technica: Private Rechtsetzung jenseits des Nationalstaats? JZ 62:755–763
Rubenfeld J (2004) Unilateralism and constitutionalism. NYU Law Rev 79:1971–2028
Rudolf W (1967) Völkerrecht und deutsches Recht: Theoretische und dogmatische Untersuchungen über die Anwendung völkerrechtlicher Normen in der Bundesrepublik Deutschland. Mohr Siebeck, Tübingen
Ruffert M (2004) Die Globalisierung als Herausforderung an das Öffentliche Recht. Boorberg, Stuttgart
Sassen S (2007) A sociology of globalization. Norton, New York
Sauer H (2018) Staatsrecht III: Auswärtige Gewalt, Bezüge des Grundgesetzes zu Völker- und Europarecht, 5th edn. CH Beck, München
Scalia A, Breyer S (2005) The relevance of foreign legal materials in U.S. constitutional cases: a conversation between Supreme Court justices. Int J Constit Law 3:519–441
Schinkels B (2007) Normsatzstruktur des IPR: Zur rechtstheoretischen Einordnung des Befehls der ‘Anwendung’ ausländischem Recht entnommener Normsätze im autonomen deutschen IPR. Mohr Siebeck, Tübingen
Schlink B (1989) Die Entthronung der Staatsrechtswissenschaft durch die Verfassungsgerichtsbarkeit. Der Staat 28:161–172
Schmalenbach K (1996) Der neue Europaartikel 23 des Grundgesetzes im Lichte der Arbeit der Gemeinsamen Verfassungskommission: Motive einer Verfassungsänderung. Duncker & Humblot, Berlin
Schmid CU (2001) All bark and no bite: notes on the Federal Constitutional Court’s ‘Banana Decision’. ELJ 7:95–113
Schmitt C (1928) Verfassungslehre. Duncker & Humblot, München
Schönberger C (2004) Die Europäische Union als Bund: Zugleich ein Beitrag zur Verabschiedung des Staatenbund-Bundesstaat-Schemas. AöR 129:81–120
Schönberger C (2009) Die Europäische Union zwischen ‘Demokratiedefizit’ und Bundesstaatsverbot. Der Staat 48:535–558
Schönberger C (2015) Identitäterä: Verfassungsidentität zwischen Widerstandsformel und Musealisierung des Grundgesetzes. JöR NF 63:41–62

Schönberger C (2016) Anmerkung zu der Entscheidung des BVerfG vom 15.12.2015 (2 BvR 2735/14). JZ 71:422–424
Schuppert GF, Bumke C (2000) Die Konstitutionalisierung der Rechtsordnung: Überlegungen zum Verhältnis von verfassungsrechtlicher Ausstrahlungswirkung und Eigenständigkeit des 'einfachen' Rechts. Nomos, Baden-Baden
Schurig K (1981) Kollisionsnorm und Sachrecht: Zu Struktur, Standort und Methode des internationalen Privatrechts. Duncker & Humblot, Berlin
Schütze R (2009) From dual to cooperative federalism: the changing structure of European law. Oxford University Press, Oxford
Schweitzer M, Dederer H-G (2016) Staatsrecht III: Staatsrecht, Völkerrecht, Europarecht, 11th edn. CF Müller, Heidelberg
Schwöbel CEJ (2011) Global constitutionalism in international legal perspective. Nijhoff, Leiden
Seinecke R (2015) Das Recht des Rechtspluralismus. Mohr Siebeck, Tübingen
Solomon D (2007) Die Verbindlichkeit von Schiedssprüchen in der internationalen privaten Schiedsgerichtsbarkeit: Zur Bedeutung nationaler Rechtsordnungen und der Entscheidungen nationaler Gerichte für die Wirksamkeit internationaler Schiedssprüche. Sellier, München
Spickhoff A (1989) Der ordre public im internationalen Privatrecht: Entwicklung, Struktur, Konkretisierung. Metzner, Neuwied
Stein E (1981) Lawyers, judges, and the making of a transnational constitution. Am J Int Law 75:1–27
Story J (1834) Commentaries of the conflict laws, foreign and domestic: in regard to contracts, rights, and remedies, and especially in regard to marriages, divorces, wills, successions, and judgments. Hilliard, Gray, Boston
Teubner G (1971) Standards und Direktiven in Generalklauseln: Möglichkeiten und Grenzen der empirischen Sozialforschung bei der Präzisierung der Gute-Sitten-Klauseln im Privatrecht. Athenäeum, Frankfurt am Main
Teubner G (1978) Organisationsdemokratie und Verbandsverfassung: Rechtsmodelle für politisch relevante Verbände. Mohr Siebeck, Tübingen
Teubner G (1996) Globale Bukowina: Zur Emergenz eines transnationalen Rechtspluralismus. RJ 15:255–290
Teubner G (2003) Globale Zivilverfassungen: Alternativen zur staatszentrierten Verfassungstheorie. ZaöRV 63:1–28
Teubner G (2006) Die anonyme Matrix: Zu Menschenrechtsverletzungen durch 'private' transnationale Akteure. Der Staat 45:161–187
Teubner G (2012) Verfassungsfragmente: Gesellschaftlicher Konstitutionalismus in der Globalisierung. Suhrkamp, Berlin
Thüsing (2006) Kirchliches Arbeitsrecht: Rechtsprechung und Diskussionsstand im Schnittpunkt von staatlichem Arbeitsrecht und kirchlichem Dienstrecht. Mohr Siebeck, Tübingen
Trautmann C (2011) Europäisches Kollisionsrecht und ausländisches Recht im nationalen Zivilverfahren. Mohr Siebeck, Tübingen
Tsagourias N (ed) (2007) Transnational constitutionalism: international and European models. Cambridge University Press, Cambridge
Tzanakopoulos A (2012) Judicial dialogue in multi-level governance: the impact of the Solange argument. In: Fauchald OK, Nollkaemper A (eds) The practice of international and national courts and the (de-)fragmentation of international law. Hart, Oxford, pp 185–215
Unruh P (2018) Religionsverfassungsrecht, 4th edn. Nomos, Baden-Baden
Vesting T (2001) Subjektive Freiheitsrechte als Elemente von Selbstorganisations- und Selbstregulierungsprozessen in der liberalen Gesellschaft: Dargestellt am Beispiel der Bedeutung der Intellectual Property Rights in der neuen Netzwerkökonomie. Die Verw-Beiheft 4:21–57
Viellechner L (2006) Amerikanischer Unilateralismus als Verfassungsfrage? Zur rechtlichen Begründung des einseitigen Handelns der USA auf internationaler Ebene. Der Staat 45:1–26

Viellechner L (2012a) Berücksichtigungspflicht als Kollisionsregel: Zu den innerstaatlichen Wirkungen von völkerrechtlichen Verträgen und Entscheidungen internationaler Gerichte, insbesondere bei der Auslegung und Anwendung von Grundrechten. In: Matz-Lück N, Hong M (eds) Grundrechte und Grundfreiheiten im Mehrebenensystem: Konkurrenzen und Interferenzen. Springer, Heidelberg, pp 109–159
Viellechner L (2012b) Responsiver Rechtspluralismus: Zur Entwicklung eines transnationalen Kollisionsrechts. Der Staat 51:559–580
Viellechner L (2013) Transnationalisierung des Rechts. Velbrück, Weilerswist
Viellechner L (2014) Die transnationale Dimension der Grundrechte. In: Vesting T, Korioth S, Augsberg I (eds) Grundrechte als Phänomene kollektiver Ordnung: Zur Wiedergewinnung der Gesellschaftlichen in der Grundrechtstheorie und Grundrechtsdogmatik. Mohr Siebeck, Tübingen, pp 295–316
Viellechner L (2015) Verfassung als Chiffre: Zur Konvergenz von konstitutionalistischen und pluralistischen Perspektiven auf die Globalisierung des Rechts. ZaöRV 75:233–258
Vogel K (1964) Die Verfassungsentscheidung des Grundgesetzes für eine internationale Zusammenarbeit: Ein Diskussionsbeitrag zu einer Frage der Staatstheorie sowie des geltenden deutschen Staatsrechts. Mohr Siebeck, Tübingen
Vogel K (1965) Der räumliche Anwendungsbereich der Verwaltungsrechtsnorm: Eine Untersuchung über die Grundfragen des sog. Internationalen Verwaltungs- und Steuerrechts. Metzner, Frankfurt am Main
Vogel K (1997) Wortbruch im Verfassungsrecht: Mit einer Bemerkung zum Verhältnis zwischen Bundesverfassungsgericht und demokratischem Gesetzgeber. JZ 52:161–167
von Bogdandy A (2009) The past and promise of doctrinal constructivism: a strategy for responding to the challenges facing constitutional scholarship in Europe. Int J Constit Law 7:364–400
von Bogdandy A, Wolfrum R, von Bernstorff J, Dann P, Goldmann M (eds) (2010) The exercise of public authority by international institutions: advancing international institutional law. Springer, Heidelberg
von Gierke O (1868) Das deutsche Genossenschaftsrecht, vol 1. Weidmann, Berlin
von Savigny FC (1840) System des heutigen Römischen Rechts, vol 1. Veit, Berlin
von Savigny FC (1849) System des heutigen Römischen Rechts, vol 8. Veit, Berlin
Voßkuhle A (2010) Der europäische Verfassungsgerichtsverbund. NVwZ 29:1–8
Wahl R (1999) Die zweite Phase des Öffentlichen Rechts in Deutschland: Die Europäisierung des Öffentlichen Rechts. Der Staat 38:495–518
Wahl R (2002) Konstitutionalisierung: Leitbegriff oder Allerweltsbegriff? In: Eberle C-E, Ibler M, Lorenz D (eds) Der Wandel des Staates vor den Herausforderungen der Gegenwart: Festschrift für Winfried Brohm zum 70. Geburtstag. CH Beck, München, pp 191–207
Waldenfels B (1987) Ordnung im Zwielicht. Suhrkamp, Frankfurt am Main
Waldhoff C (2010) Neue Religionskonflikte und staatliche Neutralität: Erfordern weltanschauliche und religiöse Entwicklungen Antworten des Staates? Gutachten zum 68. Deutschen Juristentag. CH Beck, München
Walker N (2002) The idea of constitutional pluralism. MLR 65:317–359
Walter C (2010) Neue Religionskonflikte und staatliche Neutralität: Erfordern weltanschauliche und religiöse Entwicklungen Antworten des Staates? DVBl 125:993–1000
Weber W (1949) Weimarer Verfassung und Bonner Grundgesetz. Fleischer, Göttingen
Wendel M (2011) Permeabilität im europäischen Verfassungsrecht: Verfassungsrechtliche Integrationsnormen auf Staats- und Unionsebene im Vergleich. Mohr Siebeck, Tübingen
Wendel M (2013) Richterliche Rechtsvergleichung als Dialogform: Die Integrationsrechtsprechung nationaler Verfassungsgerichte in gemeineuropäischer Perspektive. Der Staat 52:339–370
Wiater P (2012) Rechtspluralismus und Grundrechtsschutz: Das Kölner Beschneidungsurteil. NVwZ 31:1379–1382
Wielsch D (2009) Die epistemische Analyse des Rechts: Von der ökonomischen zur ökologischen Rationalität in der Rechtswissenschaft. JZ 64:67–77

Wischmeyer T (2015) Nationale Identität und Verfassungsidentität: Schutzgehalte, Instrumente, Perspektiven. AöR 140:415–460
Wolff HJ (1950) Der Unterschied zwischen öffentlichem und privatem Recht. AöR 76:205–217
Yntema HE (1963) The comity doctrine. In: von Caemmerer E, Nikisch A, Zweigert K (eds) Vom deutschen zum europäischen Recht: Festschrift für Hans Dölle, vol 2. Mohr Siebeck, Tübingen, pp 65–86
Zypries B (2012) Ist die religiöse Beschneidung Körperverletzung? Contra: Lassen wir die Kirche im Dorf! RuP 48:139

# Between Constitutionalism and Legal Pluralism: Perspectives from Greece

**Ioannis A. Tassopoulos**

**Abstract** The relationship between the Greek Constitution and European law; the bailout of Greece by combined action of national, European and international institutions; the haircut of Greek bonds to reduce sovereign debt; the compulsory application of sharia law over the Muslim population of a specific region of the country; the impact of the Judgments of the ECHR in the domestic legal order; and the refugee crisis which marks the return of territoriality associated with national sovereignty, are central fields where legal pluralism is tested, in an interplay of national, European and international law. The Greek experience highlights the current dilemma, whether the prevailing trend in the age of globalization is going to be primarily a process of constitutionalization of international law, or, rather, the reverse one. The question is particularly acute in Europe, where both visions compete with one another, and against the return to traditional European nationalism.

## 1 Introduction

Greece is a country with long-established institutional features: a unitary nation-state, founded on popular sovereignty, with a rigid Constitution as the cornerstone of the legal order; Parliament of a single Chamber; a powerful Prime Minister; polarized majoritarian politics exposed to the lure of populism; a long tradition of parliamentary elections going back to 1844,[1] and a political tradition marked by the Jacobin dimension, i.e. the "immediate and collective political action committed to the realization of an egalitarian but abstract sociopolitical ideal of citizenship

[1]Pantelis et al. (2010), p. 807.

I. A. Tassopoulos (✉)
National and Capodistrian University of Athens, Athens, Greece
e-mail: itassop@pspa.uoa.gr

 
G. Tusseau (ed.), *Debating Legal Pluralism and Constitutionalism*, Ius Comparatum – Global Studies in Comparative Law 41, https://doi.org/10.1007/978-3-030-34432-0_7

through strong and centralized state institutions."[2] Finally, in Greece, judicial review of legislation has existed since 1897, as an expression and guarantee of the rigid Constitution, in a diffused system of judicial review, of the American type, but with no single Supreme Court, given the dual system of civil and administrative jurisdictions. Nevertheless, the Council of State plays a central and increasingly important role in the Greek system of judicial review. In Greece, the guarantee of the constitutional order rests as much on democratic politics as on courts and the rule of law.

Following the collapse of the Colonel's dictatorship and the restoration of democracy, in 1974, Greece's accession to the European Communities has been a central political objective for the sake of stabilizing democracy, promoting economic growth, and improving national security through participation in the process of European integration. With the benefit of hindsight, however, it is clear that the country's first priority had been democratization and the enhancement of *input* legitimacy,[3] when the primary concern and justification of the EU was *output* legitimacy, based on the technocratic efficiency of coordinated or Europeanized policies.[4] To make things worse, the idea of democratization took all too often, in Greece, the form of party clientelism eroding the impartiality and efficiency of bureaucracy.[5] Indeed, Greece has since 1975 dismantled most forms of checks and balances through revisions of the Constitution, in order to better entrench the institutional features described above, leading to a sort of self-regulated two-party system, with no effective guarantees of the rule of law, other than judicial review.[6] Greece, where overpoliticization undermined bureaucratic efficiency, has been operating in the EU (to use Justice O'Connor's memorable phrase) within "a framework," which "is clearly on a collision course with itself:"[7] "self-referential"[8] democratic constitutionalism v. incorporation in a pluralist system of economic interdependence and coordination.

Consequently, the Greek sovereign debt crisis has been the natural outcome of this collision course, which exacerbated both the inadequacies of Greece's disregard of output legitimacy, and the democratic deficit of the EU, downplaying input legitimacy. The Eurozone crisis, however, was followed by the refugee crisis, which highlighted a reverse tendency: the former imposed a "straitjacket" framework of narrow economic and budgetary supervision of the member-states, restricting their economic discretion[9]; while the latter marked the return of territoriality and, therefore, the renewed expectations from the nation-state to fulfill its

---

[2]Tassopoulos (2013), p. 59, citing L. Jaume, Le discours Jacobin et la démocratie, Paris: Fayard, 1989, pp. 25–26.

[3]Schmidt (2013), p. 2.

[4]Lindseth (2010), p. 6.

[5]Tassopoulos (2014), pp. 31–32.

[6]Tassopoulos (2007), p. 48.

[7]Akron v. Akron Ctr. for Reprod. Health, 462 U.S. 416 (1983), J. O'Connor dissenting, p. 458.

[8]Tassopoulos (2013), p. 76.

[9]Barragia (2015), p. 268.

traditional function as guarantor of national sovereignty, being now as well European territorial sovereignty.

For a small state with the location of Greece, the choice for European integration went beyond democratic consolidation; it was also *strategic,*[10] for enhanced *security*. Instead of autarky, i.e. self-sufficiency without external assistance, the transformation of sovereignty locates power in the network of the state's international relations and alliances.[11] The Constitution's position over the relation between national and international law is not a technical legal issue. It is a fundamental one to the extent that, as Mirkine-Guetzévitch was writing in 1933, in his *Droit constitutionnel international*[12]: "le droit interne c'est la *technique de la liberté* et le droit international, c'est la *technique de la paix*".[13] The transition from a monist view of supremacy of domestic law over international law,[14] to the dualist position of two parallel and independent legal orders, which do not interpenetrate, to the monist view of preponderance of international law, or to non-hierarchical "interacting systems,"[15] marks the interplay between the *constitutionalization of international law* or the *internationalization of constitutional law,* more prominent in the tensions between universalization of human rights, democracy, and market globalization.[16] More than a dilemma between these two branches of public law, this should be understood in the sense that "each is both a condition of and a corrective to the other."[17]

The preceding tensions underlie the debate over constitutionalism and legal pluralism. The former introduced, after all, the universality of human rights in the Declarations of the French and American Revolutions. The question is whether the constitutional framework of universal rights and democracy is going to be maintained in the age of globalization, or is going to fade out, losing power vis-à-vis the markets.[18] The Greek Constitution of 1975, as amended, being extremely receptive of international law, accepts resolutely the challenge (taking also the risk), of being open to the optimistic vision of a process of European integration compatible with the values of constitutionalism.

Art. 28.1 GRC provides that the generally recognized rules of international law, i.e. customary law, as well as international conventions as of the time they are ratified by statute and become operative according to their respective conditions, shall be an integral part of domestic Greek law and shall prevail over any contrary provision of the law. Moreover, par. 2 provides that constitutional competences may

---

[10]Bobbit (2002), pp. 234–235.

[11]Chayes and Handler Chayes (1998), pp. 22, 135.

[12]Mirkine-Guetzévitch (1933), p. 8.

[13]Hathaway and Shapiro (2017), pp. 101, 336 (discussing international law's efforts to outlaw war).

[14]Rubenfeld (2004), p. 2023–2026.

[15]MacCormick (1999), p. 117.

[16]Auby (2017), pp. 19, 118–125.

[17]Walker (2013), pp. 240, 263.

[18]Scharpf (2014), pp. 93, 143.

by treaty be vested in international organizations, when this serves an important national interest and promotes cooperation with other States. A majority of three-fifths of the total number of Members of Parliament shall be necessary to vote the law ratifying the treaty. According to par. 3, Greece shall freely proceed by law passed by an absolute majority of the total number of Members of Parliament to limit the exercise of national sovereignty, insofar as this is dictated by an important national interest, *does not infringe upon the rights of man and the foundations of democracy*, and is effected on the basis of the principles of *equality* and under the condition of *reciprocity*. In practice, all the European Treaties (e.g. Maastricht, Amsterdam, Lisbon) have been ratified in Greece on the basis of art. 28,[19] without clarification of paragraph, due to the inconsistency of par. 2 and 3, where the former provides for a supermajority, while the latter sets substantive limits, requiring only absolute majority. An interpretative clause, added in 2001, did not solve the riddle: "Article 28 constitutes the foundation for the participation of the Country in the European integration process."

## 2 The Greek Constitution and European Law

In the EU legal order there is no supremacy clause, like in the American Constitution[20]; the supremacy of European law over national law is the construction of case law.[21] Some of the most interesting cases regarding the tension between constitutionalism and legal pluralism in Greece are those of the "major shareholder." Most prominent among them is Council of State (in pleno) 3670/2006, involving the conflict of a constitutional rule, which restricts participation in public procurements, with European law. Art. 14.9 GRC provides that the capacity of major shareholder or managing director of an information media enterprise is incompatible with the capacity of major shareholder or managing director of an enterprise that undertakes towards the wider public sector to perform works or to supply goods or services. This prohibition extends also over all types of intermediary persons, such as spouses, relatives, financially dependent persons or companies. The specific regulations and sanctions "shall be determined by law." A divided Court decided to submit a preliminary reference to the CJEU, under Article 267 of the Treaty on the Functioning of the European Union (TFEU), over the conformity of the constitutional rule on the "major shareholder" with Council Directive 93/37/EEC concerning the coordination of procedures for the award of public works contracts.

First, the CS, based on the original intent of the constitutional legislator of 2001, adopted a strict construction of the constitutional provision on the "major

[19]Contiades and Fotiadou (2014), pp. 718–721.

[20]Am. Con. Article VI, Clause 2.

[21]Case 26/62, Van Gend en Loos v. Nederlandse Administratie der Belastigen (1963) ECR 1. Case 6/64 Costa v. Enel (1964) ECR 585.

shareholder." Accordingly, the CS constructed the term *incompatible capacity* of GRC art. 14.9, as setting a direct and absolute exclusion from participation in public contracts of contractors involving the aforementioned suspect categories (summarily described as "major shareholder"). As a result, the statutory provision implementing art. 14.9 could not turn the incompatibility into compatibility, without rendering inactive the explicit prohibition, circumventing the Constitution. By contrast, the dissent argued that the term *incompatible capacity* set only a *rebuttable presumption*, not an absolute prohibition. Additionally, two dissenting opinions addressed directly the conflict between GRC art. 14.9 and Council Directive 93/37/EEC on the exclusion of candidates from participation in public contracts. One argued that the judicial duty is to interpret the Constitution in conformity with EU law, so as to avoid their conflict. Common legislation can, then, implement the Constitution in accordance with EU law, transforming the *incompatible capacity*, from an absolute prohibition, into a rebuttable presumption. For the other, the opposite was true: Notwithstanding the CJUE's jurisprudence, according to which the national law of the member-states, including the Constitution, must be set aside in order to give effect to EU law, one can hardly draw from the provisions of the Greek Constitution the conclusion that a Greek judge can implement the supremacy of EU law vis-à-vis the Constitution, without violating his constitutional obligation to uphold the Constitution. The Greek constitutional legislator allows the political leadership of the country to deal with the potential crisis arising from the breach of the international obligations of Greece. There is no room, therefore, for a preliminary reference to the CJUE.

The further question concerned the consequence of the unconstitutionality of the statutory provision, accepting the rebuttable presumption. The Court held that, if there were a conflict between Council Directive 93/37/EEC and national law, then the whole scheme, regarding the "major shareholder," would have to be set aside. For the dissenters, this further consideration was unnecessary; petitioners could win their case on the ground of unconstitutionality, avoiding thus the thorny question of the conflict between the Constitution and EU law, in a typical attitude of judicial self-restraint. Moreover, another dissenting opinion took an outspoken position of constitutional sovereignty, invoking GRC art. 120.4, which entrusts the "observance of the Constitution" "to the patriotism of the Greeks" (omitting, however, the concomitant right of resistance...). According to this view, a preliminary reference to the CJEU questioning a mandatory constitutional provision, like art. 14.9, is simply inconceivable. The CS, and the Greek judiciary in general, cannot set aside or invalidate the Constitution, as the latter does not recognize the supremacy of other texts over it.

The validity of the EU legal order in Greece is grounded on the accession act (law 945/1979), voted by Parliament on the basis of GRC art. 28; therefore, so the argument goes, it is not possible to recognize the supremacy of EU provisions over other explicit, mandatory and equally binding provisions of the Constitution, like art. 14.9. Otherwise, the power to amend the Constitution would be restricted by the EU legal order; in which case, art. 28 would be recognized as superior over the rest of the Constitution, although not mentioned in GRC art. 110, regarding constitutional amendment.

When the CJEU ruled that the irrebuttable presumption regarding the capacity of major shareholder in both media enterprises and public work contractors, imposed by GRC art. 14.9, violated the principle of proportionality, the CS changed course in 3470/2011 (in pleno).[22] The Court abandoned the strict construction of GRC art. 14.9 and adopted a *teleogical and evolutionary interpretation,* accepting that it should be harmonized and construed in conformity with EU law, which must be upheld in the domestic legal order, as required by the Constitution itself, establishing the principle of proportionality (art. 25.1).

The obvious question which creeps up into the mind is why follow this cumbersome route and reach the result of a constitutional construction in conformity with EU law (which after all had already been suggested as fitting and appropriate in 2006, only five years earlier), submitting a highly contested preliminary reference to the CJEU? What for this perplexity, which seems to violate every principle of procedural economy?

The answer must be found in the very foundations of Community legal order, constituted by the transfer of national sovereignty: self-contained and autonomous; but yet not composing in conjunction with the national legal orders a federal state. The CS, on the one hand, recognized the essential difference between a federal state and a supranational legal order, such as the EU; but, on the other hand, insightfully or intuitively, submitted the preliminary reference, implying the *federal principle.* The distinction was forcefully drawn by Judge Pescatore[23]:

> The methods of federalism are not only a means of organizing states. It would rather seem that federalism is a political and legal philosophy which adapts itself to all political contexts on both the municipal and the international level, wherever and whenever two basic prerequisites are fulfilled: the search for unity, combined with genuine respect for the autonomy and the legitimate interest of the particular entities.

The decision of the Greek CS has not taken position on the hierarchical relation between the Greek Constitution and EU law. Rather it captures and reflects the peculiar quality of the EU legal order—a hybrid *between constitutional and international law*—well described in Costa v. ENEL[24]*:*

> By creating a Community of unlimited duration, having its own institutions, its own personality, its own legal capacity and capacity of representation on the international plane and, more particularly, real powers stemming from a limitation of sovereignty or a transfer of powers from the States to the Community, the Member States have limited their sovereign rights, albeit within limited fields, and have thus created a body of law which binds both their nationals and themselves.

That EU law is upheld over domestic law, including the Constitution, is the legal consequence of the *federal principle*, which can operate *without* a federal constitution, or a federal state. In the supranational European structure of *dual sovereignties*, i.e. of the EU and of the member-states, one may think, not in terms of hierarchy, but

---

[22]Yannakopoulos (2013), pp. 424–434, 446.

[23]Cappelletti et al. (1985), pp. 3, 13–14. But see, Moravcsik (2001), p. 187.

[24]See above, n. 21.

of a relation of priority, or precedence, of EU law vis-à-vis the domestic legal order, resulting from the federal principle. The latter makes necessary, at least for functional purposes of coordination, the prevalence of EU law. More important than figures of speech about vertical or horizontal relations, are the functional aspects and the underlying normative considerations.[25] First, neither the EU, nor any other similar system, can survive, if its members are able to circumvent their obligations to the supranational entity by invoking their national Constitution at their wish. Secondly, from the normative point of view, this tactic would favor the intergovernmental method, where national interests tend to prevail, at the expense of the common European interest. Third, it may be possible to describe the relation between EU law and national law, as one where national law withdraws only when the legal competence for a specific issue belongs to the EU, but this does not change the hard legal reality: in this case, EU law prevails.

Participation in the EU creates two parallel and coexisting routes for constitutional change: the formal amendment process (GRC art. 110) and the supranational one (GRC art. 28) of EU legal order. The former is *direct*, formal, established and recognized; the latter is *indirect*, and as a consequence contested and problematic. Yet, not accidentally, the material limits are more or less co-extensive in both the direct and the indirect processes. The unamendable provisions of GRC art. 110.1 are "those which determine the form of government as a Parliamentary Republic," plus human dignity, legal equality, free development of personality, religious freedom, and separation of powers. According to GRC 28.3, they concern the rights of man, the foundations of democratic government and reciprocity. Democracy, human rights, and the background equality of member-states, entailed by the principle of reciprocity, set the fundamentals of Greek legal order and the conditions for its continuing participation in the EU.

The tedious and cumbersome approach of the Greek CS in the "major shareholder" cases was more than justified; it was necessary, because it recognized the structural autonomy of Greek and EU legal orders, each one with its own sovereignty—national and composite, respectively. What the Court did *not* do was to assume that the usual and regular precedence of EU law over domestic law, justified by the federal principle, means *ipso facto* the negation or abandonment and elimination of national sovereignty. Rather, the CS engaged in a structured and principled horizontal dialogue between the two legal orders. The priority recognized to EU law by Greek constitutional order is not coerced; it originates in voluntary participation and commitment to the major historical project of European integration, implementing the fundamental rule of GRC art. 2.2: "Greece, adhering to the generally recognized rules of international law, pursues the strengthening of peace and of justice, and the fostering of friendly relations between peoples and States." Were the European integration process to take a different route (e.g. imposing restrictions on voting rights in the Council for indebted countries), anti-democratic, scornful of reciprocity, and forgetful of respect for fundamental rights, the CS would

[25]Grabenwarter (2010), pp. 95, 108.

certainly react to the violation of the fundamental principles, which set the material limits to the amendment of the Greek Constitution, following a rationale similar to the German Solange decisions.[26]

## 3 The Limits of European Constitutionalization. The Experience of the Greek Crisis

The priority of EU law vis-à-vis the Constitution faces strong objections. The President of the Republic, Prokopios Pavlopoulos,[27] an eminent jurist, has argued that it is wrong to put into question the supremacy of the Constitution over EU law, as long as the EU has not developed politically to the point of having a common constitutional foundation. President Pavlopoulos continued by stressing the obligation of Greek judges to premise their analysis on the Greek Constitution. According to him, the supremacy of European law over the Constitution would violate the principle: *"nemo plus juris ad allium transfere potest quam ipse habet"*. No constitutional organ of the state can abdicate, in favor of EU law, the Constitution's sovereignty.

The aforementioned analysis employs the doctrine of *delegation* to conceptualize the relations between national and European law, in the sense that the supranational bodies act as agents of the states.[28] P. Lindseth has probably made the most forceful argument against using the term constitutionalization to describe the development of European governance: "it is a category mistake," implying an "autonomous constitutional legitimacy," which European governance lacks, being at best "administrative, not constitutional."[29] The ultimate importance of the delegation doctrine regards Kompetenz-Kompetenz, i.e. the power of national courts to declare that a European norm violates the *outer limits of national constitutional deference* to the EU legal order[30]; in the case of Greece, as already said, democracy, respect for human rights, and reciprocity.

In a way, the reverse side of the delegation doctrine is the "*ultra vires doctrine*,"[31] mentioned in the OMT (Outright Monetary Transactions) case, by the Bundesverfassungsgericht, in its preliminary reference to the CJUE.[32] Indeed, under the circumstances of the Financial Crisis, President Pavlopoulos invoked the German decision, as well as the Décision n° 2012-653 DC du 9 août 2012 of the

[26]https://law.utexas.edu/transnational/foreign-law-translations/german/case.php?id=572 BVerfGE 73, 339 2 BvR 197/83 Solange II-decision, 22 October 1986.

[27]Pavlopoulos (2017). Yannakopoulos (2013), pp. 389, 418.

[28]Lindseth (2010), p. 47.

[29]Id. p. 49.

[30]Id. p. 267.

[31]Endicott (2003), pp. 201–216.

[32]Gauweiler C-62/14.

Conseil Constitutionnel (le traité sur la stabilité, la coordination et la gouvernance au sein de l'Union économique et monétaire) to reach the conclusion that the only viable solution regarding the relation between the Greek Constitution and EU law is their interpretation in a spirit of mutual deference and consideration, so as to achieve harmony and to avoid conflicts. However, one must raise some critical questions about the delegation doctrine:

(a) Even accepting that the delegation doctrine aims at preserving the role of representative government and of the democratic nation-state as the source of legitimacy in the EU, there is still doubt whether this aim is better promoted by limiting the discourse on democracy and constitutionalism at the level of member-states, instead of extending it to the EU itself, in the form of constitutionalization of the process of European integration. (b) Is the delegation doctrine adequate and sufficient for this goal, given, first, its inefficiency in preserving the role of parliament vis-à-vis the executive in Europe,[33] and secondly, and crucially, in light of the risk of fueling the intergovernmental character of the EU, leading to a tide of nationalism, focused and directed to national interests, accountable to national constituencies, at the expense of solidarity towards the other member-states and of European common interests? (c) Last but not least, is it the *formal* or the *material* Constitution, or, possibly, *a combination* thereof, the proper legal instrument to inculcate the necessary democratic legitimacy and to guarantee the role of the nation-state as the "principal" of the European institutional "agents," as aspires the delegation doctrine, thus controlling the technocratic excesses of European bureaucracy? This question needs further clarification: the *formal* Constitution as a source of law, a *legal code*,[34] leads to conflicts between legal norms, whereas in reality the problem we are facing is hardly one of formal legality. Only for a diehard legal positivist is the question of political (and more broadly, constitutional) legitimacy, primarily or exclusively, one of formal sources of law, and not of substantive results, social ideals and normative values, reflected in the prevailing public policies, and usually associated with the *material* C*onstitution.*[35] Ultimately, *material* are the limits of constitutional amendments.[36]

The three previous questions are interconnected. Democratic legitimacy at the national level may lead to the egoistic promotion of national interest at the supranational level, without the appropriate concern for the legitimate interests of others, or of the European general interest. In the context of intergovernmental politics, where settlement and compromise result out of largely unequal negotiating power, on an expansive array of highly important sociopolitical issues, (a) democratic and constitutional legitimacy, in the formal but also in the substantive sense, are necessary both at the national and at the European level; (b) delegation, focusing in principle to ultra-vires concerns, is inadequate, in and of itself, to address substantive issues,

[33]Lindseth (2004), pp. 1341, 1361, 1372.

[34]Fletcher and Sheppard (2005), p. 111.

[35]Mortati (1998), pp. 110, 136, 139 (discussing constitutional ends).

[36]Rigaux (1985), p. 45. See also Albert (2019), p. 78.

which have to do, not with the external legality[37] of the decisions (who decides?), but with the internal one (what is decided?); (c) for this to occur, however, a combination of substantive and formal conceptions of constitutionalism is required: one not concerned indiscriminately with any norm which happens to be part of the formal Constitution, but primarily with those substantive fundamental principles which capture the gist of liberal and democratic constitutionalism. Art. 2 of the Lisbon Treaty is pertinent in this regard:

> The Union is founded on the values of respect for human dignity, freedom, democracy, equality, the rule of law and respect for human rights, including the rights of persons belonging to minorities. These values are common to the Member States in a society in which pluralism, non-discrimination, tolerance, justice, solidarity and equality between women and men prevail.

Additionally, art. 9 and 10 of Lisbon Treaty, which provide that the Union shall observe the principle of the equality of its citizens, who shall receive equal attention from its institutions, and declare that the functioning of the Union shall be founded on representative democracy, are also of the utmost importance for the constitutionalization of the EU.

If the formal notion of the Constitution is *over-inclusive* to the extent that it does not distinguish between provisions that are only technically of constitutional stature, by way of inclusion into the *legal code* (although *materially* they do *not* belong to it), and provisions which concern fundamental principles of constitutional law, yet, it can also be *under-inclusive*, if the notion of the formal Constitution is understood with dogmatic rigidity as excluding, i.e. not tolerating, any process or outcome which results out of the contemporary pluralist legal universe, in the age of globalization, but is not provided directly by the Constitution. This is, par excellence, the case of the conflict between the "major shareholder" and EU law, discussed above. Under-inclusiveness is ultimately reduced to the supremacy of the national legal order, regarding all "*legal parallelism*,"[38] at the limit, as contrary to the Constitution. However, if legal pluralism serves a purpose, this is the creativity and experimentation with new lawmaking procedures and legal forms, in an attempt to find lawful solutions at the international level to novel and unforeseen, urgent situations. Such an emergency occurred in spring 2010 during the Sovereign Debt Crisis, which made necessary Greece's bailout by its European partners and the IMF, notwithstanding the explicit prohibition of bailouts by EU law. The crisis made necessary the invention of an *ad hoc*, at the time, mechanism for the creation of norms, which would save Greece from default, circumvent the prohibition of bailout, and have the sanction of the EU![39] These objectives, difficult to harmonize, led to law 3845/2010 entitled "Measures for the implementation of the Mechanism in support of the Greek Economy from the member-states of the Eurozone and the IMF."

---

[37]Vedel (1997), par. 34, 35.

[38]Kar (2012), p. 457.

[39]Henning (2017), pp. 16, 19, 76, 184.

The law included as Attachment II the "Statement on the support to Greece by Euro Area Members States" of April 11, 2010, providing among others that:

> The Commission, in liaison with the ECB, will start working on Monday April 12th, with the International Monetary Fund and the Greek authorities on a joint programme (including amounts and conditionality, building on the recommendations adopted by the Ecofin Council in February). In parallel, Euro area Members States will engage the necessary steps, at national level, in order to be able to deliver a swift assistance to Greece.

Attachment III was the "Memorandum of Economic and Financial Policies," of May 3, 2010. The Statement of March 25, 2010 provided that: "As part of a package involving substantial International Monetary Fund financing and a majority of European financing, Euro area member states, are ready to contribute to coordinated bilateral loans [. . .]." In the mechanism of the Greek bail-out, the member-states of the Eurozone were both *partners and debtors.* The monitoring and surveillance of Greek economy was undertaken by the Troika: the European Commission, the ECB and an international organization, the International Monetary Fund with its seat in Washington, "who gave the whole enterprise the distinctive aura of globalization at its best! The sovereign debt crisis pushed Europe into a phase of experimentation."[40] Nothing comparable to this law existed in the typology of Greek sources of law. Its classification as an international treaty, or a set of measures sanctioned by EU law, or rather a piece of national legislation, was very uncertain, occupying a position in the "penumbras of sovereignty,"[41] in the grey zone of ambivalence between debtors and partners.

In judgment 668/2012 (in pleno), the CS characterized the Memorandum incorporated into law 3845/2010 as a political program of economic stabilization to be implemented by future specific legislative or administrative measures, subject to judicial review whenever enacted.[42] The political responsibility for the implementation of the Memorandum is not with the Court but the legislature. Under the circumstances, any attitude other than judicial self-restraint, for the sake of the integrity of the formal Constitution, would simply amount to a sort of unrealistic and doctrinaire legal imperialism. But then follows the dark side.

The risks of a horizontal, pluralist legal universe, where heteroclite legal norms, coming from porous legal systems, co-apply amalgamated in an unprincipled and relatively fluid manner, are well reflected in the subsequent developments which transformed the Memoranda and the underlying principle of strict conditionality, which they effectuate, from *ad hoc* emergency measures, into an established mechanism, available to the EU, not merely in cases of financial support, required by a member-state, but whenever its macroeconomic instability may have menacing repercussions for other Eurozone member-states.[43] This development occurred through the deliberate adaptation of EU strict conditionality to the corresponding

---

[40]Contiades and Tassopoulos (2013), p. 199.

[41]Id. p. 201.

[42]Id. p. 203.

[43]Regulation (EU) No 473/2013, art. 6-13.

standard of the IMF,[44] which operates as a limitation of sovereignty, where structural reforms and severe austerity are demanded by the creditor from the debtor, in exchange of money. Crucial in this regard is of course the unequal bargaining power between creditor and debtor. Introduced in Europe's economic governance, strict conditionality is intergovernmental in character and as a result it turns the creditor-debtor relation into a major cleavage separating the member-states in those who dictate and those who are bound to accept the conditions for their financing. In this situation, the Open Method of Coordination (OMC), far from opening the field for a flexible, democratic and cooperative endeavor among the member-states, is turned into a sort of arena, where technocrats press on with various measures,[45] which they name "structural reforms," free from accountability and responsibility, in case of failure; because the famous *ownership* of the macroeconomic adjustment program, so crucial in the IMF practice, shifts the burden for implementation of the agreed measures to the debtor, even when the creditor chose and imposed them on the debtor, against debtor's protests.

The same fluidity is also present at the political level. The former PM of Greece, Costas Simitis, stated in Greek Parliament in October 2008 that: "It is a common secret in the circles of the European Commission that Greece does not adhere to the directives of the EMU; [...] It would be good for Greece – they believe – to be forced to the IMF for further recourse, so that the monitoring of Greek economy will fall under its responsibility and oversight, and not that of the European Commission."[46] Indeed, the European Commission did not exercise effectively its supervisory powers, at the critical period when there was still time to take effective measures that could have prevented Greece's exclusion from the financial markets.[47] On the 14.12.2008, most of Athens dailies held reports about the spreads, the debt and the Eurozone, describing future events quite accurately.[48] In the course of the Greek Crisis, all Greek Prime Ministers have been paying visits to Berlin, holding meetings with Chancellor Merkel in repeated, but unsuccessful, efforts to initiate political negotiations to influence the more technical discussion of the Eurogroup and the Euroworking group. This is in direct conflict with the position of the CJEU[49] that: "In so far as, by their actions, the appellants sought the annulment of a Eurogroup statement, it should be noted not only that the term 'informally' is used in the wording of Protocol No 14 on the Eurogroup, annexed to the FEU Treaty, but also that the Eurogroup is not among the different configurations of the Council of the European Union [...]." Informality, i.e. lack of a specific constitutional framework of established competences, may lead to diffused political responsibility and lack of accountability.

---

[44] Khan and Sharma (2003), p. 227.

[45] Idema and Keleman (2006), pp. 108, 118.

[46] Simitis (2012), p. 19.

[47] Id. p. 25.

[48] Tassopoulos (2014), p. 318.

[49] Mallis and Malli, (C-105/15 P) par. 61.

It should be emphasized that, in the case of the Eurozone bailouts, there is no room for any sort of idealization, in terms of "directly-deliberative polyarchy," emphasizing participation and reason-giving.[50] Greece's huge sovereign debt resulted out of a twin moral hazard; first, the irresponsibility of Greek political system, accumulating debts beyond any reasonable level; and, secondly, the irresponsibility of the banks, financing the Greek loans, in an equally unreasonable manner, having then to be saved by the states, i.e. ultimately by the tax-payers. Indeed, prior to the restructuring of Greece's debt, in 2012 (PSI), mostly German and French banks held approximately Euros 119 billions out of Euros 206 billions of Greek debt.[51] Currently, in the new landscape of European governance, under strict conditionality, the arsenal of democratic constitutionalism is the only available guarantee for a principled and balanced resolution of the conflicting interests between creditors and debtors, who are at the same time partners in a community of law and order, respectful of the values of the Treaty of Lisbon (art. 2).

## 4 The Haircut of Greek Bonds: Legal Pluralism at Work

At least three European legal orders[52] had the opportunity to render major decisions on the legality of the PSI (Public Sector Involvement), from various points of view. The Greek cases (CS 1506, 1507, 1116/2014 etc.) involved law 4050/2012, providing for the replacement of Greek bonds with new ones, for purposes of reduction of the Greek debt. The CS did not submit a preliminary reference to the CJUE, holding that the statute establishing the PSI process was enacted by a sovereign decision of Greece. The old bonds (to be replaced) did not include a Collective Action Clause (CAC) and many of the applicants were holding these bonds, not as investors, but in order to secure their savings, i.e. with the mentality of bank depositors. The Statement of Reasons, supporting the statute, mentioned the "international practice" of including CAC in bonds, and justified the extension of this procedure to the old bonds as well, on the basis of public interest considerations. It cited the grave economic situation of the country and the destructive consequences of a potential default, as the successful implementation of the restructuring was set as a condition for the second bailout of Greece by its European partners. Invoking the crisis, the CS stated forthrightly that "When such things happen, then the state lawfully tries to renegotiate on the basis of the *'rebus sic standibus'* clause, which sets the limits to the general legal maxim *'pacta sunt servanda'*." Implemented with the cooperation of the Eurogroup and of the Institute of International Finance (I.I.F.), the PSI resulted into a collective decision taken by the majority of bondholders, amounting to a forcible participation of private individuals to accept the offer of the Greek state to

[50]Cohen and Sabel (1997), pp. 313–342.

[51]Zettelmeyer et al. (2013), pp. 34, 11.

[52]There were also legal suits in Germany.

exchange the old bonds with new ones, of lesser value, thus preventing Greece's default and saving the banks, at the cost of public treasury and of persons who were not investors. Finding out that the principle of equality in international trade practice takes the form of treating all creditors (bondholders) of the same debtor "on equal footing," "*pari passu*," so that satisfaction is "*pro rata*," the Court rejected the petitions.

The ECHR, ruling in *Mamatas and other v. Greece* (judgment 21.7.2016, application nos. 63066/14, 64297/14 and 66106/14) over the haircut of Greek bonds, underlined the state's wide margin of appreciation in that sphere and the reduction of the commercial value of the bonds, finding the PSI law proportional and appropriate to meet the crisis.

Finally, in *Accorinti v. ECB* (Case T-79/13 Judgment 7.10.2015 par. 86) the ECB argued that "the principle of equal treatment of creditors is not a universal rule of public international law or of constitutional law common at Member State level, still less a general principle of EU law, as its application depends on the choice of the bond issuer." In any case, it would create legal obligations only for the Greek state, and not for ECB. Furthermore, if the Greek bonds held by the Eurosystem central banks, including the Greek Central Bank, had not been excluded from the PSI, the Eurosystem's capacity to refinance credit institutions and to operate in the financial markets within the meaning of Article 18(1) of its Statute would have been undermined. "Therefore, as the situations at issue were not comparable, the applicants cannot claim that there was unequal treatment." The General Court rejected the liability of ECB for the PSI.

The preceding analysis sufficiently highlights the inherent limits of the notion of "relevance," employed by Santi Romano,[53] in order to explain the relation between the various orders in a universe of legal pluralism, because it has a rather sociological, factual dimension, instead of a normative one, to the extent that its focus is mainly on the *functional* relationship between the various orders. This functional aspect is of course influenced by notions of legal superiority and hierarchy, but it can equally be shaped by considerations of political expediency. This is so particularly in cases where the subordinate order is not eager to recognize the superiority of the superior one, at least in the juridical sense,[54] to the extent that the inferior order has not been brought into existence by an act of the superior, and therefore, being sovereign, it cannot be dissolved by the superior, albeit it depends on it, for its future existence in economic terms, or for its security from external threats.

Romano's notion of relevance, and the corresponding one of *irrelevance*,[55] can be quite helpful if they are taken in a rather normative sense, as arguments against the *excessive fragmentation* of the pluralist legal universe, particularly with regard to those orders which tend to be *closed*, *impenetrable* and *isolated* from the rest of society, as remote islands in the middle of the ocean. Such a fragmentation is very

[53]Romano (2002), pp. 106, 135.

[54]Id. pp. 113–114, 122.

[55]Id. p. 144.

nefarious especially with regard to the legal protection of human rights. Applying Hauriou's *theory of the institution*, if the "idea of work which is realized and endures juridically in a social milieu, leads to manifestations of communion,"[56] i.e. of collective conscience, which are resolutely hostile to individualism, e.g. eliminating the human face of women behind the burka, which covers the eyes and hides the expression, then the *irrelevance* of constitutionalism as a system of values is objectionable, while legal pluralism does not take the form of peaceful coexistence of autonomous legal orders mutually respectful in reciprocity, but rather a sort of "feudalism" or "tribalism,"[57] where individuals, and especially women, are bound to oppressive norms, being subjugated to the authoritarian will of their community.

## 5 The Limits of European Pluralism

Some of the negative implications of legal pluralism can be seen in the very problematic situation regarding the legal regime, i.e. the applicable law, over Greece's Muslim minority in Western Thrace,[58] exempted by the Treaty of Lausanne from the compulsory exchange of populations of 1923 between Greece and Turkey. The Areios Pagos, the Greek Supreme Court with civil and criminal jurisdiction, decided (AP 2113/2009) that the Treaty of Lausanne (art. 42, 45) secured the validity of Muslim customary law and of sharia over Muslim Greek citizens. As a result, the applicable law for inheritance is the Sacred Muslim Law, which is, for purposes of testation, the domestic law of Greece, for Greek citizens of Muslim religion in Western Thrace. Consequently, a will according to Greek Civil Code has no legal effect, because sharia does not recognize this legal instrument. However, the Court of Appeals (CtAppThrace 237/2011) accepted that a Muslim Greek citizen has the right to choose the law of the Civil Code, even silently (e.g. by going to a notary public for a will), in which case the will is valid. Otherwise, there would be a violation of statutory law; of the Constitution (art. 4, equality; art. 5 free development of personality; art. 13 freedom of religion); and of the European Convention on Human Rights (art. 14 equality; 1st Protocol, art. 1, property). After the decision had been quashed by Areios Pagos, the bequeather applied to the European Court of Human Rights, in light of the Court's judgment in *Refah Partisi et al. v. Turkey*,[59] where it held that sharia law, which faithfully reflects the dogmas and divine rules laid down by religion, is incompatible with the fundamental principles of democracy, because it is hardly reconcilable with pluralism in the political sphere or the constant evolution of public freedoms. Moreover, sharia's

[56] Hauriou (1970), pp. 99, 107.

[57] Jeffery (1956–1957), p. 648.

[58] Ktistakis (2006), pp. 78, 127.

[59] Applications Nos. 41340/98, 41342/98, 41343/98 & 41344/98, par. 123.

values clearly diverge from Convention values, particularly with regard to the legal status of women. The ECHR, in *Molla Sali v. Greece,*[60] held that "freedom of religion does not require the Contracting States to create a particular legal framework in order to grant religious communities a special status entailing specific privileges. Nevertheless, a State which has created such a status must ensure that the criteria established for a group's entitlement to it are applied in a non-discriminatory manner." Moreover, the Court emphasized "the negative aspect of the right to free self-identification," "namely the right to choose not to be treated as a member of a minority." The ECHR found a violation of art. 14 of the Convention, in conjunction with Article 1 of Protocol No. 1 (property), but it did not decide on the compatibility of sharia law with the Convention.

Another issue concerning the Muslim minority in Thrace pushed the Areios Pagos to a strong *dualist* approach with regard to the effect of Judgments of the ECHR in Greek legal order. In AP 353/2012, the Court dealt with the Judgment of the ECHR (*Affaire Tourkiki Enosi Xanthis et autres v. Gréce, 27 mars 2008, 26698/05*), condemning Greece in the case of the "Turkish Union of Xanthi," an association outlawed in Greece for its claim of being Turkish, when Greece does not recognize the existence of an ethnic, but only of a religious, minority in Western Thrace. The Areios Pagos held that the Judgment of the ECHR does not provide legal grounds to ask for the reform or revocation of the decisions of Greek courts, following the condemnation of Greece in the specific case, because the judgments of the ECHR do not constitute a change of established case law to the extent that they "lack the capacity of penetrating into the national legal order, causing in and of themselves the abolition of the decision of national courts." The Supreme Court pointed out that the obligation of Greece is to comply with the judgment of the ECHR, but it is a matter of the condemned state to choose how to implement the judgment of the ECHR. As a result, the Greek Parliament amended art. 758 of the Code of Civil Procedure and recognized the right of an applicant who won in Strasbourg to ask for the reform or revocation of the decision that had been found in violation of the Convention.

The necessity for coordinated action and the reality of interdependence, which display the limits of even regional systems of human rights protection such as the Council of Europe, is clearly shown by the refugee crisis. This marks the return of territoriality, as already said, i.e. of the nation-state in its most traditional function of sealing the borders to prevent unregulated entrance in territory under its sovereignty.[61] But what does it take for any state to secure its borders, when the Coast Guard is confronted with civilians left in the middle of the rough sea? Obviously, the primary obligation is to rescue. The traffickers must be stopped at the point of departure, not through the sacrifice of innocent lives. Furthermore, a solution is necessary to the civil war devastating Syria. Obviously, these are problems that require close and resolute collaborative action, both within the EU, among the

[60]ECHR, Molla Sali v. Greece (Application no. 20452/14) (Grand Chamber), judgment 19.12.2018, par. 157, 158.

[61]Farahat and Markard (2016), p. 945.

member-states, and with the neighboring countries. The law obliges the EU and member-states to respect human dignity and individual rights. However, instead of recognizing the urgent need for a closer union in accordance with their duty of sincere cooperation (article 4.3 TEU), many European states redeployed themselves engaging in "a race to the bottom"[62] "with the purpose of keeping refugees away." Zaki Laidi's view of Europe, where norms play a geopolitical role,[63] being an effective source of constraint, gives way to closed borders and reestablished border controls of the most severe kind.

The problems of migration, however, are not limited to the borders. They extend over a variety of issues including schooling of children, the adaptation of refugees to the social and cultural environment of the communities which host them, freedom of movement, religious practices, etc. Among the forms of normative ordering, discussed by Tamanaha,[64] community/cultural normative systems, as well as religious/cultural ones may turn out to be highly influential, if not decisive, in shaping the more formal sources of official legal systems. The Greek CS had the opportunity to deal with these issues in the *Greek citizenship* cases,[65] where it struck down a law providing the attribution of citizenship on the basis of mere fulfillment of formal criteria, e.g. elementary school attendance, to immigrants of second generation. A section of the CS came perilously close to interpreting the concept of *the people* according to the traditionally prevailing doctrine of *jus sanguinis*, in Greece, i.e. in terms of the historical continuity of the Greek *ethnos*,[66] which is based on descendance from Greek families. By contrast, the Plenum of the Court struck down the law, but it shifted the grounds of justification to the concept of *society*, instead of the *ethnos*.[67] Still, the CS demanded an individualized judgment for every prospective citizen, ascertaining the capacity to become a functional member of Greek society. The latter does not develop arbitrarily, or at random, but has a historical continuity, cohesion and structure, stated the Court. However, the CS tried to overcome any tension of its position with the existence of European citizenship, stating *expressis verbis* that its analysis was consistent with the supranational project of European integration.[68]

---

[62]Benedek (2016), p. 949.

[63]Laidi (2008), pp. 20, 63–74.

[64]Tamanaha (2008), pp. 375, 397.

[65]CS 460/2013 (in pleno).

[66]CS 350/2011.

[67]CS (in pleno) 460/2013.

[68]Tassopoulos (2014), p. 247.

## 6 From the Dilemma Between Constitutionalism and Internationalism to a Synthesis

The preceding analysis illuminated both the persistence of the democratic nation-state under the rule of law, as a crucial and indispensable framework within which modern societies can address their problems in a legitimate manner, *and* the insufficiency of the nation-state to resolve them solely on its own. The interplay between constitutionalism and pluralism reflects this reality. Instead of choosing one horn of a false dilemma, we should try to understand the valid points of each side, in order to arrive at a sustainable synthesis. Pluralists indicate that it is not any more possible to assume that the nation-state is best conceptualized in Hobbes's notion of political representation,[69] as developed in chapter XVI, on "Persons, Authors and things Personated", of the first part of the Leviathan:

> A Person, is he, whose words or actions are considered, either as his own, or as representing the words or actions of another man, or any other thing to whom they are attributed, whether Truly or by Fiction. When they are considered as his own, then is he called a Natural Person: And when they are considered as representing the words and actions of another, then is he a Feigned or Artificial person.

*The problem with this notion of representation is when an artificial and collective political body, such as the electorate, the people, or the nation, is treated as a single, natural person.*[70] Neither the sociological conditions, in terms of homogeneity and common moral or religious outlook, nor the legal ones, in terms of a closed and self-sufficient legal system of positive law, exist any longer in our times. The nature of the problems, the magnitude of the challenges, and the bitter experience of recent historical times with the totalitarian nation-state, leave no doubt that collaboration and common rules and standards are necessary to promote shared goals. Nowhere is this interdependence more obvious than in environmental concerns, or in issues that involve immigration, when desperate populations cannot survive in some parts of the globe, because of human or natural disasters.[71]

*But equally unattractive is the alternative of international anarchy.* If, as has been argued by Larry Catá Backer,[72] "Global law has no order to it; it has no object, it has no law about it" being "a system of systems, teeming with sub-systems, each autonomous, fluid, and permeable," then the resulting situation is one of old-fashioned *international realism*[73] where the stronger states or powerholders (e.g. multinational corporations) are able to dictate their will over weaker actors, using probably more sophisticated means of coercion than gunboat diplomacy

[69] Runciman (1997), p. 243.
[70] Tassopoulos (2014), pp. 226–227.
[71] Held (2010), p. 184.
[72] Backer (2012), pp. 177, 198–199.
[73] Forde (1992), pp. 372–393.

(e.g. the threat of a massive movement of capital out of a politically destabilized economy can well assure compliance).

Probably, we have to abandon the *monist* conception of constitutionalism[74] with its unilateral and dependent—or, at best, dualist—view of international law, which favors the impermeability of the legal system of the nation-state, in order to adopt a *pluralist* idea of popular sovereignty as the founding principle of the nation-state. Because "pluralism is inherent in constitutionalism,"[75] the idea is to focus, not to the apex of the pyramid of representation, as Hobbes did, but to its base, where rests the plurality of citizens, i.e. the multitude, whose action tries the legal system to coordinate in processes of collective decision-making. This view has many advantages over the traditional monist conception of popular sovereignty, which places a monolithic and homogenous idea of the nation, or of the people, as the legitimating source of pubic law: it takes the social matrix of the nation-state to be *a society of free and autonomous individuals*, whose status is defined by fundamental rights. This view is congenial with *political liberalism.*[76] It takes into account the divisions, the interdependence and the externalities, which nourish the practical problems of contemporary life; it avoids the simplistic choice of *excessive voluntarism*, which is monism's favorite approach to practical reason, placing instead proper emphasis on deliberation and cooperation; it recognizes the *federalist principle* to be the central idea (and ideal) towards plural loyalties, in concentric extended circles, for more than one normative orders, local, regional and global (e.g. Greece, the EU, international cooperation).

"The pluralist strategy [of popular sovereignty] tries to implement the deeper ideal of political liberalism. Its central concepts are the *public*, and the ability to converse; it looks for rational, functional, and practical solutions to social problems; it tries to explore and expand the common ground of consent and compromise."[77] So, its outlook is very much akin to legal pluralism's focus on governance; *albeit with an important difference.* Owen Fiss has rightly emphasized that the court's job "is not to maximize the ends of private parties, nor simply to secure the peace, but to explicate and give force to the values embodied in authoritative texts such as the Constitution and statutes. [. . .] Parties might settle while leaving justice undone."[78] The equality of litigants before the law and the equality of arms before the court are designed to neutralize, at least, three kinds of disparities: the one of *legal status*, between the government and its subjects (les *gouvernants* et les *gouvernés*); next, the difference of *political power*, between the majority and the minority; and, last but not least, the *socioeconomic* inequality between the rich and the poor.[79] Settlement

[74]Krisch (2010), p. 242.

[75]Maduro (2012), p. 18 https://www.wzb.eu/sites/default/files/u32/miguel_maduro_three_claims_of_constitutional_pluralism_hu-coll_may_15_2012.pdf.

[76]Rawls (1993), pp. 35, 40.

[77]Tassopoulos (2014), p. 28.

[78]Fiss (1983), pp. 1073, 1085.

[79]Tassopoulos (2014), p. 116.

outside the framework of the rule of law and of separation of powers is unable to sustain the values of justice. This is even more severe in the field of international relations. Pluralism without constitutionalism fails to pay adequate attention to these vital concerns.

Even the concept of judicial dialogue[80] is insufficient to secure the values of justice without an effective quasi-constitutional framework, as became clear from the Eurozone crisis. As already discussed above, with regard to the bailout of Greece, the courts of the debtor state are tightly constrained, if the CJUE does not undertake a harder scrutiny of the conformity of strict conditionality measures to the fundamental principles of the EU (art. 2, Treaty of Lisbon),[81] in order to apply the techniques and explicate the judicial virtues of legal pluralism: pragmatism, reasonableness, proportionality and subsidiarity.[82]

## 7 Conclusion

The Greek experience shows conspicuously the inadequacy of both the monist conception of constitutional sovereignty, which makes the national legal order supreme, and of the opposite view of inchoate legal pluralism, developing more or less at random, according to the changing balance of power. It is ironic that legal pluralism's focus on systems falls short of envisaging a larger system, coordinating the narrower ones. However, accepting legal pluralism's chaos and disorder would seriously undermine all the achievements of constitutionalism in the field of political legitimacy, in favor of justice and against arbitrariness. The Enlightenment offered a universal ideal of human rights, combined with a remedy against tyranny and absolutism, i.e. the separation of powers. To give up these fundamental principles in the name of pluralism is quite disingenuous, because the result would be most probably the hegemony and domination of the stronger over the weaker, without effective legal protection of the latter. The dilemma is, then, whether the prevailing trend in the age of globalization, is going to be primarily a process of constitutionalization of international law, or, rather, the reverse one. The crisis is particularly acute in Europe, where both visions compete with one another, and against the return to traditional European nationalism.

---

[80]Voßkuhle (2010), pp. 175, 178.

[81]C-8/15 P Ledra Advertising v Commission and ECB C-105/15 P Judgment (Grand Chamber) of 20 September 2016, par. 58, 59.

[82]Somek (2014), pp. 216, 222.

## References


Albert R (2019) Constitutional amendments. OUP, Oxford

Auby J-B (2017) Globalization, law and the state. Hart, London

Backer LC (2012) The structural characteristics of global law for the 21st century: fracture, fluidity, permeability, and polycentricity. Tilburg Law Rev 17:177–199

Barragia A (2015) Conditionality measures within the euro area crisis: a challenge to democratic principle. Camb J Int Comp Law 4:268–288

Benedek W (2016) Recent developments in Austrian asylum law: a race to the bottom? German Law J 17(6):949–966

Bobbit P (2002) The shield of Achilles. Penguin, London

Cappelletti M et al (1985) Integration through law: Europe and the American federal experience. A general introduction. In: Cappelletti M et al (eds) Integration through law – Europe and the American federal experience, vol 1. De Gruyter, Berlin, pp 3–68

Chayes A, Handler Chayes A (1998) The new sovereignty. Harvard, Cambridge

Cohen J, Sabel C (1997) Directly deliberative polyarchy. Eur Law J 3:313–342

Contiades X, Fotiadou A (2014) The Hellenic Republic. In: Besselink L et al (eds) Constitutional law of the EU Member States. Kluwer, pp 703–772

Contiades X, Tassopoulos I (2013) The impact of the financial crisis on the Greek constitution. In: Contiades X (ed) Constitutions in the global financial crisis. Ashgate, pp 195–218

Endicott T (2003) Constitutional logic. Univ Tor Law J 53:201–216

Farahat A, Markard N (2016) Forced migration governance: in search of sovereignty. German Law J 17(6):923–948

Fiss O (1983) Against settlement. Yale Law J 93:1073–1090

Fletcher G, Sheppard S (2005) American law in a global context – the basics. OUP, Oxford

Forde S (1992) Varieties of realism: Thucydides and Machiavelli. J Polit 54(2):372–393

Grabenwarter C (2010) National constitutional law relating to the European Union. In: von Bogdandy A, Bast J (eds) Principles of European constitutional law. Hart Publishing, London, Verlag Beck, Munich, pp 95–144

Hathaway O, Shapiro S (2017) The internationalists and their plan to outlaw war. Allen Lane, Anchor

Hauriou M (1970) The theory of the institution and the foundation. In: Broderick A (ed) The French institutionalists. Harvard, Cambridge, pp 93–124

Held D (2010) Cosmopolitanism. Polity, Cambridge

Henning R (2017) Tangled governance. International regime complexity, the Troika, and the Euro crisis. OUP, Oxford

Idema T, Keleman D (2006) New modes of governance, the open method of co-ordination and other fashionable red herring. Perspect Eur Polit Soc 7:108–123

Jeffery C (1956–1957) The development of crime in early English society. J Crim Law Criminol Police Sci 47:647–666

Kar RB (2012) Outcasting, globalization, and the emergence of international law. Yale Law J Online 121:413–477. http://yalelawjournal.org/forum/outcasting-globalization-and-the-emergence-of-international-law

Khan M, Sharma S (2003) IMF conditionality and country ownership of adjustment programs. World Bank Res Obs 18(2):227–248

Krisch N (2010) Beyond constitutionalism. The pluralist structure of postnational law. OUP, Oxford

Ktistakis Y (2006) Sacred law of Islam and Muslim Greek citizens. Athens-Thessaloniki (in Greek)

Laidi Z (2008) La norme sans la forece. SciencesPo., 2nd edn. Paris

Lindseth P (2004) The paradox of parliamentary supremacy, delegation, democracy and dictatorship in Germany and France, 1920s–1950s. Yale Law J 113:1341–1415

Lindseth P (2010) Power and legitimacy: reconciling Europe and the nation state. OUP, Oxford

MacCormick N (1999) Questioning sovereignty. OUP, Oxford

Maduro M (2012) Three claims of constitutional pluralism. In: Avbelj M, Komárek J (eds) Constitutional pluralism in the European Union and beyond, ch. 4. https://www.wzb.eu/sites/default/files/u32/miguel_maduro_three_claims_of_constitutional_pluralism_hu-coll_may_15_2012.pdf. Accessed 19 May 2019
Mirkine-Guetzévitch B (1933) Droit constitutionnel international. Sirey, Paris
Moravcsik A (2001) Federalism in the European Union: rhetoric and reality. In: Nicolaidis K, Robert H (eds) The federal vision. OUP, Oxford, pp 161–187
Mortati C (1998) La Costituzione in Senso Materiale. Giuffre, Milano
Pantelis et al (2010) Greece. In: Nohlen D, Stöver P (eds) Elections in Europe. Nomos, Baden-Baden, pp 807–872
Pavlopoulos P (2017) The contemporary meaning of sovereignty of the Member States of the European Union (22.11.2017) (in Greek). http://www.presidency.gr/2017/11/. Accessed 19 May 2019
Rawls J (1993) Political liberalism. Columbia UP, New York
Rigaux M-F (1985) La Théorie des limites matérielles à l'exercice de la fonction constituante. Larcier, Bruxelles
Romano S (2002) L'Ordre Juridique. Dalloz, Paris
Rubenfeld J (2004) Unilateralism and constitutionalism. N Y Univ Law Rev 79:1971–2028
Runciman D (1997) Pluralism and the personality of the state. CUP, Cambridge
Scharpf F (2014) Legitimacy intermediation in the multilevel European polity and its collapse in the eurocrisis, *and* Comment The eurocrisis as a victory of neoliberalism? In: Fossum JE, Menéndez AJ (eds) The European Union in crises or the European Union as crises?, Arena Reports, 2/14, pp 93–142 and 143–154. http://www.sv.uio.no/arena/english/research/publications/arena-reports/2014/report-2-14. Accessed 19 May 2019
Schmidt V (2013) Democracy and legitimacy in the European Union. Revisited. Output, input and throughput. Polit Stud 61(1):2–22
Simitis C (2012) The European debt crisis, the Greek case. Manchester UP, Manchester
Somek A (2014) The cosmopolitan constitution. OUP, Oxford
Tamanaha B (2008) Understanding legal pluralism: past to present, local to global. Sydn Law Rev 30(3):375–411
Tassopoulos I (2007) Institutional checks and balances and the revisions of the constitution. Sakkoulas, Athens-Thessaloniki (in Greek)
Tassopoulos I (2013) On the Jacobin dimension of Greek constitutional tradition. In: Triandafyllidou A et al (eds) The Greek crisis and European modernity. Palgrave, London, pp 59–88
Tassopoulos I (2014) Popular sovereignty and the challenge of impartiality. Kritiki, Athens (in Greek)
Vedel G (1997) Excès de pouvoir administratif et excès de pouvoir législatif (II). Cahiers du Conseil constitutionnel n° 2 - mai 1997. http://www.conseil-constitutionnel.fr/conseil-constitutionnel/francais/nouveaux-cahiers-du-conseil/cahier-n-2/exces-de-pouvoir-administratif-et-exces-de-pouvoir-legislatif-ii.52882.html. Accessed 19 May 2019
Voßkuhle A (2010) Multilevel cooperation of the European Constitutional Courts: Der Europäische Verfassungsgerichtsverbund. Eur Constit Law Rev 6:175–198
Walker N (2013) The post-national horizon of constitutionalism and public law: paradigm extension or paradigm exhaustion. In: MacAmhlaigh C et al (eds) After public law. OUP, Oxford, pp 241–263
Yannakopoulos K (2013) The impact of European Union law on judicial review of the constitutionality of the law. Sakkoulas, Athens-Thessaloniki (in Greek)
Zettelmeyer J, Trebesch C, Gulati M (2013) The Greek debt restructuring: an autopsy. Peterson Institute for International Economics, Working paper 13-8: 1–65. https://piie.com/sites/default/files/publications/wp/wp13-8.pdf. Accessed 19 May 2019

# Legal Pluralism in Centralist Singapore

**Jaclyn L. Neo**

**Abstract** As a former British colony, Singapore has a legal system that is very much influenced by British common law and constitutional ideas, while operating within a social-political context that is shaped by Islam, which was the majority religion in the region, and a nascent constitutional-legal culture that sits apart from more liberal legal traditions. Within this context, Singapore's legal system is distinctly and self-avowedly pluralistic, as it seeks to accommodate traditional legal systems in the form of Muslim personal laws, while resisting developments in the common law that are viewed as 'foreign'.

## 1 Introduction: Background

Singapore has a pluralistic legal system, which is largely a legacy of its experience as a former British colony. It formally received English law via the Second Charter of Justice in 1826. This was however a limited reception in two ways: first, English statute passed after the Second Charter was not to become part of Singapore law; and secondly, the reception of English law was subject to suitability to local circumstances and could be modified where its application would cause injustice or oppression.[1] There is some debate as to whether the cut-off date of 1826 also applies to the common law, particularly in light of a strain of legal thought that saw unwritten common law as "timeless".[2] This early commitment to suitability to local circumstances built into the legal system an acceptance of exceptional space and an ethos of adjustment for local customary and religious practices. Harding argues that local knowledge has an important role to play in understanding the

[1] See generally Phang (1990).

[2] Phang (1986).

J. L. Neo (✉)
National University of Singapore, Faculty of Law, Singapore, Singapore
e-mail: jaclyn.neo@nus.edu.sg



G. Tusseau (ed.), *Debating Legal Pluralism and Constitutionalism*, Ius Comparatum – Global Studies in Comparative Law 41, https://doi.org/10.1007/978-3-030-34432-0_8

developments of transplanted legal systems.[3] Among these, Islamic practices continue to be accommodated within Singapore's legal system. Besides English law, Singapore has also borrowed from other commonwealth jurisdictions such as India (from which it derived its Penal Code and the Evidence Act) and Australia (in areas of land law and company law).[4]

Pluralist sources can also be discerned in Singapore's constitutional structure. While its initial constitutional design was based on the Westminster model of parliamentary government, this was later modified to address a range of local conditions, including minority representation and the need to ensure political pluralism in the context of a dominant party state. The head of government in Singapore is the Prime Minister, who is not directly chosen by the people but by his/her party holding the majority of seats in Parliament. As a Republic, its head of state is the President. Up till 1991, the President had powers similar to those of the British constitutional monarch, i.e. he/she had mostly a ceremonial position and only had limited discretionary powers over the appointment of the Prime Minister, declaring the office of the Prime Minister vacant, and in refusing a request to dissolve Parliament. In all other instances, Article 21 of the Singapore Constitution explicitly stated that the President had to exercise his functions in accordance with the advice of Cabinet. This scheme of government that hewed closely to the British system has been dramatically changed since 1991 through a series of constitutional amendments. The amendments granted the President additional powers that are often characterized as 'custodial' in nature. The President has constitutional powers to exercise his discretion in four instances: (1) to withhold assent to drawdowns on past reserves; (2) to withhold assent to certain public appointments; (3) to exercise a swing vote in instances where the respective advisory bodies disagreed with the Cabinet over detention orders under the Internal Security Act and restraining orders under the Maintenance of Harmony Act; and, (4) to grant approval for investigations if the Prime Minister refused to consent to an investigation recommended by the Director of the Corrupt Practices Investigation Bureau.

Legal pluralism is also manifest in Singapore's pluralistic structures of adjudication. It continued a judicial system that was first established by the British colonial government. Today, there is a multi-level court system comprising the Supreme Court (Court of Appeal and High Court), the subordinate State Courts (comprising primarily the District Court and Magistrate Court), and the specialized Family Justice Courts. Notably, the Syariah courts are not part of the judicial system. Although they are called 'courts', they should be conceptualized as tribunals as they are administered under the auspices of the Ministry of Social and Family Development. Indeed, these Syariah courts are statutorily created. The 1966 Administration of Muslim Law Act (AMLA)[5] came into force on 1 July 1968, formally defining the functions and powers of the Syariah Court as well as two other key

[3]Harding (2002).

[4]Goh and Tan (2011), p. 177.

[5]Act 27 of 1966.

Muslim institutions, i.e. the Islamic Religious Council of Singapore (Majlis Ugama Islam Singapura or MUIS) and the Registry of Muslim Marriages.

It should here be observed that there are religious courts only for Singapore's Muslim minority. However, the Singapore government has also enacted several laws pertaining to the incorporation and operation of religious institutions. There are statutory laws incorporating the Catholic Church as well as several boards managing Sikh and Hindu properties. These include the Central Sikh Gurdwara Board Act 1981 (Chapter 357), which constitutes a Board "to regulate the conduct of religious services and other ceremonies customary among the followers of the Sikh religion"; the Hindu Endowments Act 1968 (Chapter 364) which constitutes a board to administer Hindu religious and charitable endowments; and the Roman Catholic Archbishop Act 1975 (Chapter 375) which recognizes the prior constitution of the archbishop and replaces it with a statutory corporation.[6] Furthermore, some of these statutes grant the government the right to directly or indirectly appoint office bearers in those religious boards. For example, members of the Hindu Endowments Board are appointed by the Minister.[7] These regulations could be justified as 'protective' measures required under article 152(1) of the Singapore constitution, which makes it the responsibility of the government to "constantly care for the interests of the racial and *religious* minorities in Singapore".

These pluralistic aspects of Singapore's legal system however is sometimes challenged by the fact that Singapore is a territorially small city-state with a dominant political party that has been in government since its independence. This means that despite these legally pluralistic structures, there is sometimes a tendency towards legal centralism. As such, whereas this may sometimes appear to diminish the salience of legal pluralism insofar as there appears to be a tendency to view the law in a dominant party state as monist (one internally coherent system), statist (the state has a monopoly of law within its territory), and positivist (what is not created or recognized as law by the state is not law)."[8] John Griffiths argues that this conception of law stems from the ideology of legal centralism, which asserts that "law is and should be the law of the state, uniform for all persons, exclusive of all other law, and administered by a single set of state institutions."[9] Within this ideology, is an exclusivist claim that law is hierarchically superior to "other, lesser normative orderings, such as the church, the family, the voluntary association and the economic organization."[10] This claim of a unified hierarchical ordering is an ideology that sees the state as "the fundamental unit of political organization".[11] In the context of

---

[6]For a full list of laws incorporating various other religions, see Bell (2012), pp. 17–18 and footnote 41. As Bell notes, most of these other laws were originally adopted by the British and continued after independence.

[7]See section 5 and 6 of the Hindu Endowments Board Act (Cap 364, 1994 Rev Ed Sing).

[8]Twining (2000), p. 232.

[9]Griffiths (1986), p. 3.

[10]*Ibid.*

[11]*Ibid.*

Singapore, as the rest of this chapter will show, this tendency towards legal centralism is very real. However, the established structures in the form of courts and a repeated commitment to pluralism contributes to the persistence of legal pluralism in Singapore.

## 2 International, Regional, and Foreign Law

In terms of its relationship to international law, Singapore is a dualist state. This means that ratified treaties/conventions are not part of domestic law until specifically incorporated. Dualism's premise is that international law is a "horizontal legal order based on and regulating mainly the relations and obligations between independent and theoretically equal sovereign States."[12] State actions on this horizontal legal order do not have direct or automatic effect on the domestic level. This contrasts with monist states, where treaties are self-executing/automatically incorporated; no additional legislative act is required. Monism thus sees international and municipal law as forming part of the same continuous legal order, whereby there is a distinct hierarchy with international law sitting at the apex, constitutional law and then statutes/common law below it.[13] This hierarchy means that international law would prevail over domestic constitutional and statutory/common law.[14] There is no such hierarchical relationship in dualist states.

Nonetheless, Denza observes that matters are more complex than a simple dualist-monist distinction. Indeed, a state's constitutional approach to international obligations, to the implementation of a new treaty, or even judicial treatment of the applicability of international law may vary across different countries.[15] One movement within dualist states is judicial adoption of international law through interpretation. Such interpretive incorporation takes many different forms[16] and may result in international law being implemented on the domestic plan as persuasive non-law, soft law, or binding hard law.[17] Thus, even the United Kingdom, from which Singapore derived its dualist approach, has treated customary international law as directly applicable as part of its common law.

Dualism therefore can be understood as encompassing several interrelated legal propositions. First, a dualist state may completely view international law as being entirely irrelevant to domestic law, a position that I have called "*absolute non-relevance*".[18] Secondly, a dualist state may see international law as relevant

---

[12]Denza (2014), p. 421.

[13]*Ibid.*

[14]*Ibid.*

[15]*Ibid.*

[16]Waters (2007).

[17]Neo (2013).

[18]Neo (2012).

but as not hierarchically superior, and thus would not override or supersede national statutes and the common law. In other words, "*domestic law prevails*".[19] Thirdly, a dualist state may see international law as relevant, but that it could not override or supersede the supreme constitution of the state. This means that the "*constitution prevails*" at all times, although international law may supersede national statutes or the common law.[20] The second and third propositions are less stringent in dividing international law from domestic law since they contemplate the possibility that international could be *relevant*. An example where this could be the case is where there is a gap in domestic law.[21]

The Singapore courts have articulated an approach towards international law that seems more closely aligned to the idea that domestic law prevails. This is reflected in the Court of Appeal's recent pronouncements in *ABU v Comptroller of Income Tax*[22]:

> Under the dualist view, international law does not form part of Singapore's domestic law "until and unless it is applied or definitively declared to be part of the domestic law by a domestic court" in the case of customary international law (see *Lim Meng Suang* at [118]); or until it has been infused into domestic law by legislation in the case of treaty obligations. . . . This is not to say that the treaty will never inform the interpretation of the domestic legislation giving effect to it. . .[23]

Even clearer in terms of the Court's prioritization of domestic law is reflected in its opinion that:

> [I]t is also a corollary of the dualist view that where legislation has been passed to give effect to Singapore's treaty obligations, the Singapore court's primary focus must be on applying the relevant provisions of the domestic legislation and not specifically on enforcing the treaty.[24]

This case concerned a challenge of a disclosure order of certain bank accounts pursuant to a request made to the Singapore government by the National Tax Authority of Japan under a bilateral treaty. The treaty was given effect under a section in Singapore's income tax legislation.

However, in terms of its effect, it is questionable whether and how international law could be relevant. In the case of *Public Prosecutor v Tan Cheng Yew and another appeal*,[25] for example, the High Court affirmed a strict dualist approach whereby it states that "Singapore's international law obligations do not give rise to individual rights and obligations in the domestic context unless and until transposed into domestic law by legislation."[26] According to the High Court, international law

---

[19]*Ibid.*

[20]*Ibid.*

[21]*Ibid.*

[22][2015] 2 SLR 420.

[23]*ABU v Comptroller of Income Tax* [2015] 2 SLR 420, paras 47–48.

[24]*Ibid.*, para 47.

[25][2013] 1 SLR 1095.

[26]*Public Prosecutor v Tan Cheng Yew* [2013] 1 SLR 1095, para 56.

and domestic law "exist on different planes."[27] Thus, even if there was a breach of treaty obligations by the government, such obligations were owed only to the treaty partner on the plane of international law.[28] Any claims on the basis of individual rights can only be derived from the implementing domestic legislation, and not the international treaty.[29] This case concerned an appellant who had been extradited from Germany to face criminal charges and who had challenge those charges on the basis that they violated the speciality rule. This strict dualist approach appears to regard international law as being not relevant.

Indeed, Singapore courts have not provided much guidance on how the courts would interpret domestic law consistently with international law. For instance, would such interpretation be available only when the domestic law is ambiguous or where there is a gap ? Or would it be possible if domestic law is vague? Where constitutional rights are involved, these provisions are usually drafted in general terms. Could not international law be used to substantiate those provisions? In the 2010 case of *Yong Vui Kong v Public Prosecutor and another matter*,[30] the Court of Appeal held that domestic law (and this includes the constitution) should, as far as possible, be interpreted consistently with Singapore's international legal obligations. However, the Court also declined to interpret the constitutional guarantee of the right to life to include an implied prohibition against "inhuman punishment". According to the Court, there are "inherent limits" to the interpretive exercise. The main obstacle here was that a proposal to include an express constitutional provision to prohibit inhuman punishment had in fact been rejected by the constitutional commission that reviewed Singapore's constitution in 1966. The Court of Appeal therefore held that it was precluded from reading into Article 9(1) a prohibition against inhuman punishment, as it would effectively 'legislate' a new constitutional right and one that had been rejected.

The Court of Appeal's holding in *Yong Vui Kong v Public Prosecutor*[31] appears to restrict international law's interpretive relevance. There, the appellant had challenged the use of caning as a form of punishment on the basis that it was a form of torture prohibited under international law and that the constitution has to be interpreted accordingly.[32] where it held that even international law norms of peremptory nature could not invalidate domestic legislation. Indeed, the Court stated that even if a customary international law had acquired the status of jus cogens, it cannot override a domestic statute whose meaning and effect is clear.[33]

---

[27] *Ibid.*

[28] *Ibid.*, para 45.

[29] *Ibid.*, para 69.

[30] [2010] 3 SLR 489.

[31] *Yong Vui Kong v Public Prosecutor* [2015] 2 SLR 1129.

[32] The argument presented in the case was not as clear as it could be on this point but this is the best interpretation to counsel's arguments with respect to international law.

[33] *Yong Vui Kong v Public Prosecutor* [2015] 2 SLR 1129, para 38.

Singapore's strong commitment to dualism coheres with the common justification premised upon the doctrine of the separation of powers. In *Tan Cheng Yew*, the Court observed that extradition involved the exercise of sovereign power and that it was the executive that has the prerogative to determine the scope and conditions of extradition. Furthermore, it is commonly argued that allowing direct incorporation of international law on the domestic plane would intrude into the legislature's law-making powers. In the context of a jurisdiction like the United Kingdom which practices parliamentary sovereignty, such an argument would have much traction. One questions whether jurisdictions that have supreme constitutions should be similarly constricted in their engagement with international law, particularly in interpreting their constitutions. In those circumstances, an alternative objection may be that having regard to international law in judicial reasoning could encourage judicial activism and undermine the autochthonous nature of domestic law, especially the constitution.[34]

Singapore courts have declined to apply interpretive incorporation, which involves judicial incorporation of treaty provisions through interpretation. Interpretive incorporation involves a range of interpretive methods. Waters identifies five of them. The first uses human rights treaties to further affirm a particular interpretation of domestic law. A second entails the courts construing ambiguous statutes in such a way that would not violate the country's human rights obligations. The third method involves updating the common law consistently with human rights standards. The fourth is applied to constitutional or bill of rights cases; it involves using international human rights treaties as persuasive sources of constitutional interpretation. Human rights treaties provide context for judicial interpretation. The fifth method also concerns the constitutional bill of rights but treats international human rights treaties as binding normative framework.[35] As I have argued in a previous article, interpretive incorporation does not always mean that treaty provisions would have binding effect. Depending on the interpretive method employed, treaty law could attain varying degrees of authoritativeness under interpretive incorporation: as non-law, soft law, or hard law.[36] Thus far, however, the courts have been extremely reluctant to interpret the constitution to give effect to international law, including international human rights treaties. This view of the legal system as being neatly delineated into the international and domestic plane is consistent with a state legal centralist approach.

[34]See Neuman (2004) and Waters (2004).

[35]Waters (2007).

[36]Neo (2013).

## 3 The Dynamics of Relations Among Legal Spheres in Positive Law

Singapore has state religious courts for its Muslim minorities. This is the main area of legal pluralism, albeit a form of state legal pluralism. The Singapore constitution obligates the legislature to enact laws to regulate "Muslim religious affairs" as well as to constitute "a Council to advise the President in matters relating to the Muslim religion."[37] Pursuant to this, the government passed the Administration of Muslim Law Act ("AMLA")[38] in 1966, providing for the administration of Muslim law in Singapore. The Act also establishes a Syariah court, a Fatwa Council, and the Islamic Religious Council of Singapore (also known as the Majlis Ugama Islam Singapura or "MUIS").

The relationship between the Syariah legal system and the general/secular legal system has been subject to some adjudication. Legislatively, there have been moves to rationalise this relationship and even, some may argue, harmonize the two systems. Under AMLA, Syariah courts (and the Kadis/religious leaders) have jurisdiction over marriage, divorce, family, and inheritance questions. Decisions of the Syariah Court can be appealed to a Syariah Appeal Board established and administered by MUIS.[39] Section 35 of AMLA provides that the Syariah court has territorial jurisdiction throughout Singapore but only where *all parties are Muslims*, or where *parties were married under the provisions of Muslims law*, and the subject matter of the dispute relates to marriage, divorce,[40] and related matters,[41] including the disposition or division of property on divorce or nullification of marriage.

In 1999, following a series of cases that came to differing results concerning the jurisdictional boundaries between the Syariah court and the secular courts, statutory changes were put in place to clarify these boundaries. Up till then, section 16(2) of the Supreme Court of Judicature Act, 1969 ("SCJA") stated that "the High Court shall have *no jurisdiction* to hear and try *any civil proceeding* which *comes within the jurisdiction of the Syariah Court* constituted under the Administration of Muslim Law Act."[42] Cases addressing the jurisdictional boundaries between the High Court and the Syariah court were initially ambivalent about the exact import of the provision. As such, there were several cases where the civil courts did hear cases that could be said to fall within Syariah court jurisdiction. In *Muhd Munir v Noor*

[37]Article 153 of the Constitution of the Republic of Singapore states: "The Legislature shall by law make provision for regulating Muslim religious affairs and for constituting a Council to advise the President in matters relating to the Muslim religion."

[38]Cap 3, 2009 Rev Ed Sing.

[39]See generally Abbas (2012).

[40]These are *fasakh*, *cerai taklik*, *khuluk* and *talak*.

[41]Betrothal, nullity of marriage or judicial separation, payment of *emas kahwin*, marriage expenses (*hantaran belanja*), maintenance and consolatory gifts or *mutaah* relating to marriage and divorce.

[42]Act 24 of 1969 (emphasis added).

*Hidah*,[43] the High Court read AMLA narrowly to decide that a civil court can hear custody disputes arising from a Muslim divorce. The reasoning was rather technical. The High Court held that the jurisdiction-conferring section of AMLA (section 35) was exhaustive. Since custody was not specified as a head of jurisdiction, but only designated as one of the orders that the court is empowered to make,[44] the High Court's jurisdiction was excluded only when there is a pending divorce proceeding before the Syariah Court in which custody would be addressed. When there are no pending divorce proceedings, the Syariah Court had no independent jurisdiction over a custody matter. The High Court is therefore not precluded by section 16(2) of the SCJA from hearing the custody issue.

The later case of *Lathibaby Bevi v Abdul Mustapha*[45] however departed from the *Muhd Munir* approach. There, the High Court held that *all* ancillary applications concerning custody of children of Muslim parents *must* be made to the Syariah Court. The case concerned a custody dispute that arose after a Muslim couple had divorced. In granting the order for dissolution of marriage, the Syariah Court also made a consent order based on parties' agreement on custody. The wife/mother later became dissatisfied with the arrangement, and applied to the High Court under the Guardianship of Infants Act for custody of her daughter whose custody, under the parties' agreement, had been granted to the father. The High Court declined jurisdiction, opining that the application was to vary the Syariah court's custody order, and that only the Syariah court has powers to vary that order. Thus, as long as the Syariah court has assumed jurisdiction to decide a custody matter, the court's view is that all further disputes concerning custody would fall within the Syariah court's jurisdiction. That is the case even if one party is no longer a Muslim, thus subjecting a non-Muslim to Islamic jurisdiction. According to the court, such ancillary matters "form an integral part of the jurisdiction conferred on the Syariah Court" under AMLA,[46] and was thus within its exclusive jurisdiction.

Several other cases sought to grapple with the jurisdictional boundaries issues. Statutory amendments in 1999 sought to clarify these issues. First, the SCJA was amended to remove section 16(2) that sought to delineate jurisdictions. Instead, a new section 17A was inserted to clarify the areas in which the Syariah court would

---

[43] *Muhd Munir v Noor Hidah & Other Applications* [1990] SLR 999.

[44] The High Court made a distinction between jurisdiction and power. It held that the Syariah Court has no jurisdiction to hear and determine issues with respect to custody of children but that it is vested with the power to make orders concerning the custody, maintenance and education of children where there is an application for divorce before it. The vesting provision, section 35 of AMLA, confers the Syariah Court jurisdiction over marriages, divorces, and disposition or division of property on divorce, but no mention was made of jurisdiction over the guardianship and custody of children. Section 52 which sets out the powers of the Syariah Court empowers to court to make such orders as it thinks fit with respect to, inter alia, "the custody, maintenance and education of the minor children of the parties" at any stage of the proceedings or after a decree or order has been made, "[i]n any application for divorce." *Ibid.*, pp. 1006–1009.

[45] *Lathibaby Bevi v Abdul Mustapha* [1997] 3 SLR 1038.

[46] *Ibid.*, p. 1041.

have exclusive jurisdiction, which are only over the validity and dissolution of Muslim marriages, betrothals, nullity of marriage, and judicial separation. The section also states that the High Court would have concurrent jurisdiction over all other matters, including ancillary matters arising from divorce (maintenance, custody and disposition/division of matrimonial property).[47] AMLA was also amended to allow the civil courts to have concurrent jurisdiction to hear ancillary disputes arising from Muslim divorces. A new section 35A grant parties the right to commence or continue civil proceedings in the secular courts on such ancillary matters: either by mutual agreement or by order of the Syariah court.[48]

In response to critics who denounced what is seen as an interference with religious autonomy, the government stated that this was necessary to give Muslims, who are also citizens of Singapore, the option of having equal access to the civil courts to resolve their ancillary matters. The government stated that to designate the Syariah courts as *the only forum* to hear matrimonial disputes between Muslims would unduly restrict the rights of Muslims to equal access to the civil courts.[49] As concession, the laws were also changed to enhance the Syariah courts' enforcement powers. Under the new provision, the registrar of the Syariah court would be empowered under the amendments to sign documents on behalf of the errant spouse. An adminsitrative framework was also put in place such that Syariah court orders can be registered in the District Courts and enforced through them.

Another round of legislative changes in 2008 further clarified the scope of Syariah family laws in Singapore. AMLA was amended to remove the administrative requirement of registering Syariah court orders for enforcement. The new laws raised the status of Syariah court orders to be treated as District Court orders for the purpose of enforcement.

Despite these legislative changes, jurisdictional and normative conflicts between these two legal systems continue to arise. Here, I will discuss three such cases. The first case goes to competing sources of law and was resolved in favour of state positivism. In the 2004 case of *Ismail bin Ibrahim v Mohd Taha bin Ibrahim* ("*Ismail*"),[50] the civil courts had to resolve the question of whether a legal device *nuzriah* endorsed by the Islamic Religious Council to allow individual Muslims to circumvent Syariah inheritance rules was legally valid. This case is particularly

[47]See section 17A of the SJCA, read with section 35 of AMLA.

[48]Under this new section, parties can agree to commence or transfer proceedings concerning disposition or division of property as well as custody of children to the civil courts. Where there is mutual agreement, the Syariah Court is required to counsel parties on their options, and if *after* such counseling, parties remain in mutual agreement, the Syariah Court would be required to issue a certificate of attendance for the proceedings to be heard in the civil courts. See section 35A of AMLA.

[49]Singapore Parliament, Report of the Select Committee on the Administration of Muslim Law (Amendment) Bill (Bill No 18/98), para 9; Singapore Parliamentary Reports (April 15, 1999), Administration of Muslim Law (Amendment) Bill (As Reported from Select Committee), col 1249–1250.

[50]*Ismail bin Ibrahim v Mohd Taha bin Ibrahim* [2004] 4 SLR 756.

interesting because the conflict was between two religious rules. *Nuzriah* allows a testator to dispose of his entire putative estate by way of a legal fiction in which his putative estate is deemed to have been transferred to designated persons 3 days or at least an hour before his death.[51] This goes against conventional Syariah inheritance rules (*faraid*) which restrict the ability of a testator to will away his property. Under the rules, one can only will away one third of his property by will, with the remaining two thirds to be distributed according to Islamic inheritance rules.[52] This one-third restriction is statutorily recognized[53] and has been applied in judicial decisions in Singapore.[54] Despite this, the Islamic Religious Council's Legal Committee declared in a fatwa that the *nuzriah* was an acceptable overriding of *faraid*.[55]

Before proceeding, a word about fatwas. In classical Islam, a fatwā is formal legal opinion given in answer to an inquiry by a religious scholar or judge, which typically does not have general binding effect, and is applicable only to the enquirer. In Singapore, the fatwa is a formal legal opinion issued by a Legal Committee constituted under AMLA. The Legal Committee may issue a fatwa in answer to a query or by its own initiative, and is composed of the Mufti, two members of the Islamic Religious Council, and two other "fit and proper" Muslims.[56] Section 33 of AMLA further specifies that any rulings "shall ordinarily follow the tenets of the Shafi'i school of law" unless the applicable tenets are "opposed to the public interest", following which other accepted schools of Muslim law may be followed.

In *Ismail*, High Court held that *nuzriah* was not a sufficient device to override the *faraid* rules, which had statutory and judicial backing. A fatwa did not have the same legal status as a statute. Consequently, even though the Islamic Religious Council, the mufti, and the Legal Committee took the position that a *nuzriah* could have legal effect, this was deemed insufficient to override a statutory provision.[57] This case is

[51]The transfer is deemed to have taken effect 3 days before his death if he dies of sickness, or 1 h before his death in the case of accidents or sudden death.

[52]All Muslims are subject to these rules. This is established under section 112 of AMLA: "(1) In the case of any Muslim person domiciled in Singapore dying intestate, the estate and effects shall be distributed according to the Muslim law as modified, where applicable, by Malay custom. (2) This section shall apply in cases where a person dies partly intestate as well as in cases where he dies wholly intestate. (3) In the case of a Malay dying intestate, the court may make an order for the division of the harta sepencarian or jointly acquired property in such proportions as to the court seems fit."

[53]See, e.g., section 60(1) of AMLA which restricts the ability of Muslims to will or gift away more than one third of his property to charitable trusts. See also *Ismail bin Ibrahim v Mohd Taha bin Ibrahim* [2004] 4 SLR 756, paras 49, 51.

[54]The High Court referred to *Shaik Abdul Latif v Shaik Elias Buz* (1915) 1 FMSLR 204, *Siti binti Yatim v Mohamed Nor bin Bujai* (1928) 6 FMSLR 135, *Re Fatimah Binte Mohamed Bin Ali Al Tway, Deceased* [1933] 1 MLR 211, *Abdul Jabbar v M Mohamed Abubacker* [1940] 1 MLJ 286, and *Re Estate of Siti bte Naydeen* [1983-1984] SLR(R) 682.

[55]Majlis Ugama Islam Singapura, Office of Mufti (2019).

[56]Sections 31 and 32 of AMLA.

[57]The will containing the *nuzriah* was certified and validated by the Mufti of Singapore. After a dispute arose among the heirs concerning the division of property, the Fatwa Committee was asked

interesting because the rule of recognition is affirmed as the exercise of the state's legislative power. Even though the Islamic Religious Council was a statutory body, it is an administrative body which does not have legislative powers. While this could be criticized as an interference with the religious autonomy of a minority group, the fact remains that there is a hierarchy of norms and powers whereby Parliament retains the ultimate law-making power in the country. The legal validity of a rule remains the exercise of legislative power, and not religious doctrine or the views of religious scholars or leaders. The ultimate rule of recognition for all laws, even religious ones, is still the state's legislative powers.[58]

A second case highlighting the relationship between the civil/secular legal system and the religious legal system is the 2010 case *Shafeeg bin Salim Talib and another v Fatimah bte Abud bin Talib and others* ("*Shafeeg v Fatimah*").[59] This case raises the issue of the relative status of legal norms within the two systems. The issue at hand was whether real property held in joint tenancy forms part of the estate of a Muslim deceased. Under the common law, the right of survivorship operates such that the property becomes vested in the remaining joint tenant (here, the wife) upon death and not part of the estate.[60] However, under Islamic inheritance law, there is no similar concept of the right of survivorship and it was argued that half-share of the property formed part of the estate. The Islamic Religious Council's Legal Committee also weighed in to rule, via a fatwa, that the property was part of the couple's matrimonial property, and that the husband's half of the property formed part of the estate to be distributed according to Islamic inheritance law.[61]

The High Court disagreed and this was affirmed by the Court of Appeal. In coming to its decision, the Court of Appeal applied a hierarchy of laws whereby legislation and the common law prevails over personal laws.[62] Thus, while Syariah laws govern the distribution of the estate, the prior question of whether a property forms part of the estate is to be governed by general laws (i.e. statute and the

---

to and issued a fatwa declaring that the *nuzriah* made in the will was valid, and determined how the estate should be divided. MUIS also ratified the *nuzriah* segment of the will. See *Ismail bin Ibrahim v Mohd Taha bin Ibrahim* [2004] 4 SLR 756, para 17.

[58]For a further discussion on the hierarchy of norms in Singapore, see Neo (2016).

[59][2010] 2 SLR 1123.

[60]On 12 May 2005, pursuant to an application of the administrators of the estate, the Syariah Court issued an inheritance certificate ("the Inheritance Certificate") under s 112 of AMLA identifying 12 beneficiaries of the estate. The deceased's wife was declared as having 10/40 shares in the estate. The deceased's children were held to be not entitled to any share as they were not Muslims at the date of death of the deceased. Despite that, the wife filed a Notice of Death at the Singapore Land Registry and became registered as the sole owner of the property. She subsequently transferred the property to herself and their two children. The children had been denied from inheriting the deceased's estate under Syariah law because they had converted out of Islam.

[61]The fatwa reads: "The Fatwa Committee is of the opinion that the estate is considered as a matrimonial property (harta sepencarian) as the deceased and his wife had jointly own [sic] it. Therefore half of the estate is considered as inheritance and should be distributed in accordance to Islamic Inheritance Law (faraidh)."

[62]*Shafeeg v Fatimah* [2010] 2 SLR 1123, paras 28, 69.

common law). Interestingly, the Court of Appeal's sent the following message in its judgment: "We hope that MUIS will take note of our observation".[63]

A third case is the 2017 case of *TMO v TMP*.[64] This case concerned the powers of the Syariah court to adjudicate over ancillary matters arising from a divorce decree obtained overseas. The Muslim couple were married under Muslim law in Singapore but relocated to Johor where they later obtained a divorce from the Johor Sharia Court. The wife sought an order for the division of matrimonial assets from the Singapore Syariah Court, which however refused as it took the view that it did not have the jurisdiction to make the division under AMLA since it did not grant the divorce. The wife later applied to the civil family courts for a division order but her application was dismissed on the basis that the family courts did not jurisdiction under the law to decide over matters arising from a Muslim divorce granted overseas. Under the Women's Charter (under which family law was governed), courts were specifically granted statutory powers to make orders for financial relief with respect to marriages dissolved by an order of a foreign court.[65] However, the Family Court and the High Court held that this does not extend to Muslim marriages dissolved overseas as the Women's Charter explicitly excluded Muslim marriages from its purview.

This was a problematic result and one that has been criticized for leaving a lacuna in the law. The matter was appealed to the Court of Appeal, which sat *en banc* (an unusual scenario). The Court of Appeal held that where a matter did not fall within the jurisdiction of the Syariah Court, the High Court retained residual jurisdiction over the matter. They took a purposive interpretation of the provision in the Women's Charter excluding Muslim marriages from its purview, and held that the provision should be construed to be subject to the qualification that it applied only where the Syariah Court had jurisdiction over the matter. Where the Syariah Court had no jurisdiction over the matrimonial dispute, the High Court would have residual jurisdiction. Furthermore, the Court held that there would be no conflict of jurisdiction in those circumstances since the High Court alone would have jurisdiction.

These cases highlight the continuing resolution of the boundaries between the civil and the syariah courts, despite the legislative changes. The results reflect a strong impetus towards legal centralism.

[63]*Ibid.*, para 69.

[64][2017] 1 SLR 585.

[65]Section 121G of the Women's Charter (Cap 353, 2009 Rev Ed Sing).

## 4 The Renewal of Legal Reasoning and Jurisprudence

Legal borrowing and engagement has always been part of Singapore's legal tradition as part of the common law world. There has always been an openness towards looking at other common law jurisdictions in how Singapore courts resolve legal disputes. Much of this engagement is based on genealogy, which can be both the common law and statute.[66] This openness towards foreign jurisprudence however appears to apply more to private law matters. Where constitutional law is concerned, the Singapore courts have developed a *four walls doctrine* which insists on interpreting the Singapore Constitution and public law statutes within the four walls of the constitution.

The leading case setting out this approach is the 1994 case of *Chan Hiang Leng Colin v Public Prosecutor*, where the then Chief Justice Yong Ping How declared that the constitution is "primarily to be interpreted within its own four walls and not in the light of analogies drawn from other countries such as Great Britain, the United States of America or Australia". The case concerned a constitutional challenge against an administrative order banning publications by the Watch Tower Bible & Tract Society, the parent body of Jehovah's Witnesses. The prohibition order was made in conjunction with the dissolution of the Singapore Congregation of Jehovah's Witnesses as a society pursuant to their refusal to perform compulsory military duty. Several Jehovah's Witnesses were charged for being in possession of prohibited materials. They challenged the underlying order on the basis that it violates their constitutional right to religious freedom. Under the Singapore Constitution, "[e]very person has the right to profess and practise his religion and to propagate it." In dismissing the challenge, the Court declined to follow judicial pronouncements in the United States on the right to freedom of religion, remarking inter alia that unlike the First Amendment to the United States Constitution, the Singapore Constitution does not prohibit the 'establishment' of any religion. Beyond textual differences, the court also observed that the social conditions in Singapore are "markedly different from those in the United States".

The four walls approach however does not entirely preclude reference to foreign jurisprudence. Indeed, as has been observed, even in the case of *Chan Hiang Leng Colin*, the then Chief Justice did refer approvingly to an Australian High Court case to support the curtailment of religious freedom on grounds of national security.[67] Furthermore, the very passage setting out the four walls doctrine was restated from a Malaysian case.[68]

The four walls doctrine has been criticized not only for its inward-looking approach but also for the fact that it obscures actual borrowing that is taking place within the sphere of constitutional law adjudication. This is especially as

[66]See Woon (1999).

[67]*Adelaide Co of Jehovah's Witnesses Inc v The Commonwealth* (1943) 67 CLR 16.

[68]*Government of the State of Kelantan v Government of the Federation of Malaya* [1963] MLJ 355. See further Tan (2017a).

engagement with foreign constitutional jurisprudence has increased in recent years. Courts have, for instance, engaged with the *Reynolds* test of responsible journalism as an expanded form of qualified privilege for defamation suits.[69] While defamation is a private tort, it impinges upon freedom of speech and is a constitutionally permitted limitation to the right to free speech in Singapore. Observers have therefore suggested that the four walls doctrine may well be regarded as having become irrelevant in constitutional jurisprudence in Singapore.[70] Nonetheless, others have argued that while there has been less resistance to referring to foreign and international law in constitutional cases, such engagement remains limited. Arun Thiruvengadam has argued that recent courts have been "less absolutist", but their use of foreign law is still closer to the "resistance" model rather than the engagement model articulated by Vicki Jackson.[71] I will discuss two areas of continuing resistance.

## *4.1 Proportionality*

One area of continuing resistance is manifest in the Singapore courts' rejection of the doctrine of proportionality. Proportionality has been called the 'most important doctrinal tool in constitutional rights law around the world for decades'[72] and 'the orienting idea in contemporary human rights law and scholarship'.[73] In recent years, proportionality analysis has spread from its German origins across Europe and into the Commonwealth systems. However, in the case of *Chee Siok Chin and others v. Minister for Home Affairs and another*,[74] the High Court emphatically rejected proportionality as a jurisprudential approach that is a "more exacting requirement than reasonableness" and which would require "the court to substitute its own judgment for that of the proper authority" in some cases.[75] The Court appeared to consider this to be an inappropriate expansion of judicial function. It further rejected the doctrine on the basis that it had never been part of the common law and therefore not part of Singapore law.

An earlier Court of Appeal case approached proportionality with less emphatic opposition, although this more accepting approach may be premised on its view that proportionality can be subsumed under "irrationality", which is a conventional ground of substantive review in English administrative law. The Singapore courts'

---

[69] *Review Publishing Co Ltd v Lee Hsien Loong* [2010] 1 SLR 52, discussing *Reynolds v Times Newspapers Ltd* [2001] 2 AC 127.

[70] See Thio and Chong (2012), pp. 87, 97.

[71] Thurvengadam (2017). See also Jackson (2005).

[72] Moller (2012), p. 709.

[73] Huscroft et al. (2014).

[74] [2005] SGHC 216.

[75] *Ibid.*, para 87 (emphasis added).

resistance towards proportionality has been criticized. Jack Lee argues for instance that the rejection of proportionality doctrine has affected the rights to freedom of expression and assembly as well as the freedom of religion.[76] Stone-Sweet and Mathews argue that Singapore appears to lag behind other Asian countries, which have adopted the doctrine.[77] That said, in a recent High Court case of *Vijaya Kumar s/o Rajendran and others v Attorney-General*,[78] the Court applied a method of reasoning which could be said to approximate proportionality analysis. This case concerned a challenge against a police order prohibiting the use of musical instruments during parts of a religious procession during the Hindu Thaipusam festival. The court upheld the ban, but through an interesting reasoning process. The Court considered the justification for the prohibition (i.e. legitimate aim). It then observed that the "music ban" did not prohibit all music during the Thaipusam procession, but that the participants were still permitted to play musical instruments on temple grounds at the start and end of the procession, to sing of religious hymns throughout the procession and to broadcast the hymns from public address systems at three locations during the procession (i.e. least restrictive means). The Court further observed that the police "had nuanced its approach over time in response to dialogue with the Hindu community."[79] The Court thus concluded that this calibrated approach showed that the government had given sufficient regard to the religious freedom rights of the applicants.

## 4.2 Basic Structure Doctrine

Another increasingly global doctrine that has been rejected, though in a less emphatic way, is the basic structure or features doctrine. The basic features doctrine was first developed by the Indian Supreme Court in the case of *Kesavananda Bharati v State of Kerala*[80] *which held that every provision of the constitution can be amended provided that "the basic foundation and structure of the constitution remains the same". Among the basic structure are the following features—supremacy of the constitution, the republican and democratic form of government, the secular character of the constitution, the federal character of the constitution, and the separation of powers.*[81]

---

[76]Lee (2014).

[77]Stone-Sweet and Mathews (2017).

[78]*Vijaya Kumar s/o Rajendran and others v Attorney-General* [2015] SGHC 244.

[79]*Ibid*.

[80]AIR 1973 SC 1461.

[81]Per Sikri CJ in *Kesavananda Bharati v State of Kerala* AIR 1973 SC 1461. Other judges identified slightly different features in their concurring judgment, such as the dignity of the individual, and the unity and integrity of the nation (per Shelat and Gover JJ).

*The basic structure doctrine was examined and rejected by the High Court in 1989 as being "not applicable" to the Singapore constitution in the case of Teo Soh Lung v Minister for Home Affairs & Ors.*[82] There the court had to consider whether there are implied substantive limitations on the Singapore Parliament's powers to amend the Singapore constitution. Parliament had amended the constitution to allow for legislative changes to its preventive detention laws that would limit the scope of judicial review of ministerial decisions. The amendment was procedurally valid and so the question was whether the amendment could be invalidated on the basis of substantive limitations to the amendment powers. The High Court declined to adopt the *Kesavananda* doctrine, holding that Parliament has the power to amend any provision of the constitution as long as the prescribed procedure was followed. Curiously, the High Court also gave a throwaway line stating that in its view, the amendments did not violate the basic structure of the constitution. That presumes that the High Court has an implicit idea of what the basic structure would be.

In recent times, the basic structure doctrine has been canvassed several times by the Singapore courts, although it is not always clear that the courts are referring to the *Kesavananda* doctrine of implied limitations to amendment powers. In the case of *Mohammad Fiazal bin Sabtu v Public Prosecutor*,[83] then Chief Justice Chan Sek Keong appeared to revive the relevance of the basic structure doctrine in stating that:

> The Singapore Constitution is based on the Westminster model of constitutional government ('the Westminster model'), under which the sovereign power of the State is distributed among three organs of state, *viz*, the Legislature, the Executive and the Judiciary. In the UK (where the Westminster model originated), the Legislature is the UK parliament (comprising the House of Commons and the House of Lords), the Executive is the UK government and the Judiciary consists of the UK judges. Likewise, under the Singapore Constitution, the sovereign power of Singapore is shared among the same trinity of constitutional organs, *viz*, the Legislature (comprising the President of Singapore and the Singapore parliament), the Executive (the Singapore government) and the Judiciary (the judges of the Supreme Court and the Subordinate Courts). *The principle of separation of powers, whether conceived as a sharing or a division of sovereign power between these three organs of state, is therefore part of the basic structure of the Singapore Constitution.*[84]

This case involved the constitutionality of an amended section of the Misuse of Drugs Act, which provided for mandatory minimum punishment of 5 years' imprisonment and three strokes of the cane for repeat offenders. The accused person argued that section 33A(1)(a) was unconstitutional as it amounted to a legislative direction to the judiciary to impose a mandatory minimum punishment on him. This, it was argued, violated the doctrine of the separation of powers. As Kevin Tan observes, this passage adopts wholesale the Westminster model of the separation and matrix of the separation of powers and also in holding that the separation of powers between

---

[82][1989] 2 MLJ 449.

[83][2012] 4 SLR 947.

[84]*Ibid.*, pp. 956–957 (emphasis added).

the three branches of government forms part of the 'basic structure' of the Singapore Constitution.[85]

In the more recent case of *Yong Vui Kong v Public Prosecutor*,[86] the Court of Appeal expounded on the doctrine and stated that "in order for a feature to be considered part of the basic structure of the Constitution, it must be something *fundamental and essential to the political system* that is established thereunder."[87] It however held that it was not necessary for the court to consider the applicability of the *Kesavananda* doctrine since the case at hand did not deal with the validity of a constitutional amendment.[88] In this case, the accused person had been convicted of drug trafficking offenses and sentenced to the mandatory minimum of life imprisonment and 15 strokes of the cane. He appealed against the imposition of the 15 strokes on the basis that caning was unconstitutional. One of the basis for challenging its constitutionality was that caning constituted torture and that the right to life and personal liberty guaranteed under the constitution impliedly prohibits torture. The Court concluded that caning, as administered in Singapore as a form of punishment, did not constitute torture. What is interesting in this case is not only that the Court did not outrightly reject the applicability of the basic structure doctrine, but suggests that unenumerated rights might arguably be read into the constitution when they could be considered part of the basic structure of the constitution, i.e. that they were fundamental and essential to the constitutionally established political system. Accordingly, there was a brief discussion suggesting that the right to vote could be part of the basic structure of the constitution. This expands the *Mohammad Faizal* dicta, which only referred to the separation of powers as part of the basic structure of the Singapore constitution.

Consequently, while the basic structure doctrine and the broader idea of unconstitutional constitutional amendments has not been fully adopted in Singapore, the courts have started to display openness to the idea that there could be certain features that are crucial to the constitutional identity of the Singapore constitutional order and that such features could be cautiously identified by the courts. How courts would decide should they be faced with a constitutional challenge over an amendment that impinges upon the basic structure of the constitution is however hard to predict. At least in the recent High Court decision of *Ravi s/o Madasamy v Attorney-General and other matters*,[89] where the petitioner challenged a recent constitutional amendment to the presidency, the court emphasized that the basic structure doctrine did not yet apply in full force in Singapore.[90] Like in previous decisions, the High Court declined to rule conclusively on the applicability of the basic structure doctrine.

---

[85]Tan (2017b).

[86][2015] 2 SLR 1129.

[87]*Ibid.*, pp. 1158–1159 (emphasis added).

[88]*Ibid.*, p. 1160.

[89][2017] SGHC 163.

[90]*Ibid.*, para 65.

What is interesting in that case, however, is that the High Court provided a "thin" conception of the basic structure doctrine, which it explained as "a broad restatement of the truism that the Constitution rests on an overarching principled framework embracing the precepts of the rule of law and the separation of powers."[91] The Court interestingly went on to decide that the impugned amendments "did not involve any curtailment of the judicial power or any other incursions into the precepts of the rule of law and the separation of powers."[92]

Set against a discernible trend in which courts in many jurisdictions have started to adopt some normative limits to amendment powers, the Singapore courts' hesitation to embrace the basic structure doctrine points to the cautious approach that judges here take towards any hints of judicial activism.

## 5 Conclusion

Broadly speaking therefore, two conditions can be said to define Singapore's legal pluralism. The first is a strong impetus towards legal centralism, which very much vindicates Griffiths' critique that state legal pluralism is weak legal pluralism and conforms to the logic of legal centralism.[93] Indeed, developments relating to the Syariah legal system reflects this pressure towards legal monism, whereby the religious legal system tends to be seen as an exceptional space but subject to the hierarchical imposition of norms and values from the secular system.

The second condition is the dominant party system whereby one political party dominates the 'democratic' government. There has only been one political party in power in post-independence Singapore. The ruling People's Action Party (PAP) has formed the government after every general elections since independence. Between 1966 and 1981, PAP members held all seats in Parliament. Since then, it has held more than two-thirds of parliamentary seats, which is the procedural threshold since 1979 for passing constitutional amendments. This has allowed the government to shape the constitutional order via amendments. This include introducing new types of parliamentarians (unelected, nominated parliamentarians and parliamentarians without constituencies), as well as changing the presidency from a nominated/ ceremonial to an elected one. Within Singapore's dominant party-political culture, it is an important way for the judiciary to negotiate and maintain a significant policy space[94] to ensure the availability of constitutional review, albeit a limited one. The Court have been careful to emphasise that the judiciary is not in an "exalted or superior position relative to the other branches of the government",[95] but simply is

[91]*Ibid.*, para 66.

[92]*Ibid.*, para 66.

[93]Griffiths (1986).

[94]Ginsburg (2003), p. 19.

[95]*Tan Seet Eng v AG* [2016] 1 SLR 779, para 90.

the branch of government with the separate and distinct responsibility of pronouncing on the legality of state action.[96] It has been argued that the dialogue metaphor may be useful to describe judicial behaviour in Singapore whereby courts seek not to strike down legislation or executive decision, which would be a form of confrontation with the political branches, but to engage in dialogue with them.[97] In a way, a largely deferential approach characterizes the courts' attitude towards legal pluralism, particularly where faced with foreign legal doctrines such as proportionality and basic structure doctrine. Nonetheless, it may be argued that the degree of deference towards the political branches has declined somewhat in recent years as the courts find its way to vindicate its role as a coequal branch of government within Singapore's constitutional order.[98]

Despite these two conditions, legal pluralism persists. The work of the Syariah courts, and the general acceptance that legal pluralism is a desirable condition supports the continuing operation of Singapore's legally pluralistic structures. Indeed, one may see how the Syariah courts and other institutions/organizations have adapted to these conditions and ensured their relevance by adopting a generally cooperative, non-confrontational stance. The judiciary has also played a significant role in ensuring that pluralistic sources and interpretations of the law can be canvassed and considered. These will ensure that legal centralism remains a myth and legal pluralism remains the norm in Singapore.

**Acknowledgement** I would like to thank Philip Teh Ahn Ren for his editorial assistance.

## References

Abbas AN (2012) The Islamic legal system in Singapore. Pacific Rim Law Policy J 21(1):163–187
Bell G (2012) Religious legal pluralism revisited – the status of the Roman Catholic Church and her Canon Law in Singapore. Asian J Comp Law 7(1):5
Denza E (2014) The relationship between international and national law. In: Evans MD (ed) International law, 4th edn. Oxford University Press, Oxford, pp 412–442
Ginsburg T (2003) Judicial review in new democracies: constitutional courts in Asian cases. Cambridge University Press, New York
Goh YH, Tan P (2011) An empirical study on the development of Singapore law. Singapore Academy Law J 23:176–226
Griffiths J (1986) What is legal pluralism? J Legal Pluralism Unofficial Law 24:1–55
Harding A (2002) Global doctrine and local knowledge: law in South East Asia. Int Comp Law Q 51:35–53
Huscroft G et al (eds) (2014) Proportionality and the rule of law: rights, justification, reasoning. Cambridge University Press, New York
Jackson V (2005) The Supreme Court, 2004 term – comment: constitutional comparisons: convergence, resistance, engagement. Harv Law Rev 119:109–128

[96] *Ibid.*, paras 1, 106.

[97] Yap (2015). See critique in Jhaveri and Neo (2017).

[98] See, e.g., Neo (2017).

Jhaveri S, Neo JL (2017) The many facets of constitutional dialogue: the case of Singapore. Aust J Asian Law 18(1):1–14
Lee JTT (2014) According to the spirit and not to the letter: proportionality and the Singapore constitution. Vienna J Int Cont Law 8:276–304
Majlis Ugama Islam Singapura, Office of Mufti (2019) Nuzriah in Islam. https://www.muis.gov.sg/officeofthemufti/Irsyad/English-Nuzriah. Accessed 21 Sep 2012
Moller K (2012) Proportionality: challenging the critics. Int J Const Law 10:709–731
Neo JL (2012) Incorporating human rights: mitigated dualism and interpretation in Malaysian courts. Asian Yearb Int Law 18:1–37
Neo JL (2013) Calibrating interpretive incorporation: constitutional interpretation and pregnancy discrimination under CEDAW. Human Rights Q 35:910–934
Neo JL (2016) Secular constitutionalism in Singapore: between equality and hierarchy. Oxford J Law Religion 5(3):431–456
Neo JL (2017) Balancing act. In: Neo JL (ed) Constitutional interpretation in Singapore: theory and practice. Routledge, Abingdon, pp 159–187
Neuman GL (2004) The uses of international law in constitutional interpretation. Am J Int Law 98 (1):82–90
Phang ABL (1986) Of "Cut-Off" dates and domination: some problematic aspects of the reception of English law in Singapore. Malayan Law Rev 28:242–266
Phang ABL (1990) Reception of English Law in Singapore: problems and proposed solutions. Singapore Academy Law J 2:20–40
Stone-Sweet A, Mathews J (2017) Proportionality and rights protection in Asia: Hong Kong, Malaysia, South Korea, Taiwan – Whither Singapore? Singapore Academy Law J 29:774–799
Tan EKB (2017a) Much ado about nothing? The enigma of engagement of foreign constitutional law in Singapore. In: Neo JL (ed) Constitutional interpretation in Singapore: theory and practice. Routledge, Abingdon, pp 289–317
Tan KYL (2017b) Into the matrix, constitutional interpretation in Singapore. In: Neo JL (ed) Constitutional interpretation in Singapore: theory and practice. Routledge, Abingdon, pp 50–75
Thio LA, Chong DGS (2012) The Chan Court and constitutional adjudication – a sea change into something rich and strange? In: Chao HT et al (eds) The law in his hands: a tribute to Chief Justice Chan Sek Keong. Academy Publishing, Singapore, pp 87–119
Thurvengadam AK (2017) The continuing resistance to foreign law in constitutional adjudication in Singapore. In: Neo JL (ed) Constitutional interpretation in Singapore: theory and practice. Routledge, Abingdon, pp 318–341
Twining W (2000) Globalisation and legal theory. Butterworths, London
Waters MA (2004) Justice Scalia on the use of foreign law in constitutional interpretation: unidirectional monologue or co-constitutive dialogue. Tulsa J Comp Int Law 12(1):149–161
Waters MA (2007) Creeping monism: the judicial trend toward interpretive incorporation of human rights treaties. Columbia Law Rev 107:628–705
Woon WCM (1999) The applicability of English law in Singapore. In: Tan KYL (ed) The Singapore legal system. NUS Press, Singapore, pp 230–248
Yap PJ (2015) Constitutional dialogue in common law Asia. Oxford University Press, Oxford

# Constitutionalism and Customary Laws in Solomon Islands

**Jennifer Corrin**

**Abstract** Constitutionalism in Solomon Islands is dominated by the written Constitution, which imports a Westminster system and the common law tradition. However, as in other jurisdictions where customary communities are strong, constitutionalism involves more than state institutions and mechanisms. At independence, Solomon Islands proclaimed an allegiance to custom in its Constitution. As a consequence of this, and its colonial history, it has a plural legal system wherein State laws co-exist with customary laws. In this context, the challenge for the idea of constitutionalism may come not only from international developments, but also from the domestic sphere. This Chapter argues that, rather than being challenged by limits imposed at an international or supranational level, governmental power is being challenged by local initiatives designed to promote the authority of traditional leaders and the customary laws which they promulgate. It commences with some background on Solomon Islands and an overview of its systems of law and government to give context to the discussion. It then proceeds to explore the balance of relations in different spheres of positive law, both generally and in respect of judicial review, freedom of contract, and the hierarchy of norms. Discussion then moves to the dynamics of the relationship between different aspects of positive law. The place of international law in Solomon Islands, the approach of legal actors, resolution of conflicts and transconstitutional dialogue, and evolution of approach to constitutionalism and conflicting norms are considered. The last part of the chapter comments on the failure of legal reasoning and jurisprudence to evolve.

J. Corrin (✉)
Centre for Public, International and Comparative Law, TC Beirne School of Law,
The University of Queensland, Brisbane, QLD, Australia
e-mail: j.corrin@law.uq.edu.au



G. Tusseau (ed.), *Debating Legal Pluralism and Constitutionalism*, Ius Comparatum – Global Studies in Comparative Law 41, https://doi.org/10.1007/978-3-030-34432-0_9

# 1 Introduction

At independence, a written Constitution[1] was made for Solomon Islands by Order in Council in the United Kingdom.[2] This Constitution is necessarily a dominant feature in any discussion of constitutionalism in the country. However, it should be borne in mind that, as commented by, Chief Justice Robert French in the context of Australia, constitutionalism is,

> a kind of conceptual envelope. It encompasses a variety of institutional mechanisms for defining and limiting governmental power in its various manifestations, adherence to those mechanisms by governmental actors and support for them by members of the relevant society.[3]

Due to its colonial history, Solomon Islands has inherited a Westminster system and the common law tradition. However, as in other jurisdictions where customary communities are strong, the envelope contains more than state institutions and mechanisms. Both traditional authority and non-State laws, referred to in this Chapter as 'customary laws', have ramifications for constitutionalism. At independence, many South Pacific island countries, including Solomon Islands, proclaimed an allegiance to custom in their Constitutions. As a consequence of this, and its colonial history, Solomon Islands has a plural legal system wherein State laws co-exist with customary laws. In this context, the challenge for the idea of constitutionalism may come not only from international developments, but also from the domestic sphere.

This Chapter considers constitutionalism in Solomon Islands and argues that, rather than being challenged by limits imposed at an international or supranational level, governmental power is being challenged by local initiatives designed to promote the authority of traditional leaders and the customary laws which they promulgate.

This chapter commences with some background on Solomon Islands and an overview of its systems of law and government to give some context to the discussion. It then proceeds to explore the balance of relations in different spheres of positive law, both generally and in respect of judicial review, freedom of contract, and the hierarchy of norms. Discussion then moves to the dynamics of the relationship between different aspects of positive law. The place of international law in Solomon Islands, the approach of legal actors, resolution of conflicts and transconstitutional dialogue, and evolution of approach to constitutionalism and conflicting norms are considered. The last part of the chapter comments on the failure of legal reasoning and jurisprudence to evolve.

[1] Constitution of Solomon Islands 1978 ('Constitution').

[2] Solomon Islands Independence Order 1978.

[3] French (2009), p. 6.

## 2 Background to Solomon Islands and Its System of Law and Government

Solomon Islands is an archipelago made up of twenty-six main islands, and about 900 small islands and islets, spread out in a 1360 km long, double chain. It lies about 1600 km north-east of Australia. The country has a land area of about 28,000 $km^2$, around one third of the size of Tasmania, and a total sea are of 1,340,000 $km^2$. The population is about 550,000,[4] speaking about 80 vernacular languages,[5] the majority of whom live in rural areas.

From 1892 to 1978, the country was a British Protectorate, known as British Solomon Islands Protectorate.[6] Until the early 1970s, legislation was made for the Protectorate, as well as Fiji, the Gilbert and Ellice Islands and the New Hebrides, by the British High Commissioner for the Western Pacific. The constituent laws establishing the structure of government, and the limits of its powers were made by the Crown.[7] At this stage in history, therefore, legislative power was held transnationally within the region, but with ultimate control reserved to Britain, on the other side of the world. In the 1960s, Britain started to prepare the Protectorate for independence, and the High Commissioner required the advice and consent of a legislative council to make laws. In addition to these locally made laws, 'the substance of the law for the time being in force in England' was applied to the Protectorate.[8] This was later replaced by the application of 'the statutes of general application in force in England on the 1st day of January 1961'.[9] In addition to legislation, principles of English common law and equity were introduced so far as appropriate to the circumstances of the country.[10]

Customary laws were not originally regarded by the State as a formal source of law, except in relation to title to customary land.[11] However the colonial administration allowed indigenous customs to be applied by customary leaders within their communities as a form of social control. Accordingly, even at this stage, there was some division of power between the national and sub-national levels of society. In

[4]The 2009 census puts the population at 515,870: Solomon Islands National Statistics Office (2009), p. 6.

[5]Sixty-six percent of the population speak a local language: Solomon Islands National Statistics Office (2009), p. 102.

[6]Pacific Order in Council 1893 (UK).

[7]Pacific Order in Council 1893 (UK), issued both under the legal authority granted by the common law to the British Crown to make constituent laws for overseas territories not settled by British citizens, and also under the legal authority provided by the Pacific Islanders' Protection Acts 1872 and 1875, and the Foreign Jurisdiction Act 1890 (UK).

[8]Pacific Order in Council 1893 (UK), s 20.

[9]Western Pacific (Courts) Order 1961 (UK), s 15.

[10]Pacific Order in Council 1893 (UK), s 20; Western Pacific (Courts) Order 1961 (UK), s 15.

[11]Because Solomon Islands was only a protectorate, not a colony, Britain and the British administration in Solomon Islands laid no claim to ownership of the land.

1942, broader recognition was given to 'native customs', which were to be applied by the native courts.[12] These courts, later renamed the local courts,[13] were established by legislation and sought to bring customary dispute resolution under the control of the state.

In 1978, Solomon Islands became independent. The independence Constitution (the 'Constitution') is not an autochthonous document, but was drafted in London by British officials, after discussion with local leaders from the Solomon Assembly, and brought into force by an Order in Council.[14] The Constitution commences with a prefatory provision, often termed a Preamble, which sets out the basic values upon which the Constitution is based. The enacting parts commence with some provisions about the nature of the state and the status of the Constitution. They then set out a bill of rights and rights to citizenship. This is followed by provisions establishing the executive, legislature and judiciary. The Constitution also provides for the public service and public finances. Express provisions about land are also included, most importantly the declaration that the 'natural resources of [the] country are vested in the people and the government of Solomon Islands'.[15] The procedure for amending, repealing or suspending the Constitution is spelt out, together with transitional provisions.

The Constitution kept in force introduced laws, together with the colonial legislation, as a transitional measure, until the newly established Parliament could replace them with local enactments.[16] It also recognised customary laws and provided for them to be applied by Solomon Islands' courts.[17] In theory, customary laws are to apply in preference to common law.[18] There is no mention of international law in the Constitution, but, as discussed below, the document contains an expression of sovereignty and statehood.[19]

## 3 The Balance of Relations in Different Spheres of Positive Law

### *3.1 General*

The essence of constitutionalism has been said to be 'the idea ... that government can and should be legally limited in its powers, and that its authority depends on its

[12] Native Courts Ordinance 1942, s 10.

[13] Statute Law Revision Ordinance 1974, s 3.

[14] Solomon Islands Independence Order 1978 (UK).

[15] Constitution, Preamble.

[16] Ibid sch 3.1-3.2.

[17] Ibid sch 3.3.

[18] Ibid sch 3.

[19] See, e.g., Constitution, s 1(1).

observing these limitations.[20] In Solomon Islands, the government is limited by the written Constitution. The Westminster model has resulted in a 'dualist' system.[21] Accordingly, international treaty law does not become part of domestic law unless specifically incorporated by legislation.[22] To date, there have been very few Acts which specifically introduce an international treaty into the internal law.[23] Examples are the Fisheries (United States of America) Treaty[24] and the Aircraft (Tokyo, Hague and Montreal Conventions) Act.[25] Also of note is the Facilitation of International Assistance Act 2003, which implements the RAMSI Treaty, a multilateral, regional treaty to assist in the restoration of law and order and security in Solomon Islands.[26] The Treaty deals with matters such as detention and disarmament,[27] seizure and destruction of weapons,[28] health and safety,[29] and sets up the mandate and limits of the Visiting Contingent generally.[30]

In the absence of ratifying legislation, conventions are not directly enforceable in Solomon Islands. However, there is an onus on the government to introduce legislation to bring domestic law into line with a convention.[31]

International Law plays an increasingly large role in Solomons, forming an additional layer of law that increases the complexities of the relationship between State and customary laws. Whilst there is a paucity of legislation directly domesticating a treaty, there is a small amount of recent legislation that is designed to bring the law in Solomon Islands into line with its international obligations. The most recent is the Child and Family Welfare Act 2017, discussed further below. Another recent example is the Wildlife Protection and Management (Amendment) Act

[20]Waluchow (2004), para 1.

[21]This is as opposed to a monist system. In the United States, for an example, a treaty becomes part of the domestic law of the country once it has been ratified according to the constitution.

[22]Solomon Islands, as a common law country, follows the United Kingdom's dualist approach: *R v Bow Street Metropolitan Stipendiary Magistrate; Ex parte Pinochet Ugarte (No 1)* [2000] 1 AC 61. See also Corrin Care (2006), p. 59. See also Farran (2009), p. 62.

[23]The only small island of the South Pacific to have done this is Vanuatu: see for example, Convention on the Elimination of all Forms of Discrimination against Women (Ratification) Act [Cap 235].

[24]Cap 39.

[25]Cap 46.

[26]Agreement concerning the operations and status of the police and armed forces and other personnel deployed to Solomon Islands to assist in the restoration of law and order and security, signed 24 July 2003, [2003] ATS 17 (entered into force 24 July 2003) ("RAMSI treaty").

[27]Ibid art 8.

[28]Ibid art 9.

[29]Ibid art 19.

[30]Ibid arts 14-17.

[31]*Raja Paksha v Attorney General* [2011] SBHC 189; *Regina v K* [2005] SBHC 80. See also, Draft Constitution (below n 91), cl 244(1)(j), which states: (j) customary international law, international conventions, treaties and agreements applicable to Solomon Islands so far as they are incorporated into domestic law.

2017,[32] which brings the law into line with the Convention on International Trade in Endangered Species of Wild Flora and Fauna, and for related matters.[33]

The attitude displayed toward international law by government and the courts is not uniform. More attention appears to be paid to human rights than to other aspects of international law, and this is despite the fact that this is an area where conflict with customary norms is most acute. Within the realm of human rights, the area that has received most attention in recent times is child protection. This is possibly because of the low threshold that has prevailed and the pressure that has been brought to bear by international child rights bodies in the wake of reports of widespread child abuse.[34] Solomon Islands ratified the United Nations' Convention on the Rights of the Child ('CRC') in 1995,[35] which committed it to the incorporation of children's human rights into all relevant legislation. Solomon Islands' first report to the Committee on the Rights of the Child was not lodged until 2002.[36] The Committee's Concluding Observations in 2003 highlighted the lack of specific legislation governing children's rights, and emphasised the need to bring domestic legislation and customary laws into line with the principles of the Convention.[37] However, it took until 2017 for Solomon Islands to do this, in the form of the Child and Family Welfare Act, mentioned above. This Act, which has yet to come into force, does not specifically domesticate the CRC, but it does incorporate many of its principles, being designed to promote,

> the welfare and protection of children and, in particular, to strengthen families and promote the wellbeing of children; to ensure that families and communities receive advice and support in caring for their children; to provide for children who are in need of care and protection and to give certain powers to social welfare officers in their role to provide for the welfare of families, and for related matters.[38]

It also provides that in making decisions or taking action under the Act, 'the rights of the child under the Convention on the Rights of the Child should be promoted and respected to the extent possible'.[39]

However, the dilemma of conflicting norms is well illustrated here, as, contrary to the CRC Committee's Concluding Observations in 2003, the 2017 legislation does

[32]Amending the Wildlife Protection and Management Act 1998.

[33]Wildlife Protection and Management (Amendment) Act 2017, long title.

[34]See e.g., 'Solomon Islands no longer safe for children'. Radio New Zealand, 23 January 2017. https://www.radionz.co.nz/international/pacific-news/322910/solomon-islands-no-longer-safe-for-children-report.

[35]*Convention on the Rights of the Child*, opened for signature 20 November 1989, 1577 UNTS 3 (entered into force 2 September 1990).

[36]Committee on the Rights of the Child, State Party Report: Solomon Islands, UN Doc CRC/c/51/add.6 (12 July 2002), available at: http://www.refworld.org/docid/3df59ecb2.html [accessed 11 September 2017].

[37]Committee on the Rights of the Child, Concluding Observations: Solomon Islands, 33rd sess, UN Doc CRC/C/15/Add.208 (2 July 2003) p. 2.

[38]Child and Family Welfare Act 2017, Long Title.

[39]Ibid s 11(j).

not make any changes to customary laws to ensure they comply with the principles of the Convention.

At the domestic level, the relationship between norms is dominated by the Constitution, which provides that:

> This Constitution is the supreme law of Solomon Islands and if any other law is inconsistent with this Constitution, that other law shall, to the extent of the inconsistency, be void.[40]

However, in addition to enshrining a Bill of Rights,[41] the Constitution also makes declarations about the importance of custom and tradition.[42] Given the disparity between the norms expressed in the Bill of Rights and the norms underpinning custom, this has given rise to what the author has called 'the constitutional conundrum'. Traditional leaders are a powerful force and therefore, the norms underpinning custom are very persuasive and in practice have operated as a limitation on governmental power. This is discussed further below.

## 3.2 *Judicial Review*

The common law system introduced during the colonial era includes the administrative law regime, which confers powers to limit governmental decisions and actions. As part of this regime, the High Court of Solomon Islands has inherited the jurisdiction of the High Court of England to conduct a judicial review of the decisions and actions of the State.[43] This includes government officials and officers acting for statutory bodies.[44] It also includes actions by private persons who are part of a framework of governmental control.[45]

The High Court of Solomon Islands has adopted the same grounds of judicial review as have been employed by the courts in England and Wales, that is, refusal to perform a public duty, lack or excess of jurisdiction (*ultra vires*), breach of principles of natural justice and fairness, error of law on the record, and fraud. An example of the exercise of the power to compel government officials to perform a public duty can be found in *Kaupai v Principal Magistrate (Malaita).*[46] In that case, a writ of mandamus was issued by the High Court of Solomon Islands to require a magistrate, in his capacity as clerk of the Malaita Customary Land Appeal Court, to accept an appeal to the court which had been made within the 3 months prescribed by s 231 of

---

[40]Constitution, s 1.

[41]Ibid ch II.

[42]Ibid preamble.

[43]Western Pacific (Courts) Order 1961 (UK), s 14.

[44]*Council of Civil Service Unions v Minister of State for the Civil Service* [1985] AC 374.

[45]*R v Panel on Takeovers and Mergers ex p Datafin* [1987] QB 815; *Simata v Goldie College Secondary School Board of Governors* [1998] SBHC 46.

[46][1985–86] SILR 95.

the Land and Titles Act,[47] but which he had mistakenly considered had been filed out of time. Similarly, in *Luifaufao'oa v Malaita Customary Land Appeal Court,*[48] the High Court of Solomon Islands ordered a Customary Land Appeal Court to consider and determine the various items of costs submitted by the party in whose favour it had made a general order for costs.

Examples of limitation of governmental action on the basis of a failure to comply with the process prescribed by law can also be found. In *R v Public Service Commission ex p Tiare,*[49] where decisions made by the Public Service Commission were set aside by certiorari because the procedure prescribed by statute for the conduct of disciplinary inquiries was not complied with. In more recent times, a decision by a Minister of Immigration of Solomon Islands to order the issue of a deportation order against a man on the ground that he had been declared an undesirable person, was set aside on grounds of unreasonableness.[50]

There are also numerous examples of limitation of the power of government agencies on the basis of principles of natural justice and fairness. These principles require that a person must be allowed an adequate opportunity to respond to allegations. On two occasions, decisions made by school disciplinary committees to expel students for misbehaviour have been held to be invalid because the students were not told where and when they could give their versions of the incidents to the committees.[51] Similarly, a decision of a Customary Land Appeal Court was quashed by certiorari because the court proceeded in the absence of the appellant and did not allow her an opportunity to respond to the respondent's evidence.[52] However, the extent of the limits imposed by natural justice on the decision making powers of government is not as broad as may first appear. It does not necessarily require that an opportunity to respond be given in any particular form. An opportunity to respond in writing, rather than a hearing, is often regarded as adequate.[53]

An example of setting aside a decision based on fraud can be found in *R v Customary Land Appeal Court (Western) ex p Pitakaka.*[54] In that case, a decision of a Customary Land Appeal Court awarding land to a party was quashed by certiorari, as one of his witness had given evidence on behalf of his deceased father; it was later established that the father was alive.

---

[47]Cap 133.

[48][1988–89] SILR 70.

[49][1984] SILR 80.

[50]*Rajapaksha v Attorney General* [2011] SBHC 189.

[51]*Kakano v Attorney General* [1992] SBHC 16; *Nimepo v Premier of Guadalcanal Province* [1996] SBHC 35.

[52]*Siope v Malaita Customary Land Appeal Court* [1985–86] SILR 255.

[53]See, e.g., *Talasasa v United Church* [1985–86] SILR 69, although the respondent was the church rather than the government.

[54][1985] SBHC 27.

Administrative law has not evolved significantly in recent times, although, as mentioned above, Solomon Islands has followed the United Kingdom[55] in extending the power of review to private persons who are part of a framework of governmental control.[56] The conventionality control doctrine, developed in *Barrios Altos v Peru*[57] has no application in Solomon Islands.

## 3.3 Freedom of Contract

Freedom of contract is a notion that prevails in Solomon Islands' legal and commercial sectors, and, subject to certain limitations, parties are free to determine their own contractual terms.[58] The government is liable for breaches of contract in the same way as private individuals and the courts will award damages against the government.[59] The common law has evolved somewhat in recent years,[60] and courts will refuse to enforce a contract that is contrary to public policy. There are several established heads of public policy under which enforceability of contracts has been challenged. The most relevant to a discussion of constitutionalism are contracts promoting corruption[61] and contracts prejudicial to public safety.[62] However, contracts which oust the jurisdiction of the court also have implications for the boundaries of government power.[63]

Another limitation on freedom of contract arises from the fact that parties in a stronger bargaining position may impose the contract terms, often through the use of standard form contracts. In such cases, the weaker party may have little choice but to enter into the contract. Solomon Islands does not have unfair contract terms legislation. However, whilst still paying lip service to the notion of freedom of contract, it adopts the common law approach and is likely to interpret exemption clauses narrowly in an attempt to prevent the operation of unreasonable contract terms. This is particularly the case where the terms form part of a standard form consumer contract. In such cases, a court may declare the contract unenforceable.[64] Further, a

[55] *R v Panel on Takeovers and Mergers ex p Datafin* [1987] QB 815.

[56] *Simata v Goldie College Secondary School Board of Governors* [1998] SBHC 46.

[57] *Merits Judgment* (IACHR Series C, no 75, 14 March 2001).

[58] *Baltic Shipping Co v Dillon* (1993) 176 CLR 344, 369.

[59] See e.g., *Suidani v Attorney General* [2016] SBHC 49, where damages were awarded against a provincial government.

[60] See the summary of this evolution in *George Mitchell (Chesterhall) Ltd v Finney Lock Seeds Ltd* [1983] 2 AC 803.

[61] *Parkinson v College of Ambulance* [1925] 2 KB 1.

[62] *Regazzoni v Sethia* [1958] AC 301.

[63] *Czarinikow v Roth Schmidt* [1922] 2 KB 478.

[64] *George Mitchell (Chesterhall) Ltd v Finney Lock Seeds Ltd* [1983] 2 AC 803.

court may intervene if the dominant party's conduct constitutes duress[65] or undue influence,[66] or is unconscionable.[67]

The common law, also renders void an illegal contract,[68] and this leaves open another possibility of the State intruding in the contractual space if a contract is detrimental to its interests. An example can be found in *Griffiths v Indian Pacific Fisheries Ltd*,[69] where it was held that the Labour Act[70] required an immigrant or non-indigenous worker to have a work permit in order to be employed. In the absence of such a document the contact of employment was 'prohibited completely'. Accordingly, the plaintiff's claim for unpaid wages was dismissed. However, there is no evidence that Solomon Islands' government has sought to interfere with contracts on the basis of illegality. Apart from these restrictions, the doctrine of freedom of contract continues to prevail.

There are also certain situations in Solomon Islands where entry into a contract is required by statute. A prime example is contracts of motor vehicle insurance to cover injury and damage to third parties.[71] There are other cases, where contract terms are prescribed by statute, for example, contracts for sale of goods.[72]

With regard to choice of law and the forum for dispute resolution, in general, courts in Solomon Islands follow the practice in other common law jurisdictions and parties may agree on the law governing the substance and validity of the contract and the forum for resolution of any disputes.[73] However, courts retain a discretion to exercise jurisdiction in cases where they consider that they are the more convenient forum. Where the court does exercise jurisdiction, it may refuse to allow diversion from requirements which they consider to be within their own domain, which includes adjectival laws, remedies, and choice of law rules.[74] In the case of arbitration, the choice is covered by legislation, and agreement to arbitrate will normally be binding on the parties and any court application stayed.[75]

It is unclear whether the law of contract has any application within the customary legal system. Traditional societies have been described as 'status based' as their rights and duties tend to be dictated by their place in society, rather than by agreement.[76] Customary transactions, at least those that consist of reciprocal

[65]See, e.g., *Cheon v Cheon* [1997] SBHC 16.

[66]*National Westminster Bank v Morgan* [1985] 1 AC 686.

[67]*Ross Mining (SI) Ltd v Roni* [1999] SBHC 5.

[68]*Griffiths v Indian Pacific Fisheries Limited Ltd* [1997] SBHC 51.

[69][1997] SBHC 51.

[70]Cap 73.

[71]Motor Vehicle (Third Party) Insurance Act [Cap 83].

[72]Sale of Goods Act 1893 (UK), ss 12 – 15, applying in Solomon Islands as an Act of general application. The Act does not prevent exclusion of implied terms.

[73]*Baltic Shipping Co v Dillon* (1993) 176 CLR 344, 369.

[74]Richardson and Garnett (2016), p. 1.

[75]Arbitration Act [Cap 2], s 2.

[76]Gluckman (1972), p. 171.

arrangements rather than exchange of goods or services, may have little to do with choice, and may be more concerned with the interests of the community as a whole than any individual.[77]

### 3.4 The Hierarchy of Norms

The Constitution declares itself to be the supreme law of Solomon Islands,[78] and sets out a hierarchy of laws. Norms encapsulated in legislation passed by the national parliament are next in the hierarchy.[79] The term 'Act of Parliament' has been interpreted as meaning an Act of Solomon Islands Parliament, so, although Acts of the UK Parliament have been kept in force until repealed expressly or by implication,[80] in theory, the courts should apply customary laws even if they are inconsistent with an Act of the UK Parliament. However, the High Court of Solomon Islands has suggested that the two sources of law rank equally. Which will prevail will be determined on a case by case basis, taking into account public policy and the circumstances of each particular case.[81]

Fundamental rights and freedoms are constitutionally enshrined in Chapter II of the Constitution.[82] The rights which are protected are:

- The right to life (s 4);
- The right to personal liberty (s 5);
- The right to be free from slavery and forced labour (s 6);
- The right to be free from inhuman and degrading treatment (s 7);
- The right to property (s 8);
- The right to privacy (s 9);
- The right to due process of law (s 10);
- The right to freedom of conscience (s 11);
- The right to freedom of expression (s 12);
- The right to freedom of association and assembly (s 13);
- The right to freedom of movement (s 14);
- The right to freedom from discrimination (s 15).

The Constitution provides that each person is entitled to these rights and freedoms, subject only to respect for the rights and freedoms of others and to the public

[77]See further Seddon (1974), p. 49.

[78]See Constitution, s 2. This includes customary laws which, while constitutionally recognised, are not to be applied to the extent they are inconsistent with the Constitution: Constitution, Sch 3, s 3(1).

[79]Constitution, s 76(2)(1).

[80]*R v Ngena* [1983] SILR 1; Corrin and Patterson (2017), p. 60.

[81]*K v T* [1985-1986] SILR 49. This case involved a custody dispute, and accordingly is arguably of questionable relevance to the interpretation of the phrase outside this area of law.

[82]Scheduled to Solomon Islands Independence Order 1978 (UK).

interest.[83] These protections have binding effect throughout the country and, in theory, take precedence over other laws. However, as discussed further below, in practice Solomon Islands courts have often been loath to allow these provisions to take precedence over customary laws.

The Constitution makes no express reference limiting the persons who may be liable under these provisions. However, the High Court has made it clear that these rights are 'principally' concerned with the relationship between citizen and State.[84] Thus they form an important limitation on governmental powers. However, the right of redress is limited by the constitutional provision that a Court may decline to grant constitutional relief if other means of redress are available.[85]

The rights chapter is modelled on the Universal Declaration of Human Rights (1948)[86] and the European Convention for the Protection of Human Rights and Fundamental Freedoms (1950).[87] Consequently, it is hardly surprising that the constitutional provisions overlap with the international documents, a fact recognised by the High Court of Solomon Islands in *R v Gua*.[88] In that case the court's decision to depart from the common law rule that rape could not occur within marriage was stated to be based partly on the Convention on the Elimination of all forms of Discrimination Against Women (CEDAW)[89] and partly on the constitutionally enshrined right to freedom from discrimination.[90] A new, federal, constitution has been under discussion in Solomon Islands since 2004. The latest version (the 'Draft Constitution')[91] contains a far more extensive bill of rights, encompassing both civil and political and economic, social and cultural rights and specific protections for women and other persons.[92]

In theory, customary laws are superior to common law and equity.[93] However, in practice, common law is often applied by the courts as a matter of course.[94] This is

---

[83]Constitution, s 3.

[84]See *Loumia v Director of Public Prosecutions* [1985-6] SILR 158 per Connolly JA (Wood CJ concurring). See also *Ulufa'alu v Attorney-General* [2005] 1 LRC 698.

[85]Constitution, s 18(2).

[86]Universal Declaration on Human Rights, GA Res 217A (III), UN GAOR, UN Doc A/810 (10 December 1948).

[87]European Convention for the Protection of Human Rights and Fundamental Freedoms, opened for signature 4 November 1950, 213 UNTS 222 (entered into force 3 September 1953).

[88]*Regina v Gua* [2012] SBHC 118.

[89]Convention on the Elimination of All Forms of Discrimination against Women, opened for signature 18 December 1979 1249 UNTS 13 (entry into force 3 September 1981). Acceded by Solomon Islands 6 May 2002.

[90]Constitution, s 15.

[91]Second Draft for proposed Federal Constitution of the Federal Democratic Republic of Solomon Islands 2014 ('Draft Constitution'). http://www.sicr.gov.sb/2nd%202014%20SI%20Constitution%20Draft%20(R)%20pdf%20-%208%205%2014.pdf. Accessed 12 December 2017.

[92]Ibid ch 4, parts II-V.

[93]Constitution, sch 3.

[94]See further, Corrin (2010), p. 2.

despite the fact that the preamble to the Constitution reflects a desire for laws encapsulating local values and objectives to be respected. It begins with an aspirational declaration of pride in 'the wisdom and the worthy customs' of Solomon Islanders' ancestors and a pledge to 'cherish and promote the different cultural traditions within Solomon Islands'. Ironically, where the norms of customary law conflict with international norms enshrined in domestic law, customary law will not always be made to give way, and this is discussed in more detail below.

Customary law still plays an important role in Solomon Islands. Traditional leaders are powerful figures and in some instances government may be loath to interfere with their vested interests. In practice, the position is often governed by pragmatism. This is particularly the case in relation to land and resources. The general belief that land is governed by customary laws, even where, according to state law, it has been alienated, holds sway amongst the majority of the population. Where there is conflict between customary laws and state law, the government has been reluctant to enforce the relevant legislation. A good example of this is ownership of the area below high-water mark, which according to common law belongs to the State.[95] However, under customary law it is regarded as belonging to the owner of the adjacent land area. Solomon Islands Law Reform Commission has recommended that the law be amended to concede ownership to the customary owners.[96] While custom continues to be recognised as a source of law by the Draft Constitution to the extent it is not inconsistent with the Constitution or other statutes, the exemptions custom previously enjoyed in respect of human rights have been removed. Whether this makes a perceptible difference to the balance of norms is yet to be seen.

The church is also a powerful influence in Solomon Islands, both locally and nationally. The preamble to the Constitution states that Solomon Islands is a democratic State, 'under the guiding hand of God'. Ninetey-six percent of Solomon Islands are Christian.[97] There are five major churches in Solomon Islands, with membership in the following percentages: Church of Melanesia or Anglican Church (32%); Roman Catholic Church (20%); South Seas Evangelical Church (17%); Seventh Day Adventist Church (12%); and the United Church (10%).[98] Although there is no one dominant Church. Christianity seems to have acted as a uniting force. The five main churches combine under the umbrella organisation of Solomon Islands Christian Association. This body coordinates religious representation at national events and plays a role in political affairs. Due to the inattention of national government to the needs of rural societies, the Church has become a surrogate authority, bridging the gap between the remote and unfamiliar Westminster style of government and the traditional authority of chiefs in remote villages. It has provided services and education in exchange for denominational allegiance. Both

[95]See e.g., *Allardyce Lumber Company Limited v Laore* [1990] SBHC 46.

[96]Solomon Islands Law Reform Commission (2012), p. 17.

[97]Ibid.

[98]Solomon Islands National Statistics Office (2009), p. 81.

in urban areas and villages, Solomon islanders announce their denominational allegiances proudly and publicly by their attendance at Church and other religious events and their contribution to fundraisings.

There is currently no system of appeal or review in place which is specifically addressed at giving force to external norms. However, there is a process provided for application for redress for contravention of the bill of rights within the Constitution, which, as mentioned above, is itself based on the Universal Declaration of Human Rights (1948)[99] and the European Convention for the Protection of Human Rights and Fundamental Freedoms (1950).[100] The High Court of Solomon Islands has original jurisdiction to hear an application by any person who alleges infringement, whether actual or potential, of their constitutional rights.[101] A subordinate court may also refer any question arising before it as to the contravention of the rights provisions.[102]

The Draft Constitution[103] provides for the establishment of a Constitutional Court[104] and Human Rights Commission.[105] It also gives preference to human rights norms over the norms of customary law, as it removes the shield provided in relation to discrimination. This is discussed further below. Apart from the changes that are flagged in the Draft Constitution, there have been no significant developments in the relationship between norms in the past few years.

## 4 The Dynamics of the Relationship Between Different Aspects of Positive Law

### *4.1 The Place of International Law in Solomon Islands*

As at 1 November 2017, Solomon Islands has acceded to the Convention on the Elimination of All Forms of Discrimination against Women[106] and the Convention on the Rights of the Child.[107] It has signed the Convention on the Rights of Persons

[99]Universal Declaration on Human Rights, GA Res 217A (III), UN GAOR, UN Doc A/810 (10 December 1948).

[100]European Convention for the Protection of Human Rights and Fundamental Freedoms, opened for signature 4 November 1950, 213 UNTS 222 (entered into force 3 September 1953).

[101]Constitution, s 18(1)-(2).

[102]Ibid s 18(3).

[103]Draft Constitution, cl 144.

[104]Ibid ch 18, pt 11.

[105]Ibid ch 22, pt IV; cl 49.

[106]Convention on the Elimination of All Forms of Discrimination against Women, opened for signature 18 December 1979 1249 UNTS 13 (entry into force 3 September 1981). Acceded by Solomon Islands 6 May 2002.

[107]Convention on the Rights of the Child, opened for signature 20 November 1989, 1577 UNTS 3 (entered into force 2 September 1990). Acceded by Solomon Islands 10 April 1995.

with Disabilities,[108] and has succeeded to the International Covenant on Economic, Social and Cultural Rights[109] and the International Covenant on the Elimination of All Forms of Racial Discrimination.[110] However, as discussed above, it has implemented very few of these conventions through domestic legislation.[111]

With regard to human rights, as discussed above, these norms are enshrined in the Constitution. This has led to conflict with the norms of customary law. The key areas of friction have been between the patriarchal and status based norms of customary law, which conflict with the constitutionally protected rights to protection from discrimination[112] and to freedom of movement.[113] In these cases, the courts appear to take a narrow view of the application of human rights.[114] Some cases demonstrating this are discussed below. There has also been conflict between freedom of religion and the authority of traditional leaders,[115] and between the customary penalty of 'payback' and the right to life.[116] In these cases, the court has been more inclined to uphold international norms.

With regard to other international norms there is little evidence of serious conflict. However, where conflict does arise, as a result of the dualist legal system, explained above, the domestic law of Solomon Islands will prevail. Overall, it cannot be said that there has been a 'reshuffle' of the interactions among norms imposed by globalisation. Where there has been some movement, it cannot be described as natural or chaotic or conflictive in Solomon Islands. Instead, the more appropriate descriptor is *'ad hoc'*. There is some evidence of international law operating as an influence on the law through its use by the courts as an aid to interpretation.[117] Some instances of this can be found in the cases discussed in this chapter. However, the courts do not take a uniform approach to application of the international norms

---

[108]Convention on the Rights of Persons with Disabilities, opened for signature 30 March 2007, 2515 UNTS 3 (entered into force 3 May 2008). Signed by Solomon Islands 23 September 2008.

[109]International Covenant on Economic, Social and Cultural Rights, opened for signature 16 December 1966, 993 UNTS 3 (entered into force 3 January 1976). Succeeded by Solomon Islands 17 March 1982.

[110]International Covenant on the Elimination of All Forms of Racial Discrimination, opened for signature 7 March 1966, 660 UNTS 195 (entered into force 4 January 1969). Succeeded by Solomon Islands 17 March 1982.

[111]See e.g., *Lobo v Limanilove* [2002] SBHC 110.

[112]Constitution, s 15.

[113]See also Brown and Corrin Care (1998), p. 1334.

[114]See e.g., *Tanavulu v Tanavulu* [1998] SBHC 4. Aspects of this decision are also discussed in Brown and Corrin Care (2001), pp. 668–670.

[115]*Lobo v Limanilove* [2002] SBHC 110.

[116]*Loumia v DPP* [1985/6] SILR 158.

[117]See generally *Hatilia v Attorney General* [2014] SBHC 125; HCSI-CC 456 of 2011 (13 October 2014) where *Thornhill v AG of Trinidad & Tobago* [1981] AC 61 is drawn upon when discussing the interpretation of the constitution. See, e.g., *R v Rose* [1987] SBHC 1; [1988] LRC 369 (21 September 1987); *Kelly v Regina* [2006] SBCA 17; CA-CRAC 019 of 2006 (25 October 2006); *Tii v Regina* [2017] SBCA 6; SICOA-CRAC 14 of 2016 (5 May 2017).

encapsulated in the Constitution or to the use of international norms as a guide to interpretation.

## 4.2 *Consistency in the Approach of Legal Actors*

Before considering whether legal actors take a similar approach to the interrelationship of different sources of law and authority, it is noteworthy that a separation of powers between the executive,[118] legislature[119] and judiciary[120] is established by the Constitution. The legislature's power to make laws are explicitly set out in the Constitution,[121] as is the judiciary's mandate to administer them.[122] This demarcation of powers allows the judiciary and the legislature to adopt differing ideological approaches to the application of international norms. The lack of an homogenous approach to the interaction of norms makes it necessary to discuss these bodies separately.

### 4.2.1 The Executive

Executive authority is vested in the Head of State, who is the Queen of England, acting through the Governor-General.[123] The Governor-General acts on the advice of the Cabinet and is to be kept informed of the general conduct of government by the Prime Minister. The system of responsible government is specifically referred to in the Constitution,[124] which establishes a Cabinet consisting of the Prime Minister and other Ministers, which is 'collectively responsible to Parliament'. The Prime Minister is elected from members of parliament. Ministers are appointed from MPs by the Governor- General on the advice of the Prime Minister. In practice, there is little consistency in the approach taken by the executive. Cabinet changes occur frequently reflecting the view that decisions are often driven more by a desire to stay in power than by state policy or philosophical commitment. Whilst political parties exist, it is more common for votes to be cast for individual 'Big-Men' or 'wantoks' from voters' communities.[125]

---

[118]Constitution, ch V.

[119]Ibid ch VI.

[120]Ibid ch VII.

[121]Ibid cl 59-74.

[122]Ibid ch VII, pt II.

[123]Ibid s 1(2).

[124]Ibid s 35.

[125]Alasia (1997), pp. 15–16.

### 4.2.2 The Legislature

Solomon Islands Parliament is established by the Constitution as the national legislature.[126] It has a single house, charged with a mandate to 'make laws for the peace, order and good governance of Solomon Islands.'[127] As noted above, with limited exceptions, Solomon Islands' parliament has failed to incorporate international norms into domestic law. While accession may be a manifestation of consent to be bound by the treaty,[128] the lack of domestic implementation of international norms means that, in a strict legal sense, except in the case of constitutionally enshrined human rights there are no competing norms to be reconciled.

There has been little discussion on why Solomon Islands has not domesticated any of the core treaties.[129] It has had ample opportunity to do so, and its Parliament continues to pass legislation every year.[130] However, there are a number of factors which may explain this. With regard to human rights, a human rights regime, modelled after the Universal Declaration of Human Rights European Convention on Human Rights, is incorporated within the Constitution.[131] As discussed, this includes rights to life,[132] liberty,[133] expression,[134] assembly and association.[135] This lessens the impetus to legislate to implement human rights conventions domestically, and if implemented would create a duplicity of human rights regimes. However, relying on a domestic Bill of Rights does not expose Solomon Islands to external scrutiny, and shields it from the benchmarks and rulings of the various human rights bodies established to adjudicate disputes arising out of international human rights instruments.[136]

Further, with regard to human rights, in the circumstances of Solomon Islands, there is a disconnect between normative and empirical universality.[137] Whilst, the ideals of international human rights instruments are said to be universal, in reality such ideals are constrained by the signatory's capacity to implement them. Village

---

[126] Constitution, s 46.

[127] Ibid s 59

[128] Vienna Convention on the Law of Treaties, opened for signature 23 May 1969, 1155 UNTS 331 (entered into force 27 January 1980), art 11, 15.

[129] Corrin (2013), p. 108.

[130] See University of the South Pacific Law School, 'Pacific Islands Legal Information Institute' (web site). www.paclii.org.

[131] Constitution, ch II.

[132] Ibid s 4.

[133] Ibid s 5.

[134] Ibid s 12.

[135] Ibid s 13.

[136] Corrin (2017), pp. 88–89.The extent to which state agreement to be bound by the convention, or possibly even the Charter of the United Nations justifies intervention by the UN under international law depends on whether this involves some abdication of sovereignty: see, e.g., Best (1995), pp. 775–799.

[137] Corrin (2013), p. 103.

societies in Solomon Islands are dominated by patriarchal and status-based norms.[138] The focus is on the community, rather than the individual and on duties, as opposed to rights.[139] This conflicts with the foundation of human rights treaties, which aim to protect the rights of the individual, in accordance with liberal theory.[140] Customary law in Solomon Islands is, in many ways, ideologically incompatible with international human rights instruments. It is bound up with the culture and traditions of each individual community, and lacks the institutional structures to interface harmoniously with international norms. This forms a barrier to the implementation of human rights; it restricts access to remedies and creates significant evidential problems.[141] For example, a complainant may be ostracised by a local community for seeking relief for breach of rights that do not accord with the mores of the traditional system. As pointed out by Kabutaulaka, in the case of women, they have been 'flooded with international instruments', however such instruments are in desperate need of modification to fit the circumstances of Solomon Islands.[142]

Politically, Members of Parliament, whose main concern is often re-election, are unlikely to pursue policies such as the ratification of international treaties, if such matters are of no concern to their constituents.

One possible supranational influence on development of laws reflecting international norms comes from Solomon Islands membership of the Pacific Islands Forum. Established in 1971, this is the dominant regional political grouping.[143] Its membership comprises Australia, Cook Islands, Federated States of Micronesia, Fiji, Kiribati, Nauru, New Zealand, Niue, Palau, Papua New Guinea, Republic of Marshall Islands, Samoa, Solomon Islands, Tonga, Tuvalu, Vanuatu, and, since September 2016, French Polynesia and New Caledonia.[144] The Forum's object is the economic and political governance, security, and fostering of regional coordination and integration in the Pacific.[145] The Forum's Secretariat has introduced the 'Pacific Plan: For Strengthening Regional Cooperation and Integration'.[146] The Plan includes streamlining legislation to bring it into line with international treaties.[147]

[138]See Corrin (2009), p. 57.

[139]Corrin (2013), p. 129.

[140]Tamata (2000), para 2.

[141]Corrin Care and Zorn (2005), particularly pp. 159–160.

[142]Kabutaulaka (2004), p. 23, citing the views of Ruth Maetala, former Secretary General of the National Council of Women. See also Zorn (2000).

[143]https://www.forumsec.org/who-we-arepacific-islands-forum/.

[144]Tokelau and Wallis and Futuna are Associate Members: see 'Pacific Islands Regional Organisations', Department of Foreign Affairs and Trade. http://dfat.gov.au/international-relations/regional-architecture/pacific-islands/Pages/pacific-islands-regional-organisation.aspx. Formerly the South Pacific Forum.

[145]'Forum Secretariat Mission Statement', Pacific Islands Forum Secretariat. https://www.forumsec.org/pacific-islands-forum-secretariat/. Accessed 17 March 2019.

[146]Pacific Islands Forum Secretariat (2007), p. 1.

[147]Ibid p. 20, initiative 12.5.

### 4.3 The Courts

There is no constitutional court in Solomon Islands. However, such an institution is included in the Draft Constitution, which is now in its second draft form. If given the force of law, the Draft Constitution would introduce a provision for a Constitutional Court to review the constitutionality of a Bill passed by Parliament, on the referral by the President.[148] The President would be mandated to make such a referral if, after making reservations to the Bill, Parliament had not accommodated those reservations.[149] If the Constitutional Court found that the Bill was constitutional, the President would be compelled to assent to the Bill.[150]

Under the current Constitution, the High Court wields unlimited original jurisdiction to preside over and determine, 'any civil or criminal proceedings under any law and such other jurisdiction and powers as may be conferred on it by [the] Constitution or by Parliament.'[151] This includes proceedings against the government, and as mentioned above in relation to freedom of contract, the High Court is prepared to give judgment against the government. The High Court also exercises a supervisory jurisdiction over lower courts[152] and government. The Constitution also establishes a Court of Appeal.[153] The Local Courts Act provides that the Chief Justice may establish local courts for the purposes of adjudicating minor disputes and customary disputes as he or she sees fit.[154]

As foreshadowed above, the approach of the courts to reconciling international norms with the domestic legal system has been ad hoc. There is no discernible principled approach that has been adopted. The main instances where the court has been faced with reconciling international and domestic norms have arisen in the context of human rights. As discussed, this is due to the fact that the constitutionally enshrined rights conflict with the norms of domestic customary law. In some instances, courts have affirmed Solomon Islands' commitment to international human rights.[155] In *R v Loumia*,[156] for example, the Court of Appeal had to consider whether a rule in Kwaio[157] custom that sanctioned the killing of an individual who was responsible for the death of a close relative was a 'legal duty' for the purposes of s 204 of the Penal Code.[158] Section 204 provides that the killing of a person will be manslaughter where the offender, 'acted in the belief in good faith and on reasonable

[148]Draft Constitution, s 144.

[149]Ibid s 144(4)(b).

[150]Ibid s 144(5).

[151]Constitution, s 77(1).

[152]Ibid s 84(1).

[153]Ibid s 85.

[154]*Local Courts Act* [cap 19].

[155]See e.g., *Regina v K* [2005] SBHC 80.

[156][1984] SILR 51. See further Brown (1986), p. 133.

[157]An area within Malaita Province.

[158]Cap 26.

grounds that he was under a legal duty to cause the death or do the act which he did.' The court held that to kill, even if sanctioned by customary law, was inconsistent with s 4 of the Constitution, which enshrined a right to life. It did not engage with the possibility that a customary rule might inform s 204 of the Penal Code. On this basis, it upheld the offender's murder conviction.

In a small number of cases, commitment to international human rights norms has been by direct reference to international law, as opposed to constitutionally enshrined rights. For example, in *Ambrose v Keioi,*[159] the High Court stated that:

> The local court decision would clearly recognise the equality of rights afforded both conflicting parties for they stem from the same genealogy. The manner in which the tribal paramount body approaches the difficulties as shown by the statement of David Ma'ai may be seen as threatening breach of an International Convention against Human Rights for the statement would appear to prevent the basic right to sustenance from ones own land. Underlying custom needs to recognise these principles of rights if in fact there is a risk.

These cases can be contrasted with decisions where the courts have refused to apply human rights provisions in preference to customary laws.[160] A prime example is *Pusi v Leni.*[161] In that case, the plaintiff had been abusive to local chiefs and alleged that, as a consequence, he had been banned from going to the village. The chiefs had subsequently refused to accept his attempts to apologise, on the basis that they did not comply with the customary protocols. The plaintiff applied to the High Court for compensation for breach of his constitutional rights to, *inter alia*, personal liberty and freedom of movement. In refusing to grant constitutional relief, Muria CJ observed:

> The Constitution itself recognises customary law as part of the law of Solomon Islands and its authority therefore cannot be disregarded. It has evolved from time immemorial and its wisdom has stood the test of time. It is a fallacy to view a constitutional principle or a statutory principle as better than those principles contained in customary law. In my view, one is no better than the other is. It is the circumstances in which the principles are applied that vary and one cannot be readily substituted for the other.

Another example can be found in the case of *Tanavalu v Tanavalu*,[162] where relief was sought on the basis that the customary rules of inheritance of money from a statutory fund was discriminatory. In that case, it was held that a customary law that was discriminatory would not be invalidated by s 15 of the Constitution, which ordinarily protects individuals from discriminatory laws.[163] Awich J, found that the phrase 'no law shall', as it appeared in s 15, was prospective in nature such that it only applied to laws that were to be enacted in the future. Customary law, having

---

[159]*Ambrose v Keioi* [2016] SBHC 172; HCSI-CC 213 of 2014 (5 October 2016).

[160]See, e.g., *Pusi v Leni* [1997] SBHC 100. This case is discussed in Corrin (2007), p. 151.

[161][1997] SBHC 100. This case is discussed in Corrin (2007), p. 151. See also Corrin Care (1999), p. 135.

[162][1998] SBHC 4.

[163]Constitution, s 15.

'evolved from time immemorial'[164] did not fall within this ambit. On appeal, the ruling was upheld on different grounds, but the Court of Appeal stated that the Constitution contemplated and accepted that the application of certain customary laws might result in some level of discrimination.[165]

The form of these judgments and the reasoning adopted in both categories of cases is of little assistance in elucidating the reasoning process of the courts. In practice, the day to day decisions of tribal authorities are unlikely to be based on international norms.

As noted above, Solomon Islands' courts will often utilise international treaties as interpretative aids.[166] In particular, human rights treaties have, on a number occasions, been used to interpret the human rights chapter of the Constitution.[167] By way of example, in *Regina v Su'u*,[168] the court considered the Universal Declaration of Human Rights and the International Covenant on Economic Social and Cultural Rights in ascertaining the content of the constitutionally enshrined right to life.[169] Consideration has also been given to the European Convention on Human Rights.[170] On occasion, the courts have gone so far as to take account of conventions to which Solomon Islands has not signified agreement. In *Regina v Su'u*,[171] the High Court also considered the International Covenant on Civil and Political Rights, which Solomon Islands has neither signed nor ratified. This approach is somewhat paradoxical given that Parliament does not seem interested in ratifying the instruments to which Solomon Islands is a party. It also emphasises an inconsistency between the attitudes of the legislature and the judiciary to the domestic implementation of international norms.

The Solomon Islands courts' approach also raises the question of whether they are entitled to engage in such an interpretative frolic, given that they are constituted to administer the law of Solomon Islands. Unlike some countries, Solomon Islands' Constitution does not require courts to consider public international law that is applicable to its constitutionally enshrined rights.[172] However, the common law has long recognised that the Constitution must be interpreted in a different manner to ordinary legislation. This was noted in *Minister of Home Affairs v Fisher*[173] where Lord Wilberforce observed that constitutions were sui generis documents and that the 'provisions protecting human rights and freedoms call for a generous interpretation avoiding what has been called "the austerity of tabulated legalism", suitable to

[164]*Pusi v Leni* [1997] SBHC 100, per Muria CJ.

[165]*Tanavalu v Tanavalu* [1998] SBCA 8.

[166]See e.g., *R v Rose* [1987] SBHC 2.

[167]See e.g., *R v Rose* [1987] SBHC 2.

[168][2007] SBHC 144.

[169]Constitution, s 4.

[170]*Loumia v DPP* [1985-6] SILR 158; *R v Rose* [1987] SBHC 2.

[171][2007] SBHC 144.

[172]Cf, Constitution of Fiji 2013, s 43.

[173][1980] AC 319.

give the individual the full measure of the fundamental rights and freedoms'.[174] This case has been followed in Solomon Islands in *Hatilia v Attorney General*,[175] where Apaniai J also drew on the statements of Lord Diplock in *Thorhill v AG of Trinidad & Tobago*,[176] who identified a principled concordance between the Fundamental Rights chapter of the Malaysian Constitution, a constitutional document, and international conventions:

> The provisions contained within the Fundamental Rights chapter were not described with particularity that would be appropriate to an ordinary Act of Parliament nor are they expressed in words that bear precise meanings as terms of legal art. They are statements of principles of general breadth and generality, expressed in the kind of language more commonly associated with political manifestos or international conventions.[177]

Relying on these authorities, Apaniai J held that the court 'must apply an interpretative approach that serves and protects [constitutional] rights and freedoms'.[178] This decision seems to provide a warrant for Solomon Islands courts to utilise international instruments when interpreting domestic law.

In *Tii v Regina*,[179] the Court of Appeal went even further in seeming to suggest that had s 5(1)(g) of the Constitution not been available to qualify s 200 of the Penal Code, it would have relied on the Convention on the Rights of the Child to do so. The Court stated that:

> To the limited extent prescribed in s. 13, the mandatory sentencing rule in s. 200 is impliedly repealed or confirmed or required by s. 5(1)(g) of the Constitution, and, if need be, also by international treaties and conventions on the subject. Indeed, if s 13 of the Act is not given the interpretation adopted here, it serves no purpose at all, and might as well not have been enacted. Some meaning and effect must be given to it, and in our view it is to be read as qualifying the mandatory terms of s 200 of the Penal Code as regards life imprisonment in the case of the grave crime of murder committed by a child or young person.[180]

In rare instances, the High Court has gone beyond the use of international instruments to which Solomon Islands has acceded to, but not ratified, as an aid to interpretation. In *Rajapaksha v Attorney General*,[181] the High Court noted that the 'fact is there has been accession by Solomon Islands. That means the Solomon Islands Government must ensure that domestic law carries into effect all that is set out in the convention.'[182] Despite the fact that Solomon Islands Government had not so ensured, the Court applied CEDAW in an abstract way, although it was ultimately found that there had been no violation. In this way, the courts may be viewed as

---

[174] Ibid 328.

[175] [2014] SBHC 125.

[176] [1981] AC 61; [1980] 2 WLR 510.

[177] Ibid 516.

[178] *Hatilia v Attorney General* [2014] SBHC 125, [37].

[179] [2017] SBCA 6.

[180] *Tii v Regina* [2017] SBCA 6, [20], quoting *Kelly v Regina* [2006] SBCA 17.

[181] [2011] SBHC 189.

[182] *Rajapaksha v Attorney General* [2011] SBHC 189, [33].

ameliorating the stagnancy of the Parliament in implementing international norms into the domestic legal order.

In stark contrast, there are a number of instances where Solomon Island courts have refused to consider international instruments. For example, in *Re Appeal by Cable and Wireless PLC*,[183] Awich J considered it unnecessary to look to the United Nations Double Taxation Convention 1996 to determine the meaning of the phrase 'through permanent establishment'. His Honour considered that domestic law was sufficient to supply an answer, stating:

> Parties devoted some time of their submissions to urging the Court to apply or not to apply the meaning of the phrase, through permanent establishment, given in the 1996 United Nations Model Double Taxation Convention. I considered it unnecessary to apply or rely on the definition in the Convention because the Income Tax Act at article 4 of the Arrangement was, in my view, adequate for the determination of this case. It was not necessary therefore, for me to decide whether or not the definition in the Convention was applicable.[184]

Clearly, it is difficult to identify a unifying thread to tie together the jurisprudence of Solomon Island courts, either in relation to direct application of international law or its use as an interpretative aid. The conflicting approaches of Solomon Island courts to international law, can only be described as *ad hoc*.

## 4.4 Resolution of Conflicts and Transconstitutional Dialogue

There is little opportunity for transconstitutional dialogue, as there are few avenues for external appeals or referral of disputes from Solomon Islands to supranational bodies. Ironically, as mentioned above, during the colonial era, there was a transnational court, in the form of the High Commissioner's Court, based in Fiji. From 1877 through to 1976, that body heard appeals not only from Fiji, but also from Solomon Islands, Gilbert and Ellice Islands and the New Hebrides.[185] In 1962, the High Commissioner's Court was renamed the High Court of the Western Pacific and relocated to Solomon Islands.[186] This Court was abolished in 1976, but until 1975 an appeal still lay from there to the Fijian Court of Appeal.[187] At one stage, there was also an appeal from Solomon Islands courts to the Privy Council, but that was abolished from 7 July 1978.[188] There has also been discussion at various points in

---

[183] [2001] SBHC 180.

[184] *Re Appeal by Cable and Wireless PLC* [2001] SBHC 180.

[185] Western Pacific Orders-in-Council 1877; Pacific Order-in-Council 1893.

[186] Western Pacific (Courts) Order in Council 1961.

[187] Solomon Islands Courts Order 1975.

[188] Solomon Islands Independence Order 1978, s 3(1), repealing Solomon Islands (Appeals to Privy Council) Order 1975.

Pacific history of a regional Court of Appeal.[189] However, that has never eventuated, partly due to the fact that Pacific Island countries fiercely defend their sovereignty.

There has also been discussion of the possibility of establishing a regional human rights organisation.[190] The Asia-Pacific is the only region worldwide where no regional rights protection system exists.[191] There have been a number of United Nations-sponsored initiatives designed to look into this.[192] In 1996, the Commonwealth Secretariat organised a workshop on human rights education in the South Pacific. The attendees recommended that a Pacific Charter of Human Rights be adopted and that a South Pacific Centre for Human Rights be established.[193] However, this was not taken further. More recently, there has been some support for a Pacific regional human rights mechanism in the 'Pacific Plan', which, as mentioned above, has been created under the auspices of the Pacific Islands Forum.[194] Nonetheless, it remains the case at present that there is no Pacific human rights organisation for Solomon Islands to join.

As mentioned above, the Draft Constitution provides for the establishment of a national Human Rights Commission as an 'Independent Commission under Chapter 12 of [the] Constitution.'[195] Clause 195, in Chapter 12, provides that its purpose is to, *inter alia*, protect the sovereignty of the people,[196] uphold the rule of law,[197] and maintain constitutionality and integrity.[198] More specifically, the proposed Human Rights Commission would be charged with promoting and protecting the observance of and respect for human rights in public and private institutions,[199] monitoring observance of human rights,[200] and receiving and investigating complaints about alleged human rights abuses.[201] Further, cl 49(5)(b) provides that the Human Rights Commission would also be responsible for, 'education about the rights and freedoms recognised in the Bill of Rights, as well as other internationally recognised rights and freedoms'.

As a consequence of the fact that most conventions are not part of domestic law, few conflicts arise. The exception is in the field of human rights due to the fact that

[189]See Pulea (1980), p. 1 for a discussion of the historical perspective. See Mataitoga (1982), p. 70 for a discussion of some of the problems which favour the present system in preference to a regional appeal court. See also Boyd (2003), p. 303.

[190]On the need for such a commission, see Imrana Jalal (2009), p. 191.

[191]Chiam (2009), p. 128; Imrana Jalal (2009), p. 187.

[192]Chiam (2009), p. 128. See also Imrana Jalal (2009), p. 180.

[193]See Wickliffe (1999), para 12.

[194]Imrana Jalal (2009), pp. 182, 185–186.

[195]Draft Constitution, cl 49.

[196]Ibid cl 195(2)(a).

[197]Ibid cl 195(2)(b).

[198]Ibid cl 195(2)(c).

[199]Ibid cl 49(5)(a).

[200]Ibid cl 49(5)(c).

[201]Ibid cl 49(5)e).

the constitutional bill of rights incorporates international norms. Where conflict has arisen, as explained, there is little opportunity transconstitutional dialogue. However, from examination of the body of case law discussed above, it is possible to extrapolate some observations about how conflicts are managed.

Firstly, as stated above, the Constitution of the Solomon Islands is *lex superior* in the domestic legal system.[202] In *K v Regina*,[203] the Court held that international instruments must be read subject to the Constitution and other domestic legislation. However, this subjection was in the context of an 'overlap' between the Convention on the Rights of the Child and the domestic legislation; it was not a case of direct conflict. However, as noted above, once the Child and Family Welfare Act 2017 commences, it will require the rights of the child under the CRC to be 'promoted and respected to the extent possible', and the propensity for conflict with the norms of customary law will increase.

Secondly, the Constitution is silent on the question of international law, and how it is to be treated by the courts. Unlike customary law, international law is not expressly recognised as a source of law. As the Constitution is the supreme source of law domestically, even if an international human rights instrument has been incorporated in legislation, it cannot override the Constitution, and in cases of conflict the Constitution would prevail.[204] A more problematic conflict sometimes occurs between domestic customary law and the Bill of Rights in the Constitution. The approach to such conflicts has been discussed above.

In some cases, the treaties to which Solomon Islands has become a party contain express dispute resolution mechanisms. One example is the RAMSI Treaty which was the governing document of the Regional Assistance Mission to Solomon Islands. The Mission involved 16 countries, including Solomon Islands, and was led by Australia.[205] The Mission was started in response to the deteriorating 'law and order and security in Solomon Islands pos[ing] a threat to good governance and economic prosperity of Solomon Islands.[206] The Governor-General of Solomon Islands also expressly requested such assistance on 4 July 2003, on the advice of the Cabinet.[207] While the Mission initially played a larger role in Solomon Islands' law and order, it was not solely a policing mission.[208] Solomon Islands incorporated the RAMSI Treaty into its domestic legal system via the Facilitation of International Assistance Act 2003. Article 12 of the RAMSI Treaty provided that in 'giving effect to this Agreement, the Parties shall act in a manner consistent with their obligations under international law.'

---

[202] Constitution, s 1.

[203] [2005] SBHC 150, affirming *Regina v K* [2005] SBHC 80.

[204] See Constitution, s 2. This includes customary laws which, while constitutionally recognised, are not to be applied to the extent they are inconsistent with the Constitution: Constitution, sch 3, s 3(1).

[205] 'About RAMSI', *RAMSI* (Web Page). http://www.ramsi.org/about-ramsi/.

[206] RAMSI Treaty, preamble.

[207] Ibid.

[208] 'About RAMSI', *RAMSI* (Web Page) http://www.ramsi.org/about-ramsi/.

Section 24(1) of the Act created a modest conflict resolving mechanism, which gave it primacy over any other law of Solomon Islands, save the Constitution:

> Subject to the Constitution, this Act and any regulations or other subsidiary legislation made under this Act shall have effect notwithstanding any other law of Solomon Islands.

This was a clear example of a harmonising provision that might resolve collisions between two positive law instruments brought into conflict by globalisation. Analogies might be drawn with art 103 of the UN Charter, which provides that:

> In the event of a conflict between the obligations of the Members of the United Nations under the present Charter and their obligations under any other international agreement, their obligations under the present Charter shall prevail.

However, while art 103 of the UN Convention might be used to systemically harmonise conflicts between constitutional regimes, such as between the European Convention of Human Rights and Security Council Resolutions passed under the auspices of the UN Charter, the RAMSI Treaty lacked this constitutional characteristic.

Another treaty which contains a harmonising provision is the Pacific Agreement on Closer Economic Relations,[209] which Solomon Islands has signed[210] and ratified.[211] The object of the Agreement is to,

> establish a framework for the gradual trade and economic integration of the economies of the Forum members in a way that is fully supportive of sustainable development of the Forum Island Countries and to contribute to their gradual and progressive integration into the international economy.[212]

The Agreement provides for, *inter alia*, guidelines for terms of trade agreements,[213] and an obligation to periodically review tariffs with a view of liberalising trade.[214] Article 15 provides a practical, rather than legal mechanism for dispute resolution. It states that:

> **Article 15**
> Consultations
> If a Party considers that:
> (a) an obligation under this Agreement has not been, or is not being, fulfilled;
> (b) any benefit conferred upon it by this Agreement is being, or may be, denied;
> (c) the achievement of any objective of this Agreement is being, or may be, frustrated;
> (d) a change in circumstances necessitates, or might necessitate, an amendment of this Agreement;

---

[209]Pacific Agreement on Closer Economic Relations, opened for signature 18 August 2001, [2001] PITSE 1 (entered into force 3 October 2002) ("PACER").

[210]Signed 6 August 2002: see 'Status Report: Pacific Agreement on Closer Economic Relations', Pacific Islands Legal Information Institute. http://www.paclii.org/pits/en/status_pages/2001-1.html.

[211]Ibid, ratified 2 June 2003.

[212]Ibid s 2(1).

[213]Ibid s 7.

[214]Ibid s 8.

> it may notify any other Party, through the Forum Secretariat, of its wish to enter into consultations. The Party so requested shall enter into consultations in good faith and as soon as possible, with a view to seeking a mutually satisfactory solution.

The article makes provision for parties to enter into consultation in good faith and, without the courts intervention, and come to a mutually satisfactory solution in consideration of any relevant competing legal regimes. In cases where the non-fulfilment of obligations under the Agreement is a function of adherence to a competing legal regime, dispute resolution articles akin to this might be viewed as practical, indirect means of reconciling different legal regimes.

Solomon Islands has also been a member of the World Trade Organisation ('WTO') since 26 July 1996 and the General Agreement on Tariffs and Trade ('GATT') since 28 December 1994.[215] When parties become a party to the WTO Treaty, they accept the terms of the Dispute Settlement Understanding ('DSU') that is annexed to it. That DSU creates a Dispute Settlement Body,[216] and an Appellate Body.[217] The Dispute Settlement Body and the Appellate Body exist to,

> preserve the rights and obligations of Members under the covered agreements, and to clarify the existing provisions of those agreements in accordance with customary rules of interpretation of public international law. Recommendations and rulings of the DSB cannot add to or diminish the rights and obligations provided in the covered agreements.[218]

Solomon Islands has never been a complainant or respondent in any matter before the WTO.[219]

As discussed above, there is no impediment to a referral to arbitration. Conflicts are unlikely as the choice is covered by legislation, and agreement to arbitrate will normally be binding on the parties and any court application stayed.[220]

---

[215]World Trade Organisation, 'Solomon Islands and the WTO', *World Trade Organisation* (Web Page), https://www.wto.org/english/thewto_e/countries_e/solomon_islands_e.htm. Accessed 17 March 2019.

[216]Generally, the primary objective of the system is not to make rulings or to develop jurisprudence, but to settle disputes, preferably through a mutually agreed solution.

[217]Understanding on the Rules and Procedures Governing the Settlement of Disputes, signed 15 April 1994, 1869 UNTS 401 (entered into force 1 January 1995), art 17.

[218]Ibid art 3(2).

[219]World Trade Organisation, 'Solomon Islands and the WTO', *World Trade Organisation* (Web Page), https://www.wto.org/english/thewto_e/countries_e/solomon_islands_e.htm. Accessed 17 March 2019.

[220]Arbitration Act [cap 2], s 2.

## 5 Failure of the Approach to Constitutionalism and Conflicting Norms to Evolve

Unlike many other countries outside the South Pacific region, there is no discernible evolution of the legislative approach to constitutionalism. The one area where parliament seems to have taken a stance to curtail the abuse of government office is in relation to leadership. The Constitution contains a Leadership Code,[221] which states that a leader must not engage in conduct which creates a conflict of interest, demeans the office or position; allows the leader's integrity to be called into question; or endangers or diminishes respect or confidence in the integrity of the government. It provides that,

> a person to whom this Chapter applies shall not use his office for personal gain or enter into any transaction or engage in any enterprise or activity that might be expected to give rise to doubt in the public mind as to whether he is carrying out or has carried out the duty imposed by the preceding subsection.[222]

The definition of leader is broad, covering not only a list of named officers but also those failing within the category of public officers'.[223] The Constitution empowers parliament to strengthen these provisions, which it has done by passing two Acts, the latest being the Leadership Code (Further Provisions) Act 1999. The government has also followed up with regulations[224] and rules.[225] An example of a successful prosecution for breach of the Act can be found in *Regina v Musuota*,[226] where a cabinet minister had accepted the use of a hire car from a person who had an interest in matters within his portfolio. However, it is notable that gifts which are, 'offered at or in connection with a custom ceremony' do not have to be declared.[227] This highlights the importance of custom in Solomon Islands, which is often more influential than introduced laws and the norms they encompass.

As discussed above, an area of particular contention between competing regimes lies in the conflict between constitutionally enshrined human rights norms and customary law. The case law reveals an ad hoc approach to conflicting norms, rather than any discernible evolution. As discussed above, the Constitution, is the supreme law of Solomon Islands.[228] However, particularly as regards the position of customary law, the hierarchy of laws is contentious and the outcomes of conflicts uncertain.

---

[221]Constitution, ch VIII, ss 93-5.

[222]Ibid s 94(2).

[223]Ibid s 93(g).

[224]Leadership Code (Further Provisions) Regulations 2000.

[225]Leadership Code Commission Rules 2000.

[226][1997] SBHC 9. See also *Regina v Siapu* [1993] SBHC 14.

[227]Leadership Code (Further Provisions) Act 1999, s 9(4)(b).

[228]Constitution, s 2.

Perhaps the best illustration of the reverence accorded to customary law is to be found in decision of Muria CJ in *Pusi v Leni,*[229] discussed above. Ultimately, it was not necessary for Muria CJ to consider the conflict between the constitutional and customary law regimes as his Honour found, factually, that there had been no restriction of the applicant's freedom of movement. However, His Honour took the opportunity to state that constitutional and statutory principle were not superior to the principles of customary law. His Honour went on to add that:

> I have made these observations because it appears to the court that this case is a classic example of an attempt to use the Constitution to circumvent the lawful application of custom, a course of action that may well engender disharmony in society. Such a course must not be allowed to flourish in this country.

As discussed above, in other cases, the approach to customary law has not been so sanguine. In *R v Loumia,*[230] for example, the Court of Appeal refused to engage with the possibility that a customary rule might override the right to life enshrined in the Constitution, even to the extent of reducing murder to manslaughter. Give the ad hoc approach of the courts, it is difficult to predict with any certainly the outcome of future applications for enforcement of human right provisions where the act complained of is in accordance with customary law.[231]

## 6 Stagnation of Legal Reasoning and Jurisprudence

There is no sign that globalisation has had an impact on legal reasoning in Solomon Islands. Nor has a cohesive body of principles governing the relationship between different legal spheres emerged. The country remains protective of its sovereignty and determined to promote domestic culture and custom in preference to 'foreign' ideals. This is reflected in the Draft Constitution, which, whilst strengthening the Bill of Rights, continues to emphasise the importance of tradition, founding the document on 'the authority of our traditional clan and tribal systems and leadership' and declaring a 'determination to live together in harmony, to preserve ... wisdom and customs, and to establish a system of government that will uphold ... customs and traditions'.[232]

There is limited evidence that reference to international norms is on the increase as an aid to interpretation of domestic laws. However, it would be overemphasising this to say that this constitutes a standard or structured approach.

There is no discernible 'dialogue' in the jurisprudence driven by globalisation. Generally, there is an absence of discussion of these issues outside academic circles. Nor have concepts or tools appeared to assist in negotiating between the domestic

[229] [1997] SBHC 100.

[230] [1984] SILR 51. See also Brown (1986), p. 133.

[231] See also *Tanavalu v Tanavalu* [1998] SBHC 4, discussed above.

[232] Constitution, preamble.

and international legal spheres. This may be due to the lack of engagement by Solomon Islands government with international law and failure to incorporate international laws into the domestic legal system. For most villages, traditional values have more relevance than international norms, whether contained in international law or the Constitution. In fact, it is fair to say that the majority of the population outside urban centres do not engage with the state legal system, let alone international law. As a result, the legal pluralism discourse has concentrated on in the interaction between State law and customary law.[233] It is only in this context that the concept of law has been discussed and broadened. The failure of many legal reform programmes which have ignored the local context and, more specifically, traditional authority and customary laws, has led to a greater attention being paid to the local than to the international. One manifestation of this is the increased awareness that legal transplants are often inappropriate, particularly where they incorporate foreign norms.[234]

## 7 Conclusion

In Solomon Islands, there is very little discussion of constitutionality or the issues discussed in this chapter. One reason for this it that the country is still emerging from a tribal society and searching to find itself as a nation. Legal positivism and the theory of constitutionalism are themselves foreign concepts, far removed from the everyday experiences of Solomon Islanders. Traditional leaders often have more influence than government officials, and in this context customary law is far more relevant than state law. For many, international laws are not even on the horizon, and even constitutionally enshrined norms are at best aspirational concepts, rather than a reflection of practical reality. As stated by Hassall:

> As the modern constitutions of South Pacific states remain divorced from traditional order so too does the origin of law in the will of the people remain, in large part, a fiction. This issue is at the heart of the failure of the legitimacy of the rule of law in the Pacific Island states.[235]

## References

Alasia S (1997) Party politics and Government in Solomon Islands. Research School of Pacific and Asian Studies, discussion paper 97/7. https://openresearch-repository.anu.edu.au/bitstream/1885/41732/3/ssgmalasia.pdf. Accessed 17 Mar 2019

Best G (1995) Justice, international relations and human rights. Int Aff 71(4):775–799

Boyd S (2003) Australian judges at work internationally. Australian Law J 77:303–308

---

[233] See e.g., Brown (2005); Corrin (2009), p. 31.

[234] Corrin (2019), p. 34.

[235] Hassall (2010), p. 57.

Brown K (1986) Criminal law and custom in Solomon Islands. QUT Law J 2:133–139
Brown K (2005) Reconciling customary law and received law in Melanesia: the post-independence experience in Solomon Islands and Vanuatu. Charles Darwin University Press, Darwin
Brown K, Corrin Care J (1998) Conflict in Melanesia: customary law and the rights of women. Commonwealth Law Bulletin 24(3–4):1334–1355
Brown K, Corrin Care J (2001) More on democratic fundamentals in Solomon Islands: Minister for Provincial Government v Guadalcanal Provincial Assembly. Victoria Univ Wellington Law Rev 32(3):653–673
Chiam S (2009) Asia's experience in the quest for a regional human rights mechanism. Victoria Univ Wellington Law Rev 40:127–148
Corrin J (2007) Breaking the mould: constitutional review in Solomon Islands. Revue Juridique Polynesienne 13:143–168
Corrin J (2009) From horizontal and vertical to lateral: extending the effects of human rights in post colonial legal systems of the South Pacific. Int Comp Law Q 58(1):1–39
Corrin J (2010) Accommodating legal pluralism in Pacific Courts: problems of proof of customary law. Int J Evidence Proof 15:1–25
Corrin J (2013) Cultural relativism vs universalism: the South Pacific reality. In: Arnold R (ed) The universalism of human rights. Springer, Dortrecht, pp 103–125
Corrin J (2017) Human rights are not our business: legal pluralism and the South Pacific's constitutional conundrum. In: Hourquebie F (ed) Pluralisme Juridique et Droits Fondamentaux. Fondation Varenne, Bordeaux, pp 83–97
Corrin J (2019) Transplant shock: the hazards of introducing statutes of general application. In: Breda V (ed) Legal transplants in East Asia and Oceania. Cambridge University Press, Cambridge, pp 34–62
Corrin Care J (1999) Customary law and human rights in Solomon Islands. J Legal Pluralism Unofficial Law 43:135–144
Corrin Care J (2006) Negotiating the constitutional conundrum: balancing cultural identity with principles of gender equality in post-colonial South Pacific societies. Indigenous Law J 5:51–81
Corrin Care J, Zorn JG (2005) Legislating for the application of customary law in Solomon Islands. Common Law World Rev 34:144–168
Corrin J, Patterson D (2017) Introduction to South Pacific law, 4th edn. Intersentia, Cambridge
Farran S (2009) Human rights in the South Pacific: challenges and changes. Routledge-Cavendish, Abingdon
French R (2009) The future of Australian Constitutionalism. Unpublished speech, 27 November 2009. Centre for Comparative Studies, Melbourne, p 6
Gluckman M (1972) The ideal in Barotse jurisprudence. Manchester University Press, Manchester
Hassall G (2010) Governance, legitimacy and the rule of law in the South Pacific. In: Jowitt A, Newton T (eds) Passage of change. ANU Press, Canberra, pp 51–69
Imrana Jalal P (2009) Why do we need a pacific regional human rights commission? Victoria Univ Wellington Law Rev 40:177–194
Kabutaulaka T (2004) Beyond intervention: navigating Solomon Islands future: report on post-conflict nation rebuilding workshop. East-West Centre, Hawaii
Mataitoga I (1982) South Pacific court of appeal. Pacific Perspect 11(1):70
Pacific Islands Forum Secretariat (2007) The Pacific Plan for strengthening regional cooperation and integration. https://www.adb.org/sites/default/files/linked-documents/robp-pac-2010-2013-oth01.pdf. Accessed 14 Dec 2016
Pulea M (1980) A regional court of appeal for the pacific. Pacific Perspect 9(2):1
Richardson M, Garnett R (2016) Choice of law and forum in international commercial contracts: trends in common law jurisdictions (A Non-European Perspective). www.ialsnet.org/meetings/business/RichardsonMegan-Australia.pdf. Accessed 14 Nov 2017
Seddon N (1974) Reciprocity, exchange and contract. Melanesian Law J 2(1):48–65
Solomon Islands Law Reform Commission (2012) Review of the law that applies to land below high water mark and low water mark report. SIG, Honiara

Solomon Islands National Statistics Office (2009) Census 2009, Volume 2. https://www.statistics.gov.sb/statistics/demographic-statistics/census. Accessed 17 Mar 2019

Tamata L (2000) Application of the human rights conventions in the Pacific Islands courts. J South Pacific Law 4:2000. http://www.paclii.org/journals/fJSPL/vol04/12.shtml. Accessed 3 Dec 2009

Waluchow W (2004) Constitutionalism. In: Zalta EN (ed) The Stanford encyclopedia of philosophy. Center for the Study of Language and Information (CSLI), Stanford University, Stanford. http://plato.stanford.edu/entries/constitutionalism/. Accessed 17 Mar 2019

Wickliffe C (1999) Human rights education in the Pacific. J South Pacific Law 3. https://www.usp.ac.fj/index.php?id=13148. Accessed 17 Mar 2019

Zorn J (2000) Occasional paper 5: women, custom and international law in the Pacific. University of South Pacific, Port Vila

# Accommodating Legal Pluralism and "Pluralizing" the Constitution: The Example of the United Kingdom

**Athanasios Psygkas**

**Abstract** This chapter argues that the forms that the normative encounter between domestic and supranational constitutionalism has taken in the United Kingdom (UK) are intertwined with fundamental domestic constitutional principles. Even as the UK legal order ceded ground to external normative sources as a matter of practical outcomes, the key national constitutional actors self-consciously justified this move, as a matter of formal constitutional principle, by express reference to domestic constitutional principles and sources. In the attempt to accommodate legal pluralism in the constitutional edifice of the UK, the constitutional architecture itself became more plural and textured. This constitutional reconfiguration is ongoing and has come to the forefront as the UK is currently at a moment of constitutional reckoning owing to Brexit. This maps onto a long-standing debate on the position of the UK in the international sphere, most notably with respect to the European Convention on Human Rights. The chapter argues that Brexit and similar impulses highlight the interface between domestic and external legal orders (international or supranational). This interface cannot be nullified easily, contrary to what some proponents of Brexit may have expected or wished for. Rather, these recent developments add impetus to constitutional self-reflection; instead of negating constitutional pluralism they move the inquiry to the domestic sphere forcing national constitutional actors to reflect explicitly on the forms that pluralism ought to take.

A. Psygkas (✉)
University of Bristol, Bristol, UK
e-mail: a.psygkas@bristol.ac.uk



G. Tusseau (ed.), *Debating Legal Pluralism and Constitutionalism*, Ius Comparatum – Global Studies in Comparative Law 41, https://doi.org/10.1007/978-3-030-34432-0_10

# 1 Introduction

The British constitution has been described as an "awesome mess"[1] drawing on a multitude of sources of varied historical pedigree. As supranational constitutionalism expanded and the United Kingdom (UK) engaged increasingly with international organizations and the European Union especially in the second half of the twentieth century, the textured domestic constitutionalism encountered new sources of norms. This enhanced the multi-layered nature of the UK constitution[2] and added complexity to the constitutional architecture. It further created the need for the normative accommodation of this "constitutional pluralism"[3] as multiple constitutional sites made claims to authority.

These constitutional sites, domestic and supranational, claim authority autonomously thus sustaining a horizontal, heterarchical relationship.[4] In the absence of an uncontested hierarchy, this constitutional plurality of valid claims can generate tensions. These tensions become more salient against the backdrop of a parliamentary sovereignty system, as is the UK, where the fundamental normative tenet had been the idea that Parliament has "the right to make or unmake any law whatever," and "no person or body is recognised by the law of England as having a right to override or set aside the legislation of Parliament".[5]

This contribution argues that the forms that the normative encounter between domestic and supranational constitutionalism took in the UK are intertwined with fundamental domestic constitutional principles. Even as the UK legal order ceded ground to external normative sources as a matter of practical outcomes, the key national constitutional actors self-consciously justified this move, as a matter of formal constitutional principle, by express reference to domestic constitutional principles and sources. Briefly put, the simplified version of the argument was that it is "*our* Parliament and *our* courts" making the conscious decision to establish links between these normative spheres which, in turn, may result in national law being set aside. Perhaps the most interesting aspect of this story is that in the attempt to accommodate legal pluralism in the constitutional edifice of the UK, the constitutional architecture itself became more plural and textured: the domestic constitutional enterprise of tackling legal pluralism stemming from external sources "pluralized" the constitution itself. This constitutional reconfiguration is ongoing and has come to the forefront as the UK is currently at a moment of constitutional reckoning. The referendum of 23 June 2016, which resulted in 51.9% of the electorate voting in favor of the UK leaving the EU, has been interpreted as pushback against external legal orders, a decision to "take back control." This maps onto a long-standing debate on the position of the UK in the international sphere, most notably with respect to the European Convention on Human Rights. I

---

[1] Wright (2013), p. 19.

[2] Walker (2002) and Avbelj and Komárek (2008).

[3] Bamforth and Leyland (2003).

[4] Walker (2002), p. 337.

[5] Dicey (1959), pp. 39–40.

will argue that Brexit and similar impulses highlight the interface between domestic and external legal orders (international or supranational). This interface cannot be nullified easily, contrary to what some proponents of Brexit may have expected or wished for. Rather, these recent developments add impetus to constitutional self-reflection; instead of negating constitutional pluralism they move the inquiry to the domestic sphere forcing national constitutional actors to reflect explicitly on the forms that pluralism ought to take.

Section 2 describes this complex normative landscape and outlines the dynamic relations between the domestic and external spheres as a matter of positive law. Section 3 argues that the process of accommodating this normative pluralism stemming from external sources has enhanced the pluralistic nature of the internal constitutional arrangements. Section 4 concludes by examining the conditions under which normative pluralism can generate consensus and conflict.

## 2 The Dynamic Relations Among Legal Spheres in Positive Law: Accommodating Pluralism

The relations between international and municipal law in different jurisdictions are generally described as falling along a spectrum between monism and dualism.[6] Dualism emphasizes the "distinct and independent character of the international and national legal systems. . . . Monism postulates that national and international law form one single legal order, or at least a number of [coherent] interlocking orders [whereby] international law can be applied directly within the national legal order".[7] As each national legal system determines the terms of its engagement with international and transnational law, the distinction between monism and dualism is analytically useful as a starting point; however, the image that emerges in terms of practical operation is a pluralist one where the specifics of the interface between international and municipal law reveal almost as many models as there are legal systems.[8]

Schematically, the UK is a dualist system[9] but with important qualifications that have led to its more accurate description as a "partially dualist" system.[10] This section begins with a discussion of international law where the dualist filters are in clearer operation (Sect. 2.1). I describe this as the "default" to highlight subsequently the special position of EU law (Sect. 2.2). Brexit further complicates this picture (Sect. 2.3). Section 2.4 concludes with a discussion of other types of pluralism, notably through transnational dialogue. I argue that these multifaceted interactions between the domestic and international spheres reflect a pluralistic normative

---

[6]Feldman (2015), pp. 140–141.

[7]Crawford (2012), p. 48.

[8]Denza (2014), p. 418; Crawford (2012), pp. 110–111.

[9]Crawford (2012), p. 63.

[10]Feldman (2015), p. 142.

landscape. However, a common theme running through this discussion is the conscious attempt of domestic institutions, mainly courts, to act as "a gatekeeper governing the 'normative traffic' which flows between the international and the domestic legal orders".[11] The judiciary recognizes this role for itself but, importantly, for Parliament as well.

## 2.1 *The "Default": The Position of International Law in the Domestic Legal Order*

The normative accommodation of international law rules varies depending on whether these are treaty-based or part of customary international law. However, as we will see, there are indications that this conventional distinction may "have been altered to become one which rests upon the subject-matter of the dispute".[12] Moreover, the gatekeeping function of national institutions manifests itself across both categories of international norms.

Customary international law relaxes the traditional dualist position. Lord Denning described this clearly in *Trendtex*: "the rules of international law are incorporated into English law automatically and considered to be part of English law unless they are in conflict with an Act of Parliament."[13] This is the doctrine of incorporation which Lord Denning endorsed over the doctrine of transformation; under the latter, customary international law becomes part of English law once it has been adopted as such by a court decision or a statute.[14] The implication of the doctrine of incorporation, Lord Denning noted, was that the rules of international law, *as existing from time to time*, form part of English law. When the rules of international law change, the courts can give effect to the changes without any Act of Parliament.[15]

Later cases added important qualifications to the operation of customary international law in domestic law. In *Jones*,[16] twenty individuals were charged with various offences, including criminal damage and aggravated trespass. These offences were allegedly committed on British and US military bases in the UK in February and

[11]Capps (2007), p. 459.

[12]Capps (2007), p. 469.

[13]*Trendtex Trading Corporation v Central Bank of Nigeria* [1977] QB 529, 553.

[14]Id. See also Crawford (2012), p. 67.

[15]*Trendtex*, supra note 13, at 554 (also stating "I now believe that the doctrine of incorporation is correct. Otherwise I do not see that our courts could ever recognise a change in the rules of international law. It is certain that international law does change. I would use of international law the words which Galileo used of the earth: 'But it does move.' International law does change: and the courts have applied the changes without the aid of any Act of Parliament. Thus, when the rules of international law were changed (by the force of public opinion) so as to condemn slavery, the English courts were justified in applying the modern rules of international law" (internal citations omitted).

[16]*R v Jones (Margaret)* [2006] UKHL 16.

March 2003 to disrupt the military preparations against Iraq. The defendants (appellants before the House of Lords) asserted that they were legally justified to act as they did because they wished to impede the commission of the crime of aggression by the UK and US governments. They argued that crimes recognized in customary international law, such as the crime of aggression, were (without the need for any domestic statute or judicial decision) recognized and enforced by domestic law.[17] The House of Lords rejected these defences. Lord Bingham accepted that "a crime recognised in customary international law may be assimilated into the domestic criminal law of this country. The appellants, however, go further and contend that that result follows automatically. The authorities, as I read them, do not support that proposition."[18] The crime of aggression was not proscribed in domestic legislation and this lack of any statutory incorporation was not, for the court, "a neutral factor, for two main reasons. The first is that there now exists no power in the courts to create new criminal offences ... The second reason is that when it is sought to give domestic effect to crimes established in customary international law, the practice is to legislate."[19]

*Jones* highlights the gatekeeping role of courts identified earlier,[20] a role which in turn activates the similar gatekeeping function of Parliament. Under the principle in *Trendtex*, there was no need for positive parliamentary intervention for the operation of customary international law but rather a negative form of intervention only where customary international law is not consistent with statutory law. In the specific context of *Jones* which involves criminal law, the House of Lords, citing the unanimous decision in *Knuller*,[21] requires a positive parliamentary intervention: new criminal offences can only be created by statute. There are constitutional principles underpinning this judicial pronouncement. Lord Bingham agrees with Berman's observation that "it would be odd if the executive could, by means of [customary international law], acting in concert with other states, amend or modify specifically the criminal law, with all the consequences that flow for the liberty of the individual and rights of personal property."[22] Consequently, the House of Lords reaffirms that customary international law cannot alter the "important democratic principle ... that it is for those representing the people of the country in Parliament, not the executive and not the judges, to decide what conduct should be treated as

---

[17]These defences were based on s. 3(1) of the Criminal Law Act 1967 providing that "a person may use such force as is reasonable in the circumstances in the prevention of crime" and s. 68 of the Criminal Justice and Public Order Act 1994 Act providing that (1) a person commits the offence of aggravated trespass if he trespasses on land and does there anything which is intended by him to obstruct or disrupt lawful activity. (2) Activity of a person or persons on land is 'lawful' for the purposes of this section if he or they may engage in the activity on the land ...without committing an offence.

[18]*Jones*, supra note 16, at [23].

[19]Id., at [28].

[20]Capps (2007), p. 459.

[21]*R v Knuller (Publishing, Printing and Promotions) Ltd* [1973] AC 43.

[22]*Jones*, supra note 16, at [23] citing Berman (2003), p. 11.

lying so far outside the bounds of what is acceptable in our society as to attract criminal penalties."[23]

The nuanced position of customary international law and its interface with domestic norms were captured in a more recent decision of the UK Supreme Court. Lord Mance reiterated that customary international law, "once established, can and should shape the common law, whenever it can do so consistently with domestic constitutional principles, statutory law and common law rules which the courts can themselves sensibly adapt without it being, for example, necessary to invite Parliamentary intervention or consideration."[24]

The dualist features of the UK system are clearer in the example of unincorporated international treaties, which are not recognized as sources of rights and obligations in municipal law without domestic legislation.[25] Courts early on had held that treaties affecting private rights required the sanction of the legislature.[26] More recent case law has reiterated this principle: "as a matter of the constitutional law of the United Kingdom, the Royal Prerogative, whilst it embraces the making of treaties, does not extend to altering the law or conferring rights upon individuals or depriving individuals of rights which they enjoy in domestic law without the intervention of Parliament. Treaties, as it is sometimes expressed, are not self-executing. Quite simply, a treaty is not part of English law unless and until it has been incorporated into the law by legislation."[27] The implication of this principle is that international treaties do not have direct effect and cannot be invoked by individuals before domestic courts prior to the enactment of domestic legislation incorporating these treaties.[28] For instance, individuals could not seek the enforcement of rights provided in the European Convention of Human Rights (ECHR) before domestic legislation, the Human Rights Act 1998 (HRA), had come into effect.[29]

The UK Supreme Court recently summarized two key components of the dualist theory: "The first is that treaties between sovereign states have effect in international law and are not governed by the domestic law of any state.... The second proposition is that, although they are binding on the United Kingdom in international law, treaties are not part of UK law and give rise to no legal rights or obligations in domestic law."[30] The rationale for the dualist theory is that the principle of parliamentary sovereignty would be bypassed if the executive could exercise its

---

[23] *Jones*, supra note 16, at [29].

[24] *Keyu v Secretary of State for Foreign and Commonwealth Affairs* [2015] UKSC 69 [150].

[25] Denza (2014), p. 424.

[26] *The Parlement Belge* (1879) 4 P.D. 129.

[27] *JH Rayner (Mincing Lane) Ltd v Department of Trade and Industry* [1990] 2 AC 418, 500 (Lord Oliver).

[28] Sales and Clement (2008), p. 397.

[29] *R v Secretary of State for the Home Department, ex parte Brind* [1991] 1 AC 696; Feldman (2015), pp. 147–148.

[30] *R (Miller) v Secretary of State for Exiting the European Union* [2017] UKSC 5 [55].

prerogative powers to enter into a treaty that would produce direct effects altering domestic law.[31] As the Supreme Court explained, "the dualist system is a necessary corollary of Parliamentary sovereignty, or, to put the point another way, it exists to protect Parliament not ministers."[32] Therefore, Parliament, with the support of the courts, will exercise the gatekeeping function determining which international treaties will develop legal effects domestically. Moreover, under a constitutional convention known as the "Ponsonby rule," treaties would normally not be ratified until they had been laid before both Houses of Parliament for 21 says.[33] This convention was placed on a statutory footing by Part 2 of the Constitutional Reform and Governance Act 2010, which gives to the House of Commons an effective veto to treaty ratification.

There are exceptions to the dualist theory, e.g., in the case of peace treaties.[34] Furthermore, some senior members of the judiciary have argued that an additional exception should be recognized for human rights treaties. In the *SG* case, which examined a welfare benefits cap, one argument relied on the United Nations Convention on the Rights of the Child (UNCRC), which had not been incorporated by Parliament into UK law. The majority reiterated the general rule that UK courts have no jurisdiction to apply unincorporated international treaties.[35] Lord Kerr, in dissent, found "no logical reason to deny to UK citizens domestic law's vindication of the rights" protected in human rights treaties. "If the government commits itself to a standard of human rights protection," he continued, "it seems to me entirely logical that it should be held to account in the courts as to its actual compliance with that standard."[36] This approach has also found support in the literature. Bjorge argues that international law treaties to the benefit of individual rights should in certain circumstances be a source of the common law similar to customary international law rules.[37] This is a normatively attractive proposition. As a matter of positive law, most relevant cases prove the negative side of the proposition, i.e., that treaties adversely affecting individual rights require parliamentary intervention, rather than the affirmative side, i.e., that treaties enhancing rights, do not require statutory incorporation. Even under this proposal, domestic courts would still determine which provisions of unincorporated treaties apply and would thus carry out the gatekeeping role identified previously.

Indeed, UK courts have played this gatekeeping role to ensure that the dualist filters apply properly as a means of safeguarding constitutional principles. *Ahmed* is

[31]Sales and Clement (2008), p. 399; Denza (2014), p. 424.

[32]*R (Miller) v Secretary of State for Exiting the European Union* [2017] UKSC 5 [57].

[33]Feldman (2015), pp. 148–149.

[34]*The Parlement Belge* (1879) 4 P.D. 129.

[35]*R (SG) (Appellants) v Secretary of State for Work and Pensions* [2015] UKSC 16 [90] (Lord Reed), [115] (Lord Carnwath).

[36]Id. at [256] (Lord Kerr).

[37]Bjorge (2017).

an illustrative example.[38] Article 41 of the UN Charter provides that the UN Security Council may call on UN Members to apply measures not involving the use of armed force. In such cases, the UK government is empowered by a domestic statute, s. 1 of the United Nations Act 1946, to issue Orders in Council as "necessary or expedient for enabling those measures to be effectively applied." The Orders can be made by the executive without any kind of parliamentary scrutiny. Under this statute, the Terrorism (United Nations Measures) Order 2006 and the Al-Qaida and Taliban (United Nations Measures) Order 2006 ("the Al-Qaida Order") were issued to give effect to Security Council Resolutions, which were designed to suppress the financing of terrorist activities. These Orders provided for the freezing of the financial assets of persons who were designated for the purposes of the Orders. Article 3(1)(b) of the Al-Qaida Order provided, in particular, that persons on a list compiled by the sanctions committee of the Security Council were "designated persons." These individuals could not challenge the basis upon which the sanctions committee had placed them on the list. When these Orders were challenged before the House of Lords, the court reasserted the principle of legality and protection of fundamental rights (Feldman 2015, pp. 152–153). It held that the general words of s. 1 of the 1946 Act did not authorize several provisions in the Orders overriding the fundamental rights of individuals to use their property and doing so in a way which deprived individuals of any real possibility of challenging their listing in the courts. The case added an interesting wrinkle to the dualist approach. As Lord Mance explained, the purpose of s.1 of the UN Act 1946 was to address the consequences of the dualist view by facilitating the implementation at the domestic level of the UK's international legal obligations under Chapter VII. However, the case turned on whether s. 1 "covered any and every Security Council Resolution that might be passed, including even a Resolution directed at what would otherwise be regarded as basic constitutional rights under domestic law."[39]

## 2.2 *Complicating the Picture: The Special Status of EU Law*

The default dualist position does not apply neatly to the status of EU law in the UK legal order. The main "challenges" came from the application of the EU principles of supremacy and direct effect in a system of parliamentary sovereignty. The picture is further complicated by Brexit; the constitutional implications of the UK's withdrawal from the EU can be appreciated better against the historical backdrop of the original reception of EU law.

From the perspective of domestic constitutional law, the statutory foundations of the UK's membership of the EU are found in the European Communities Act 1972 (ECA). Section 2(1) of this Act is the "domestic counterpart" to the EU doctrine of

---

[38] *Ahmed v HM Treasury* [2010] UKSC 5.

[39] Id. at [244].

direct effect.[40] Section 2(4) ECA is the domestic counterpart to the doctrine of supremacy. It provides that any Act of the UK Parliament, whether enacted before or after the UK, "shall be construed and have effect subject to" EU law. The principle of supremacy resulted in the landmark *Factortame (no 2)* decision.[41] In this case, the House of Lords issued an injunction to disapply temporarily the Merchant Shipping Act 1988, a statute that had been enacted after the ECA and under the traditional doctrine of parliamentary sovereignty would have taken precedence over the earlier statute that was the ECA. The unprecedented nature of this decision and the "challenge" to the Diceyan notion of parliamentary sovereignty prompted scholars to describe the judgment as a technical legal revolution.[42] Other accounts described this development as a "principled legal evolution".[43]

For present purposes, the key point is that *Factortame (no 2)* as well as later cases have acknowledged the role of Parliament and domestic legal principles as the foundations of any modifications to the orthodox conception of parliamentary sovereignty. In *Factortame (no 2)* itself, Lord Bridge explained: "If the supremacy within the European Community of Community law over the national law of member states was not always inherent in the EEC Treaty it was certainly well established in the jurisprudence of the Court of Justice long before the United Kingdom joined the Community. Thus, *whatever limitation of its sovereignty Parliament accepted when it enacted the European Communities Act 1972 was entirely voluntary*. Under the terms of the 1972 Act it has always been clear that it was the duty of a United Kingdom court, when delivering final judgment, to override any rule of national law found to be in conflict with any directly enforceable rule of Community law."[44]

In a later case, *Thoburn*, Laws LJ stressed that if the traditional doctrine of sovereignty is to be modified, "it certainly cannot be done by the incorporation of external texts," such as EU law. The conditions of parliamentary supremacy, Laws LJ continued, "necessarily remain in the United Kingdom's hands." In fact, they had been modified "by the common law, wholly consistently with constitutional principle."[45] Laws LJ continued that the common law should recognize a hierarchy of Acts of Parliament: "ordinary" statutes and "constitutional" statutes. He defined a constitutional statute as one which "(a) conditions the legal relationship between citizen

[40]Elliott and Thomas (2017a), p. 363. Section 2(1) ECA reads: "All such rights, powers, liabilities, obligations and restrictions from time to time created or arising by or under the Treaties, and all such remedies and procedures from time to time provided for by or under the Treaties, as in accordance with the Treaties are without further enactment to be given legal effect or used in the United Kingdom shall be recognised and available in law, and be enforced, allowed and followed accordingly."

[41]*R v Secretary of State for Transport, ex parte Factortame (no. 2)* 1 AC 603.

[42]Wade (1996).

[43]Craig (2015) and Allan (1997).

[44]*R v Secretary of State for Transport, ex parte Factortame (no. 2)* 1 AC 603 at 658-59 (Lord Bridge) (emphasis added).

[45]*Thoburn v Sunderland City Council* [2003] Q.B. 151 [59].

and state in some general, overarching manner, or (b) enlarges or diminishes the scope of what we would now regard as fundamental constitutional rights."[46] The implication of this recognition was that constitutional statutes can only be repealed by "express words in the later statute, or by words so specific that the inference of an actual determination to effect the result contended for was irresistible."[47] According to *Thoburn*, the ECA was clearly a constitutional statute and thus not subject to implied repeal.

The gatekeeping role of the UK Parliament identified by Lord Bridge in *Factortame (no 2)* was also reaffirmed by statute. Section 18 of the European Union Act 2011 reiterated that "directly applicable or directly effective EU law (that is, the rights, powers, liabilities, obligations, restrictions, remedies and procedures referred to in section 2(1) of the European Communities Act 1972) falls to be recognised and available in law in the United Kingdom only by virtue of that Act [i.e. the ECA 1972] or where it is required to be recognised and available in law by virtue of any other Act."

While previous cases, including *Factortame* and *Thoburn*, involved a potential clash between the ECA as a constitutional statute and a later ordinary statute, in a more recent case, *HS2*, the Supreme Court in interesting dicta referred to a different type of clash, that between two constitutional statutes. With a clear nod to the gatekeeping role of domestic law, Lord Reed argued that the clash cannot be resolved "simply" by applying the doctrine of supremacy "since the application of that doctrine in our law itself depends upon the 1972 Act. If there is a conflict between a constitutional principle, such as that embodied in article 9 of the Bill of Rights,[48] and EU law, that conflict has to be resolved by our courts as an issue arising under the constitutional law of the United Kingdom."[49] Lords Neuberger and Mance were even clearer in their opinion: "It is, putting the point at its lowest, certainly arguable (and it is for United Kingdom law and courts to determine) that there may be fundamental principles, whether contained in other constitutional instruments or recognised at common law, of which Parliament when it enacted the European Communities Act 1972 did not either contemplate or authorise the abrogation."[50]

[46]Id. at [62].

[47]Id. at [63].

[48]Article 9 of the Bill of Rights 1689 states that "the Freedome of Speech and Debates or Proceedings in Parlyament ought not to be impeached or questioned in any Court or Place out of Parlyament." This provision has been described as "the most important statutory expression of parliamentary privilege" (Joint Committee on Parliamentary Privilege, *Parliamentary Privilege* (2013-14, HL 30, HC 100) para 16).

[49]*R (on the application of HS2 Action Alliance Limited) (Appellant) v The Secretary of State for Transport* [2014] UKSC 3 [79].

[50]Id. at [207].

## 2.3 *Complication Squared: Brexit*

The emphasis on domestic law as the normative foundation of the UK's membership of the EU, with all the modifications of parliamentary supremacy that EU membership has entailed, is most salient in the debates around Brexit. Supporters of Brexit had advanced their cause using slogans such as "taking back control," and repealing the ECA is one step in this process. The complex process of withdrawing from the EU brings to the fore yet again the links between EU and domestic law. These links are evident in two landmark legal texts—a court judgment, *Miller*, and a statute, the European Union (Withdrawal) Act 2018.

In *Miller*,[51] described as the "constitutional case of the century",[52] the Supreme Court addressed whether a formal notice of withdrawal from the EU under Article 50 Treaty on European Union (TEU) could lawfully be given by ministers through the exercise of prerogative powers, namely without prior legislation. All eleven serving justices sat en banc to hear the case—the largest panel since the Law Lords were created in 1876.[53] By an 8-3 majority, the Supreme Court held that legislation was required before the government could formally trigger Article 50 TEU. A detailed examination of the case is beyond the scope of this chapter. The majority recognized that the government has the prerogative power to enter into and withdraw from treaties. However, under the UK constitution, "unless primary legislation permits it, the Royal prerogative does not enable ministers to change statute law or common law," or to "frustrate the purpose of a statute . . . by emptying it of content or preventing its effectual operation."[54] The majority then highlighted the special nature of the European Communities Act 1972 which constituted "EU law an independent and overriding source of domestic law." While the eight justices accepted that the ambit of the rights which are incorporated into domestic law through section 2 of the ECA varies with the UK's obligations from time to time under the EU Treaties, they noted the "vital difference between changes in domestic law resulting from variations in the content of EU law arising from new EU legislation, and changes in domestic law resulting from withdrawal by the United Kingdom from the European Union." They concluded that "the EU Treaties not only concern the international relations of the United Kingdom, they are a source of domestic law, and they are a source of domestic legal rights many of which are inextricably linked with domestic law from other sources. Accordingly, the Royal prerogative to make and unmake treaties, which operates wholly on the international plane, cannot be exercised in relation to the EU Treaties."[55]

By contrast, Lord Reed in his dissent explained that the ECA "creates a scheme under which the effect given to EU law in domestic law exactly matches the UK's

---

[51] *Miller*, supra note 30.

[52] Eeckhout (2016).

[53] Neuberger Lord (2017).

[54] Id. at [50]-[51].

[55] Id. at [61]-[65], [76], [78], [86].

international obligations, whatever they may be." The effect of EU law on domestic law is conditional on the UK's membership of the EU. If the EU Treaties "do not apply to the UK, then there are no rights, powers and so forth which, in accordance with the Treaties, are to be given legal effect in the UK."[56]

Interestingly for present purposes, both the majority and the dissent recognized that the ECA is the normative foundation for EU law to take effect domestically, and thus the ECA has not altered the rule of recognition.[57] However, the majority proposed a "realistic approach," whereby "so long as the 1972 Act remains in force, its effect is to constitute EU law an independent and overriding source of domestic law."[58] There is an internal inconsistency in this position: if EU law relies on domestic legislation to develop legal effects, it cannot at the same time be described as an "independent" source of law from a domestic perspective.[59] What is driving the majority here may be something else: by requiring parliamentary sanction, the majority introduces Parliament as a gatekeeper, in addition to the executive. In this case, however, the gatekeeping function does not *introduce* normative pluralism in the direction that we saw earlier in this chapter. Rather the majority prevents the *termination* of a source of this normative pluralism without the considered judgment of both the executive and legislative branches, described by the majority respectively as the "junior" and "senior" constitutional partners in this exercise.[60]

A more recent development indicates how the process of reducing normative pluralism through Brexit still introduces normative pluralism in a different format. On 26 June 2018, the European Union (Withdrawal) Act 2018 ("2018 Act") received royal assent. Section 1 of the Act repeals the European Communities Act 1972 on exit day. As the Explanatory Notes indicate (2018, para 74), "the main effects of repealing the Act are to reflect the end of supremacy of EU law in domestic law and to remove the mechanism which enabled the flow of new EU law into UK law." A detailed examination of the 2018 Act is beyond the scope of this chapter.[61] However, for present purposes, it is important to highlight that the statute creates a new category of domestic law for the UK: retained EU law.[62] More specifically, section 2 continues in force all "EU-derived domestic legislation," the most important example being primary or, more commonly, secondary legislation passed under the ECA 1972 to give effect to EU directives. Section 3 converts all "direct EU legislation" (namely, EU regulations, decisions and tertiary legislation) into domestic law Section 4 converts all other "rights, powers, liabilities, obligations,

[56]Id at [177], [189], [191].

[57]Id. at [61], [228]. See also Young (2017a), pp. 293–294.

[58]Id. at 65.

[59]Elliott (2017a).

[60]Id. at [90].

[61]For a more detailed discussion of the 2018 Act and its implications, see Elliott and Tierney (2019), Craig (2019) and Segan (2018).

[62]House of Commons Library (2017).

restrictions, remedies and procedures" recognised and available by virtue of section 2(1) ECA 1972 (e.g. relevant EU Treaty provisions) into domestic law.

Under section 5, the EU supremacy principle will apply to retained EU law vis-à-vis pre-exit but not post-exit domestic legislation.[63] Therefore, post-exit day laws will take precedence over retained EU law. Section 5(4) stipulates that the EU Charter of Fundamental Rights is not part of domestic law on or after exit day. However, this provision does not affect the retention in domestic law on or after exit day of any fundamental rights or principles which exist irrespective of the Charter (section 5(5)). However, this caveat is of "limited utility".[64] Schedule 1 of the Act provides that there is no right of action in domestic law on or after exit day based on a failure to comply with any of the general principles of EU law, and no right to damages in accordance with the rule in *Francovich*. These provisions, "hidden away in Schedule 1, are likely to prove more significant than the exclusion of the Charter, given that the Charter tends only to be used by courts to reinforce rights which it is also able to locate in other international human rights instruments, and in the general principles of EU law".[65]

The Act includes instructions for courts to which the following section will return. The pluralist implications of the EU (Withdrawal) Act will be considered in Sect. 3. However, suffice it to say for now that this Act has added complexity to the status of retained EU law post-Brexit. Under section 7(1), EU-derived domestic legislation under section 2 of the 2018 Act continues to have after the exit day the same legal status it had pre-Brexit. This part was not complicated. However, complexity arose with respect to the status of retained EU law under sections 3 and 4 of the Act. When the Bill was published, the Government's original view had been that this second category of "retained direct EU law" should be ascribed a sui generis status that is neither primary nor secondary legislation; this approach was criticized by the House of Lords' Constitution Committee.[66] Section 7 was added to address this criticism. Section 7 distinguishes between "retained direct principal EU legislation" (in practice, EU regulations and directly effective Treaty provisions) and "retained direct minor EU legislation" (in practice, EU tertiary legislation) and provides rules on how each of these can be modified. However, section 7 has been criticized as introducing complexity and not directly answering the question of the status of retained direct EU law as such but rather only the question of how this law can be modified.[67] Consequently, Elliott and Tierney have concluded that this category of law is still "sui generis vis-à-vis the established domestic distinction between primary and secondary legislation [and] leaves open some difficult questions that it will now necessarily fall to the courts to resolve".[68]

---

[63]Elliott (2017b).

[64]Elliott (2017b).

[65]Syrpis (2017).

[66]Elliott and Tierney (2019), pp. 41–42; Craig (2019), pp. 324–325.

[67]Craig (2019), pp. 326–327.

[68]Elliott and Tierney (2019), p. 43.

## 2.4 Other Forms of Pluralism: Transconstitutional Dialogue

The previous sections sketched out the interface between domestic and supranational norms with an emphasis on the gatekeeping role asserted by national constitutional actors to accommodate the pluralistic normative landscape. At the core of these interactions, which may in turn generate normative tensions or conflicts, lie the apex courts in the respective jurisdictions. Since its establishment in 2009, the UK Supreme Court—and its predecessor, the Appellate Committee of the House of Lords—has had a "strategic objective" to develop dialogues with courts overseas.[69] The most formalized links are those with the European Court of Human Rights (ECtHR) and the Court of Justice of the European Union (CJEU).

From an international law perspective, under Article 46 ECHR the UK has the obligation to abide by the final judgments of the ECtHR in cases to which the UK is a party. However, from a domestic constitutional law perspective, under s. 2 HRA all courts applying Convention rights "must take account" of ECtHR judgments. As Lord Bingham explained the case law under s. 2 HRA in the *Ullah* case,

> While such case law is not strictly binding, it has been held that courts should, in the absence of some special circumstances, follow any clear and constant jurisprudence of the Strasbourg court... This reflects the fact that the Convention is an international instrument, the correct interpretation of which can be authoritatively expounded only by the Strasbourg court. From this it follows that a national court subject to a duty such as that imposed by section 2 should not without strong reason dilute or weaken the effect of the Strasbourg case law... It is of course open to member states to provide for rights more generous than those guaranteed by the Convention, but such provision should not be the product of interpretation of the Convention by national courts, since the meaning of the Convention should be uniform throughout the states party to it. The duty of national courts is to keep pace with the Strasbourg jurisprudence as it evolves over time: no more, but certainly no less.[70]

This approach has been labelled the "mirror principle." However, the relationship between UK courts and the ECtHR is not hierarchical and there are examples "where the national courts will refuse to follow a clear and constant line of case law, as well as examples of where the national courts are more willing to go beyond the current case law of the ECtHR".[71] In a 2014 case, Lord Neuberger distinguished from the *Ullah* principle cases in which the ECtHR has held that there is a wide margin of appreciation accorded domestic authorities, and consequently national courts must reach their own judgment on how to apply Convention rights. In such cases, Lord Neuberger continued, "the national courts therefore must decide the issue for themselves, with relatively unconstraining guidance from the Strasbourg court, albeit bearing in mind the constitutional proprieties and such guidance from the Strasbourg jurisprudence, and indeed our own jurisprudence, as seems

[69]Paterson (2013), p. 221.

[70]*R (Ullah) v Special Adjudicator* [2004] UKHL 26 [20].

[71]Young (2017b), pp. 260–261.

appropriate."[72] The Court in *Nicklinson* tried carefully to disclaim any broader implications of its decision for the *Ullah* principle.[73] However, commentators have observed that these statements can have "wide-ranging ramifications" as the Court's approach can apply "in other contexts, even when a narrower margin of appreciation may be in question".[74]

As a unanimous Supreme Court had explained in an earlier case, this relationship between the UK Court and the Strasbourg court facilitates judicial dialogue:

> This court is not bound to follow every decision of the European court. Not only would it be impractical to do so: it would sometimes be inappropriate, as it would destroy the ability of the court to engage in the constructive dialogue with the European court which is of value to the development of Convention law... Of course, we should usually follow a clear and constant line of decisions by the European court... But we are not actually bound to do so or (in theory, at least) to follow a decision of the Grand Chamber.[75]

In other words, for the transconstitutional dialogue to develop its deliberative potential, this communication must be a two-way street with both domestic courts and the ECtHR contributing to this conversation. Indeed, the Department for Constitutional Affairs had acknowledged the "positive dialogue between UK judges and those at the European Court of Human Rights."[76]

By contrast, the dialogue between the UK Supreme Court and the CJEU has been described as "more akin to sequential monologues".[77] The main procedural vehicle for these interactions is the preliminary reference procedure under what is now Article 267 Treaty on the Functioning of the European Union. The primacy of EU law renders the CJEU the authoritative arbiter of cases involving EU law on which the CJEU is asked for a ruling. This suggests a more hierarchical relationship. However, as the literature has suggested drawing on cases such as *HS2* discussed earlier in this chapter, UK courts have asserted their ability to determine the relationship between EU law and national law.[78]

Brexit adds a layer of complexity to the relationship between the CJEU and domestic courts. Section 6(1) of the European Union (Withdrawal) Act 2018 stipulates that UK courts will not be bound by CJEU decisions made on or after exit day, and that they will no longer have the power to refer questions to the Court. However, under section 6(2) a domestic "court or tribunal may have regard to anything done on or after exit day by the European Court, another EU entity or the EU so far as it is relevant to any matter before the court or tribunal." Section 6 (3) provides that all relevant case law of the CJEU decided *before* Brexit day,

[72] *R (on the application of Nicklinson) v Ministry of Justice* [2014] UKSC 38 [70], [73].

[73] Id. at [70] ("In those circumstances, it does not appear to me that the dictum quoted above from *Ullah* is in point. (For this reason, this is not the occasion to address the question whether, and if so how far, the principle enunciated by Lord Bingham in *Ullah*, para 20, should be modified or reconsidered)").

[74] Ferreira (2015), pp. 370–371.

[75] *Manchester City Council v Pinnock* [2010] UKSC 45 [48] (Lord Neuberger).

[76] Department for Constitutional Affairs (2006), p. 10.

[77] Paterson (2013), p. 224.

[78] Young (2017b), p. 277

including the general principles of EU law, should be used by the courts to determine the "validity, meaning and effect" of retained EU law.[79] This retained EU case law will be given the same precedent status as decisions of the Supreme Court. This means that under section 6(4), the Supreme Court/High Court of Justiciary are "not bound by any retained EU case law," and in deciding whether to depart from any retained EU case law, each "must apply the same test as it would apply in deciding whether to depart from its own case law" (section 6(5)). Therefore, the 2018 Act establishes a new relationship between the evolving case law of the European courts and courts in the UK which "will occupy lawyers, and invite litigation, for years to come" (Syrpis 2017). It is also relevant to add that in one of the "Brexit papers" issued by the UK government, the government noted the example of agreements between the EU and third countries, which specify that "account is to be taken of CJEU decisions . . . where both parties agree that divergence in interpretation would be undesirable".[80]

The emphasis in this section has been limited to the formalized links with the ECtHR and the CJEU. However, UK courts have drawn on other jurisdictions as inspiration for the development of the common law and human rights protection.[81] Another interesting study of the use of comparative law by the House of Lords and the Supreme Court in tort cases has found that these courts have drawn extensively from other common law jurisdictions, primarily Australia, the US, Canada, and New Zealand. By contrast, civil law jurisdictions have featured at a much lower level which appears to have declined in recent years (Stanton 2013). Last, even though space limitations preclude a more detailed treatment of this point, cross-border dialogue is not only judicial but involves other actors, notably administrative authorities. There are regulatory networks in the EU, of which the UK is (still) a member, and the effect of EU law on domestic administrative systems has had important implications for the nature of governance in the member states.[82]

## 3 The Renewal of Legal Reasoning and the Constitution

Section 2 described the legal interactions generated by globalization as the domestic UK legal order encountered and sought to accommodate external legal sources. These dynamic interactions have had implications for national legal reasoning, both in terms of the reasoning tools employed by domestic legal actors (e.g., proportionality analysis) but, perhaps more importantly, in terms of domestic constitutional law. Section 3 draws on examples of three developments—the revival of common law principles, the emergence of constitutional statutes, and the reinvigoration of the

[79]Simson Caird (2017).

[80]HM Government (2017a), para 46.

[81]Feldman (2015), pp. 156–158; Paterson (2013), pp. 221–222.

[82]See, e.g., Psygkas (2017).

territorial constitution—to showcase that legal pluralism beyond the national sphere has had ripple effects on the nature of constitutional law domestically.

## *3.1 Pluralizing the Constitution I: The Revival of Common Law Constitutionalism*

As argued earlier in this chapter, European law, broadly understood to cover both EU law and the ECHR, has influenced considerably the UK's approach to rights protection by enhancing the powers of courts.[83] EU law, with its attendant primacy over national law, and the HRA, especially sections 3, 4 and 6 expanding the toolkit of UK courts, became a salient feature of rights litigation arguably displacing the common law. However, in a series of more recent cases, the UK Supreme Court has reasserted the significance of the common law as a dynamic source of rights protection and an affirmation of "authochthonous constitutionalism".[84] I suggest that this development should be seen not as relegating external sources of law to secondary status but rather as exemplifying the influence of external normative spheres in a two-way interface prompting a reinvigoration of common law principles.

An examination of this line of cases reveals this dynamic. In *Osborn*,[85] the Supreme Court examined whether the Parole Board could lawfully recall to prison or not release from prison different prisoners without affording them an oral hearing. Lord Reed, writing for a unanimous court, noted that the submissions on behalf of the prisoners had focused on Article 5.4 ECHR, and "paid comparatively little attention to domestic administrative law." However, this approach, he continued, "does not properly reflect the relationship between domestic law (considered apart from the Human Rights Act 1998) and Convention rights."[86] Speaking to the interface between domestic and international norms, Lord Reed explained that "the values underlying both the Convention and our own constitution require that Convention rights should be protected primarily by a detailed body of domestic law."[87] In other words, the common law can concretize Convention principles. The two-way interface between these two sources of law is further reflected later in the judgment: "The importance of the [Human Rights Act] is unquestionable. It does not however supersede the protection of human rights under the common law or statute, or create a discrete body of law based on the judgments of the European court. Human rights continue to be protected by our domestic law, interpreted *and developed in*

[83]Stephenson (2015).

[84]Stephenson (2015), p. 398.

[85]*R (Osborn) v Parole Board* [2013] UKSC 61.

[86]Id. at [54].

[87]Id. at [56].

*accordance with the Act* when appropriate."[88] Ultimately, the Supreme Court held that had the Parole Board acted in accordance with the common law requirements of procedural fairness, it would have also complied with Article 5.4 ECHR.

*Kennedy*,[89] a case involving disclosure of information and freedom of expression, similarly reasserted the significance of the common law. However, again the image is not one of isolation but one of engagement and eventually a synthesis with the ECHR. In the words of Lord Mance (with whom Lord Neuberger and Lord Clarke agreed):

> Since the passing of the Human Rights Act 1998, there has too often been a tendency to see the law in areas touched on by the Convention solely in terms of the Convention rights. But the Convention rights represent a threshold protection; and, especially in view of the contribution which common lawyers made to the Convention's inception, they may be expected, at least generally even if not always, to reflect and to find their homologue in the common or domestic statute law... In some areas, the common law may go further than the Convention, and in some contexts *it may also be inspired by the Convention rights* and jurisprudence (the protection of privacy being a notable example). And in time, of course, *a synthesis may emerge*.[90]

These cases illustrate that the revival of common law constitutionalism far from rejects normative pluralism. The normative accommodation of external sources, such as the ECHR, does not replace but expands or "pluralizes" the domestic constitutional sphere. The HRA has had a catalytic effect in creating new or expanding existing common law rights.[91] Indeed, the reaffirmation of common law principles may be partly a judicial response to attempts to reduce the influence of external pluralism by repealing the HRA or even withdrawing from the ECHR.

In a similar vein, the reaffirmation of common law principles may respond to the main current attempt to reduce normative pluralism via Brexit. In the recent *UNISON* case,[92] the UK Supreme Court reviewed the lawfulness of an Order introducing fees for proceedings brought to Employment Tribunals and appeals to the Employment Appeal Tribunal ("Fees Order"). The Court invalidated unanimously the Fees Order relying primarily on common law principles. Drawing on previous case law, the Court stressed that the "constitutional right of access to the courts is inherent in the rule of law" and concluded that the Fees Order was unlawful as it effectively prevented access to justice.[93] Given this conclusion, the Court stated that "the other issues arising in the appeal can be dealt with very briefly."[94] These "other issues" included the EU law principles of effectiveness and effective judicial protection

[88]Id. at [58] (emphasis added).

[89]*Kennedy v The Charity Commission* [2014] UKSC 20.

[90]Id. at [46] (emphasis added).

[91]Stephenson (2015), p. 401.

[92]*R (UNISON) v Lord Chancellor* [2017] UKSC 51.

[93]Id. at [66], [98].

[94]Id. at [98].

since the Employment Tribunals enforce EU-derived employment rights.[95] On another interesting note which echoed the interface between the common law and the ECHR discussed earlier in this section, the Court also stated "the case law of the Strasbourg court concerning the right of access to justice is relevant to the development of the common law."[96]

One last illustrative example of the dynamic relations among legal spheres as reflected in the development of legal reasoning domestically, is the application of the proportionality framework in the national legal order. The UK courts had introduced the proportionality test in cases with an EU law or a HRA/ECHR dimension. However, in "purely domestic" cases the standard for substantive review was the so-called "Wednesbury unreasonableness" test whereby a decision by a public authority is invalidated when it is "so unreasonable that no reasonable authority could ever have come to it."[97]

In a series of dicta in recent cases,[98] several justices of the Supreme Court have indicated their willingness to recognize proportionality as a common law ground of review, especially when fundamental rights are involved. In *Kennedy*,[99] Lord Mance cited with approval Paul Craig's work and noted that both reasonableness review under the *Wednesbury* test and proportionality "involve considerations of weight and balance, with the intensity of the scrutiny and the weight to be given to any primary decision maker's view depending on the context." However, "the advantage of the terminology of proportionality is that it introduces an element of structure into the exercise, by directing attention to factors such as suitability or appropriateness, necessity and the balance or imbalance of benefits and disadvantages. There seems no reason why such factors should not be relevant in judicial review even outside the scope of [ECHR] and EU law."[100]

A year later in *Pham*, Lord Mance reiterated his position that the tool of proportionality is "both available and valuable" for the purposes of reviewing a "radical step" that is the removal of British citizenship implicated in the case.[101] Lord Carnwath, who had been more cautious the year before, noted that the majority in *Kennedy* had endorsed a flexible approach to principles of judicial review, and that the considerations in that case applied "with even greater force" in *Pham* which concerned the removal of the fundamental status of citizenship.[102] Lord Sumption noted that courts had applied a proportionality test in cases involving EU law or the ECHR but not endorsed the test generally as a principle of English public law.

[95] Id. at [105]-[117].

[96] Id. at [89].

[97] *Associated Provincial Picture Houses Ltd v Wednesbury Corporation* [1948] 1 K.B. 223.

[98] Elliott (2016) provides an elucidating timeline of these cases with links to detailed blog posts on each of the cases in the series.

[99] *Kennedy*, supra note 89.

[100] Id. at [54].

[101] *Pham v Secretary of State for the Home Department* [2015] UKSC 19 [98].

[102] Id. at [60].

However, "with the progressive enlargement of the range of issues which are affected by EU law or the Convention (or, increasingly, by both), this has produced some rather arbitrary distinctions between essentially similar issues, depending on the source of law which is invoked as a ground of challenge."[103] Lord Reed's support was more explicit: "where Parliament authorises significant interferences with important legal rights, the courts may interpret the legislation as requiring that any such interference should be no greater than is objectively established to be necessary to achieve the legitimate aim of the interference: in substance, a requirement of proportionality."[104]

The following year in *Youssef*, Lord Carnwath, writing for a unanimous Court summarized the position: "there is a measure of support for the use of proportionality as a test in relation to interference with 'fundamental' rights." However, he went on to note that "in many cases, perhaps most, application of a proportionality test is unlikely to lead to a different result from traditional grounds of judicial review"[105] Finally, in *UNISON*, in the context of examining the common law right of access to justice, the Supreme Court applied a test "analogous to proportionality" to examine whether the Fees Order could be justified as a "necessary intrusion" on the right.[106]

The move toward the recognition of a common law doctrine of proportionality, albeit not completed yet, demonstrates how external normative influences in a pluralistic landscape resulted in the renewal of legal reasoning and forms of argumentation. In this case, the normative accommodation of EU law and the ECHR, which employ proportionality as a key reasoning tool, led to the courts' increased familiarity with this method which will likely prompt the formal adoption of proportionality as a common law standard of review. As a result, domestic constitutional law, in terms of both doctrine and legal reasoning, has been "pluralized" and is likely to remain so even after Brexit.

## 3.2 *Pluralizing the Constitution II: Constitutional Statutes*

The interface with external normative sources has also led to a more pluralistic understanding of UK constitutional law through the explicit recognition of constitutional statutes. While stating that constitutional rules, in terms of their substantive content, can be found in statutes may sound intuitive, the common law implications of labeling a statute as "constitutional" are noteworthy. Section 2 outlined how *Thoburn* developed the common law construct of "constitutional statutes" and its implications, namely the protection of these statutes from implied repeal. The concept of constitutional statutes was endorsed by the Supreme Court in *HS2* and

[103]Id. at [104].

[104]Id. at [119].

[105]*Youssef v Secretary of State for Foreign and Commonwealth Affairs* [2016] UKSC 3 [56]-[57].

[106]*UNISON*, supra note 92, at [99]-[102].

later did some of the work in the *Miller* litigation supporting the argument that Article 50 TEU could not be triggered through the use of prerogative powers. More specifically, the Supreme Court in *Miller* reiterated that the European Communities Act 1972 has a "constitutional character" and "constitutes EU law as an entirely new, independent and overriding source of domestic law."[107] The majority went on to state that withdrawal from the EU "will constitute as significant a constitutional change as that which occurred when EU law was first incorporated in domestic law by the 1972 Act... It would be inconsistent with long-standing and fundamental principle for such a far-reaching change to the UK constitutional arrangements to be brought about by ministerial decision or ministerial action alone. All the more so when the source in question was brought into existence by Parliament through primary legislation, which gave that source an overriding supremacy in the hierarchy of domestic law sources."[108]

The European Union (Withdrawal) Act 2018 is similarly a constitutional statute. The Act will remove EU law as a source of law but, as Sect. 2.3 detailed, will also introduce a new domestic category of law, retained EU law. This is another example of the ripple effects of supranational legal pluralism on the nature of constitutional law domestically. The entanglement of the UK and supranational legal orders over the past four decades has been such that an attempt to separate them neatly is fraught with difficulty. As a result, domestic constitutional law is faced with complicated questions outlined previously, such as the position of retained EU law in the domestic normative architecture or the role of the CJEU case law after Brexit. In effect, the supranational and domestic legal orders will still operate simultaneously to a certain extent and for some time in the future. Admittedly this interaction is mandated by a domestic statute; however, this formal veneer should not obfuscate the important external driver of changes, namely the UK's long membership of the EU, the need for a smooth transition, and potentially the future need for a "special partnership" between the UK and the EU-27. In this process, domestic constitutional law is faced with the task of clarifying how this, now internal, pluralism is to operate in practice as well as with the need of a serious debate as to how the national legal order may evolve in response to these external pressures. Contrary to what some proponents of Brexit may have expected, these pluralistic normative interactions neither ceased to exist after the 2016 referendum nor will they do so automatically on exit day.

[107] *Miller,* supra note 30, at [67], [80].

[108] Id. at [81]. The High Court, the decision of which was appealed to the Supreme Court, had made this point even more clearly: "Since in enacting the ECA 1972 as a statute of major constitutional importance Parliament has indicated that it should be exempt from casual implied repeal by Parliament itself, still less can it be thought to be likely that Parliament nonetheless intended that its legal effects could be removed by the Crown through the use of its prerogative powers" ([2016] EWHC 2768 (Admin) [88]).

### 3.3 Pluralizing the Constitution III: The UK's Territorial Constitution

Last, the interaction between domestic and supranational normative spheres may reverberate back onto the domestic plane by enhancing geographical/jurisdictional pluralism. Indeed, Brexit has brought to the fore the UK's territorial constitution and will likely reinvigorate the debates around domestic territorial pluralism. The following observations will be kept brief as any new forms of territorial pluralism will depend on how Brexit unfolds.

The June 2016 referendum "highlighted the fragility of the UK's territorial constitution".[109] The majority of voters in England and Wales voted Leave but a majority in Northern Ireland and a substantial majority in Scotland (62%) voted Remain. The EU (Withdrawal) Act 2018 introduces amendments to the devolution legislation. Under the current regime, the devolved legislatures cannot legislate contrary to EU law. Section 12 of the 2018 Act removes this requirement and gives UK Ministers powers to apply, by regulations, a temporary "freeze" on devolved legislative or executive competence in specified areas, so that in these areas devolved institutions cannot modify retained EU law.[110] These "freezing powers" are subject to sunset provisions and constitute a transitional arrangement while the UK political actors decide whether areas which are currently covered by EU law will come under the competence of the devolved nations or be "re-reserved" to the UK Parliament.[111] However, the "freezing powers" do not apply to modifications of retained EU law so far as such modifications would, immediately before exit day, have been within the legislative competence of the devolved institutions.

Therefore, the EU (Withdrawal) Bill, which was ultimately enacted in 2018, would change the scope of devolved competence. In turn, this meant that under the "Sewel convention" (a constitutional convention now written down in the devolution legislation), the UK Government sought legislative consent from the devolved legislatures.[112] After an agreement between the Welsh Government and the UK Government, which resulted in amendments to what is now section 12 of the Withdrawal Act, the Welsh Assembly gave legislative consent to the Withdrawal Bill. However, the Scottish Parliament did not.[113] Despite the Sewel convention[114] and the lack of the Scottish Parliament's legislative consent, the UK government pushed the bill through the UK Parliament.

---

[109]Elliott and Thomas (2017b).

[110]Explanatory Notes (2018), para 36; Elliott and Tierney (2019), pp. 53–54.

[111]Explanatory Notes (2018), para 37; House of Commons Library (2017).

[112]Elliott and Thomas (2017b).

[113]Elliott and Tierney (2019), pp. 55–56.

[114]It should be noted here that the Sewel convention, like all constitutional conventions, is not judicially enforceable. This did not change after the statutory recognition of the Sewel convention in the devolution legislation. On these points the Supreme Court was unanimous in *Miller*, supra note 30, at [136]-[151].

The saga continued when the Scottish Parliament passed the UK Withdrawal from the European Union (Legal Continuity) (Scotland) Act 2018 ("Scottish Continuity Bill"). The purpose of the Bill, following the intense disagreement between the UK and the Scottish Government, was to ensure the continuity of laws relating to devolved matters in Scotland which are now the subject of EU law but will cease to have effect after Brexit. The Scottish legislation made largely parallel provision to the UK Withdrawal Act but also, in other important parts, deviated from the UK Act.[115] For example, section 5 of the Scottish Bill provided that the EU Charter of Fundamental Rights would be part of Scots law after Brexit, whereas the UK Withdrawal Act provided that the Charter would not be part of UK law. The Attorney General and the Advocate General for Scotland ("the UK Law Officers") challenged the Scottish Bill by bringing a reference to the UK Supreme Court under section 33 of the Scotland Act. The UK Law Officers argued, among other things, that the Scottish Bill in its entirety was outside the legislative competence of the Scottish Parliament, and that a series of specific provisions of the Bill, such as section 5 on the EU Charter, were also outside competence. The UK Supreme Court rejected the first challenge but accepted that several provisions of the Scottish Bill were outside competence.[116]

Both the UK Government's decision to proceed with the EU (Withdrawal) Act 2018 without Scotland's consent and the *Scottish Continuity Bill* case are part of broader developments in the relations between the UK Government and devolved institutions that have been triggered by Brexit. These developments suggest that the UK may soon face a moment of constitutional reckoning with respect to its territorial constitution. The resolution will involve multiple constitutional actors at different levels of government and will be political. This process could result, for instance, in a new devolution settlement that would move the UK closer to a federal model. An alternative result could be a second independence referendum in Scotland. The Government has expressed a commitment to work "closely with the devolved administrations on an approach to returning powers from the EU that works for the whole of the UK and reflects the devolution settlements of Scotland, Wales and Northern Ireland."[117] Regardless of the outcome of these negotiations, this brief analysis suggests that as the UK is negotiating its new relationship with the EU, it will have to reconfigure its territorial constitution. This process may further pluralize the internal constitutional architecture with a view to accommodating the plurality of views in the constituent nations and preserving the Union.

---

[115]Elliott (2018).

[116]*The UK Withdrawal from the European Union (Legal Continuity) (Scotland) Bill – A Reference by the Attorney General and the Advocate General for Scotland* [2018] UKSC 64.

[117]Government (2017b).

## 4 Legal Pluralism: Consensus or Conflict?

The last question raised in the report is whether the dynamic landscape outlined in the previous sections reflects a multiplication of spheres of actors likely to promote universal human values or a source of conflicts. We can rephrase the question as follows: does normative pluralism lead to consensus or dissensus?

Some brief general observations are in order before drawing conclusions from the UK case. I would propose as our starting point the argument that normative pluralism across jurisdictions may over time evolve into normative convergence. If we use comparative law to capture cross-jurisdictional pluralism and an emerging global law to capture normative convergence, the picture I would paint is that of a two-way interaction. I use the term global law in the sense of what Waldron has described as *ius gentium*. Waldron suggests that "convergent currents" of foreign rules sometimes "add up to a body of law that has its own claim on us" by virtue of this commonality between the positive laws of particular states.[118]

I argue that Waldron's account reflects an emerging trend with respect to values but less so with respect to rules. A value is as an "ethical imperative expressed at a high degree of abstraction, and possessing the quality of an ultimate goal".[119] Rules, on the other hand, apply in an "all or nothing fashion"[120] providing concrete behavioral prescriptions. One advantage of values being formulated at a level of abstraction is that they can "travel" well. However, it is this same feature of abstractness that can hinder their practical effectiveness. By contrast, the benefit of rules is their practical bite. Conversely, it is much more difficult to garner consensus of the relevant actors around concrete rules. Empirically, we see convergence especially during the later waves of constitution-making around certain fundamental values. For instance, there are references to human dignity in 77% of the world's constitutions.[121] More tellingly, equality guarantees were included in 71% of the constitutions in 1946; 60 years later, in 2006, this percentage had risen to 97%.[122]

This empirical observation may give rise to the following plausible critique—let us call it the "indeterminacy problem." The reason there might be broad consensus on values as part of the *ius gentium*, the argument would go, is that these values represent a bare minimum. As Allan and Huscroft have put it, "agreement at the level of moral abstraction allows widespread disagreement and dissensus down at the level of drawing difficult social policy lines to be finessed."[123] In other words, there might be consensus around certain universal values but (interpretative) conflicts as to how these should be applied concretely.

---

[118]Waldron (2012), pp. 3, 28.

[119]Davis et al. (2015).

[120]Dworkin (1978).

[121]According to the Constitute project, the number is 146 out of 190 constitutions: https://www.constituteproject.org/search?lang=en&key=dignity.

[122]Law and Versteeg (2012), p. 773.

[123]Allan and Huscroft (2006), p. 36.

Indeed, to link this general framework to the analysis in previous sections, Brexit could be viewed as backlash against a perceived normative convergence or even homogenization at the level of *rules*. One argument in favor of Brexit was that the UK would be able to "chart its own way in the world"[124] free from the rules emanating from Brussels. In a similar vein, arguments in favor of a "British Bill of Rights" (or even withdrawal from the ECHR) promise a reduced influence from the ECtHR and its extensive case law. At the same time, proponents of Brexit and a British Bill of Rights reiterate their commitment to values such as international cooperation or human rights. In other words, there is broader consensus around these values but dissensus on the EU rules or ECtHR judgments concretizing them. Yet a commitment to these values necessitates genuine discussion on how to operationalize them, which reintroduces the need to engage with these external legal spheres. In the context of Brexit, this engagement takes place through the EU Withdrawal Act and future legislation that will give effect to the potential withdrawal and other agreements with the EU-27. In the context of a potential repeal of the HRA or even a withdrawal from the ECHR, this engagement would take place through a "British Bill of Rights" or common law principles which could mirror the previous case law.

Consequently, the complex normative landscape that was sketched out earlier and involves a plurality of legal spheres may engender consensus and conflict at different levels. However, ultimately even if the consensus emerging from this normative pluralism is limited to the level of certain values, this approach can still encourage serious engagement with the necessary process of translating these values into more concrete rules. In this process, as the UK example demonstrates, domestic legal orders themselves may become more pluralized to accommodate these necessary interactions with other legal spheres.

**Acknowledgement** I wish to thank Tony Prosser for helpful comments on an earlier draft.

## References

Allan TRS (1997) Parliamentary sovereignty: law, politics, and revolution. Law Quarterly Rev 113 (Jul):443–452

Allan J, Huscroft G (2006) Constitutional rights coming home to roost? Rights internationalism in American Courts. San Diego Law Rev 43(1):1–59

Avbelj M, Komárek J (2008) Four visions of constitutional pluralism. Eur Constit Law Rev 4:524–527

Bamforth N, Leyland P (2003) Public law in a multi-layered constitution. Hart Publishing, Oxford

BBC (2017) Theresa May's general election statement in full, Available at http://www.bbc.com/news/uk-politics-39630009

Berman F (2003) Jurisdiction: the state. In: Capps P, Evans M, Konstadinidis S (eds) Asserting jurisdiction: international and European legal perspectives. Hart, Oxford, pp 3–16

[124]BBC (2017).

Bjorge E (2017) Can unincorporated treaty obligations be part of English law? Public Law 2017:571–591

Capps P (2007) The Court as gatekeeper: customary international law in English Court. Modern Law Rev 70(3):458–471

Craig P (2015) Britain in the European Union. In: Jowell J, Oliver D, O'Cinneide C (eds) The changing constitution, 8th edn. Oxford University Press, Oxford, pp 104–133

Craig P (2019) Constitutional principle, the rule of law and political reality: the European Union (Withdrawal) Act 2018. Modern Law Rev 82(2):319–350

Crawford J (2012) Brownlie's principles of public international law, 8th edn. Oxford University Press, Oxford

Davis D, Richter A, Saunders C (2015) Introduction. In: Davis D, Richter A, Saunders C (eds) An inquiry into the existence of global values: through the lens of comparative constitutional law. Hart Publishing, Oxford

Denza E (2014) The relationship between international and national law. In: Evans M (ed) International law, 4th edn. Oxford University Press, Oxford

Department for Constitutional Affairs (2006) Review of the implementation of the Human Rights Act (DCA 38/06), Available at http://webarchive.nationalarchives.gov.uk/+/http:/www.dca.gov.uk/peoples-rights/human-rights/pdf/full_review.pdf

Dicey AV (1959) Introduction to the study of the law of the constitution, 10th edn. Macmillan, London

Dworkin R (1978) Taking rights seriously. Harvard University Press, Cambridge

Eeckhout P (2016) The UK decision to withdraw from the EU: Parliament or Government?, Available at https://ukconstitutionallaw.org/2016/10/15/piet-eeckhout-the-uk-decision-to-withdraw-from-the-eu-parliament-or-government/

Elliott M (2016) *Youssef*: another Supreme Court decision, another set of *obiter dicta* on substantive judicial review, Available at https://publiclawforeveryone.com/2016/01/28/youssef-another-supreme-court-decision-another-set-of-obiter-dicta-on-substantive-judicial-review/

Elliott M (2017a) Analysis: the Supreme Court's Judgment in *Miller*, Available at https://publiclawforeveryone.com/2017/01/25/analysis-the-supreme-courts-judgment-in-miller/

Elliott M (2017b) The EU (Withdrawal) Bill: initial thoughts, Available at https://publiclawforeveryone.com/2017/07/14/the-eu-withdrawal-bill-initial-thoughts/

Elliott M (2018) The Supreme Court's judgment in the Scottish Continuity Bill case, Available at https://publiclawforeveryone.com/2018/12/14/the-supreme-courts-judgment-in-the-scottish-continuity-bill-case/

Elliott M, Thomas R (2017a) Public law, 3rd edn. Oxford University Press, Oxford

Elliott M, Thomas R (2017b) Brexit, the separation of powers and devolution, Available at https://publiclawforeveryone.com/2017/10/05/public-law-update-4-brexit-the-separation-of-powers-and-devolution/

Elliott M, Tierney S (2019) Political pragmatism and constitutional principle: the European Union (Withdrawal) Act 2018. Public Law 2019:37–60

Explanatory Notes to the European Union (Withdrawal) Act (2018) Available at http://www.legislation.gov.uk/ukpga/2018/16/notes/division/1/index.htm

Feldman D (2015) The internationalization of public law and its impact on the UK. In: Jowell J, Oliver D, O'Cinneide C (eds) The changing constitution, 8th edn. Oxford University Press, Oxford, pp 134–165

Ferreira N (2015) The Supreme Court in a final push to go beyond Strasbourg. Public Law 2015:367–375

HM Government (2017a) Enforcement and dispute resolution: a future partnership paper, Available at https://www.gov.uk/government/uploads/system/uploads/attachment_data/file/639609/Enforcement_and_dispute_resolution.pdf

HM Government (2017b) Response to the Sixth Report from the Public Administration and Constitutional Affairs Committee, the future of the Union, Part Two: Inter-institutional relations in the UK, Session 2016–17, Available at https://publications.parliament.uk/pa/cm201719/cmselect/cmpubadm/442/44202.htm

House of Commons Library (2017) Briefing Paper Number 8079, European Union (Withdrawal) Bill
Law D, Versteeg M (2012) The declining influence of the United States Constitution. New York Univ Law Rev 87(3):762–858
Neuberger Lord (2017) Twenty years a judge: reflections and refractions. Neill Lecture 2017, Oxford Law Faculty, Available at https://www.supremecourt.uk/docs/speech-170210.pdf
Paterson A (2013) Final judgment: the last law Lords and the Supreme Court. Hart, Oxford
Psygkas A (2017) From the "Democratic Deficit" to a "Democratic Surplus": constructing administrative democracy in Europe. Oxford University Press, Oxford
Sales P, Clement J (2008) International law in domestic courts: the developing framework. Law Q Rev 124(JUL):388–421
Segan J (2018) The European Union (Withdrawal) Act 2018: ten key implications for UK law and lawyers, Available at https://ukconstitutionallaw.org/2018/07/26/james-segan-the-european-union-withdrawal-act-2018-ten-key-implications-for-uk-law-and-lawyers/
Simson Caird J (2017) The European Union (Withdrawal) Bill: constitutional change and legal continuity, Available at https://ukconstitutionallaw.org/2017/07/18/jack-simson-caird-the-european-union-withdrawal-bill-constitutional-change-and-legal-continuity/
Stanton K (2013) Comparative law in the House of Lords and Supreme Court. Common Law World Rev 42:269–296
Stephenson S (2015) The Supreme Court's renewed interest in autochthonous constitutionalism. Public Law 2015:394–402
Syrpis P (2017) European Union (Withdrawal) Bill: paving the way towards a very uncertain future, Available at https://legalresearch.blogs.bris.ac.uk/2017/07/european-union-withdrawal-bill-paving-the-way-towards-a-very-uncertain-future/
Wade HWR (1996) Sovereignty - revolution or evolution? Law Q Rev 112(Oct):568–575
Waldron J (2012) "Partly Laws Common to All Mankind": foreign law in American Courts. Yale University Press, New Haven
Walker N (2002) The idea of constitutional pluralism. Modern Law Rev 65(3):317–359
Wright T (2013) British politics: a very short introduction. Oxford University Press, Oxford
Young A (2017a) R. (Miller) v Secretary of state for exiting the European Union: thriller or vanilla? Eur Law Rev 42(2):280–295
Young A (2017b) Democratic dialogue and the constitution. Oxford University Press, Oxford

# Reconciling Legal Pluralism and Constitutionalism: New Trajectories for Legal Theory in the Global Age—Questionnaire

Guillaume Tusseau

## 1 General Perspective

In constitutionalism today, the constitution is understood as a type of law that prescribes what agents should do. Like any other norm, a constitution cannot be automatically efficient. Only a system of implementation can guarantee that its prescriptions are complied with. In *Marbury v. Madison*, John Marshall established the necessity for a jurisdictional guarantee of constitutions in order for constitutional norms to really impose themselves as "the supreme law of the land". From a formal point of view, the constitution closes the legal system. It defines the characteristics that all the other elements of the system must have to belong to it. Moreover, it presents itself as a superior norm because of both its active capacity to repeal other norms and its passive capacity to resist being repealed by other norms. From a substantive point of view, the constitution is considered to be a document in which the most important values, main commitments and most fundamental principles that society wants to protect are established and guaranteed. It is indeed in that respect that human rights protection is provided for in it. Today however, the link that used to connect all those concepts is distended. It is not exceptional nor illegitimate anymore to think of a multiplicity of non state-related contexts through the ideas of constitution, constitutionalisation, constitutional law etc.

At the international or supranational level, a supra-national sort of constitutionalism is emerging. Increasingly numerous international norms relate to human rights, which gives them a constitutional dimension. They overlap in many respects with the *jus cogens* norms which, being at the apex of the pyramid of international norms, confer upon the international legal system the formal structure of a constitutional system. Treaties that do not belong to the strict framework of inter-state reciprocity

G. Tusseau (✉)
Sciences Po Law School, Paris, France
e-mail: guillaume.tusseau@sciencespo.fr

 
G. Tusseau (ed.), *Debating Legal Pluralism and Constitutionalism*, Ius Comparatum – Global Studies in Comparative Law 41, https://doi.org/10.1007/978-3-030-34432-0_11

and favour forms of majority decision-making are multiplying. Several authors do not hesitate to consider that the United Nations Charter is a world constitution and the World Trade Organisation Agreement the economic constitution of the world, while the European Court of Human Rights and the European Court of Justice present themselves as agents of a form of constitutionalism.

What is most remarkable is the emergence of what some authors analyse as spontaneous forms of constitutionalisation and constitutionalism which are appearing independently of states. Private law and private actors find themselves involved in the protection of fundamental rights. Under what is called "corporate social responsibility" or "corporate citizenship", many norms which belong to soft law thus aim to make sure that economic agents protect human rights. Regarding institutions, Gunther Teubner has identified several forms of autonomous constitutionalisations in different sectors (economy, health, tourism, sports, culture, new technologies, etc.). He accounts for them in the idea of "societal constitutionalism". As he remarks, "Here we are, [...] faced with a curious phenomenon – stateless self-constitutionalisation". Sectors of the global society are progressively developing their own constitutional norms. Urgent social problems which appear within autonomous global systems engender social conflicts which lead to legal norms being conferred constitutional features. Over time, those norms are then brought together under the form of sectorial constitutions of the global society.[1] Those spheres become *de facto* relevant from the perspective of global governance. They have stable relationships the one with the other, agree on behavioural standards and conflict settlement, for themselves and in relation to third parties, develop a set of fundamental principles that all their other decisions must comply with, and settle their conflicts in a way that is close, in diverse degrees, to that of a jurisdictional process. Important parts of the *lex digitalis*, of the *lex constructionis*, etc. thus turn out to be real "transnational corporate constitutions".[2] Lastly, at the infra-national level, the dynamics of the "new constitutionalism"[3] as it is emerging in Latin America leads to the identification of new forms of acknowledgement of the constitutional autonomy of the first nations because it goes beyond the forms of normative autonomies that have hitherto been granted to entities such as churches or professional organisations when they collectively decide on labour conditions.

Today, the very grammar of constitutionalism is quite clearly being redirected towards other legal, political and social spheres which introduce multiplied forms of legal pluralism in opposition to the traditionally bilateral relation that used to exist between the concepts related to the organisation of State power. Those norms first claim formal and substantive (value-based) primacy in their own legal sphere. Then the constitutional systems assert their independence and autonomy towards other legal spheres. That is why they do not have hierarchical relations the one with the other—on the contrary, their relations are "heterarchical". The fact that legal spaces

[1]Teubner (2010).

[2]Teubner (2011).

[3]See e.g. Storini and Alenza García (2012) and Corrêa Souza de Oliveira and Luiz Streck (2014).

that were unused up to now are adopting similar self descriptions indeed implies the implementation of specific links among them. Thus the simple plurality of constitutional and constitutionalised spheres, which is quite static, also quite naturally includes a more dynamic dimension of pluralism. They are revealed in the way the actors try to comprehend one another when, quite unavoidably, they have to regulate, each from its own point of view, a same set of facts. The pluralism of constitutional norms, which has become quite apparent, calls for an *aggiornamento* of legal practices and reasoning. Potentially important conflicts result from it. It is not difficult to imagine a situation in which, regarding a professional sportsperson, the constitutional law of a State (e.g. the principles of tax collection or the workers' fundamental rights), sports constitutional law (e.g. the principles of repressive measures against doping or measures for equality among clubs) and European constitutional law (e.g. the principle of free movement of workers) are in conflict. The absence of a hierarchy among the different systems does not make it *a priori* possible to foresee any obvious solution. The situation becomes even more complicated and tensions stronger when some of the multiple constitutional spheres are able to assert what Pedro Cruz Villalón presents as forms of "meta constitutionality".[4] That word refers to the capacity for a constitutional system to assert something about another and require that it comply with its demands, while, very often, the targeted system is also able to make meta constitutional claims towards the other. In such a situation, the constitutional interwinings and the tensions that result from them distort in quite a serious way the analysis grids that are associated to the classic constitutional paradigm. The reflection that has developed about "global constitutionalism",[5] "constitutional pluralism",[6] "transnational constitutionalism",[7] "multilevel constitutionalism",[8] etc. precisely aims to face that issue.

Manuel Atienza underlines to what extent "constitutionalism" and "globalisation" are both phenomena and ways of conceptualising those phenomena.[9] That double dimension is at the core of this report's topic. The objective of this form on "Reconciling legal pluralism and constitutionalism: new trajectories for legal theory in the age of globalisation" is to measure to what extent the mutations of legal systems today are upsetting the operation of positive law. At a deeper level, what it aims at is understanding how the intellectual or cultural backgrounds, which are at the basis of the perception of those mutations, are affected. Its objective is to determine and understand how legal phenomena, when tackled through "constitutional pluralism", presuppose, trigger, accompany, impose or hinder the development of renewed ways not only of finding practical solutions to cases, both within a legislative and litigation framework, but, at a deeper level, of questioning the

[4]Cruz Villalón (2004), p. 73.

[5]Fischer-Lescano (2005) and Schwöbel (2011).

[6]Avbelj and Komárek (2008).

[7]Stein (1981) and Tsagourias (2007).

[8]Pernice (1999).

[9]Atienza (2013), pp. 31–60.

theories, concepts, categories, methods, intellectual tools, reasonings and arguments which have been called upon to conceive, analyse, understand and describe them. Its goal is to allow the presentation of the new reasonings and elements of legal theory that have been implemented, invented from the beginning or rediscovered in the light of the history of legal practices and jurisprudence—in other words, to try and comprehend whether there is any emergence of a new legal rationality (e.g. the idea of *jus commune*, of *comitas gentium*, the theories of legal pluralism, etc.).

## 2 The Role of Special Rapporteurs

The general report, and, depending on their quality, a maximum of 20 special reports, will be published in the Springer editions "Ius comparatum - Global Studies in Comparative Law" collection. So as to ensure the preparation of that book and especially of the general report that I must send to the AICD several months before its general assembly, I would be grateful if you could send the special reports, in a version that may be slightly modified in view of the final publication, as soon as possible, and on September 17th 2017 at the latest, to the following email address: guillaume.tusseau@sciencespo.fr. For practical reasons, I would like to make the following recommendations. Special reports must have the form of academic contributions. Their title should significantly reflect their content, and not mention only the State or organisation concerned. They must be in Word format, in French or English, and about 10,000 words long. Formatting should comply with that used in the Springer collection (https://www.springer.com/gp/authors-editors/book-authors-editors/book-manuscript-guidelines). To that end, the rapporteurs, without being forbidden to depart from the following general directions or to complete them depending on the answers to the situations to which they want to draw the attention, should follow them in their preparation of the special reports. It is quite possible that positive law or the jurisprudence of States or legal spheres that are the objects of the special reports call for specific and complementary developments, or, on the contrary, do not call for any particular part on one specific aspect. Nonetheless, the absence of any element that is in the form should be underlined, precisely because it may reveal an original orientation. Insofar as the comparison is about both positive law and jurisprudence, rapporteurs should not hesitate to mention and provide detailed analyses of concrete cases and developed bibliographic illustrations. I am of course available, via email, for any further information and am delighted that we are given the opportunity to work together on that important project.

# 3 Questionnaire

## *3.1 The Balance Among Legal Spheres in Positive Law*

What is the position of national law regarding international and transnational law? Is it open or closed (e.g. monistic or dualist), and to what extent, to their interference in terms of regulation of behaviours? Is its attitude uniform or does is vary depending on the types of international norms (e.g. customary law, principles of international law, international treaties, EU law, international human rights law, etc.)? What type of hierarchy of norms (e.g. place of international and supranational law regarding the constitution or the law) or norm combination (e.g. degree of contractual freedom in the choice of applicable law and litigation resolution, autonomy granted to professionals in collective bargaining, admission of normativities from traditional cultures, native communities or churches, etc.) is established? Are relations among norms mainly founded on the idea of a binding force of the norms of other legal spheres or rather on the idea of a weaker "persuasive"[10] force? Are specific appeals organised at the internal level in order to give external norms prevailing force (e.g. distinction and combination of conventionality review and judicial review; preliminary rulings; consequences of the concept of public order on contractual freedom, etc.)? Have those aspects of the relations among legal norms evolved over the past few years?

## *3.2 The Dynamics of the Relations Among Legal Spheres in Positive Law*

Has the reorganisation of the interactions among norms imposed by globalisation happened in a natural, consensual way and "softly" or "smoothly", or in a more difficult, chaotic, or even conflict-ridden way? Have all the legal actors (constitutional courts, ordinary courts, legislative bodies, administrations, local authorities, etc.) adopted a homogenous attitude in that respect? Is there any consistency between the hierarchy of norms and models of interaction, articulation and collision of norms that have thus been set up and those established, suggested or imposed by the other legal spheres, or is each sphere trying to impose its own supremacy or way of understanding the combination of legal systems upon the other? How are conflicts solved? Is there any idea of transconstitutional "dialogues"? Are they vertical types of dialogues (e.g. between a national and a supranational court) or horizontal ones (e.g. between two national or supranational courts)? Is it possible to perceive substantial influences, that is, ways for different actors to draw inspiration from one another? Are those types of interaction explicit and openly claimed or are they

[10] Glenn (1987) and Flanders (2009). On the distinction between "must-", "should-", and "may-" sources of law, see also Peczenik (2009).

rather implicit, or even hidden? Has the case-law or the (constitutional or infraconstitutional) legislation gone through a spasmodic evolution? Has this evolution been marked by important decisions, or even by the existence of periods of time or phases that were characterised by different attitudes?

## 3.3 *The Renewal of Legal Reasoning*

Have the legal interactions that globalisation implies led to a change in both the form and substance of legal reasoning and arguments? Has legal reasoning undergone changes, either in litigation and cases related to the issue of pluralism, or because of some spillover effect in other domains? To give an example, has there been an important development of reasoning in terms of principles, proportionality control or balancing? Is there a strong opposition between syllogism and weighing? Have the "methods of interpretation" been modified depending on the multiplied audience which the different legal spheres now address? Have the concrete working methods of legal actors (constitutional courts, ordinary courts, legislative bodies, individual legislators, administrations, local authorities, companies and their legal services, arbitration courts, law firms, etc.) evolved (e.g. by setting up international relations services, comparative law services, etc.)? Is the idea of "dialogue" used in jurisprudence (and which jurisprudence: constitutionalist? internationalist, etc.?) and/or by legal actors (normative authorities, courts, law professionals, etc.) themselves? Have concepts or tools enabling the interconnection and limitation of the interconnection among legal spheres appeared (e.g. *controlimiti* in Italy or constitutional identity in France and Germany)? Do these concepts tend to replace arguments founded on sovereignty? Even more fundamentally, has it been necessary to think anew the concepts of "law", legal "system", or "order" (e.g. so as to take into account the multiplication of sources of law, soft law, the fragmentation of the law, etc., or to highlight the emergence of a law which has a less determining importance, is based on autonomy, reflexivity, self-coordination, and operates in mobile and dynamic networks, and not according to the vertical model of the pyramid of norms)?

## 3.4 *The Renewal of Jurisprudence*

Have specific teachings and works appeared following the emergence of new normative interactions? Are they related to foreign jurisprudence and law professionals? Have new theories emerged or has the dominant approach consisted in adapting traditional theories? Have elements of other subjects (and if so, which ones—social sciences [ethnology, sociology, etc.], logics, linguistics, systems theory, complexity theories, fuzzy logics, etc.) been called upon? In what proportion? Is this leading to a reorganisation of disciplinary boundaries (e.g. distinction between public and private law, constitutional and international law, etc.)? Is it possible to observe the development of research projects, journals, research centres that are specifically dedicated to the themes of global constitutionalism? Is there a metatheoretical awareness of the very evolution of concepts and theories? Are there specific studies on that subject? Is the movement of identification of multiple constitutional or constitutionalised spheres admitted or is their constitutionalisation the object of debates, or is it even radically questioned as illegitimate from an intellectual point of view?

Have theories of legal pluralism been called upon to face the mutations that the globalisation imposes on legal systems? With what degree of precision (generic reference to pluralism, reference to a specific author, e.g. Santi Romano and his theory of the *rilevanza* of multiple legal systems, reinvention of new theories of pluralism, etc.)? What did the national tradition use to be in that respect (acknowledgment of pluralistic theories or theoretical centralism)? What representation of the theories and concepts that are being called upon is it possible to suggest to face "global normative disorder"?

## 3.5 The Ideological Dimension of Legal Rationality

How important and numerous are debates on this report's topics? Is it possible to find a date or time division for the interest they have kindled? Are the different jurisprudential directions and practices thus described ideologically marked, in any way (right v. left; conservative v. progressive; nationalist v. internationalist; public v. private law supporters, etc.)? Is the issue of the impact of considerations on the factual power rather than the direct normative authority of legal norms being debated (e.g. for economic or social reasons, it is hard for national constitutionalism to resist sports constitutionalism, while EU constitutionalism, which does not participate in competitions, might be more likely to counter it by putting forward its own claims)? Is the current dynamics perceived as a multiplication of spheres of actors who are likely to promote universal human values or as a source of conflicts and a form of more or less hidden imperialism, related in particular to Western financial capitalism? Is the objective of giving birth to a new real pluralism which would lead to the enrichment of perspectives developed on either sides of the fundamental interests of political societies, or is it of hiding a form of covertly developing hegemony?

## References

Atienza M (2013) Podemos hacer más. Otra forma de pensar el derecho. Pasos perdidos, Madrid

Avbelj M, Komárek J (2008) Four visions of constitutional pluralism. Eur Constit Law Rev 4:524–527

Corrêa Souza de Oliveira F, Luiz Streck L (2014) El nuevo constitucionalismo latinoamericano: reflexiones sobre la posibilidad de construir un derecho constitucional común. Anuario iberoamericano de justicia constitucional 18:125–153

Cruz Villalón P (2004) La constitucion inedita. Estudios ante la constitucionalización de Europa. Trotta, Madrid
Fischer-Lescano A (2005) Globalverfassung. Die Geltungsbegründung der Menschenrechte. Velbrück Wissenschaft, Weilerswist
Flanders CW (2009) Toward a theory of persuasive authority. Okla Law Rev 62:55–88
Glenn HP (1987) Persuasive authority. McGill Law J / Revue de droit de McGill 32:261–298
Peczenik A (2009) On law and reason. Springer, New York
Pernice I (1999) Multilevel constitutionalism and the Treaty of Amsterdam: European constitution-making revisited? Common Market Law Rev 36:703–750
Schwöbel CEJ (2011) Global constitutionalism in international legal perspective. Martinus Nijhoff, Leiden
Stein E (1981) Lawyers, judges and the making of a transnational constitution. Am J Int Law 75:1–27
Storini C, Alenza García JF (eds) (2012) Materiales sobre neoconstitucionalismo y nuevo constitucionalismo latinoamericano. Thomson, Reuters, Aranzadi, Cizur Menor
Teubner G (2010) Constitutionalising polycontexturality. http://www.jura.uni-frankfurt.de/42852930/ConstitutionalisingPolycontexturality_eng.pdf
Teubner G (2011) Self-constitutionalizing TNCs? On the linkage of 'Private' and 'Public' corporate codes of conduct. http://www.jura.uni-frankfurt.de/42852833/CSR_conference_bremen.pdf
Tsagourias N (ed) (2007) Transnational constitutionalism. International and European models. Cambridge University Press, Cambridge

CPSIA information can be obtained
at www.ICGtesting.com
Printed in the USA
BVHW010215270220
573500BV00001B/3

9 783030 344313